P. W. P Fagerstjerna

The Light of Messiah

On the Gospel of Freedom and the Order of Messiah

P. W. P Fagerstjerna

The Light of Messiah
On the Gospel of Freedom and the Order of Messiah

ISBN/EAN: 9783743395039

Manufactured in Europe, USA, Canada, Australia, Japa

Cover: Foto ©Lupo / pixelio.de

Manufactured and distributed by brebook publishing software (www.brebook.com)

P. W. P Fagerstjerna

The Light of Messiah

PREFACE

BY THE MESSIAH.

This work is not only an extraordinary effort from the eternal world to bring light down on earth, but a circumscribed prospect of what the future will bring. The spiritual world is descending gradually into the conscious life of the human mind, and the kingdom of God is coming as a divine reality of man's actual and positive progress in spirit communion. The spiritual world has reason to expect that the medium for the Messiah will be sustained in earth life, as the hope for his usefulness is under the guaranty and protection of the Ancient of Days. However, the work will be done by that messenger or by others. It consumed all life to mature him, and the most formidable obstacles were thrown into his way, but he conquered them all in the strength of God, knowing he was guided by the man from Golgotha, and looking into His suffering for support. Once by extraordinary conditions of circumstances, the Ancient of Days saved His messenger during the early days of his development, twenty years ago, when his friends and relations opposed and persecuted the truth of communion in the Spirit. Man's natural life is undeveloped and closed up against the spiritual evidences, and hence comes purgatory, which follows darkened souls after the death in the flesh. The love of God is not within man, but he is turned away from the light, and in the perdition of darkness for gain's sake, without hope, and filled with selfishness and crime. This spirit of the world has no heavenly aspiration, but is earth-bound and of the flesh, and shapes man's life, plays on his tongue, and consigns him to misery after death.

Spiritualism has done a noble work in the service of the Gospel of Freedom, in a period when doubt of immortality covered the souls of humanity in a gloom without hope, and the pulpits of the christian churches were captured and bound in ignorance, superstition, bigotry and cunning priestcraft, deserted of angels and of the spirit of grace and truth. The manifestations of spiritualism gave to humanity a new influx and a new impulse of spiritual light and harmonial philosophy.

The power of inspiration returned to man by the restoration of the primitive principles of truth, and it pleased God to raise that high up which was low down, and make that to be naught which the world honored as divine. The reality that materialized spirits appear is a fact given to man as the evidence of the resurrection from death. The crime which the world has committed against the movement of spiritualism is appalling, thousands of mediums are incarcerated in insane asylums, and are suffering a prison life without hope of release, but by death. They cannot deny their testimony that spirits are seen and speak to them, but that very fact declare experts on medical evidence for manifest insanity. Rapping and writing mediums who have no personal agency in the manifestations are removed to insane asylums by friends and relations, who pay liberally to keep them there, because the clergy and the doctors sustain the general belief, that all spiritual manifestations are freaks of a diseased brain, serious idiocy of the mind, or hopeless insanity. However, God's work has been going on, and the cries of martyrs have called legions of angels to the standard of the crucified Messiah, until now the hosts of the Lord are marching the earth, and the churches have to follow the spirit or crumble down, because redemption is at hand.

Persons who never saw a judge; who never were given one moment for self-defense; who never were examined; have been adjudged insane on account of the light of God, and are kept in the dungeons of insane asylums, public or private in California, as all over the world, but more especially in the United States of America. Those who honor the prophets with their lips will kill the prophets of their own generation, and build tombs and monuments over the dust of those their ancestors killed. Therefore I said to my disciples: "Men shall kill you and believe they serve God by it." I am the corner-stone in Zion, and the rock of the Order of Messiah, and whosoever dashes against that rock shall be broken to pieces. Spiritualism has raised high up the torch light of spiritual communion, and given a new infusion of light and life to man. I am the great center-light, and that light is radiated in the spirit to the circumference. The eternal world above cannot change the programme of heaven, nor can I am that I am change his being—only the folly of man's childhood must change into sober manhood, and make progressive steps of obedience to the truth by taking refuge in the love of God, and be adopted by the spirit of that love. The ignorance of man is fighting against that knowledge which is in God's love. Therefore my messengers be fearless. Go out into all the world and proclaim freedom from bondage to creeds and priestcraft, and live in God's light. The three crosses shall be a sign of deliverance from thraldom, ignorance and superstition. Teach how to live in the strength and health of the body, to attain spiritual power. Observe the daily cold sponge bath. Pray always in your hearts, and anoint your heads with oil in the name of Messiah. Give thanksgiving to God in your souls, that the gifts of inspiration and healing shall not depart from you. Wash your feet with cold water in my name, and you shall walk much and not be tired, nor suffer pain, nor enter the ways to destruction, for the Holy Spirit shall be by you as a cloud of light, and the heavenly messengers shall follow you. By that shall the Knights of the White Cross understand the philosophy of the first heaven, and how to conduct earth life in health and strength, and truth of that heaven.

You Knights of the Red Cross are called the Knights of Love, or the Knights of the Red Rose. All philosophy in the summer land belongs to you. Teach by your own lives, and live that heavenly love which is in thé eternal companionship—a love between two souls for which the human tongue has no name, but can only be lived never to be expressed in any language, and blessed are mine elect who live it.

The red cross on the white ground is the emblem of my innocent blood from the cross on Golgotha, where I died full of that love to man which I have in the love of my heavenly Father.

Lift high up and floating under the sky the flag of the red cross, and let your battle-cry be heard all over the earth. Be girded with the word of life and the two-edged sword of truth for a weapon, fighting the battle of heaven, because the Son of Man is fighting by you. Preach the spirit of life and peace on the streets, in halls, on fields, and acquire knowledge, filling your souls with mental ammunition, and perfect weapons to conquer the world as faithful soldiers of the king.

The three crosses on Golgotha represent the three heavens. The first, including the earth sphere, is in much ignorance because it is not much developed in love. To the second heaven or Paradise one of the thieves followed me in love, and on the day of the crucifixion we were together in the summer land. The third heaven I went to greeting my eternal Father, before I descended to the spirit planet Hades.

Save not your earthly lives. Keep the red cross in your hearts, and preach the philosophy of love about the companionship of the summer land. You represent the sphere of love, and the rosy light which adorns the planet Mars, the emblem of martial strength, permeates the atmosphere of the summer land. Breathe that heavenly love with all the fragrance from the red rose permeating your soul. Be valiant in your crusade against mistakes in the Utah church, but do not condemn in teaching; because love opens the heart for the truth, when condemnation closes it up. Your warfare is against the falsehoods and stagnation in all churches. Do not love the world with the love of the world within you, but love the world with the love of God within you, and you shall not be a prey for the world, but be the conquerors of the world. I fought the battle with the spirit of Baal and the world, and laid down my life for truth's sake, that my followers should be where I am in the glory of my Father's love. Fight the same battle of defense, and your life shall give life to the world, even as I am the light and the life of the world. Preach in the spirit of power and charity, and may your lives be the emblems of your words and the teachings of the summer land. Serve the messengers, serve the churches in the world, serve each other, and the spirit of holiness shall rest upon you in the perfection of my Father's love, dedicating to Him the work of the king. Eternity is listening to your words, therefore love the truth, that heavenly fruit of love, and mankind shall receive it in my name as though you were angels from the Most High God.

Blessed shall those be who follow you, because they are following after me, and the hosts of heaven shall follow you, and serve you, and guide you.

Now the Son of Man speaks :—When the world rejects His messengers my Father will speak in cyclones, pestilence, earthquakes, droughts, wars, famine, fears, consternation and death upon earth.

Gather in my elect and teach them how to build my temple at Independence, that they may prepare the world for my Father's glory, and I will open the hearts of the rich men to donate of their means for my work. They shall give to you what they would have given to me, and they shall not lose their reward. When the world is fighting, remember it is not my work nor that power you are fighting for, because I have called you to peace and not to war.

Bloodshed shall come on this continent, and the spirit of the flesh shall be very angry, but ye shall not rise up after the world's pattern for conquest and plunder, because I have called you to holiness, and your power and your riches shall be in God.

When the days of desolation shall come upon the American nation, you shall protect the helpless with a strong arm. You shall shield the fugitive and give the suffering rest. You shall be a shelter for women and children, and clothe the naked, and feed the hungry, and bury the slain. The Knights of the Red Cross shall be the protectors of the defenceless all over the world. Mighty shall you be in the heart of this continent on that day, when you shall restore peace between the bleeding parties.

In the daybreak before the sunrise of my second advent I hail you sons and daughters of the golden rays, the Knights of the Golden Cross. Glorious shall your host come to the temple. From east to west, and from north to south shall the light of prophecy flash over the world. Inspiration is your inheritance to govern by. Truth is your sceptre which the world will honor, because you are mine elect and in the love of God. An Order of prophets are the Knights of that Golden Cross which is raised in the third heaven, raised in my triumph over death and the grave. You are the earthly embodiment of God's eternal love, as His love reigns in the golden light of the celestial world. Therefore His will be done on earth as it is done in heaven, and in His kingdom to come. You are the princes of the glorious kingdom of God. The kingdoms of the world shall try to ensnare you, but the angels from my Father shall protect you.

Remain friendly to the catholic and protestant churches, because mine elect are to be found in all of them. The world shall condemn and persecute, but my Father's work shall go to the churches of christianity, and to the Jews, and to mankind generally. The re-organized church is a link between the churches and the Order; upon the same principle as the Order is a link between the combined churches and the kingdom. God's work is a cosmopolitan movement, and not confined to any church, but it became necessary to clear the ground from the beginning as laid down in the spiritual messages, and finish up in the outlines of the Order without a creed, but originated in the Gospel of Freedom. The Order is not based on books, but on the living word of inspiration, as in the primitive christian church, when nothing of the new testament was written. Nor do books govern the Order, but are good for knowledge and exhortation, as the spirit is the rule for faith, truth, and love in God. The Knights of the Golden Cross are watchmen, and the perpetual succession of prophets by the gifts of prophets sustained within the degree.

The third heaven is the perfection of companionship into the sphere of wisdom, and this eminent excellency should be the emblem of your lives, adorned with the golden cross, that you should be governed by the golden rule of a superior intelligence. Being the representatives on earth of such a lofty altitude, you have to walk humbly, and love in the love of God. No person can attain into the spirit of prophecy or the mind of God, except by a continued devotion and constant prayer in the heart and soul for to meet God, and after a reception in the Father's house as the son who was lost, but found again and restored to the household as a royal prince.

When the Knights of the Golden Cross meet the king with arms cross laid over their breasts, it is an emblem of the spirit of inspiration in prayers and prophecy. Prepare yourself in the spirit to meet the Messiah by being one with His mind in your mind. Then He shall be where you are in His love, and you shall live where He is, and in His home.

Triumphant is the Golden Cross in heaven, and triumphant shall it come down to earth as the emblem of victory in my Father's love. Love man in God's love, by that love I love you. The churches shall cry out at your words and say, spiritualism! And I answer: "yes, the spiritualism of the Messiah in my Father's kingdom." The churches do not know their own spiritual ignorance and death, because they became imbued with the spirit of the world. They cry out, "devil," against spiritualism as they will do against you, but the Gospel of Freedom is my Father's spiritualism, even as I am the Messiah and have the spiritual light, but the Jews said I had the devil, and I did my healings by the devil. Destruction will come upon the world by rejecting the truth, because my Father's light to this generation of man is in His love which is rejected. In repelling that light it recoils in the spirit of anger, and war, and destruction comes upon the nations.

Receive all the truth and despise none. Greet your spiritual brethren in my love. I am sending you as lambs amongst howling wolves. The world shall hate you, but it hated me worse than it hates you. I will crown the Order of Messiah with spiritual power on earth, and the angels of heaven and the Messiah will transfigure visibly, and I shall address you audibly standing in your midst, even as I shall stand visible and audible before the eyes of Israel. Therefore do not despise materialization, because the Messiah reveals Himself in that before the world, as He does before His elect in His Father's love, with the power as Lord of Lords and the King of Kings.

INDEX.

	TIME.	PAGE.
From Messiah, CONCERNING PRIESTHOOD,	June 11, 1882.	5
The Ancient of Days, THE CHURCH AT UTAH, Ogden,	Sept. 30, 1882.	16
Messiah, ATONEMENT,	Wyoming Ter., Oct. 3, 1882.	19
Ignatius Loyola,	Oakland, April 14, 1884.	31
Messiah,	Hyde's Park, Iowa, Nov. 12, 1881.	33
John, the Apostle,	Point City, Cal., March 4, 1884.	36
Messiah,	Hyde's Park, Iowa, Oct. 2, 1883.	39
Messiah, ZION'S NEW BIRTH,	Humboldt Lake, July 14, 1885.	42
From Messiah,	Independence, Mo., April 8, 1882.	43
To build the Temple,		44
The Sixth Seal,		45
From John Stuart Mill,	Oakland, March 15, 1885.	46
Jehovah,	San Antonia, Cal., July 27, 1885.	47
Ancient of Days,	Oakland, March 26, 1885.	50
Nephi,	Oakland, Dec. 26, 1886.	56
Lemuel,	Oakland, Dec. 27, 1886.	60
Laman,	Oakland, Dec. 27, 1886.	61
Messiah to John Taylor,	Hyde's Park, Aug. 27, 1882.	66
Messiah to the Church,	Hyde's Park, May 12, 1882.	68
Messiah to George Q.,	Crescent City, Iowa, April 3, 1882.	70
Messiah to the Messenger,	Crescent City, Iowa, April 3, 1882.	71
Messiah, ON GATHERING,	Independence, April 8, 1883.	72
David Patten,	Independence, Mo., Dec. 6, 1885.	75
Messiah to John Taylor,	Hyde's Park, Aug. 6, 1883.	76
P. P. Pratt,	Independence, Mo., Dec. 29, 1882.	86
Temple to be built,		87
From Messiah, about DECEPTION,	Oakland, May 8, 1884.	88
Dr. Martin Luther,	San Antonia, Cal., April 21, 1884.	94
Peter the Apostle,	Brooklyn, Cal., April 7, 1884.	95
Messiah to Joseph Smith of Lamoni,	Oct. 28, 1883.	99
Messiah, ON ATONEMENT,	San Francisco Bay, Feb. 21, 1883.	102
Messiah, ON THE FIRST PRINCIPLES,	Peterhof, Feb. 4, 1885.	105
Moses,	Peterhof, Cal., Feb. 15, 1885.	108
Messiah, concerning Joseph Morris and others,	Aug. 11, 1884.	113
Messiah, THE CHURCH,	Oakland, Jan. 7, 1885.	119
Messiah, THE CHURCH PRIESTCRAFT,	Nebraska, Oct. 6, 1882.	137
The Apostle Paul,	Independence, April 9, 1882.	141
Messiah, THE SPIRITUAL CHURCH,	April 10, 1882.	143
Messiah, SICKNESS AND RICHES,	Hyde's Park, May 25, 1883.	147
Mahomet the Prophet,	Independence, Aug. 24, 1882.	149
Messiah, TRUTH,	Terre Haute, June 15, 1882.	150
Given at Temple Block,	Independence, Dec. 29, 1882.	152

INDEX.

	TIME.	PAGE.
From Joseph the Seer,	Oakland, July 26, 1886.	154
Michael, to the Archangel,	Hyde's Park, March 16, 1882.	154
Messiah, THE MESSENGER,	Independence, April 1, 1882.	156
Messiah, CONCERNING BAPTISM,	Hyde's Park, Dec. 14, 1882.	157
Messiah, Concerning Joseph Smith of Lamoni,	Sept. 25, 1882.	160
The HOLY GHOST,	San Francisco, March 11, 1882.	163
Concerning Spiritual Power,		165
The New Jerusalem,		173
Adam and Eve,		181
Spirit Control,		185
The Adversary,		188
The Birth of Adam and Eve,		191
The Birth of Cain,		191
Oceania,		193
The Moon,		202
Spirit Spheres,		214
Domain of The Adversary,		215
The Sun,		218
The Globe, Eve, and The Pyramids,		220
Kolob, or God's Mansions,		221
The Velocity of Spirit Travel,		222
The Spirit Spheres,		226
Chinese and Egyptians,		227
Hades, Merijam, Baal, and Gehenna,		228
Gehenna, Utter Darkness,		229
Spirits,		233
Monads,		234
The Principles of Life,		240
Incarnation,		243
One Man and One Woman,		251
Silent Prayer in the Spirit,		253
Spirit Communication,		253
Prayers,		254
Male and Female Guardian Angels,		255
The Principle of Love,		257
Spirit Worlds,		259
Summer Land, or Second Heaven,		260
Third Heaven,		261
The Spiritual Sun Kolob,		263
Women with Masculine Nature,		264
Men with Feminine Nature,		265
Monads and Astral Spirits,		265
The Fourth Heaven,		266
Rebellious and Obedient Children,		268
The Son of the Morning Glory,		270
The Sun's Rays,		272
A Journey from the Earth into Space,		273
The Celestial Sphere,		277
Man's Relation to God,		280

INDEX.

			TIME.	PAGE.
From Messiah.	Judgment.	. . .	Peterhof, Jan. 1, 1885.	286
Messiah.	Faith.	. . .	Hyde's Park, Nov. 15, 1882.	287
Messiah.	Gospel of Freedom.	.	San Francisco, Feb. 4, 1885.	288
Messiah.	Fasting.	. . .	Point City, Cal., Dec. 22, 1884.	290
Messiah.	Pre-existence.	. .	Fruitvale, Feb. 21, 1885.	291
Messiah.	The Coming Kingdom.		Terre Haute, April 30, 1882.	292
Gautama Buddha.		. . . .	July 12, 1882.	295
Messiah.	VICTORY.	. .	Kansas City, Mo., April 5, 1882.	296
Messiah.	THE LAW.	. .	Independence, Mo., Nov. 17, 1882.	297
John Taylor,	. .	.	West Point, Cal., Aug. 3, 1887.	299
Messiah.	. . .		Salt Lake City, Utah, Sept. 25, 1882.	300
Messiah.	CHURCH AUTHORITY.	.	Kanesville, Aug. 7, 1882.	304
Messiah.	REJECTION.	. . .	Point City, April 28, 1884.	306
Messiah.	THE ORDER OF MESSIAH.		Peterhof, Cal., May 25, 1887.	320
Messiah.	DISCIPLINE of the Order.		San Francisco, Aug. 20, 1887.	364

Message from Jeshuah, the Messiah.

Concerning the Priesthood.

Hyde's Park, Iowa, June 10, 1882.

The priesthood was not instituted because man and woman should be governed by it, but because they should be guided by it. It was not intended to be a ruling power, as there is only one Ruler, and it is God; but it should be a starlight shining in the dark, by which earthly advice and earthly counsel could be obtained by a more ripe experience. However, it did not so happen to be understood. The priesthood has at all times transgressed the law of its boundaries, and disrespected its true limit of control.

The so-called holy priesthood is not exactly the same power as the Holy Ghost; one with the Father in power and dominion, as a spiritual companion is one with her mate. The Holy Ghost is also represented by legions of angels, and as the Father is the Lord of Hosts, also do the angels serve man as the Father and his anointed Son, and the archangels do distribute the spiritual missions. Therefore, do not be filled with errors, and do not think that the priesthood on earth can officiate as a substitute for the Holy Ghost, nor do his work, which is the work of God, and the angels there serve him.

Whenever this point is settled in your mind, I will tell the brethren, and all friends of the Messiah, that they shall not worship idols, nor bend down before them in divine reverence; nor shall they do it before any living priesthood, neither that in heaven or that on earth.

Even so was John, my messenger at Patmos, commanded by the angel to arise, and not kneel down, nor worship him, being only a fellow-servant, and a messenger of Messiah. The law which keeps good in heaven shall also be kept good on earth.

Therefore I command you not to make idols out of a priesthood, nor to worship it, as it is written: "Thou shalt not have other gods before me, says the Lord thy God."

The starlight cannot fulfill the mission of the sunlight, and the mission of the priesthood on earth cannot fulfill the work of the priesthood in heaven, the hosts of angels and spirits directed by the power of God, and working by the same power, which flows to all, and is in all according to the conception of his love. Therefore, do not give offenses, nor willfully mislead or deceive even the lowest one amongst you.

The work of the Holy Ghost is to guide and instruct the new-born soul into the spiritual kingdom, and as it is in heaven, also it shall be done on earth, the will of my Father.

It is the duty of the priesthood to go out and teach all men and women of all nations on earth, and preach the gospel of truth, and freedom, and light from above, and my peace shall be with them, and follow at their heels, and the victorious battle-flag of the Holy Ghost shall be spread, flying before their sight as a banner in the white of heaven with a drawn sword resting on its ground.

The mission of the priesthood is not to build up any kingdom of this world, nor any state in this Union, nor to exercise a church rule, as those in the church are at liberty and not in bondage, but in the hands of the Messiah and in the freedom of his love. One is your Father in heaven, and one is your guide, Jesus, the Messiah; and his angels are before you and behind you, and at your right and your left side, and the hosts of heaven are serving you until the work is done, which is the work of my Father who is in heaven.

The eternal Father is great in heaven and on earth, but he does not allow himself to be flattered, and in all his glory he says: " I am that I am, that I am. Therefore, if you can endure
" my presence, do not kneel, and be not cast down, but stand
" erect on your feet, and look at me face to face, that I am,
" that I am, the spirit of the eternal truth, which has made this
" heaven and the earth, and worship my God, the power of
" eternity, beyond all perception of man, and not to be ap-
" proached in words, but in the spirit, which power being
" beyond all comprehension of the human brain, and can only
" be perceived as a principle the Father represents, and is iden-
" tified with in power to man on earth, that man may know the
" great eternity, which has no beginning and is without any
" end."

That is the endless ascension of God above God, or God in that unity manifested to man, and in man into endless perfection of eternal development, never to be found out where the last link is to be, nor the beginning of life in its primitive formation. That is wisdom; blessed are those who hear it and understand it, for they shall not want, nor shall their souls starve into a death-like stupor, as in the churches of Christianity, where ministers are crying out that heaven has been shut up as a tent made of brass, and without windows. I have not called them, and they have preached in my name. I have not sent them, and they have walked on, and been doing my errands. "Blessed art thou!" cries out a spirit to you, because you write by the power of Messiah. Yes, blessed are those who hear and read these words, and receive the truth on account of its being the truth. There shall be strife and discontent on earth as long as the Messiah is not revealed to man in his second coming, when he shall be revealed as he is, and not as he is supposed to be, and his disciples shall receive him as the Messiah, and be as he is in their conduct of life, and in the spirit of their doings. That time is not yet, but has to come. When the tree has ripe fruit, then you are going to gather it, and not at the time when the fruit is green; but the second harvest is at the door not as the first one by my servant, Joseph, but as the second harvest shall be, not only in preaching, and in faith, and in signs, and in expectations, and in the obedience to commandment of love ye one another, but in power, and in the sight of heaven, when the hosts of heaven shall be revealed, and appear with me, and this earth shall sing its hallelujah: Blessed be the eternal God, and blessed be his name, because he has turned the hosts of the ancestors to the hosts of the children, and taken the curse away which blasted this planet. Amen.

That little church in heaven, but large church on earth, called the Catholic church, has lifted my cross high under the sky, and it has honored me with lips and songs and customs and ceremonies, but it has bowed down in dust before idols of its own make, and it has been wandering far away from me and the spirit of truth. A living priesthood is as a stream of living water, which flows as a stream of living power out from God, filled with the Holy Spirit of life to comfort those before the altar—the officiating priesthood—as those under the altar, those whose blood was shed as a testimony to that truth of heaven, to be the truth and to dare to be the truth. In that sense has the Catholic church utterly failed, as it has built up an edifice on a foundation which is not me, nor of me, because I am the truth, and not the policy of the appearance of the truth. The pontiff at Rome has not the power in the church to change the channel of hierarchical teachings, even if he knew that they were all but falsehoods.

Such a condition is a petrifaction of cold, lifeless, bygone superstitions, and handed-down legends and traditions, without power to remodel man and woman to be God-like, in the spirit of a union with God. That penalty of a servitude has to come to an end, as centuries have put it on the scales and tested its apparent value, and found it to be lacking of almost every claim and every pretension.

Blessed are those who hear me when I say now, the gospel of delivery from bondage, or the gospel of freedom shall be revealed to earth, and it shall be a salvation to men and women in the Catholic church. The barrier of an arrogant and self-conceited priesthood shall be broken asunder as it were of glass, and justice shall once more be done on earth—justice to the dignity of that to be a man and of that to be a woman, even conceived in imperfections, and reared in sins, altho' aspiring to the perfection of my Father in heaven, who is perfection.

Be not misled, as your cardinals, and archbishops and monks, and nuns and priests are of dust, and shall be to dust again. They are of the earth, and altho' their souls shall not die, I say to you that the Catholic hierarchy is an institution of this world, and shall perish with the world, as any earthly condition shall cease to be. These have received the personal worship of being divine, but shall be abhorred and despised, as though they were devils, even with all their honesty, and their followers shall reproach them, and say: "Did we not depend upon your words; did we not feed you and your hosts of disciples? And we depended on you, and you did not save our souls from error— we are deeper in the mire than we ever were, and you are stuck as we are, and cannot come to our rescue." They shall answer them: "We served you for money of the world, and we gave you whatever we had of the world, and if we had possessed something else, or something better, we should have served your souls with it. *Our* souls were starving, and you cried for bread, and where should we get it from? We comforted *ourselves*, and sung a hymn for *you*, and sung a cradle ballad, and rocked you to sleep."

A loud voice was heard out of heaven, as a thunder rolling from across the firmament: "O, ye hypocrites, why did you not humble yourselves, and by day and at night ask for light and truth from the Father of Heaven, who gives readily, and reproaches none for his prayers. Silence has now befallen you, for you are cut off from the Holy See of prejudice and abominations, as it is stagnated in errors, only fit to be burned up by the eternal fire of its own combustible material, in the presence of the light of the gospel of freedom and truth."

The Vicar of Christ is an impossibility in itself, as to be Christ is to be the embodied principle of the Messiah manifested in the world. This principle has moved humanity in and by my person. To be a follower of Christ is to be one with Christ in that principle, altho' the person, Jesus, remains a distinct individual. If the Pope claims himself to be a Vicar of Jesus, then he might accept such a position by having a literal and direct appointment from me in person to sit where he does, and act as he does as a prince. I never gave the Roman Pontiff any such power of attorney to act for me, nor in my name. The tradition handed it down that Peter was the first presiding elder in Rome, and that to him I had committed the presiding power of the church. Let it be known, in the first place, that the message about Messiah was carried to Rome by my apostle Paul, and others, a long time before Peter ever arrived there, and the congregations there had their presiding elders a long time before Peter lived and preached at Rome. The next point is that the apostles appointed by me were to go out into the world as general messengers, and I never had any knowledge that any of the twelve ever settled down as a presiding elder, or bishop, over any single congregation, but they preached the gospel of truth from door to door, and from city to city, even as it was commanded them to do; and when they had ordained presiding elders, they went on and on, to new places and other towns. This, in itself, implies that Peter did tarry at Rome, even as Paul and numerous others did, but only as a sojourner, and not as a presiding elder, or bishop.

Now I will argue the third point, that of Peter having received the keys of heaven, or the supreme authority as the Vicar of Christ.

What is the key of heaven? It is an instrument by which heaven can be unlocked. What do you call that instrument or key? Inspiration! Did Peter have it? Yes, in such a degree that he unlocked heaven and saw the Messiah, and lived in the Messiah principle of truth, and it became identically verified in his person, so that in perceiving it he could identify me as Messiah, the son of the living God.

For this Christ principle there is no vicar; it can only be lived as a vital part of man himself, and blessed are those who attain to it because they have the key to heaven. Therefore, among other things, I said to Peter: "Blessed art thou, Simon, Jonas' son, because not flesh and blood, it is no human knowledge has revealed it unto you that I am the Messiah, but the spirit of my Father has done it. To possess that spirit in such a degree that persons live in it by the gifts and power of heaven, by the gifts of healing, and visions and dreams, and trance, speaking in tongues, and inspirations, and interpretations sufficient to discern the principle of Messiah as part of themselves, those men or women know the Messiah, and are in possession of the key to heaven; and what they make free on earth by the power of that key shall also be made free in heaven, because by that power of being the ambassadors of heaven, they shall have the key to heaven to manifest their power by." What I said to Peter individually, I say to all men and all women: Be ye as I have been in the world, and walk as I have done, and follow after me in the same spirit, and ye shall carry in the bosom of your souls that power which is to possess the key of heaven, and more than that, the key to the kingdom which is to come to earth.

Any ordination of the priesthood can only confirm you in that power, but cannot give it. This is the perfection of my Father's work on earth, for the salvation of man, even the Gospel of Freedom.

The Pontiff of Rome has no such mission to officiate in the name of Messiah. I am the Messiah, the son of the living God, because I am one with the Father, but not one with the Pope. If I was one with the infallible pontiff, I should not be that I am now, identified with the spirit of truth.

My successor on earth is the Holy Spirit, and hosts of messengers to earth. The Holy Spirit has ever been present and active wherever doors and souls have been kept open to receive him and his representatives, the holy angels and spirits sent from God to man, and the gates of hell have not been able to quench out that power and gifts from heaven to man. The spirit was ever active among mine elect, the chosen of God, after the order of Messiah, even when the world reigned supreme in its own political churches, professing my name, but filled with deception, and with death to all spiritual truth.

The Pope, as an individual, has not been further away from me than most men have been, but he has not been near to me. Arrogance, bigotry, political intrigues, and cares of this world and its vexations, have blinded the most of all the pontiffs, and put them into a deep slumber, and desire for power and worldly aggrandizement, greatly to be deplored, and detestedly abhorred by the angels in heaven, because the Popes became a greater imposition to themselves than most men, as their claims were the greatest; also many of them have fallen the deepest in the spirit world. They became indeed what they were in their earthly lives, a deception to themselves, and a living lie, carrying the crucified truth on their breasts. As it went with Babylon, also shall it take place with the Vicar at Rome, the first signifying the power of this world's glory, and the second signifying this world's spiritual pride and arrogance, or glory of imposture, under the mocked name of Christ. They have preached in my name, and I did not ordain them with my spirit to do the work. They have called people into my fold, and I did not send them, but they went on and did their own errand, and claimed it to be from God.

Blessed are those who receive the truth and keep it. Amen.

Now is the time come when the Son of Man shall have his power revealed to earth.

The Mormon priesthood at Utah is as arrogant as the Catholic priesthood ever was, even in the point of claiming an eternal authority, and inflicting a despotic torture of ruling power to be exercised in the church. I say arrogant, because they have shut up their eyes and ears, and cry out as loud as the priesthood did in my days among Israel: "We have Moses and the prophets." But I was sick, and they did not visit me. I was hungry, and they did not give me food or drink; and I was naked and in rags, and without a home, and they did not clothe me, nor give me a shelter to sleep under, and they professed my name with their tongues, and with long sermons at the tabernacle, but they never knew me, nor had they ever seen me, nor had I ever shown them my Father in heaven.

They proclaim to the world that they have power and authority from me, given under the hands of the angels. Then let them do the work of angels, and let them have among the twelve the spirit of angels, and the authority from angels in my name shall abide with them; but angels have departed from their midst, and they have been blinded by their own misdeeds, and their ways among the mountains have been stained with blood, and persecutions have come upon the church, and all kind of ill sayings have reached the church, and laid heavy chains upon my people.

Brigham Young is now in the spirit, and is in the presence of the church which he presided over, and I have laid the plumb in his hand to discern by the depth and height of the church, as he led the people for a little while. Therefore I have put him as a line on his own work, and he is finding it as it is, and wanting in the length, and breadth and depth.

Wo shall come upon all the people of the church there honor the memory and deny his mission that I have appointed him to fill to the church, and in the spirit form above. I have given him a work to perform, another work than my servant, Joseph, has been appointed to fulfill in his mission from the spirit, and to man on earth, and another work different from that of any of my servants.

Wo shall befall you, my people, who are my disciples, and profess my name, if you with my name on your lips refuse to listen to my voice.

I am calling on you with a lamenting voice, as from a lonely bittern among the rushes at the seashore, and I have commanded my servant, Brigham, to be a guide to the messenger whom I have called upon to do my errand to my people, he shall be at the right and at the left side of my messenger, when he does my work amongst my people which are hiding up amongst the mountains; and you shall know that it is my voice which sounds to you on earth, coming as the words from my messenger, and sounding before the final coming of the Son of Man.

The Mormon priesthood at Utah has left its first inheritance, and prostituted its first love.

Therefore return speedily, and return with haste in the spirit where you came from, when you were driven out from Missouri, and do your former works, or my love, that love by which you love me, shall be wedded to your brethren of the reorganized church, and to him you despise, my servant, Joseph Smith, at Lamoni. I have called him by the spirit of revelation to be the presiding elder, and the first elder before my church on earth; and if you will harken to my voice, then I will take both of the churches by my hand, and make them one by my hand, and I will teach them how to follow after me. On that day you shall know that it was my love, that love by which the spirit loved you, there gave you strength to possess in the spirit that pearl to your soul, there gave you the inspiration, so your life and power was found to be one with the life and power there is in God. For the purchase of that pearl have many of you given away all that you possessed in the world of earthly treasures.

Blessed are you, when you are calling upon God in the name of Messiah; and blessed shall your inheritance be with Israels on earth, as with my elects in the heavens. AMEN.

Message Given by the Ancient of Days.

About the Church at Utah.

Ogden Canon, Utah, Sept. 30, 1882.

I am by you, not because I wish to give any new commandment; but because I want to call attention to what already is well known. I do not want to dissolve, but to build up and strengthen what already exists. I wish the people of Utah, and of the church of Messiah, to understand more fully the necessity of being of one accord in regard to what they have called the church of God. Joseph Smith was young, and not experienced by any ripe age in earth-life—even he was an inspired prophet—and it caused much vibration in the church in his days, and his premature death, which was all the legal consequence of his want of caution, and not of courage. He did not entirely absorb the idea that the government of the church is a spiritual power, to be exercised over all nations, and not a power of this world, nor a principality after the world's pattern. Therefore he had the pain to see the church driven out from Independence, Mo., and from Nauvoo; therefore he had to fight and contend with the political power of the world; therefore has the same spirit been pursued at Utah, and things and affairs have got into a focus, and the fight is going on.

The government of this earth has a right to exist, and the church has a right to exist; but each one on its own platform. Collision is not necessary when each remains in each own domain; as once has been told you, to render that to God what is to be rendered him, and to the world what has to be rendered to the world. In that respect there can be no collision, and the church has no legal right from heaven to override the governments of the earth, nor has this government such liberty given it from above. The contest at present, headed with the fight about polygamy, has the church forced upon the United States government, as the church intended to compel the people of the United States to recognize polygamy, a recognition very arbitrary as a command to legislate on. No such power can be invested, or has been invested, in the church, nor has the church any such command from heaven to preach polygamy as an institution to be recognized of the world, which in fact must appear as such by claiming it to be recognized by the congress of the people. This is the bottom of the evil from which there is no outlet but defeat or retreat. If the priesthood were wise men in the wisdom of heaven, something they claim to be, they would at once discover that they have gone too far, and would be willing to retreat in good order. Good order would be wisdom, as a state against a state, within a state, is a disorder in that state, and rebellion in the heart of the government. All and every government must fight the battle of self defense, or be broken asunder.

It was not intended that the church of God on earth should be annihilated within and amongst a free people, as this government represents; therefore was the church organized here, and the gospel has been preached and believed and established here. There is the great failure of the church, which has dwarfed its growth, that it became mixed up with the world's institutions, not worth fighting for nor aspiring to. If the church at once could divest itself of all political power or aspiration, then the contest could and would cease. As it is, the fight will go on till another exodus will take place, and then again another exodus, and the movement will dwindle down to few families, and the church will fail in its mission, which is the spiritual development and domain in the hearts of all nations. Only in this way and manner can it possibly be the stone, which cut off from out of the mountains, shall fill the earth with a superior governing power. This petty quarreling about the supremacy is unworthy the church of God, as it does not serve any person's or pretender's individual interest; nor does it represent any power or government on earth.

Polygamy has publicly been made a disgust to the people of the United States and government; therefore, let it not be so any longer, by putting it before the world as an institution practiced in the world's domain, or imposed on the world and the governments of the world to decide upon. The world has the power to put it down, as obnoxious and disgusting to its governments. Only in such an acceptation is the power in the voice of the people, that the church must keep all such practice as offenses given to the world, and has to remain within its own domain of love and not of lust.

The spiritual companionship in heaven stands as the Omega, or the last; never understood by the Saints, and less by the world, and it became a curse to the Saints more than a blessing. Be not confounded. Conquer first the world by the living word of truth. Teach the world the first principles, and the letters of the alphabet belonging to the gospel, but do not commence with the last letter. Keep the last to the last. You cannot teach a child the alphabet in the manner you have acted, and much less the executive, and officers, and congress of the United States government. Some of you have contested congress to enact laws against a church institution, even the church of God. This has not been done, as you have not lived according to my laws, which went out from Zion. Therefore, your polygamy is of the world and not of me, nor according to the spirit of my law, and as your deeds have been, so also have you defended them. Therefore, repent, and let the world have the right to judge its own institutions; because what is of the world belongs to the world, and the world has the right to judge it, and do with its own as it will. God's love was not within it, and polygamy was practiced according to the spirit of the world. The world claims to control that which rightfully belongs to the world.

Some persons have ideas that they are wronged, and their spirits get filled with bitterness and gall against the world, which they should love, and convert from darkness to light; but you are fighting darkness by darkness, being yourselves in darkness, and from that is nothing derived; as darkness can only be fought by a superior light, as the only method by which you can conquer the world.

A warning voice is reaching you from the Patriarch of heaven, and the Father of mankind and Ruler of the earth. The Ancient of Days speaks to you with his own voice and you ought to listen, because of its superior truth. He is warning you to abolish what power you have borrowed from the word, because all flesh is only grass, and all unions which are not in the spirit shall perish as grass. Polygamy came into the church, and the spirit of the world, which is the spirit of the flesh, it crucified the church in the world. Let that curse be banished, and the world will honor and respect you. If you are the friends of Messiah, you are the friends of peace, and as such salute each other. Leave politics alone. Spread the gospel over all the world. Build temples over all the world. Preach life, peace and truth over all the world. Monogamy or polygamy does not concern the gospel in the world, as all marriage belongs to the world, but the gospel is the life eternal. It does not solve governments, but was preached alike to the Jews in polygamy as to the pagan Romans and Greeks in monogamy. Governments are not affected by it, except by what truth there is in it to give light and life to new ideas. The heavenly companionship is not the monogamy nor the polygamy of the world, but belongs to the gospel of freedom, as it is understood in heaven, and as it will be understood in the second coming of Messiah, but now is misunderstood on earth; therefore, let polygamy be abolished, because you are a chosen people, and not a people of the world. My name is forever, and will last forever.

The Ancient of Days, the Patriarch of heaven, is the God of Abraham and Isaac, and Jacob and Daniel. With a warning voice he says in time to you, abolish polygamy; and do it before my warning voice does not speak any longer, or you shall feel the force of the world put upon you, and there shall be no escape, and another people shall step into your place and do your work, and you shall be left outside the door, and in darkness and in pain.

Give unto Cæsar that which is Cæsar's, and render unto God that which is God's. Amen. The world shall not hate you if you do not steal from the world.

MESSAGE FROM JESHUAH, THE MESSIAH.

CONCERNING THE ATONEMENT.

LARAMIE PLAINS, WYOMING TER., Oct. 3, 1882.

There has been an idea presented to the church that I was unjustly crucified, and for that reason needed to be avenged. That gave birth to another equally erroneous idea, that the prophets, and even Joseph, my servant, was unjustly slain, and ought to be avenged. It led to a third tremendous error, that people who embraced the faith were deprived of their free agency, and if they committed any crime, or apostatized, they were deprived to depart in peace, and some were killed to perfect my atonement for them, which was supposed to have been made imperfect to them by their apostasy from a body of believers, or the church. However, a person may apostatize from the church, and at the same time not apostatize from me. In this manner crept that error into the church, that the atonement by me for such a dissenter could not be perfected except by the shedding of his own blood, or by being murdered. Murder thus became the royal court crime among the priesthood, and the most refined method by which I could be served by them.

This rank heresy of all truth in heaven or upon the earth, was more becoming the church of demons than any body of men and women calling themselves after my name. Brigham is now present in the church of light, as you see him standing by us, and hear his defense. He says that he did it in reverence and faith, and obedience to my holy sacrifice to the world, and not because he wished to torture his brethren and sisters. Also that a death warrant was executed more on persons who committed adultery and were full of lust, than on those who had lost their faith in the gospel.

I shall answer Brigham, my servant, personally, as I know this bottom evil of all evils in heaven and on earth must cease, and at least in the kingdom of Messiah, murder shall not be found even in name.

My sacrifice for man and to man was a sacrifice of love—nothing but love to humanity made me come into the world and do what I did, and say what I did, and suffer what I did, and die as I did. Let it forever and forever be settled in your mind that it was a free and willing sacrifice of my life on the altar of truth and love to humanity, in that love by which the Father loved the Son.

From childhood I was fully aware of what was going to happen, and the spirit of God revealed it in dreams to my mother, Marie. Also you have read that Moses and Elias were revealed to me on the mountain, visible and audible, in the presence of the apostles, and they heard their voices, that they spoke to me about my death and suffering upon the cross.

I said the same thing to my disciples times and times again, that the Son of Man had to suffer all this humiliation from a darkened and perverted generation, and enter through suffering and death on the cross into his glory in heaven.

Now I ask any person in heaven or on earth, where the avenging me could get into any human soul who believes in me? That question I give to all, as well as to my servant, Brigham. On the principle of avenging, the Jews have been persecuted from country to country, and from city to city, and their blood has been shed by those who believed in my blood, or in the blood shed of my body on the cross. Be not confounded with what you call the atonement and in what it consists, because even so did God love the world that he did not save me, his only begotten Son in the flesh, but made the light of heaven to be the light of the world—and I became the light of this world, as he is the light of heaven, through suffering.

The next part of the atonement to understand, is that man loves himself, and called forth the demand of my death, but that God loves the human family, and in the fullness of time, when the race had received such a development that the truth could find followers, and not only believers, I came into the world, flesh of flesh, and God of God, and, that the human family should not be confounded about my presence in the world, I became as one of the lowest and meekest among men on earth. This was the destination of love made in eternity as an atonement between light and darkness, or between God and man. Such a conception of my birth makes it an atonement for man. Such a childhood and such a youth of my being in the world, and yet being conscious of my glory in heaven, and the spiritual messengers and angels of light who surrounded me and served me, made my presence on earth an atonement of God's love to man.

The manifestations of my appearance into the world, with all the spiritual power which attended it, is the atonement of God's love to man—and there is no single act of mine, or point in my life, on which you can balance the atonement, not even by the blood, except on my entire life. I am the atonement from the beginning to the end, altho' it was finished in an earthly sense when my last breath was hushed in the silence of death. That very point that God was manifested in flesh, reconciled the flesh with God, and made the atonement as a reconciliation with the nature of man fallen away from God in the possibility that flesh and blood became reunited with heaven.

That is the very point that I want to get deeply rooted in your mind, that the atonement is not a single act, or concentrated in any drops of blood, but it was in blood that my last act between God and man was sealed as the seal of God's love to man. In that blood the new testament, or the new covenant, was made with man, as the last act of my life, giving myself away as a sacrifice of God's love, to give life to the world, and my life, as my words came from that love, and were of that love, even that of my Father who is in heaven. Therefore, each and every one who believe in me, and follow after me as I was in the world, shall not perish, but have everlasting life, because that is life eternal to be found in God, the fountain of happiness, and the glory and assurance of immortality, to know thee, the only true God, to man, as I have shown thee to him in the perfect knowledge of thee by which I have known thee from eternity, and thou sent me into the world that the world might know thee by knowing me.

There has been a general acceptance by theologians that my blood was shed once for all time as the perfect washing away of all sins, and the simple acceptance of such a construction of ideas was sufficient for each and all.

I assure you it is altogether a fallacy born of the fancy of man, and not of God, as it, also, is inconsistent with the laws and the love of truth and life, and was never taught by me, or by mine apostles, who **were personally my followers on earth,** and such an idea was never entertained as a creed during the first centuries of the church, even if the words of the saints from that period had been translated and construed to any such end.

During the years of my teaching that to be in the world was a greater suffering to me than pains I endured upon the cross— I say a greater suffering, as I might have escaped the cross by fleeing from the country of Judea, but it would have been turning away from my mission, for which I was born and came into the world.

There has been a dissertation that my death on the cross might have been averted, and the human family might have accepted me without any such sacrifice, by having the Jews as a nation converted to my mission. I shall answer that argument, as it has once brought a schism among the twelve in the church at Utah.

If I could have been accepted of man, I should never have been born on earth, and never have been made flesh and blood in the world. The fact to be born on earth, and get into the world, precluded from eternity all my suffering and death. It could not be otherwise when the eternal truth from heaven embodied in the world of falsehoods and sins, except it had to suffer death and be rejected of the world. I could not be triumphant except through suffering and death. It was then to me as it is to-day to others, the legal consequences of suffering from the state in which the world is living, as the light could not be known to a world blinded by its own darkness.

Could the world have received me as the light of heaven, then heaven would have been on earth, and heaven would have been open to the vision of man. There would have been no falling away, nor any such evidence as the fall of man, or the degradation of the human family, and my presence on earth would have been superfluous. The angels would have walked from heaven to earth, and taught man, and my heavenly messengers would always have been by you, and the ignorance of man would never have been.

Therefore, let no one confound you, as the death on the cross was more of a relief to me from the misery of a rejected love, than any additional suffering. The hate of the world to the revealed light from above, gave the testimony to God of the darkness of man's nature, and his love for darkness rather than light, that God became reconciled with man's spiritual infirmities, and in his love atoned himself with the race, that light should not be taken entirely away from out of the darkness of man.

Death in itself gives that relief which pain is seeking after. The seal and finish to my death on the cross, by which the covenant of salvation came from darkness to light, is stamped and made acceptable to my Father in heaven, by his love which is in my blood, that love to the world, even in the moment of death, and in obedience to the commandment of my Father. This love should not be in vain, but give light and life to the world. It is not because the seal was made in blood, but because the seal my blood was stamped with his love, and it did not need any such sacrifice from me. The blood of his only begotten Son bears testimony to heaven against the cruelty of man, and that I was faithful unto the last moment in finishing my work, and establishing the truth and light to man on earth.

It is not in blood that the work was done, nor was it accomplished with blood, but it was finished in blood. It was not in the blood that man should find the saving principle, but it was in following after me in the same spirit, which dwells in me, and in the example of Christ to be Christlike, and sons and daughters of God, bearing the seal of the blood, or God's love manifested on the cross, which is the new covenant of peace with God in their hearts and souls, that they may see heaven open, and have the fellowship with Messiah at his second coming to earth in the glory of all truth. Amen.

I say again, be not confounded, as many false teachers have been into the world, and they have laid expressive stress upon the blood theory of salvation, and because they were not inspired, they could not give to the world what they were not in possession of. It has been the cause of much cruelty and persecution among the Jews, as among the Christians, and of cruelty and intolerance in the church at Utah, and made its history among the mountains, as well as outside of them, stained with blood. That has been the cause of blotting out nearly all true Christian spirit among mankind, and of that terrible blood curse and massacres among those who profess my name, and also of the Catholic inquisition. It has been the cause that blood atonement crept into the church at Utah, as among the Catholic orders. This doctrine presented to the world about my Father, who is love, that he was a bloodthirsty tyrant, and could not be appeased but by having men slaughtered as a sweet sacrifice before him, even I, his only begotten Son, is a doctrine of the devils from eternity, as all creeds are falsehoods in the light of heaven.

There are teachings on earth from the prince of darkness, and doctrines of falsehoods pasted on the name of my Father, who is of heaven, and in heaven. Man must get low down in the desire of spirituality to accept as a social order such a degrading philosophy, which even sound reason rebels against — but modern theology is rooted in labyrinths of falsehoods. To be truthful and of truth, and to be the truth itself, is sufficient suffering to an existence in the world, but ten-fold more when truth has to live and breathe and exist in a society which is ruled by professional hypocrites. Man is naturally born into existence on earth without being born spiritually by the natural parents, and persons of his surroundings may not report with God by the Holy Spirit. Sufficient has been said on that subject at other places, so it explains itself to all who wish to have the light and nothing but the light, that man's spiritual darkness is the natural element to man, and the adversary was a murderer and a liar from the commencement, and man loved his spirit more than holiness and the spirit of God.

The blood atonement in the church at Utah is a double-headed error, there appearing as the lamb with the two horns. It speaks as a lamb, but does the work of the dragon. These terrible errors already mentioned are red in the colors of hell, and as the symbol of murder and blood, too awful to be mentioned by any inspired pen, yet it has to be done.

The church did not conceive what a monstrous crime it is to shed human blood for any pretense or in any name, and ten fold more monstrous and more accursed is it to put such a dark patch on the garment of the Savior of the world, and make his cross to be a scaffold.

I said the Savior of the world, because the ultimate result of the eternal plan laid down and matured in heaven, is the perfect redemption of all the human species, embodied or disembodied, according to their own state to belong to, and of the creation, and of the earth itself, and it is accomplished by the truth, and the development of truth, and the appliance of truth, and the obedience to truth and the laws of truth, which are the laws of life there permeating the creation, which is the nature of God.

This testament which I left behind me in the world was sealed by my blood, as a testimony to that truth, that none can open the seal except the one who sealed it in the love of God, and my Father who is in heaven, and in whose hands I commended my spirit at death, he will by me open it once, when my mission is finished in heaven as it was finished on the cross, and when it is finished in the gospel of freedom as it was in my resurrection. Then it shall be known that it was a work of the most intense love, by which only God could love the world, and not, as some bloodthirsty apostles have called it, an atonement in blood and for blood and to blood, and at the same time they have called themselves after my name, when they were the apostles of Satan, but I have trodden the winepress alone and there was none to help me, nor was there any bloody sacrifice demanded, but that I brought not to God, but to the ignorance of the world, as I died for the sins of the world. Nor did heaven, nor did angels, nor my Father, demand any such sacrifice, but the love demanded it, and in that love which is in the Father, and in the Son, and in the Holy Spirit, I gave my life away and took it again, and I did it myself. The Utah church apostles have stained with blood the reputation in the world of the church of saints, and they have drenched in blood and fear and terror that free spirit of God's love which is born of the Holy Ghost in the hearts of the saints, who are the children of my Father who is in heaven.

It is the reason why I told my disciples when on earth, that false teachers should arise, and claim to be sent to men and women in my name, and I should never have known of them, nor have heard of their mission in my name, and they should be known of their works, as they walked in their own name, and spoke in their own name, and the wolves hailed them, because the church became of the world, and did the works of the devils, and these men made deep and cunning covenants, and laid heavy oaths upon each other, to be powerful as a political body in the world, and they spoke falsehoods, that they might get power to govern the blinded souls by all kind of politics and cunnings of this world, and they captured the minds of their followers, and bound them over to do their will and work for that purpose, and in their own short-sightedness, and in thraldom to the spirit of the world, even as Israel became captivated and kept in bondage by the Egyptians, that these apostles of the church at Utah might vindicate their own design, and they were all the time calling on my name in the spirit of the adversary, who is not of me, and I did not even take the pains to hear their voice, as I knew their hearts that they were dark and evil, and their ways were full of blood, and they served the adversary with murders which they pronounced to be sacrifices to me.

When my holy angels kindled the spirit of love in a man's or woman's heart, and they were found together socially, according to the dictation of the Holy Spirit, then these apostles of perdition, which some of them are even as Judas was, and will progress through much suffering in the spirit world, they made victims and a bloody sacrifice of such persons, and said holiness to be sin, and dug their graves, and cut their throats, that they might be saved by shedding their blood, even as those apostles were themselves guilty in bloodshed, serving their master of perdition, not knowing that they had perverted my gospel of peace, and made it a terror and a by-word among all nations, and the falsehoods in the place of truths went out from Utah with a stench that fumigated heaven, and made the holy angels weep over the corruption, and depart from the presence of the church, and handed such apostles over to the guardianship of devils. Therefore has tribulation been powerful in the church, and therefore has my Father given the world a sway over the church at Utah.

Let it be known to all who pray to the Father in my name, that no burnt offerings or bloody sacrifices are demanded. The symbols of offerings belong to the sons of Levi, or to the Aaronic priesthood, and the gospel of righteousness, as a substitute for that the Father wished to receive in the spirit of a meek and humble mind, as the only true offering acceptable in heaven. Offerings were signs of submission and of humility, and not the symbols of the blood of the Son of Man. Nothing in the church has been more misunderstood than the covenant made by the gospel of grace and sealed with my blood. When it comes, which is now at hand, then shall the decay of the churches be revealed, and it shall be made evident that they have the seal and prestige of the world, and not of the Son of Man. It shall come to pass that those who are low and humble in their own estimation shall receive the truth, and those who are high up, and claim to be apostles, shall be counted among the prostitutes of the truth.

The blood of Jesus of Nazareth is a historical fact, and that he was crucified became a part of the past history of humanity, but in that knowledge is no salvation to be found; it is in the covenant of truth, which your souls make in my name with God, you arrive in a saving relation to yourself, and you get wedded in your soul with the eternal principle of truth, which gives to you the admission to the gifts in heaven, and to have them by you in earth life. You are accepted by God's love and in the obedience to the spirit of Messiah. This testament have I made with all men who are willing to do my work, and once they shall find out that the work was their own work of salvation, as it was finished and sealed for them until I shall open it myself in the gospel of freedom, sealed until that hour in my blood. This covenant in my blood is not an external gift, but a reality internally in your soul, that you are in possession of the spirit of truth, and have been received of the truth. In that way are you made free, and when you are in the freedom of the Father, and in his kingdom, then you are free indeed in his spirit.

Therefore all blood atonement and teaching about it in the church has no root in me, but in him who was a murderer from the beginning, and the father of murderers. The apostles of Messiah are familiar with the spirit of the commandment: "Thou shalt not kill," and in that spirit is no blood atonement. I have proven by my own acts and words on earth that I did not endorse the letter but the spirit of the law, and I did not sanction capital punishment to be executed on persons accused for adultery, but the church at Utah pronounced such a judgment in my name, and did not know that its own soul was full of lust. With that judgment you judge shall you be judged again, so be careful how you judge during your life on earth, as none of you can stand before me and cast the first stone, and be justified by my Father in heaven. I am standing between the priesthood and the people. The stone you are casting at your brother or sister you are casting upon me, and the knife you use against them you are using against me, and the bullet you are sending after them you are sending after me, and the grave you are digging for them you are digging for me, to plunge me into.

Long and dreadful has your journey been among the Rocky Mountains, and your footprints are as dark spots marked with cruelty and blood.

Such have your records been to the world, and the history of the priesthood among the mountains, and at last you have made it impossible to preach with success the gospel of peace among the nations, as you pray with uplifted hands, and they are red with the blood of my people. I have counted your years and days, and the hours in which you are scattered, and I am weary of looking at the church.

A new chapter of God's dealing with man is to roll up before the world, and it will roll down on the church at Utah. Because my anger is kindled against you, therefore I will drive you out of the holes where you have grown fat, and out of the chambers of the mountains, where you have been hiding with ease for years, and been living with safety, as the time for your redemption is now at hand, and you shall hear the voice of my servants who are calling on you in my name, and I will send your enemies at you, and they shall follow you up as bloodhounds do a flock of sheep. In that way I will drive out those of my flock, and I will herd them by my right hand, and gather them around me, and make them come and worship in spirit and in truth at my temple at Independence.

Thus says the Lord your God: "I will make an end of your mischief and of your ill-doings, and the remnant of you shall praise my name in honesty and truth, and in an upright spirit, and of a pure heart," says the Lord your God, "and you shall have no other God before me, nor any other blood before mine, nor any person else to assist me in the perfect redemption by blood atonements. Blinded are you and in darkness, as you went all over the world, and invited the elect to come and receive the hospitality of Zion, and when they came you killed some of them, because the spirit of God came as a witness to them against the priesthood, that it had lost the spirit of the Holy One, and that Zion had become a servant under the law belonging to the rejection of Israel, and the consequent judgment which the Jews came under in their days of unbelief and idolatry, and in the days they rejected the Messiah.

Warfare has the church at Utah waged against the truth and against the strangers who visited it in good faith to its hospitality, and trusted in Zion for protection and safety, but they were cruelly massacred, and even the sucking babes at their mothers' breasts did the priesthood not spare. Therefore the avenging angel has descended upon the church, because its people have been faithless in their hearts, even as the Jews were, and hardened their souls until they are now stagnated in errors. A crusade shall the priesthood at Utah preach against my servants, because the measure of the church is filled with superstition, and its darkness shall be great on that day. Awake and be ready and careful, my elect among the people, when you read these words, and how you will receive my servants, and how you will accept the truth as the living manna coming down from heaven to be a food for your souls. The Spirit says: "Do not on that day make a covenant in your hearts with the darkness in the church, to serve the angels of darkness, and to be obedient to the spirit of malice and blood and persecution, and false accusations against my servants. My people, do not follow the evil-doers in the church at Utah, or, my elect, your redemption shall be as through a great fire, because you followed those who waged war against the light. Remain the children of God, that you may be the children of the light. Amen.

Just now, by writing down these words, the messenger discovers in a vision his hands pierced, and as covered with fresh blood from the wounds. He also discovers next to me an altar of white marble, but there is nothing on it. I am standing by it, and am asking him now: "What do you love the most, my words, my spirit or my blood?" Truly he answers me in the spirit, that he cannot divide these three emblems of my person. Therefore, when the present generation is crying for blood, and glory in blood, it shall have the blood, as that generation and their generation got blood after I was condemned to die on the cross, as they cried out for my blood to come on theirs and their children's heads, and it came as they asked for it, and blood was running in streams when Jerusalem was destroyed, and of the Jewish nation the tribes of Judah and Benjamin were scattered, and they received blood, and such shall be my testimony to the church at Utah. It shall not be raised up by blood, but it shall be humiliated by its blood atonement, which it did in the spirit of the adversary, as Israel did it to Baal on the hills at Samaria. The blood of the saints, and the innocent blood which the apostles allowed to be shed, shall not raise up the priesthood, but cast it down, and it shall not save the people, but be a curse upon them, but those who receive me shall be saved, because I am the truth, and have the everlasting life which my father shall give to those who call on him in my name, with a pure heart and a humble spirit, and of all their strength. Amen.

My people asked the priesthood for the living bread from heaven, and the apostles poured out upon them the spirit of the serpent. O, my people, when they fight you down with the power of the adversary, then the apostles have invited the spirit of the world within themselves, and when they fight you they have turned against me, who they say ordained them to be apostles, but they called themselves, and amongst themselves, as it pleased their pride, and my words did not magnify their calling in the spirit of my Father. Because they persecuted my elect when they spoke the truth, therefore departed the spirit of revelation from the church, and the spirit of prophecy was hushed down and driven out from all its meetings, and soon it became a by-word to receive the gifts from heaven, but if they had remained in the spirit of the gifts, they had remained in me, and would have been of me, and the apostles would not have turned against my elect. Your days among the mountains are counted. I have the scales in my hand, and I have put the apostleship in the scales and rejected it. I have measured them with my lines, and I have given the spirit of their calling which they robbed from me, and the spirit of prophecy which they denied and quenched in their midst, to apostles called after my own heart, and I will give the power of revelations to another people, which I will gather together from all over the country, and they shall go forth in my power, and by Joseph, the son of the Seer, they shall build up the temple at Independence.

On that day shall my elect come out from the mountains, and not be bound any more to the rocks, and come forth with great joy, but the Utah church shall have no part in my work if it do not repent hastily, and return to its first love, and unite with my people. Therefore, abstain from political prestige after the world's pattern, and from the spirit of blood and lust, and cruelty and thraldom, and the building up of cities and governments according to the spirit of the world.

MESSAGE FROM IGNATIUS LOYOLA.

OAKLAND, CAL., April 14, 1884.

I wish to impress my friends with that freedom cannot exist without order. Freedom has its existence in order, and has to obey order, which comes from the Author of order, and the Father of all order in the universe, and he is by obeying his own nature of order in the freedom personified by himself. Therefore you shall remain in order and in freedom, if you remain in God, who is the truth and the love of all order, and of the freedom in his holy kingdom.

I am addressing you by the consent of the Messiah, our Lord, and I say to you, be of no little hope, as you now are discontented, because many years and a bright future, according to the spirit of God, even if it shall be in much toil, lays before you.

I am Ignatius Loyola, the founder of the Jesuits, or the Society of Jesus. We were only a few, and scattered and persecuted by the enemies to our devotion, when the Lord appeared before me, and I beheld the holy Son, and I conceived the idea by the Holy Ghost to be his messenger on earth, to mankind generally, as to the church. The work however was done, and blessed be his holy name in all eternity. I shall be brief with my message to you at present, and will say that Catholicism has done a work of regeneration to mankind, even with many and most severe mistakes, and my disciples in the Savior's name have not been any exception. They have failed and not done the least fault, because they became mixed up with politics, and became the servants of kings and princes and rulers of this world, and became as it appears in many instances the very devils, because they served the princes of the world and not the Most High God and his beloved Son.

This evil did I not discover, nor could I prevent it, as I was not inspired with it before too late, only too late.

Another difficulty arose from the society's disposition and chances to accumulate property and power. I said: "Be "powerful in God," but the Jesuits became powerful in the world, and weak in God. I said: "Serve the church above all "things on earth, and be in submission unconditionally to his "Holiness at Rome," but they served their own power in the church above all things on earth, and became arrogant and aggressive to the Vatican, and forgot the submission for to be dictating, and they became feared of all in the place of being beloved of all in the church as out of the church.

Their wealth and colleges and riches have been a prey and a bounty for their enemies to aim at. This part of their mission was not of the spirit but of the world, and the failure, was not in the Lord's government, but because they were associated with his enemies. The failure came not in being the Society of Jesus, but in converting it into a power different from that the Lord exercised and permitted to be exercised towards mankind. As it stands now, there is very little prospect to be otherwise, but Rome will not always be Rome. Another power is exercising its authority, and the collision of the different elements in the church will cause a spiritual explosion to be heard and known all over.

Then will my Society of the Friends of Jesus be the followers of Jesus, and the Catholic Church will in many respects be sifted, and be more liberal and broad than at present.

I say to you, my fellow-servant, "May the benediction of "Messiah follow you, even as it is sealed upon you." My blessing I give to you. Amen.

April 16, 1884.   IGNATIUS LOYOLA.

P. S. All spirits or angels are not united with you in the same harmony, but in a various manner connected with you, and that accounts for the apparent conflict which arises at times around you, as a tempest was raging, or a battle was fought. At the same time there is not any conflict at all, as in fact there is none, but the exchanging mental soul or nervous forces belonging to different spiritual individuals widely apart are associated with different people and societies in heaven, and becomes therefore exactly as differently attached to earthly conditions as to friends left behind on earth.

IGNATIUS LOYOLA.

MESSAGE FROM JESHUAH, THE MESSIAH.

HYDE'S PARK, IOWA, Nov. 12, 1881.

"Look!" says a voice, and I see the mountains covered with the hosts of the Lord. Thousands and thousands descend from the snowy peaks. Down they come in garments white, and with belts around their loins, and swords at their sides, as the legions from the Ancient of Days. Wagons are rattling with thousands of dashing chains, and heavy cannons are pushed and rushing over the high edges of the Rocky Mountains. There is a cry before and a cry behind that man is only dust, and all his pride is only vanity. The angel who sounds the trumpet is a cherub, and he says: Dark is the cloud in the east, war is poured out on the people, a shadow is covering the plains. Darker and deeper as you descend towards the east is night poured out on the people. Wo! wo! wo! A three times wo! is heard from out of the clouds, because the people have hidden their souls in darkness, and despised the light, and have said: " Shut up the " heavens above us, because we will hear no news and no tid- " ings from our Heavenly Father, nor will we learn wisdom or " love from our God any more. Angels are not any more to " speak, nor any great works to be done on earth, because we " are the kings, and the earth is our inheritance."

The Lord has looked out from his hiding place, and shall speak by his servants, the prophets, as he did in olden time, and the earth shall tremble by his presence, and those who were in safe places shall start up and shudder, and pains shall come upon them, as painful and as quick as upon a woman at a month before her birth-time, when she expected it not, and said nothing, but considered herself safe. Wo! wo! wo! shall be heard all around, and there shall be war and sickness, and hunger, and great consternation among the people, until their measure is filled, and their own indignation is emptied out, which they have filled with pride, and poured out on their own heads, because they said: "There is no God who rules above us; we are the God ourselves, and shall rule as we please to do, and there is no death which leads into life, but death is death everywhere." Therefore shall this generation suffer much pain and agony.

How beautiful are the glittering walls of the Rocky Mountains. Silvery and sparkling, they reflect the light from above towards the west. Peace is in the valley, and in the high places is peace given to many souls. Oh, Zion! thy herds shall graze in peace, and be led to the brooks filled with silvery streams of refreshing water from the mountains. Out from thy borders shall peace reign on earth, and in thy valleys shall be no war before the Lord shall march up his hosts of hosts of warriors, with their countless banners and carriages, and they shall be as clouds on the mountain sides, as when a storm is raging, but peace shall be in your hearts, thou little flock; thou shalt not perish if all the nations became thy enemies, and were set loose on thee, for my word's sake. I am the Lord of Hosts, and I will fight thy battles, therefore grieve not.

When thou shall plant thy stakes at the promised soil, then thou shalt read these words, and know that I am that I am. Glorious is the message thou shalt bear. It shall sound in the dust under thy feet, it shall speak in the wind which touches thy garments, and thy voice shall sing as the silvery tunes from a thousand bells, and thy enemy who wages war upon thee, and who hated thee most fiercely, shall say: "Blessed art thou who comes in the name of the Lord!" Then thou shalt answer this nation, and say: "Blessed are those who preach liberty and truth, and tolerance and good will, and love towards all men, and malice towards none, nor anger, nor hate, nor any ill feeling, as that thou hated me with. Blessed are those who are the messengers of the Most High God, the God of Moses, and the patriarchs and prophets, and blessed be his name, but you hated his words and persecuted his people, because he kept his words."

This is a commandment to the church in the mountains and in all the states, and to all conferences and branches, and all states on earth, wherever my people are dispersed, and call upon my name, and worship the Father in the name of Jeshuah the Messiah, that they follow after me, and preach according to the gift of prophecy in the power of the spirit and inspiration from God. All my disciples who believe in the new dispensation by Joseph the Seer, my servant, and Brigham the Leader, my servant, and John Taylor, my aged servant, and Joseph Smith at Laramie, my servant, who have all been doing my work to humanity by preaching my gospel of eternal glory and peace, let all my disciples unite in the same effort to give light to all people. Darkness is supreme in millions of human souls. Light is only dim in many souls, as in a dark lantern. Preach to all men and women, that there may be light, and there shall be light, that the light may shine, and men may become conscious about the light. I am the light of every man, that light which gives light to every human soul, and even so God loved the world that he sent the light to be a man among men, but the world loved darkness more than light, and hung the messenger of light on a cross, that the light might be blown out in the darkness of death. Therefore shall my disciples, who take my name upon themselves and follow after me, be persecuted in this world of darkness and strife, but rejoice, as in my spirit they shall have peace, that peace which I have in the Father, and nobody need to mourn, as the world of worlds belongs to him, and is in his power, and I have conquered this world, and you shall have the same power in me to conquer the world, that the world may not perish, but be redeemed to light from its own natural darkness, and glory in the light of the Messiah.

Let my work be done as my servant, Joseph, now is doing it at Lamoni: let it be done in every state of the Union, and among all the nations on earth, and by-and-by the new message, at the last hour before supper-time, is to be preached to all people, and the end of darkness shall come, which is the end of this world's rule, and the kingdom shall come. Lift up your voices, and the time shall come when that which is hidden shall be revealed, when your enemies, who cursed you, are all hushed into death and oblivion, and the Son of Man shall appear on earth as he is seen in heaven, and in the glory of the Father. That power is not of himself, but of the Father, and the friends of Messiah shall appear with him, and he shall come and dwell on earth, as he did formerly, during forty days, before the eyes of his disciples, and as he did when he blessed them and went to the Father, also shall he come back to earth again.

When the kingdom comes, and the Son of Man appears, then shall all saints know me, that I am that I am, and touch me with their hands, and I shall eat and drink with them, and the doubting soul shall rejoice as Thomas, my messenger, did, and joy shall spring forth within their hearts, as a fountain filled with life everlasting to all nations to drink from. There they shall know that God is the living God, and this is life everlasting in heaven and on earth, to have his life, the spirit of his household, resting upon them, and they shall see him and know him who speaks these words, that he is alive, and is the Redeemer of the world, who now stands face to face with the world, which being without his spirit is waging a war upon his holy name. Amen.

Message from John, the Beloved Apostle.

Point City, Cal., March 4, 1884.

I am not he who was the light from the beginning, but I bear witness about him, that you may have the same knowledge, and partake of his glory in your souls, even as we have received it by following after him, that you may do as we have done, and we have remained in his love.

This is the testimony I bear to you on earth, that he lives, and that we are by him, whom we followed through the narrow gate of regeneration, and that we have been able to re-assemble with him in heaven, and through the long period of century after century we have not been idle nor tired of his presence, but we have received all the promises fulfilled, which he gave to us, and our hope became not blighted.

We found in the spirit of his kingdom, as it is in heaven, and shall come to you on earth, all of that we hoped for. Be of good cheer. He is your best friend, and the comfort of all mankind, and even as the Father loves him, also He has loved us with the same love, that we may abide in the same love one with another, and be perfected in his image, even as He is his Father's image.

Now my children in the faith of Messiah be not discouraged, because your enemies are by you, and they are around you, for so it has to be. There is no development of your souls except by contentions, and the offences have to come, or it could not be to you the promises have been given. Be brave on the battle-field of Jehovah, and fight the good fight for liberty and truth to humanity. Be not discouraged, nor be you double-minded, nor without hope, as though you were left alone in a wilderness, but be patient, and filled with perseverance, always remembering that after midnight comes daybreak, and the glory of the noonday sun. Some of you have gone to sleep, and some will be gathered home in your dwellings at the spirit land and at paradise, but it matters not when the final advent sounds over all the earth, you shall all be there, and the myriads of heaven shall meet and shake hands with the little flock on earth, not to be counted for many in comparison with the multitudes of heaven. We have followed him, whom you love, through the throngs of heaven, as we followed him when on earth, and we know him, and we know his Father, and we know that you shall know him, as many as follow after him, that you shall have the knowledge, even that which we have. Amen.

Blessed are those who read these words, and believe them, as it shall come to them as a light from the presence of the Father, even as He is glorified by the Son, and the Son is glorified by the Father, and we are glorified by the Son and by the Father, and that is my testimony to you, that the light and the glory shall rest upon them, and dwell within their souls. Amen. I have not called you friends, but you are my friends, if the love of the Messiah dwells in you and follows you in all your doings. Love not only by the profession of words, but by your deeds of charity, as it shall cover a multitude of sins. Let there amongst you be none naked who are not clothed. Let there be none hungry, and thirsty and sick, who are not provided for. Let there be no reckness deed, which is not corrected by love first, and above all by forbearance, before such a person is cast off on account of darkness to sad experience in the world, from which condition the Lord will help him in his own appointed time. My friends, those found in the Lord cannot be cast away from him by any power vested in the church, nor by any power of man, or given to man from above.

Remember as far as the love of the Holy Spirit reaches ought surely the forbearance of the priesthood reach, but some have been cast out from the church, while the spirit of God was manifested to them, and resting upon them, and the spirit had left the church, and long ago departed from the officiating priesthood. Therefore you have grieved heaven, because you rejected its love, and its long-suffering, and angels hid their faces before the church, and Jesus, the redeemer, wept over the church, and his tears fell as fire in the souls of the apostles and prophets, that the saints might be saved.

Therefore have you had tribulation. Therefore have you had anguish and gnashing of teeth amongst you, and therefore shall the days of the saints among the mountains be shortened, as the church of Messiah shall be redeemed.

It is not for me, nor for any angel or prophet to tell the day and hour when it shall take place, but a great assembly shall go up to the temple, and be seen around Independence, and at Jackson Co., Mo.

Your enemies shall not be prepared on that day to meet you there again. Therefore be not alarmed. There shall be wars and rumors of war and much strife on earth, but our prayers are always ascending before Jehovah in your behalf. He is the ruler of the nations, and the reins are resting in his hands. He is the God of the destiny of many people, and the earth belongs to him. He locks the door and nobody can open it. He opens the door and nobody can lock it. Even so mote it be, the blessing of heaven follow you, that the adversary shall not find your footprints. Amen.

JOHN, THE BELOVED.

MESSAGE FROM JESHUAH, THE MESSIAH.

[MOSAIC YEAR 5,645.]   HYDE'S PARK, IOWA, October 2, 11 A. M., 1883.

The Son of man has the power to do what he wishes to do in harmony with his mission to the earth. Therefore as the Father does, also does the Son, and that power has been invested in his being from eternity, and this he calls his own as the Father calls it his own, so the Son by that love, which is in the Father, shall be glorified in the world, as the Father is glorified by him.

I am by you this morning, because I am commanding you to call by and by on the presiding elders and friends of the church at large, that you may be a witness and bear a true testimony to man vested in the crucified Jesus. Certainly I have drawn the multitudes to me, and many have been called upon and invited to the Lamb's nuptials, but only few are to be the chosen friends and my elect. The garments from your endowment house must be me in whom you are clothed, if they shall profit your souls, and your baptism must be that of the Holy Ghost, or your baptism in water shall profit you nothing, although you became subject to the watery grave.

Live in the spirit of the faith of Messiah, and let the spirit of the holy signs on your garments rest upon you, or they shall profit you nothing, and above all things love one another, forgive one another, and be long-suffering one with another, as by that the angels have conquered devils and opened the gates of hell. Let the crown of all faith abide with you, that you may be living witnesses, filled with charity and good works. Many are your enemies, and many are your friends, but be of good cheer, and never get disheartened, as the Son of man is in power and in the majesty of heaven, and you are of him if you remain in the garments which are his, and in the Spirit of Messiah, that you may be recognized as his own, and he shall not leave you alone on the day of your trials and your persecution, but his Father will turn all for the best, and to the comfort and progression of the church.

Be prepared. Only a few can at present receive my personal, tangible appearance, and heavenly forward testimony. I say again be prepared, and seek and you shall find, and knock early and late in constant prayers, and the door, which I am, shall be opened before your sight.

This people of Latter Day Saints are slow of hearing, and dim is their eyesight, and dull is their understanding. Many are sleeping and do not know their own faces, and they are scattering on their own ways, and are departing far from me, who is the way, and they leave even not their former footprints behind them to be known.

They scatter also in the spirit of the holy communion with each other and with the saints of heaven. They depart far off even in their own houses, and their homes become desolate for the Holy Spirit, and a desert place, where angels not any longer enter, and they are sneering at each other, are fault finding and bound under the spirit of anger according to the world's pattern, hating the sight of those they once loved, and yet clothed in garments, which are having the cut of being made for saints, but they were long ago singed by the fires of hell because the people professed to know me and know my Father, and they turned away from our presence, and did the works of the adversary. Many persons are weak amongst you for whom I pray always, as I do for the honest of heart and for the church of mine elect.

There are men and women, who are eagerly wishing to know my day, and for the salvation of those I say, none shall suffer more than the apostles at that day, as I will try their spirits and pass their life through a fire, to test their work and secret intentions, how their hearts were made either of brass or of gold.

For my friends' sake, who call on the Father in my name, I have appeared before the messenger, whom I have called to do my work, as I did before Saul, the persecutor, that my kingdom may come to the church in signs and power and abide with you, as I visibly shall abide with you. Call with a loud voice, as from a bassoon, which calls the sleeping soldiers to battle, and let them arise from slumber, and be clothed into the bright-shining steel and armor of heaven, and the bassoon shall sound from one mansion of my father's world, and echo into the other, and the secret of the sixth seal shall be revealed to the world, and those who hate you shall say, " how became this handful of imposters and mounte-" banks to be a mighty people, and why did the blessing of pro-" vidence not follow us, but went with those we despised."

Sing ye mountains filled with eternal dews on your heads, because it has pleased the Father to gather a people, who was counted not to be a people, and made them rich and prosperous in the valleys and on the hills of this continent, and this is to be rich, when you are rich in God, and his spirit is resting mightily upon you; then you have an everlasting blessing. Are you to be prosperous and possess the fat of the land in the heavenly Canaan given to the children of Israel, then prosper in the spirit, and lives upon lives shall be given to you as an inheritance eternally, and you shall greet the patriarchs and prophets at your dwellings.

Be therefore always careful how you do my work, that my work may be your work, and last forever.

Leave the blessings of my Father to dwell in you, that blessing which he bestowed on my person, as the son of man and the Messiah. May that follow you, as I follow you, and you follow after me, and as I am one with our Father. Amen.

MESSAGE FROM JESHUAH THE MESSIAH.

HUMBOLDT LAKE, July 14, 1885.

The last shall be the first in the kingdom to come, says the Lord, and the time is near at hand when all the Lord's people shall be prophets, and Zion shall be a people of prophets.

Only a little while, says the Lord to his elect on earth, and your suffering shall be converted into joy, but for the sake of Zion's new birth it is so to be, that pains shall come over Zion, and she shall shed tears in her pains before the regeneration, when she is born into the kingdom. It is not her that shall be broken asunder, but I have put a cornerstone in Zion, which is my name, and every nation shall mourn and be filled with sorrow when it turns against her, and breaks its power asunder against her.

I will pour my spirit out over Zion, when she is the deepest in mourning, and I will forget her transgressions, because she loved me through all her humiliation.

Thus says the Lord, I will put my strength as a girdle around her loins, when her enemies come up against her, if she abide in my name, and her enemies shall turn against me, and not against her, and I will blot out the name of any nation for her sake, and for my name's sake she relied upon, but if this nation of the United States will make peace with Zion for my name's sake, then I will preserve this nation, and make its name great on earth. Amen. On the contrary, I will strike the first born and the children of every family, even as I did in Egypt, if this nation stretches out its hand to destroy my people. I will make them mourn all over the land, and will allow pestilence and death to do its work among the old and the great men among this nation until Zion is redeemed.

If they take arms up against Zion to destroy her, then I will strike lame the arms carrying the weapons, and I will reveal myself out of heaven, and strike those with fear and consternation who rise up against my people. Even as Zion has sinned I will accept her repentance, and will not allow her enemies to triumph.

Therefore, thus says the Lord, I will shake the earth and make her tremble on her way through the space, and in the clouds of heaven shall my chariots and the hosts of hosts be seen, and I will dash this nation with the palms of my hands, and it shall know the anger from Golgotha, even as at the destruction of Jerusalem, and the fall of my holy Temple, and was Israel not saved, neither shall this nation be saved if it goes to war against the Holy One, and his elect, or his household, or his Zion. Amen.

Message from Jeshuah the Messiah.

INDEPENDENCE, Mo., April 8, 1882.

In the measure you have a desire in your souls to serve the truth, inasmuch are you my servants. Remain on the pathway of truth and you shall never be confounded, but be the children of the light. Many shall come to me and say Lord, Lord! but I have never known them to walk on the way which gathers into life, nor have they known my Father, because they have not known me. I am the road to life and salvation, as I am the truth of life.

Be not of a narrow mind, and imagine that all knowledge is given to the church, and all truth is revealed to man on earth, or as much as humanity ever shall need. In that you all have erred stupidly, because you have now only the introduction to my advent on earth. Therefore be humble, and meek, and pray, that wisdom may come to you, and you will receive news in abundance and according to the meekness of your hearts.

Be always ready as little children to receive the bread of

heaven from my Father's hand, and as I have honored him even so does he honor me, and my honor on earth is in those he has given me and he receives from me again. Therefore remain faithful to the spirit of truth, called the Holy Spirit, the Holy Messenger from above. I have spoken to you, until I am now getting weary and tired of warning you, because you did not hearken to my voice, nor did you follow my council, and you were driven as lost sheep and scattered in all directions, and your enemies were as wolves in your midst, when you departed from Independence.

Now after one hour and a-half I warn you again not to go asleep among the mountains, or where you are scattered in the States like the foolish virgins who all went asleep, and at the cry they tried to make their lamps ready for use by the heavenly oil of myrrh, and burning by the light of love, but darkness prevailed and they could not follow at that hour. When I shall appear personally amongst my friends, and shall be known at In_dependence, from there I will sound the sixth bassoon to all the earth. From there is the sixth seal to be broken, and its reign to go out over all the earth.

Prepare yourself and be ready. You and your children, and your children's children, and be prepared for the journey and have your clothes bound up, as Israel had in the night the people left Egypt. Leave your homes from far off, and the mountain valleys in small companies, and redeem the land of Zion by purchase, as its soil is a holy place for my use and purpose. Let there be no confusion, and no quarrels, and let mine elect enter on the passage along the long line of railroads, when you hear the bassoon sounding. "The Lord has visited Zion, and has appeared " at the holy place." So says the Lord and master: "I shall know " my elect by the desire which is burning in their hearts, to do " my will, and they shall come as doves from all the states and " visit at Independence, with joy and eternal songs, and the " glory of angels following them, and the blessing of the spirit " resting upon them, and the people at Independence shall repent " in deep humiliation, even as the people at Nineveh did, and say, " ' blessed are you, who come in the name of the Lord.' Amen."

When you see the sinking sun, then you know that night is at hand, and wickedness goes to sleep. Therefore be prepared, when the enemy sleep, and come my elect, be moving to Independence and build my temple, and Zion shall follow my people, and be with them and amongst them and within them, and Zion shall be restored in its place, and be brought back again from out of the wilderness. Therefore before many days, there shall be a great cry at midnight and the world shall tremble, and a great shake shall awake my people, and those also who are not of me, but shortly after they shall sleep with the world, as they did in the days of Noah, and the temple shall raise its towers at Independence, and be built in the same days, as the ark was built in similar days, and suddenly the Son of man shall appear wrapt in a morning glory of the heavenly light belonging to the Millennium, and the world shall know that I am that I am the only begotten son of the Father. Therefore I want my servant Joseph and the church to build the temple, and so shall it be that a lamenting voice, a warning voice, is calling on every one of you my people to do the will of the Father, that the love of the Father may be in your hearts, that love by which he loved the world, when he sent me into the world, that the world shall not perish in darkness and misery, but have the light that is full of grace and life everlasting.

Be ye in that love, work ye in that love, and the blessing of heaven shall guide the steps of each of you to build up my temple on the everlasting hill at Independence.

Take with you gold and silver in the world's money and redeem Zion by purchase, and raise up the grand and central standard of Zion before all the world. Preach these tidings before the church, and mine anointed will hear the voice and obey it, and mine elect shall know the spirit moving their hearts with intense joy and happiness, and they shall be ready to go and fulfill the pleasure of my heavenly Father and build the temple. Lift up your voices with the silver sound of the sixth bassoon, and say, the sixth seal is broken, and the contents of the sixth message has to be read. Come to the feast, come ye my elect, and spare not, as I have spared nothing in making all things ready for your welcome, and the power which follows you shall convert the people at Independence and Kansas City, and the earth around shall sing Hallelujah, when Zion is redeemed, and its temple walls are built, and those who were my enemies shall come loaded with presents, and gold, and gifts to finish the central structure of the edifice before the nations. Amen.

MESSAGE FROM JOHN STUART MILL.

OAKLAND, CAL., March 15, 1885.

Please mention my name ahead. I am John Stuart Mill. I wish to pass my opinion on your conversation. Mohammed was a true man, and he was a man in the strongest sense of being a man. From the standpoint of a Christian he has been pronounced an imposter, but he was no imposter in his own sphere of truth. He was as true as a man could be to his own guide and to his own convictions. He was not commissioned by spirits, but he was controlled by one principal intelligence, who to him was Allah. Mohammed was a man and only a man, true to one spirit and one God.

Jesus appeared to him not as a divine personage, but as a good man and a prophet, who suffered death as many prophets have done before him, and the Christian claim about Jesus was to Mohammed only an exposition of Judaism.

Mohammed could not bow down before Jesus, and he could not believe in him with much more reverence than he did in Moses or in Zacharias. Jesus became not Mohammed's center of worship, because he was his own center, and raised up by the Almighty God, represented by his own individual guide to do the work he did, and as he succeeded in doing it.

This guide Allah was not Jehovah, but a Jewish Rabbiner of most eminent rank, who wished to destroy Christianity. He acted all right from conviction, and we have nothing to say about his effort. This guide of Mohammed was his spiritual father, exactly as Jehovah was the spiritual father of Jesus, and it means his control or power.

Jesus is individually a plain, powerful and free-minded intelligence, which all who know him will admit, but he is the personified truth of his teachings, and exactly the same is the Father.

I had no idea of immortality during my earthlife and I did not believe in it, but I have learned the truth of it after death or the transition to this world of mind. Lately I have gained much by coming in contact with men from the higher spheres of spirit life, who visit my friend here, and intrust him from time to time. Good-bye, my friends. God bless you.

MESSAGE FROM JEHOVAH.

SAN ANTONIO, CAL., July 27, 1885.

Live, and thou shalt not die, but be the life, because this is the life everlasting, that you live in Him, who has the life, and who is the life, even your Lord and Master. His voice have you heard as a strong sound in the wilderness and as the sound of a bassoon where it sounded over barren and desolate plains, and it sounded into the great city and into the palaces of princes.

There is no time, as the time of times is over, and the sun is setting and the night is approaching. Therefore be prepared, as the cry at midnight will find the multitudes asleep. A deep slumber has befallen this race, and a deep sleep has come into the midst of millions, and they are as drunken and asleep, and they hear nothing and see nothing, neither do they perceive their own nakedness or need.

High up over the mountains and at the foot of the mountains are noises of horses and chariots and wagons, and rattling with chains and cannons, and the sounds of swords and spears, and the mighty thunder of guns and fire-weapons. They move as a dark cloud over the mountain peaks. Who shall tell us the truth, and who shall explain this vision?. The righteous in his soul, who don't sit in trickster's council, but loves an upright people and the Lord his God. That man shall learn wisdom and understand the signs of heaven.

Rejoice thou fallen horde of Israel, because thou who art low down shalt be put high up, and those who are rulers and govern thee shall serve the daughters of Zion. Thou shalt not perish in thy weakness, nor shalt thou seek after thy redeemer and not find him. He shall be on thy right and on thy left side, and seraphs clothed with light shall shine before thee. Descending from the heavens angels shall prepare thy way and shall level the soil upon which thou shall place thy feet.

Therefore be bold, O daughter of Zion, and let not thine enemies see thy tears, as though thou wast a forsaken virgin, because even so saith the Lord thy God : I will deal with thine enemies as with my foes, and I will give them their own flesh for daily meat, and let them devour one another on the day they shall wage war upon Zion, or shall attempt to destroy mine inheritance out of the nations on earth, or my chosen people in the new covenant.

Therefore be filled with joy, thou little flock in the east and west, in the heart of the continent and among the mountains, because the Lord thy God shall wipe away every tear from thy cheek, and show thee his tender mercy as his beloved, and as thou wert his betrothed, most dear before all people. Therefore did he separate thee in the jealousy of his love from those who hate him, and from thy friends and relations, and tried thy faith and obedience and strength in his love and willingness to do his work.

As a cloud shall thy people, O Zion, be moving over this country and in the valleys among the mountains, and the song of angels shall be heard in the canyons strong as a sweeping storm-wind, and give thee strength, and thou shalt sing : Praised be the Lord of hosts, he shall prepare his hosts to battle, and none shall be able to obstruct his ways. He shall march his hosts into the mountain passes, and give the bodies of his enemies to be a prey for wolves, and to the wild animals of the high mountains. Who can fight the Lord of hosts, and who can conquer his armies ?

At the same time he is the Father to all, and his love is extended to all persons, and his care is to the lowest of all his beloved creatures, that all may live and be redeemed into his blessed light and eternal presence. He has sworn an oath by himself and his holy name, that Zion shall not perish, nor shall it again be taken away from the earth. Even so shall it truly come to pass.

Therefore rejoice, O Zion, for thou art not alone, neither art thou a forsaken maid, but thou art clothed in the raiment of heaven, though thou art named the despised on earth, and as the nations hate me, also shall they hate thee. I have put a measure on the people of the United States, and upon their hearts, and upon that love by which they say they love me, and I have found them wanting, and in the darkness of self-love and hypocrisy. O Zion, I will put thy name written on my wings, and on my high flight I will shelter thee by that power, and I will give thee power to destroy as by the dash of my wings, and thou shalt sweep the earth with the feathers of my power, that thou shalt know that I am that I am, and all the nations shall know it and tremble. Therefore let it not concern thee when thy enemies are treating thee with contempt, nor when they make threats and say angry words to thee, nor when they cast thy sons into cold and dark prisons for my word's sake, because they have done it to me and not to thee. Let it not concern thee, when my enemies shall raise up the power of this world against Zion, as they are not fighting thee, but they are fighting me, and my holy name, and the hosts of heaven. This thou mayest know as a sign and testimony for thy salvation.

Blessed are those who bless thee, and cursed are those who curse thee. Even as I have made thine enemies dust, also shall I make thy cause cry out of the dust to govern the earth, and the dust shall sing under thy feet, when thou shall build up Zion, and Canaan shall be redeemed, and the city of Jerusalem shall rejoice. Even so shall it be. I am the one who dashed the earth with my strength, and as I said to my servant Moses, also pestilence, and plagues, and misery came upon men. I am raising the cyclones, and I am breaking the crust of the earth and making cities tremble, and am filling nations with consternation and fear, and Jehovah is my name, and that I am that I am, but my covenants with Israel shall never be forgotten, and I will bring Israel forth out of captivity and into their own country. Zion I will gather from wherever she is dispersed, and I will build her up in places of safety, and in holy places raise temples among the mountains and at Independence, and they shall not be polluted as the temple at Nauvoo, nor shall they fall into any other people's hands, but I will lift a shield of protection over your work, and over your fields and over your herds, and your doings, until you shall gather strength and go to work and offer me an acceptable offering in sending out deputations and colonies of workmen to build the temple for my name at Jackson County, Missouri.

Let it not be done in haste, but commence and work by night and by day, and the light shall not be extinguished from the commencement to the end. It shall burn at noon and at midnight, and it shall burn as a holy fire for the Lord thy God, and thou shall build the temple according to the pattern given to my servant, Joseph the Seer. Amen.

MESSAGE FROM THE ANCIENT OF DAYS.

OAKLAND POINT, CAL., March 26, 1885.

I am with you; my name is known to the world from eternity to eternity; but I am with you; what I have to say about marriage is already said in a message sent to the people at Utah, and given at Ogden. Let it be understood as it was given to the messenger, at the Ogden Canyon: I am the God of Abraham, and Isaac and Jacob, and of Moses, and Daniel, and the prophets, as I am the God of Joseph, and Brigham, and the martyrs, and the modern prophets and saints; but at the same time, I am the ruler of the nations on earth, and the "Ancient of Days" is my name, and I am that I am: God the Almighty.

When I say to my people, "Sit down and count out what it will cost to go to war," then I say to you, "Be prepared;" but not for war, but for defence, at a moment's warning. You are not going to war, but are watching for a defence. And I will rule your enemies, and I will use the hate of your enemies to fight themselves with, until they are consumed by their own hate, and their own ignorance, because they despised the light, and wanted to remain in ignorance, and could not see the truth on account of their own darkness. Let me, however, repeat to you again and again that the polygamy of David, and of Solomon, and of the many kings of Judah, and of Israel, was according to the heathens, and was an abomination in my sight, for I delight in chastity, and in purity and love, in the relations of the sexes, and in all social intercourse; and man shall respect woman, and not treat her as his inferior, because, I am that I am, and you should love one another.

The tears from women have fallen as curses upon many men, and it would have been better for such never to have entered into any marriage, either in the church or in the world.

The Catholic church is seeking the supremacy among men, but I have decided in favor of Zion—from the time of her birth again on earth; however, the Catholic church will rejoice, for the time is at hand, and the days of Messiah are coming, and he will send his messengers to all the churches and denominations on earth, and invite them to come and attend his nuptials.

Read over the message given at Ogden, and let it be impressed on your minds, every word I said, as with indelible ink on your garments. As the heavenly law on companionship is a great mystery, and not even known to all of the angels, but you have perverted it, and taught it as a doctrine before the world, and yet don't know it yourselves, nor its application to the spirit, which should be amongst you if you were not of the world; therefore, you are harvesting the fruit of your own folly.

Nothing can be said to the prophets, except the church perverts it, and in its perverted form gives it to its enemies. As a people, surely the church is like children, who betray the secret of their parents' conversation, and without my love they are not matured to meet the Messiah, but remain as spiritual children in their reasoning. The power the serpent promised man, was to know good from evil; but much more belongs to God's gifts—as wisdom to be God-like. Therefore obey wisdom, and correct any mistake, and pull in the lasso which you have thrown into the hands of your enemies, with which they are now wishing in their hearts to strangle Zion. Abolish nothing but errors. Apostatize from mistakes, but make no concessions from the truth. As you cannot abolish from the faith that you did not issue yourselves, nor can you concede to the tenets of the regulations of the world's ignorance for the pleasure of men, who would, in spite of your humiliation, even hate you the more, because they are the children of the flesh and the passions, and not the children of the Spirit, nor of the regeneration. Let the word " heavenly " be written on the nail of your left thumb, but hide it before the world within the palm of your left hand, until Messiah comes and shall make all things right.

I am the voice which spoke to Moses, and to my servants the prophets, and to John the Baptist, in the wilderness, when he arose before the enemies of the Lord, and spoke the truth, when Herod took his living brother's wife to be his wife, the mission then was done step by step ; through execution and crucifixion, it gained spiritual victory, and now the battle has to be fought by perseverance and caution. The hour of challenge has passed away, but the hour of defence has not passed. The so-called " heavenly law to the church," was not given to challenge the world by, nor to be presented and preached before the world, nor did my servant Joseph ever receive a correct understanding of it—as he perceived it or conceived it, it was a perversion of the truth ; therefore, abolish your present practice of poligamy, as it is of the flesh, and the purity of the spirit is not in it, nor the life of the truth, nor is it in love. Abolish the love-lorn wicked lust, which has crept into the church, for in Zion's people's own households there is no peace. Your souls have lost the spirit of love, and the Holy Ghost has departed from you ; and you have become the servants of the flesh to please passion, according to the desire of the flesh, ruling out the spiritual inclination of your natures. Being not familiar with the principle of love, and less with living under its law, which should govern all the saints, as they can never enter into the spirit of truth except by the heavenly love.

The apostles have made the doors wide open, and broad as the gates to hell, when the heavenly law is the most narrow path to paradise, and many here have entered, believing themselves to be on that pathway, and found themselves before the gates of hell, and they gained nothing but suffering, and lost their inheritance with Israel, and sold their birth-rights in the spirit as cheap as Esau did.

If you do not abide in the love of faith, which gives light and wisdom, you can not comprehend the law of love, nor can you be blessed by that which is heavenly. The church being rejected deceived itself; therefore, you lived according to the world, and said you lived by the heavenly law, and so it became a damnation and a destruction to you. Such people have to be educated in the marriage of one man and one wife, and there are some who are so organized from birth that it would be better for them never to enter into any marriage, and others who, in marriage, can only harvest the fruit of misery, and disorder, and death.

The church at Utah played with a sacred hope, as a parrot does with a piece of sugar; and talked heavenly words, as a parrot can be taught; and lived according to the flesh, and did the works of the devil. Therefore shall peace depart from the people, and they shall be troubled with much agony, until they abolish polygamy. I am the Ruler of the nations moving on earth, and I have given the Territory of Utah into the hands of this nation, and I will chasten the people of Utah and its borders until they shall come low down, and shall consent to abolish polygamy. Act not in defiance of the government of the republic, as it represents the people among whom you are living; nevertheless it shall be known to them that the spirit of this nation will soon wreck all its manhood by a constant violation of the original constitution, and be led away captive by women, into national suicide; as the men of the nation shall be beguiled by women, and by her extremes and her extravagances, which shall bring on destitution not to be healed, and culminate in riots, strikes, all kinds of crimes, and death, and rebellion in their midst.

Its hand was not lifted up as a protection over the church of God. Even the government of the United States is bound by the constitution to give protection to all churches. It allowed men and women in the New England States to be burnt at the stake as witches, and to be cast in the rivers for no other cause than their visitation by angels and spirits in the name of Messiah, and because the spirit of God rested upon them. Also, were the Mormon people driven away from Independence by a horde of mobs. The church had committed no crime to the world. The saints had grieved the Spirit by their ignorance and folly, and want of caution, and their entire misunderstanding of the dealings of God with his people. Zion has suffered by her own misconception of the truth and corresponding deeds; but it is all counted in from the beginning. As I know that which is in man, and that it is evil by nature ; and that the repentance and the new birth did not make my people wise, for they prayed for power in the world to crush their enemies, and they did not pray for power in the Spirit to convert them by, as the only method to conquer the world. It is on the rock of divine inspiration the world shall suffer shipwreck by its superstition, evil disposition, and dark propensities to do evil. This rock of divine inspiration the world can not abolish, because it will be in the world to the end of its days, and all the nations and all the governments of the earth will eventually be remodeled by collision with that rock, into the unity and peace of God.

The natural condition of the human heart is to go to war with heaven, and with every new light that comes down from heaven, and persecute to the bitter end all messengers from heaven. Therefore are the saints persecuted, and also the Spiritualists. But the work goes on, and the Spiritual movement is in every hamlet, and in every city of this broad country, and it will spread until the Protestant churches are filled with light ; and it is manifested with wondrous works in the Catholic church, and the Messiah shall be revealed to head the entire movement when the harvest is ripe for the Gospel of Freedom in the Kingdom of heaven upon earth. On that day shall the enemies of Spiritualism be silent, and the enemies of the Saints be forgotten, and even their graves shall be long forgotten ; and the people shall read the history of this country, and smile, and say one to another, " How was it possible ?" A long line of witnesses shall stand up against the people of this century, in this country, and say, " we were incarcerated in insane asylums, and suffered death on account of our religious convictions, but we would rather have suffered death in the flames from the fagots, and mercy was not shown to us;" and they shall march up in lines upon lines, and be counted by the thousands, and be seen in long white robes, with palms in their hands, praying for peace to be given to their tormentors, and that the evil done against them may be returned in good, and the light be given to the enemies of the light, and to those not hardened in their souls against him who is sitting on the throne of eternity. On account of crimes committed against the light in marriage, have many blessings been converted into exactly as many curses, such as dishonesty, and treachery, and the spirit of murder, and the spirit of egotism, and the lust of the flesh spell-bound in marriages devoid of passion, and without love in them. All these conditions cover the soul of humanity, and lead to various crimes to man's own destruction; and woman is more goverened by the spirit of the Serpent, which drifts into infanticide, than by the spirit of God. Marriage was given for a blessing, but is now a curse to many. Therefore, let Zion arise in her weakness, and be strong in her God, that she may bring forth a mighty people to dwell on earth, and be powerful in the order of the Sons of God. Let thy treasure be the mysteries of heaven, and close thy thumb into the palm of thy hand, and by that sign shalt thy children be known by sea and by land, and let it rest there, what the world cannot know, as in the days of scattering from the tower at Babel.

Don't go to war with the world about the heavenly conception of companionship, as neither man nor woman can enter into its perfection on earth, except by being matured in God's love, by the Gospel of Freedom in the Kingdom of Messiah, when wisdom shall be given to earth to raise holy offspring. Companionship belongs to the angels of heaven, and will be given to the Council of Zion in the kingdom, and not to the present church organization. The laws of the country, and the regulations and institutions of the world, wheresoever the church is dispersed, shall be a regulation for the saints to live by till Messiah comes.

That love which is of heaven belongs to heavenly institutions; and that love which is of earth belongs to institutions governing the earth. Don't prostitute the teachings of the Spirit of God, before sinful judges, governed by gold and the gains of the world, even as Pilate was, when Jesus remained silent; because, Pilate was spiritually blind, and deaf to all spiritual arguments, and finished at last his life on earth by suicide, as also the entire Roman nation later on did also, in their battle against light. Be prudent, be careful, and ever observing; be frugal, temperate and abstinent in all things, and what you do let it be done in that love which is in God, your Father, and his beloved Son, that you may be the beloved, and followers of the beloved Messiah. Awaken, therefore, O, Zion, from thy sleep with the world, and arise in the strength of the Spirit; because the Kingdom is coming, and the churches of christianity and spiritualism are ripened into the Gospel of Freedom and deliverance in one union, with the followers of Gautama and Mohammed as the rear guard ; but thou go out to meet the King, for he is coming with the Hosts of heaven to dwell on earth, and to sift his Saints from the world, and to measure the strength of this world's governments and redeem those in bondage to the world, and give to the downtrodden justice, and freedom to the captive, and open the prison doors for sacred reforms, when He lays the balance in his hand and by the weights of eternal justice and wisdom shall put the institutions of the world on the scales, and find them wanting, even as Babylon was found wanting, to fill her urgent want of defence in the night of her destruction. Amen.

MESSAGE FROM NEPHI.

OAKLAND, CAL., Dec. 26, 1886.

I am Nephi ; I did not engrave the plates ; but I came to this country from my native home in Judea. Beneath the big stone lays the world's heaven, as behind the big tombstone was the Savior once laid wrapped in death's linen. Who shall lift the stone? Who shall imbue the world with a new stream of important thoughts? The man whom the Lord will raise up, and whom He shall call upon out from the hidden chambers of His council—him shall He raise up, and he shall do His work. The plates of Nephi shall once more shine in the broad daylight, and before the eyes of man ; they shall once more be lifted, and weighed, and be given to be a testimony to the world, and the world shall be as deaf and dumb as ever ; they will only be received as a testimony by a few—only the elect of the Lord shall take any interest in the " gigantic fraud," as the world will call it. But the kingdom shall grow prosperous and mighty, and the church will not be defeated any more. And in its defeat, as in the defeat of the Lamanites (because they exterminated Nephi's people), shall be the harvest of seed, strewn by the present labor of the church.

Thy kingdom come, which is the Gospel of Freedom, shall be hailed by all men and all women, in the spirit of Messiah.

My tears have been shed over the tombstone which covers the lost records of my people—they are beneath the cover. But the second Nephi stands by your side ; he who engraved the records that the history of my lost people should not be destroyed, but come forth with power, and by the gift and strength of God. He shall administer to you in your second advent, in your native country, as he shall administer to Israel, the son of Joseph, at Lamoni. Then the political record of Jared, on governments, and the control of the nations, shall be given to you by the power of God, even as the full history of the church of God, and His dealings with my people shall be given to Israel, when the angel shall break the second seal, in the establishment of the kingdom on earth.

Blessed are you, because the spirit of prophesy rested on you when you took both of the sons of Joseph by the hand and prophesied, saying of David, " He is great, but his brother Israel is greater, because to him, to Israel, who is the youngest, belongs the power and strength. David shall the Lord take to himself to advance His work among the multitudes of the spirit world. But Israel shall lead the church into the kingdom of Messiah. When he shall live and see the Messiah, he shall be a man in the spirit of Joshua, and be zealous in the work of the Lord, and the soul of *his* spirit shall burn within him ; he shall see the days of the kingdom. When he shall have seen the Lord, the Lord shall appear visible for many in Zion, and he shall wheel the church into the power of heaven upon earth, when all the nations shall be tired of war, and ask Zion to make peace between them, that peace may reign on earth as it does in the Kingdom of the Lord, and then shall the writings of Israel be restored to man." These words are the sayings of Nephi, who came out from Jerusalem with his father, Lehi, and his brethren and their families. Amen.

Earth to earth, life to life, and spirit to spirit, is the power in the world to come—even the power which is the Lord, who shall send forth the Gospel of Freedom to all nations from the kingdom on earth. Amen.

MESSAGE FROM LEHI.

OAKLAND, CAL., December 27, 1886.

My name is Lehi : I am a man more powerfully built than you see my son Nephi. We have all a brown cast of the skin ; we are not of a dark skin, but we are naturally as you see us now; so were we in our earth lives—as brown as the Arabs of to-day. My son Nephi is slender, and tall, and of a feminine build, and of a very meek disposition, on which account you see him remain at a distance, with eyes looking down on the ground. The reason is, that he does not consider himself worthy to look up at the Lord, whom he discovers in your presence. I am naturally of a bold temperament, and of a fierce disposition, and I am not easily changed, but delight in being as near the Lord as possible, because I feel that his strength is my strength.

Many years have passed away, and century after century is gone, but our hopes have not vanished, as one day with the Lord is only to him as a thousand years would be to us, and he said to us : "Be not disheartened, for I will visit Zion on earth, and restore all your hopes and desires within two days."

So it came to pass that we have been contented that the restitution should come ; and our hope did not vanish, even when the church of the Lamb was driven into destruction by the power of Satan, and the saints were scattered, and a remnant of them was banished in the council of the Lord to wander far off into the wilderness. Times and times have rolled on until the hope of all Israel has ripened, and the restoration is at hand— even now at hand. Amen ; and blessed be the Lord in all eternity. Amen ! Yes, Amen is his name forever.

My son Laman will speak a few words to you ; now you see him coming. I am tall, with broad shoulders, and large chest, and jet black eyes, and curly black hair ; my weight, three hundred and fifty pounds.

Nephi had silken, long, chestnut brown hair, and a long face, long nose, and large, dark blue eyes, and a light olive complexion. My face is more round and broad, and nose is short, and I have high cheek bones. Nephi's weight on earth was only one hundred and sixty pounds; but he was a stately man to look at, with a prophetic spirit resting on him.

Now my son Laman will speak to you. He is as you see him represented to you as he appeared on earth; his weight was two hundred and fifty pounds, and of a very powerful build all over, without being portly, but very muscular. He was earth of earth, with a fault-finding and quarrelsome nature; his face was short and round as you see mine, but without the freedom of the Spirit beaming on his countenance. He is now leaning over some and looking down on the ground with scowling face, and nearly closed eyes, dark and small, and a wrinkled forehead; his eyes are not steady, and he never looks at any person for a long time, even when conversing with them. He is of a melancholy, lymphatic temperament, and has a tyrannical disposition, and not much spiritual power resting on him; but in the spirit world he has progressed some, and takes some interest in the faith he has in coming events. Good-by, my son Peter; as the Lord calls you by that name, I presume I may do the same.

When you shall receive the plates of Jared, remember they are not to the church, but to the world first, and then to the Kingdom. The inspired writing on the plates you shall receive in your native country, and there shall the principles of governments be taught, in lessons given by you to all nations. The mystery of the tower of Babel will be explained, and the effect of such a diplomacy and its history will be known. The angels Moroni, Gabriel, and Daniel will do each one his own mission, as Michael shall direct it. Maroni to the Kingdom; Gabriel to the Jews, and Daniel to the nations. Your work as forerunner before the forerunner to the kingdom, will be done in the publication of the messages to the church. Your mission to the world will be done in doing the work of Messiah to your native country first, and to the nations generally afterwards. The translation of the works and engravings of Jared, about his people, and times, and doings, &c., is to the world, but it shall cause the power of the Kingdom to be recognized as supreme by the world. Amen.

LEMUEL'S TESTIMONY.

OAKLAND, CAL., December 27, 1886.

My name is Lemuel. Excuse me; I come ahead of my brother Laman, but with his permission. I am a jolly fellow, of a disposition something of a mixture between the good and bad of the entire family. As my father was particular in giving the weights of all, I must also give my weight; it was about one hundred and seventy-five pounds—often a little less. I had no especial mission to perform when on earth except to cheer up my brethren; and do not know of anything especial now, except to let people know that I am alive, as usual, very much as lively as a fish in the water; therefore my spirit name became "Life of life." Laman is "Earth of earth," and my brother Nephi is "Spirit of spirit."

I have a great many jokes to tell you when you get over on our side, because, what is life worth without jokes? When a person is not laughing he is mostly grumbling over something.

That is the matter,
That I look like my father
In a contrary way,
To my own dismay.

He is sober and sullen,
But he looks like a mullen
In golden array,
As a king in his sway.

So my soul's life is hidden,
So it eats the forbidden—
The royal made dish.
To laugh and be merry,
And in fun to make query
And be gay as a fish.

If you can think such a man in the Kingdom to be of any special use, then you can rest assured that I will be there. Good-bye.

No, I am not ready yet. I have to introduce my brother Laman. He is a very bashful fellow when in the presence of the Lord's people; otherwise he is not apt to be retired in his habits, nor sensitive to the sight of his superiors, for he will always straighten up his full figure in the presence of fair women. He is able to speak for himself, so I will retire in good order, as Moroni did before the Lamanite forces, even if I should be as I am—very lonely, and the last surviving warrior; however, it would look as if I had run away from the battle—or rather the massacre.

Moroni was a wise man, and wisdom is worth acquiring, so that we can do the works of wisdom. Therefore, again, good-by. Laman will work a slaughter on you I am sure. Good-by. My name is Lemuel, the son of Lehi.

MESSAGE FROM LAMAN.

OAKLAND, CAL., December 27, 1886.

Ha, ha, ha! My brother is a jolly fellow. He is a man filled with wit enough to make me sorry and to cry that I was not born with the same qualities of soul and body. I was named Laman, which is Earth of earth, and he was named Life of life— so has it been.

The earth became an inheritance to Laman's people, and the Lamanites became mighty and prosperous for more than one day of the Lord's time, or a thousand of human years. God raised up many prophets among my people, but the spirit did not prevail. They were as my blessing was inherited by them, earth of earth, and so they remained, because they had quenched out the Spirit in going to war with the church of the Lamb, and destroyed the saints of the most high God, and drove *his* seed out from the land of promise, whose blessing was pronounced to be the son of the spirit of spirit.

I labored hard to save my people from internal contentions and bloodshed, but history tells that I did not succeed in my efforts, but to keep them from idolatry and in the true worship of the great Spirit of nature, or Jehovah our God. Otherwise, they intermixed with the Tartars, or Jared's people, who came from the great tower by sea, and by crossing the narrow strait at the North sea; and my people united with those who came from the north, and they became one people, and a very blood-thirsty and war-like people, who lost all positive knowledge of the records my father brought forth with him out of Jerusalem. So it came to pass, that they became bound up in many tribes, and the blood of Israel became lost in the blood of the Tartars, or Jared's people, who came in a multitude from the north down upon them, and made peace with them; and they became a dark and wild people, with a red, copper colored skin, and lost their native brownish, oriental color.

My people are now wilting away before the art of war and civilization belonging to Japhet's people. As God did not save my people, because they persecuted the church of God, so this great nation who have destroyed my people, shall not be saved, because they have been conspiring to destroy the church of God in your days, and to lay waste the holy places, that the Lamb of God should have no foothold, when He in His second coming shall step again upon the earth. "Therefore," says the Spirit, even the great Spirit to us, "that the great nation that dwells upon the graves of my people, shall come low down; as they have brought the church of God low down, and have persecuted the saints, also, shall persecution be upon the land of Joseph, and Ephraim shall weep in the valleys and on the hills of Zion, over all the contention and blood-shed which shall come as a deluge in the midst of this great nation, by which they shall destroy themselves."

Be not disheartened when you shall see the commencement of all these events, as the kingdom shall come in righteousness to bring peace and prosperity again to earth, by giving to man the Gospel of Freedom.

I have been low down as earth of earth, and so have we spoken by the voice of the prophets as out from the earth. Also shall this great nation come low down when safety shall not be found on the face of her land except in Zion. For blood shall run as brooks in her streets, and fire shall consume her cities; and her great cities, and her great mansions shall be destroyed by earthquakes and sink into the ground as you read about in the record given to you by the hand of Mormon. Now, peace be to you.

Only a remnant of my people are scattered amongst you, and Laman shall not any longer go to war with the pale faced tribe of Japhet. Ephraim shall be gathered, and the sons of Laman shall serve him, and the kingdom shall come. Not that which succumbed before the arms of war when the saints were destroyed, but the kingdom of the most High shall be established in the very midst of that land upon which you dwell, and it shall not be given to another people, or to another power; but the Lord shall be the power, and he shall dwell in the midst of Zion, and be worshipped as the Lamb of God who was slain, and the saints who were slain for his name-sake shall dwell there with him visibly, before the sons and daughters of the kingdom.

This is Laman's faith, as I have received it, and as my people rejected it, and as it will be restored to them again. Amen.

Blessed be the most high God, even the great Spirit of all the earth; and blessed be His holy name who remembered us in our transgressions, because of His love to Israel. His be the glory and worship always. Amen. I am Laman the son of Lehi, and the brother of Nephi. The records will some day be given in their fullness, as they once were known to his people in those bygone days, when Laman's children rebelled and went to war on account of a desire to destroy those sacred writings.

The soul of man must repent from bloodshed, and from the thirst and desire for blood, or every nation shall be destroyed, even as my people have been destroyed. Therefore, repent all ye nations, and pray by day and by night, and pray always. Let the spirit of prayer never depart from your souls lest the destroyer shall come upon you as a thief in the darkness of the night, and there shall be no escape.

Thou down-trodden daughter of Zion, be not without hope, because, in your desolation and sorrow, and in the darkest of all thy hours shall thy Redeemer knock on the door, and the hope of all thy aspirations shall be fulfilled. It shall not be as a wild and weary dream to thee when the Lord shall appear, but it shall be as a great light, and in the midst of the light thou shalt see Him who is clothed in power, even as the great Spirit is clothed in power. Amen.

Laman is redeemed. His people on the big hunting grounds on earth will be redeemed, even as those are who are in the spirit world, who are hunting over the big hills. Now, good-by. Nothing can hinder the work of God. Go ahead and do the work, and the glory be to the great Spirit and the Lamb of God who was slain, but shall govern and live again on earth, in the majesty of the Spirit, and in the power of His Father. Amen.

MESSAGE FROM JESHUAH, THE MESSIAH.

INDEPENDENCE, April 30, 1882, 7: 30 P. M.

In your weakness I have given you strength, and in your desolated condition I have been a rock and shelter to you, that you should not perish. Therefore, be of good cheer, and the time will come when you shall not glory in your own strength, but in your weakness, and that work which I am doing with an out-stretched and far-reaching arm before all the people of my flock, and before all the world, is a wonderful work and shall be done in the broad daylight and not in the dark, nor in the shade ; but the nations shall see it and wonder, and shall tell each other : " How was it that this people could be saved, as they were few, and only a breath of their enemies would have consumed them;

but Jehovah's angel has been walking before them, and been sitting before their face at day time, and peace was taken away from the earth, but abideth in mine angels' presence."

Before your vision is a valley rolled up as a panorama ; it is the south. When you are ready at Council Bluffs in July, and you have returned from the west, then direct your steps late in the fall towards the south and remain there all winter. I have a work for you to finish there ; a work you know nothing about now, but will be revealed to you in time. You will not do much out in the west but pay a visit, and lecture, and heal the sick at Ogden, Salt Lake City, San Francisco, and Los Angeles, until October, and you will return to Omaha, and leave again for the south ; we will not leave you alone on your travels, and my work will be done. There shall come many from east, and west, and south, and north, and say, "Come here and come there ;" but you shall go where the Lord, by His spirit of truth, shall dictate you to travel. We have only a limited time to allow you to travel in. Most of your work will be by your pen, and more in writing than in words, as the time has arrived for wonders in the heavens above, and in earth below. There shall be a preaching as a roaring thunder, which shall follow your messages to the people of my flock, and I will make signs in the heavens above, and in the earth below, and I will give the words which are sent to earth by the angel world of spirits a new, and strong, and powerful meaning. All the mediums which have, and are now working under the influence of the Spirit of prophesy, will be able to discern what is to come—the materialized revelations and manifestations of heaven coming down on earth, and the union of the two worlds into one, which is the first resurrection, and the commencement of the millenium. As my ways are above all the other creations on earth, so are the ways of God above all the wisdom, and all the cunning contemplation of man ; and what he thought to be a sure thing shall I prove to him to be his own deception, or the imagination of his own dream of vanity. I would rather that you would go to Independence and lecture, and be engaged in writing these and other messages, to be printed in a book somewhere, as the Spirit will instruct you. He comes from me, and is by you, as a guide from me. It will be on your way from Lincoln to the south. You will tarry at Independence in October or November of this year. Be not astonished because I tell you these things, as you are to be guided in such a way that your time and usefulness will not be consumed, nor your life be without fruit. There are many angels who descend from heaven to earth to see you, and to see me by you. Those you now see before you are angels clothed in light, who have a desire to see the opening of the fifth seal; and blessed are they who are greeted by the angels of the light, as the light shall shine around you, and before the world, and nations shall wonder, and be comforted in their hard struggle for liberty from despotism, and from hierarchical tyranny of priests. That despotism of souls which comes from ignorance and blindness, in all spiritual affairs of man, and acuteness in earthly doings, which is only foolishness to heaven, when applied to the wisdom and knowledge of heaven, and its law, and its treasures—so mote it be. Amen.

I am your redeemer from all your need, and it shall be your desire to be my apostle to my friends, who shall hear the voice of Messiah, and be comforted. Amen; yes, amen.

MESSAGE FROM JESHUAH, THE MESSIAH, TO JOHN TAYLOR.

HYDE'S PARK, August 27, 1882.

MY FRIEND GEORGE:

Let it be read aloud before my servant, John Taylor, and by thine own voice; and when this is done let it be copied in ink and kept in safe keeping. The time is near at hand when you shall have unveiled before your vision the mysteries of heaven. My peace be with you. My blessing is the peace of heaven. Live in this blessing and the world cannot harm nor hurt you. Amen.

It is not wisdom in me, that my servant who writes these lines from me shall give up his name to you. The church must receive the truth, as it loves the truth, in one concord, and I will pour out the spirit of prophesy on your heads, and my prophets shall be as the hosts of heaven among you. Therefore, let it be sufficient to you, that you receive what you do, and I will look at every one of your acts, and the motives in your soul, until I stand revealed before your sight, and ye shall know my messenger. My father's footsteps are on the earth now, and from the east and to the west shall they come, and from the north and to the south shall they come, and center together at Independence, Mo., where the Ancient of Days shall be revealed to all mankind as the Patriarch of Zion. Therefore, I warn you, and I warn you again: "Be careful how you receive my words." A message to the church was given in March, this year; that message you will shortly receive, and it will teach you what I want you to know. Other messages shall follow as you will need them. Wars, and rumors of wars shall not be taken away from the earth until you see me. Be not confounded by the threats of the world. Time shall come and time shall go, but my throne shall last forever. A king I was called when men lifted me on the cross, with pierced hands and feet, and a king I am in heaven, where my Father lifted me above the world; but lifted above the earth I shall draw all mankind to me, and blessed are those who understand the drawing of the Spirit, and will enlist in the cause of the Son of man, because the man is your Father and your God; and how my heart is burning that you should all know Him and His love, even as I know Him, that your lives could be one with His who has all power, that it could be given to you on earth. Blessed shall you be on that day. Amen.

I am the bright morning star which is shining before daybreak. Be prepared and awake, because the world is asleep and in darkness, and shall hear at my hour a midnight cry, and be raving and confounded, but ye shall walk in the light. I am the light. Amen, amen, amen.

MESSAGE FROM JESHUAH, THE MESSIAH, TO THE CHURCH.

HYDE's PARK, IOWA, May 12, 1882.

I honor my Father, but ye do not honor me, but as I honor the Father, also shall I be honored, because the Father is greater than I; but I shall be given the honor which is by Him as I love the Father, even as He loved me from the beginning, that His love was in me and remained by me. Therefore, I say to you: "Love one another in the same love by which I have loved you, and you shall remain in my love, as I am in the love of my Father, and shall be honored by him with the same love. Also ye shall be honored of me, by that love which is in me, and was in my Father; and He has loved you in me from the commencement of your lives, or before your birth, which is to you before the commencement of all things.

There is a love of the world which shall perish: a love for fame, and for honor and glory of this world, and for those things which shall vanish by death, and in the great revolutions and changes of nature. I say, "Don't work for the honor or glory of that which you cannot possess eternally. If it so happens to be given to you, then receive it from the hands of God and your fellow beings as a short, and very uncertain gift, that at any moment may be taken from you. Don't allow your souls to love it more than you are at any time able to lay down for my sake, or ye can not know me, nor can ye know my Father; but as I honor Him, so He is honored in you, if my love abide in your heart, and you remain by him in soul and life, as I did in the world and have done ever since."

Now, my last and greatest commandment to all my friends is: "Follow after me; take up your cross and follow me." My burden is truly easy, and my cross you can travel with, and be filled with joy and glory. Live in the world and be among the world's children; enjoy the things in the world, but as if you were not of the world.

There is no sin in love, and if you remain without sin you shall grow into perfection; and the love of my Father is His perfection, for which we all honor Him; and if you remain in Him you shall remain without sin, and ye shall not sin if you are born of Him, as His sons and daughters in the new light of the Gospel of Freedom, which is the crown of the harmonial philosophy, and the end of my mission, before I shall personally again appear on earth. In that consists our love to Him, that He loved us, and in that consists your love to me, that I have loved you, and have called on you to perceive His wonderful love which sent me into the world as a witness about His love to the world. Therefore do I honor Him, as I know Him, but ye do not know Him, and therefore you don't know me. If you knew Him you would honor me, because I came out from Him as a messenger into the world; and the world was in darkness and could not see the light, and could not know me on account of the darkness; and it dishonored me and hung me on the cross, and it dishonored my friends, the apostles and my disciples, and it put to death my witnesses. But as many as received the testimony have got the eternal record in His kingdom, which will be established on the earth, and materialized, we shall be together once more, and eat of the lamb of the passover, and drink of the new wine on earth in my Father's kingdom, and the testament shall be to an end—that last *will* made to mankind by the authority of my sacrifice. That *will* shall have its testament finished at that day, when I shall drink with you of the cup in the Gospel of Freedom, and I shall eat of the bread, and of the passover lamb in the Gospel of Freedom. And ye shall honor me, even as I honor my Father shall you honor Him with me, and the nations of the earth shall honor you, even as you have honored me shall you be honored. And as the world shall receive the least of my messengers who walk in my love, and I shall abide with, the same shall carry my peace with him to them. I have led you from earth to heaven, and I will lead you from heaven to earth, or make heaven descend on earth, and peace shall be on earth—that peace which is in heaven. Amen.

MESSAGE FROM JESHUAH, THE MESSIAH.

To Geo. Q. C———

CRESCENT CITY, IOWA, April 3, 1882.

I have not called you, and I have not sent you, and I have not shown you the way which you walk on, therefore, be not comforted, and be not healed of the wound inflicted on you. As I have said to my servant before you, also do I say to you : "Repent, and do your former works, or I will come speedily and remove you from the place where you stand." There shall come many and say Lord, Lord ! And I shall look at them and shall not remember even to have seen them doing my work, nor to have heard of them. Let the church know that my voice has sounded on earth, and let those be refreshed who mourn ; but to those who take my name in vain I have nothing to say except that they have turned a blessing into a curse by calling themselves after my name. I have allowed my Father to put your enemies on you, as it is to your blessing to be chastened, or you would quench the Spirit out from your midst.

Blessed are you if your grief is not for this world's sake, nor for the failure of this world's glory ; but that your heart and soul is mourning over your own faithless condition, and over the failure of the church as a body to accomplish the work and destiny ascribed to the saints in the world. Be not astonished when I say to you, "that the time will come when you will kill the prophets, and stone them that I send unto you, on account of your wickedness, and the pride in the hearts of the people." But if you keep my commandments, and do these things which I shall call upon you to accomplish, then I will save you from your enemies, and keep you in the hollow of my hand, and you shall be blessed beyond all your desire, or that which is possible for you to understand. Amen.

MESSAGE FROM JESHUAH, THE MESSIAH.

TO THE MESSENGER.

CRESCENT CITY, IOWA, April 3, 1882.

I will put thee as a line on my people who call themselves after my name, even the name of Jesus, the Christ; and I will stretch thee out upon them from east to west, and from north to south; and I will measure them with their own measure, and deal with them as they shall deal with thee; and as they have rejected my servants so they shall be rejected as a church, and only few shall be allowed to stand in their places and see the coming of the Lord of heaven as the Son of Man. Ye have refused to be comforted, and ye shall not be comforted. Ye have expelled the righteous from your midst, and unless your hearts become as wax, and your souls get clothed in mourning, ye shall perish in your sins. I will put a tape-line upon you; a chosen tape-line which you have lost off from your midst, but I have gathered up to be put on your length and breadth, and your hearts and inclinations will I measure by that. And your faithfulness, and your willingness, and your obedience will I measure by the way you receive him, and accept the words which I speak to him.

Blessed are those who hunger and are thirsty, who are needy and meek. Blessed are the souls with a torn and ragged garment, because they shall have the glory of God resting upon them. But woe to those who shall call themselves after my name, and count themselves as the saints of God, but are hypocrites, faithless—swelled up and big in their own imaginations,—liars, impostors, covetous, defamers, and whose hearts are burning after the riches of this world, wishing to sit in high places in the tabernacle as a damnation to themselves, worshipping the devil of perdition and retrogression in the image of God. Woe to those who barricade the way of God by their own foolishness and childish ignorance, and who persecute the saints and the righteous amongst them, only for the sake of power and dominion. Blessed are those who love me, and keep in my ways, for to them I will give the keys to the palace of heaven, and they shall open the door, and none can enter into that house, but by me ; therefore be not deceived. Amen.

MESSAGE FROM JESHUAH, THE MESSIAH.

ON GATHERING.

INDEPENDENCE, Mo., April 8, 1883, 9 A. M.

Surely there shall come many from all countries of the earth, and sup with me at this place, when the fulness of time and times are passed; and these which my Father gave me out of the world shall be gathered into one fold, and there shall be one shepherd. I am speaking now about my visible appearance on earth in the last days of the world's government; not in the last days of the present nature, but the last days of the present state of affairs on earth, when the spirit of this world's government is ruling the nations. Look at the political horoscope as it stands ; and it is indicating the conflict between the powers of darkness and light, and in the struggle the nations will hail the kingdom to come, and the Son of man with a world of heavenly light, and peace, and spiritual truth and happiness to all mankind. Then shall peace be given for the scattered to be called into Independence and build up Zion. And I will gather mine elect from all over the earth, by sea and by land, to come as delegates from the nations to meet me at this place. There are some of my people dwelling among the mountains, as all over the earth, east and west ; to those I am calling with a loud voice, saying : "Be ready and come, by sea and by rail, from far off, and make you ready, because the time will be at hand suddenly, as a flash of lightning, or a dash of the wind, and you will be moving toward this place. And those who persecuted you will be dead, and their sons and daughters will call you blessed as those who come in the name of the Lord."

Surely your inheritance has been bought with blood, and shall be redeemed by money, and a full possession shall be given to you, and the anger of your enemies shall be taken away, and the sting of the scorpion shall have lost its poison. In the same days shall the Central Temple at Independence, Mo., be built as a standard for the world to look upon, and as the Cathedral of heaven on earth ; but let it not trouble your mind, as your faith and good will in doing the work has been accepted, and shall be put into a heavenly active power; and in doing the work the church shall see it done, and there shall be workmen in heaven helping it on as well as on earth. When your hands, and shoulders, and strength, and prayers are put into such an undertaking I will personally appear visible, and face to face I will speak to you, and you shall hear my voice as my disciples did at Jerusalem, and during the forty days after my resurrection from death. It is my will and pleasure that you shall consider all these things, and not be in haste, nor be troubled in your mind, nor lose your faith in God, nor your love and honesty in seeking after truth wherever you find it. And I say to you: "There is a messenger amongst you, and you don't know him." But he is a forerunner of him who comes before me at my second coming, and he is in the spirit of the priesthood of John the Baptist; but you know him not, and he cries from afar off to you, and you hear his voice as a lonely bird moaning in the grass at the lake-shore, as the sun of this present dispensation is sinking behind the western mountains. He has not the Gospel of Freedom, but he bears witness of it, which is the mission of Messiah to be given in his second coming, when Zion is prepared, and the messenger bears a true testimony of it. He had to come, and blessed are those who hear his voice, and prepare their hearts for events which already are pressing on, and which you can not receive in your present darkened and hardened condition. Blessed are those who will hear him, and will receive my messenger. I have raised up my messengers one after another amongst you, but some have you driven off, and others have you killed ;

and the innocent blood by which the church is stained and sprinkled has called down a judgment to be executed on you, as your enemies have grown powerful. Now, I have sent one messenger and I will send another, and I will multiply my messengers until all the people from the lowest to the highest shall see me as my messenger sees me, and know my voice, as many as call on my name. The work has to be done by the Order of Messiah, or by thousands and thousands of heavenly messengers filled with the Spirit of prophesy.

Spiritualism is making way for the glorious entry of the Spirit of progress, and is preparing the nations for great events, and is lifting up hope in the minds of those who are in darkness to shout a hallelujah filled with joy and immortality. Therefore, my people in Utah and all over the world, do not shut up your ears, and close your eyes from seeing these grand stepping stones over which the nations of the earth will pass to hail Zion, and cry out: "Blessed art thou who comest in the name of the Lord." The work of the Lord is not one thing, but many things; not one design, but many designs, and He cannot conform to your pattern of church rule, as He is in freedom, but you must conform to His ways. Be not bigoted; be not narrow minded; be not in hatred one to another, but be long suffering, and broad of heart, or I will come suddenly as a flash of lightning and find you asleep; therefore, be awake, as the midnight cry comes in the Order of Messiah, and it is near at hand. Be ready for the call by day and by night, as the adversary goes not to sleep, nor do your enemies or opposers go to sleep except you keep awake early and late, and awake in the spirit of truth, which is the spirit of salvation.

I am your redeemer and your friend, and as I was with my disciples when on earth, even so I will be with you. Amen.

MESSAGE FROM DAVID PATTON.

INDEPENDENCE, Mo., December 6, 1885, 10 P. M.

Here you are again, where Joseph, the prophet, came more than fifty years ago with a handful of men, women and children, who had received the new light, even it was the old light or the gospel of Jesus. He was not a learned man, but an honest man; he was not a wise man, but a tool in the hands of God; he was not a man of age, but a youth; he was a ridicule amongst mankind as in the spirit world, and only a few on earth and a few amongst the spirits on earth greeted his advent except with sneers and contempt; but the angel world had called upon him, and he obeyed not as a slave does his master, no; but because it had become a second nature in him to live in his Father's spirit, and do the work of the only begotten Son, the Redeemer, until he was killed as I was killed on the battlefield of Jehovah in this vicinity, so that our blood could cry out under the altar of the Lamb as a witness to this generation about the cross, and the power of the cross upon which our Master hung. New light upon light, and knowledge upon knowledge will be added to the gospel, as testimony upon testimony shall be given from heaven to all who are the chosen seed, or the elect on earth in this dispensation—the second advent of Messiah.

I want you, to-morrow, to pay a short visit to my old home at the north-east corner, near the Temple Block. Tell my friends that I am alive; that I spoke to you. Tell them that we live—all who are dear to them and were lost to man's natural eyesight behind that thin veil which mankind calls by the name of "death." Tell them there is no such a thing as death, but life is swallowed up of life, and they shall rejoice at the testimony which you shall bring forth to them. Life on earth is such a very short concern, and it appears as such a small speck to the eternal life which is in store for us. We hope yet for the restoration of all things; we pray always that our aspiration shall be fulfilled to appear on earth again with a body of refined matter, spiritualized as well as it is materialized, and immortal in heaven as it will also be on earth, visible and tangible, which shall not any more see corruption, but shall be seen in that perfection in which we live ; and also, shall be heard, and seen, and believed in by immortal mankind in the similitude of the Lord's dwelling of forty days on earth after the crucifixion and resurrection. Also, shall we dwell with Him, and be as He is, and appear as He did, and be known as He is known when the fulness of time is come. Therefore be not of little hope, as the kingdom belongs to you who are His elect friends whom the Father has drawn to Him out of the world, and none were lost,-not even Judas who betrayed Him, as in the Lord's time the redemption came and he followed his Master the more eagerly, that none of the chosen ones should be lost, though he had become a devil while in the flesh.

There is very little to say about Independence in a local sense, but eighteen ninety-five and up to nineteen ninety-five will all be done whatever in our most sanguine expectations we have dreamed about. There will be built a real temple of stone and mortar, and it will adorn the Temple Block ; and it will be raised up and be seen of this generation—so mote it be. Amen.

I am David Patton, the apostle.

MESSAGE FROM JESHUAH, THE MESSIAH.

To John Taylor.

Hyde's Park, Iowa, August 1, 1883.

I have called you " friends," and inasmuch as you keep my commandments you are my friends, and the children of the light ; and your prayers and supplications are acceptable to my

Father. Live in the spirit of your prayers and you will not be confounded. Wisdom shall come down from heaven and abide with you if you seek it with an earnest soul to be a star light on your way, and a burning lantern before your feet, that you may not tremble, nor stumble in the dark, but lead the people by my hand as I am your redeemer, and the light of the world. Be not discouraged in your tribulations, as they are for the benefit of the church, or it would have been otherwise. Lonely has heaven left you for years, that your hearts might be filled with love, and longing, and long suffering, and meekness, that you might receive and not reject me, nor my messengers, and not persecute them. For that reason I have kept the seers out of your midst, but in time the faithful in Zion shall hear my voice, and not reject my testimony, nor persecute my witnesses. Amen.

Far off have you gone from the path which my spirit taught you, and you have followed your own inclinations, and have built cities in the spirit of the world, thinking to do God a service. Many have gone behind the veil because they had no faith nor spirit to live by, and many are asleep amongst you. You have cast the pearls of heaven before swine, and the Holy of Holiness before dogs, and now they turn against you and are ready to tear you asunder. You have begged your enemies for peace, because the peace of heaven—that peace by which I blessed you—had departed from your souls. In a long and weary time have your footprints been seen among the Rocky Mountains, and you have grown in prosperity according to the world, but not according to the spirit of the gospel after my name. I am the peace, and as many as remain in peace shall remain in me, and I in them, and they shall not be removed from their habitations. Riots shall be amongst you, because you have not been the children of peace; and those who shed blood will go down in death with a blood-stained soul, because there was no peace in their ways. Blessed are you if you keep the spirit of peace among the brethren, for some will go out from your midst and grasp the sword, supposing by that to be saved, and grasp the gun, meaning by that to arrive at exaltation. I say to you: "If you will keep my commandments, and walk in the spirit of my work, I will be on your right and on your left side, and I will be before and behind you, and I will confound all your enemies; and not a hair of your heads shall be lost except it be by my will, and it shall be found in my safe keeping." Amen.

Therefore, be of good cheer, and lift up your hands, as it is through much tribulation in this world that you shall be saved from the world, and receive an everlasting inheritance out of the world, and be gathered into mine own place, and see the Temple erected in Independence, Missouri, even as I have shown it to my messenger—he who now sends these messages to you. I have kept him away from you that his inheritance should not be spoiled; but I have made him a chosen tape-line by which I will measure the length, and the breadth, and the depth of your minds, that you may find out the short-comings of the church, and be saved from much tribulation. As the cloud in the east is rising towards the meridian of your home in the mountains, so comes the future dark upon you; but fear not if you are my friends, because I am the conquerer of the world, and the destiny of the nations on earth is resting in the hands of my Father. I say: "Fear not the thunder of man, neither the cannons, nor the mighty armies, but fear the thundering voice of Jehovah;" because He speaks and the earth trembles, and the universe obeys Him, and He will dash the dust of the earth, and pestilence will spring forth and stay those who fight against the will and blessing of heaven. He will make the great and self-conceited men of the world to be counted as fools among His children. Powerfully shall His work be done. Myriads are the hosts of His angels. Spirits out of all nations serve Him. As ants are moving at their nests, so are His chariots many; they are clouding the foot-hills of the mountains. Glorious are His ways over the hills as the light of flames also are His footsteps. When He speaks the air is quivering as before an earthquake, and His voice makes the earth rend as if it was wrestling with chills. Woe to the enemies of the most high God, but woe more to those who call themselves after His name, and make it a mockery and a sham to be a saint. As I will deal with the enemies of the church, also will I deal with the faithless and the traitors in your midst; they shall be left to their own fate, and empty the cup according to their own desire. My sheep will hear my voice, and flock around me; and they who are not of me will hear the voice of the world, and flock in with the world, and will lose the blessing I had bestowed on their heads—that blessing to be mine anointed, even as I am the anointed of my Father in heaven.

My son John, thou art now old, and thy days have been counted till thy head is as the snowy peaks of the mountains. Lofty and serene has thy old age been, and when I gather thee into my home thou shalt not say that I have been a miser in my dealings with thee. Now, my words come to thee in obscurity as to a man who is whispered to in the ears in the silence of the night. And I say to thee, " be prepared;" because I will hold thee and my people accountable on my own day for how thou dealest and how thou shalt deal with my messengers, even my chosen messengers whom I shall send to thee, and shall, within a short time from now, be with you. He who now sends my words to you is asking no favor of you, as he has my favor, and that is sufficient for him. Only thou shalt teach the people of the church that they may obey my words, and shall not persecute any messenger whosoever he may be, who comes to you in the name of the Lord thy God, and with " Thus saith the Lord," sounding from his lips to you. The Holy Spirit bears witness, that severe trials are to come to the church, and are near at hand, unless the saints humble themselves, and do not fall under the curse of old Israel. They must abstain from persecuting one another, and banishing one another from the church only for vanity sake, quenching out the spirit of brotherly love. They must abstain from hatred against a dissenting brother or sister, and cultivate freedom and tolerance, as heaven is built up in freedom, and its perfection is the Gospel of Freedom, which breathes nothing but tolerance to all creation. Let it be known as my will to the church, that they abstain from that dreadful sin against the holy angels, and against my messengers in heaven, and on the earth, of which you have been guilty in shedding the blood and killing the prophets, and those of mine elect out from your midst—those of my messengers who are raised up and sent into your midst to your exhortation, and comfort and joy, that when they shall come to you they shall not come as sheep among wolves and be torn asunder, and their spilt blood shall not cry from the ground, and angels shall not weep over the church as I wept over Jerusalem, and as heaven wept over Cain when he, stamped with the sign of perdition, fled into the wilderness. Woe unto you on that day which is to come, if the back of my hand shall be turned against you, because, the destroyer shall come upon you, and there shall be nobody to save, but only to devour your riches. My work has only fairly commenced on earth in the last days, and you have seen the commencement, but you have not seen the end. Only a few of my people who entered the mountains in the days of the pioneers, are left to see and hear what is to come, as among Israel who left Egypt, only two received an inheritance in the land of Canaan. Therefore, be meek and lowly in your own estimation, as my servant, Moses, was meek. With him I spoke face to face as I have done to my messenger, and if thou shalt ask for it thou shalt receive a testimony from me—an everlasting testimony which shall follow my words to thee, and thou shalt know of a surety that they were sent from me. I will give thee a lesson from above and a lesson from below, and both shall join together in one cross of conviction about the crucified Jesus who is the one, I am, who bears His testimony to thee, and blessed art thou if thou shalt receive it, and blessed is the church if it receives it, and blessed shalt your children's children be for many generations if they receive it. And a halo of light shall descend upon you, and rest on you, and abide with you as soon as you are sanctified as the Zion on earth, and identified as such by the Zion in heaven. Blessed art thou, my son John, if thou shalt keep my commandments, and two-fold more blessed shalt thou be if thou shalt lead the church into the path of all truth, and do the work which thou hast promised to do—the work of the spirit of God, even the Holy Spirit, represented to man by legions of holy angels and spirits which thou shalt discern, ascending and descending, and the heavens open, and the Son of man in great power at the right hand of Jehovah, in communion with and ready to come to his elect.

Give not your tithing to please men, but before God, neither shall you offer it to men, nor as a sacrifice given to men, but to God.

Tithing shall be a holy offering to the Lord for the benefit of the poor and needy—those who are suffering, and cripples, and the weak among you, that you may praise God in your doings, and thank Him who spared you, that you came not unto the same judgment.

Tithing is the Lord's money, and has to be used in His spirit, and according to his mind. In the Gospel of Freedom it has to be a free gift, and not according to commandment; but the will of God has to be in the freedom which comes from love.

Tithing was not instituted under the restoration of the gospel, as a fund by which families or persons should be supported. It was not given to the Lord for any such purpose or it would be converted into a curse, and the blessing of the Lord would depart from it.

It was said to Moses, that the priest should live off the tithing, even as the tribe of Levi did. And it was said to Joseph Smith when he tarried at Far West, that tithing should be given as a surplus of all property, and then that one-tenth of all interest or surplus gain should be tithing, that it might not tread down the poor, nor take the bread away from wives and children, as the interest is of the surplus gain of the capital employed. Out of that, only, has one-tenth to be given to the Lord, that the sick, and needy, and suffering might be relieved by your offering to the Lord of your surplus funds. It was in an emergency of the church, that the first ordinance about using tithing was given as a rule for the church, as David, when in need, was allowed to eat the bread before the altar, and it was not accounted to him to be a sin. Also was the church at Far West allowed to cover debt, and administer of the tithing to the presidency and the priesthood. But it was not so in the beginning, nor shall the foundations of Zion be laid from tithing, but shall from its surplus fund build homes of comfort for the poor, and houses of hospitality for the traveler, that the sojourner among you may find a home of rest, where he can stop over and be given food and shelter, that the blessing of the stranger may rest on Zion, that he may go home to his own people and bless you, and not curse you all his days.

The old saying was: " When Messiah comes he shall put all things right." And that is right, that you do all things in the church according to the spirit of the commandment, and not fulfill the letter of it only because the Spirit shall justify you if you have acted according to the Spirit, which is the Gospel of

Freedom. For the letter justifies no person, as the letter is only the body, and both carnal and of the world. Therefore, pay your tithing according to the spirit of the law, and you shall be justified by the Spirit; and use the tithing according to the spirit of the law, and the blessing of God shall abide with you ; but if your tithing is to please men and not God, your reward is gone. Be, therefore, careful how you consume God's household for the poor and needy. Apostles shall have nothing from the tithing house, as they are special messengers to the world and in the church, and I have sent you without money and without salary, to preach the gospel to the poor and the rich. Also, it is my will, that the priesthood shall do that work, not for money, nor for price, nor for support, but in faith and obedience to the work of salvation from error to truth, and from darkness to light, and their reward, and money, and food, and clothes, and eternal riches shall follow them.

If you build a house to my name, whether it be a temple, or a tabernacle, or any other house dedicated to my name, then it is my will that the expense shall not be from tithing, but from a special fund called the "Public Church Fund," and there will be plenty of money, as my blessing shall follow it. Set a box at the entrance of each meeting house for the purpose of collecting free contributions, that all can give who wish to; and it shall be done in freedom, and in love, and in truth, as God is truth, and His spirit is love, and his works are all done in the Gospel of Freedom ; therefore, be ye perfect, as the Father in heaven is perfect.

The expenses of the church shall be taken from the free church fund, and not from that of tithing, which is sanctified to the Lord's poor and needy ; but the Church Fund, or the treasure of the church, has to provide for its own necessities and missions abroad, and has to be sustained by free contributions, or in cases of urgency, by assessments levied on each ward and township all through the states ; it shall not be called a tithing to the Lord, but a payment to the church. The tithing shall be kept holy, as the Lord your God is holy; and what you sanctify to His household on earth shall be to you, as the holy of holiness to the Lord, only for the helpless, the sick, the needy beggar, or the aged man or woman, either he or she who is a stranger amongst you, or a sojourner, or a brother, or a sister in distress. Thou shalt let the hand of the Lord reach them from the tithing house. Thou shalt seek after the orphans, and the widows, and the destitute among you, and give shelter to the homeless, and food and clothes from the Lord's storehouse to the needy. You shall not cast the sick out from your midst, but remember to pray and anoint with oil in the name of the Lord, and I will be by you with the spirit of healing. Therefore, seek the spiritual gifts, and next to the spirit of prophesy and clairvoyance, seek the gift of healing, and ye shall lay hands on the sick, and they shall be healed. Administer to the sick poor, from the tithing house, as well as by your prayers, and the laying on of hands, that my spirit may not be grieved by looking at you.

The tithing fund shall be a perpetual treasure sanctified to the Lord, laid up, and the surplus kept at interest, that there shall be found no needy poor amongst you.

Houses for the poor in the wards, and townships, and counties, may be built out of that fund, and be large and comfortable as you could wish the rooms to be for yourselves.

This is the voice of the Lord concerning tithing and its appliance for the future, with a great many additions which the spirit of God shall dictate to your minds, as you shall be taught all things, and remember the teaching of the Spirit, even as He shall move upon your minds. You shall not walk in the paths of ancient Israel, and persecute the prophets, or the seers when I shall send them unto you ; you shall not hate them, nor slay them, nor drive them out from your midst because they are not the great men of the earth, or because it may be a poor or despised woman, as my glory among the saints is now abundant in such persons. I am the Lord thy God, and do not look at a man's clothes, nor at his possessions in life, but at the sincerity and honest meekness of his soul, and willingness to be a medium for my spirit, and to be subject to all privations because he loves me. Therefore, condemn none, because they do my errand and come to you in all meekness as my embassadors.

You shall care for the insane among you, as you would for a friend, or a sick brother or sister, and you shall not treat them as enemies ; you shall not bind them with ropes, or inflict punishment upon them, be they male or female. Remember always yourselves, that heaven might strike any of you down in your pride, and you may be as one of those you despise. As discord and disharmony in body and soul is the sole cause of all insanity and obsession, you shall provide all possible freedom for insane persons, as formerly was done among Israel, and surround them with the beauties and peace of a serene nature. Do not pattern after the world, as their insane asylums are "holes of abomination in my sight," says the thundering voice of Jehovah. Let your prayers for the insane reach heaven, and let heaven descend and surround them, that they may be healed. Seek into the cause of the evil, and remove the person from the place and the circumstances, and the persons who caused the discord. Your insane asylums are an abomination unto me, because they are prison holes in the place of hospitals, and not homes filled with peace and comfort, and conducted in the spirit of the good Samaritan. Therefore, I am touching the walls with my fingers, and I will break down the walls, and the windows, and the iron bars, and the strong doors will I open, and the chains and the ropes will I break asunder. You are my people, do my will and continue to call upon my name. My hands from the cross of Golgotha are lifted up against all such institutions as the insane asylums of the United States. Be not guilty of the mistakes of this world. Discord shall be soothed and healed by harmony, when it is not any longer accountable for the situation of its own condition, or able to care for its own welfare, or its own conscious I am, or God's image in man.

Utah has copied the world, and not the church of Messiah. Let the world have its own sway, and be not grieved, as the world is in darkness, but you have received the light—that which will give you the knowledge, and peace, and glory as jointheirs, and sons and daughters of the truth; and I am the truth. Therefore, praise the infinite God in the name of the Father, as you praise Him in the name of the Son, that you are not struck under the same judgment of insanity, like your unfortunate brethren and sisters. Do unto them as you would be done unto, and let love claim its own relations, and provide for their necessities; because, I say to you, that when you shall stand face to face with such persons in the spirit world, you would rather wish not to have been born than recollect and repeat before your own souls all the wickedness and abominations you have been guilty of, in the heartless and cruel murder of dear relatives, made thus to perish in the flesh within the walls of modern insane asylums. Let such inhuman conduct not be found as a blot upon the reputation of the church of the saints. For the church of Messiah, under the Gospel of Freedom, has already washed its hands and said : " I am not guilty of any such abomination in the sight of God, the Almighty." But the insane shall be kept in the bosom of a harmonious nature, away from busy life, at Riverside, or Lakeshore, or in the mighty forests of the mountains in the solitude, where angels can approach the insane persons, and heal the soul and body by their spirit force full of power—that divine element which sparkles in the sunbeams, and blazes around the throne of God, and is every where infused into the church as the holy Spirit, in proportion as the church is able to receive it by the ministration of holy messengers as angels or spirits from heaven ministering to my people on earth, for they are not left alone. So shall it be a law and regulation for all generations to come, that my people, and sons, and daughters of God shall not be cast with evil influences into dungeons of hell, and holes of pestilence, and so-called insane asylums, and all that evil be done under the false and corrupt banner of misguided philanthrophy.

Now, my son John, I bid you farewell in your earth life Your predecessor, Brigham Young, has a few words to say to you, and I say, " listen to him." Amen.

I am your old friend and brother, in the same hope and circle of brotherly love. My soul is not aroused against you, as you might suppose it to be. Failure on earth is generally our spiritual advancement, and our fortune on earth is generally our loss in heaven. Guide the church better than you could wish to guide your own family, and your own household; and blessed shall you be if you arrive here as a servant of servants, rather than as a king. If you have served the saints as a father, as a brother, as a counsellor, and as a helper and not for gain, nor for money, but for love, then as you have loved them so shall they love you, and your mansion in the world of spirits shall be a glorious one. There are points in the gospel that you shall not quarrel about; because human imperfection is found in the best garments of truth on earth, for the church creeds are only different garments of the truth.

When baptism is performed in the name of the crucified Master, Jesus, let it alone, and do not repeat it, that your lives may be as His was in the world, and your redemption shall be in a silent peace with God. Baptism once properly performed cannot be mended, neither can you improve the grace of God shed abroad in your souls. If any of you have sinned against the law of truth within them, and lost that peace which is of God, let them humble themselves before the divine fountain of their being, and wash themselves all over with fresh, cold water, as pure as you can obtain it, and let it be a symbol and a sacrifice given before your own conscience with God, that your desire is to remain in the covenant with Him as His servant.

Tithing is better for the church, but worse for the priesthood; and it would be better for all that we could dispense with it at present, if not used in the spirit of its donation, as the church is prosperous, and it can do little good, but much harm by giving you the means to do evil, but let it be as Jesus, the Messiah and our Lord has decided in His message.

BRIGHAM.

MESSAGE FROM PARLEY P. PRATT, THE APOSTLE.

INDEPENDENCE, Mo., December 29, 1882.

As we believed on earth, so do we believe in the spirit world, that Zion must be redeemed. For that purpose do we work now behind the veil. We do not send this epistle to the church in Utah, because we do not recognize the church any longer to be circumscribed by any territory, but extending its boundaries all over the earth, and not limited under the circle or control of the mountain priesthood, but extending in the hearts of all who ever heard, and who ever obeyed the gospel, and remained honest to their convictions either in allegiance to the high priesthood or not, if they remained in allegiance to God, and Christ, and the holy Spirit of truth, and the holy angels, and not to men nor any set of men, whosoever they might be, as the obedience to the spirit of the gospel puts all men and women into freedom under the heavenly rule of the Redeemer from the world, and into the freedom of the city of the New Jerusalem. To-day we are in council together at headquarters, and from the Temple Block assigned by the finger of God we say : "The law of love in freedom shall go forth from here to all nations." The law shall go forth out of Zion, and the word of the Lord from Jerusalem, and as the word went forth to all nations, and they became blessed by it in the seed of Abraham, so shall the law of love go out from Zion, or Independence, Mo., and give freedom, and love, and redemption to all saints, and all men and women who receive it, and to the soil of Independence and Adam ondi Ahman.

Therefore, we call on the first presidency to understand the precious moment which is at hand, and to remember that this place was bought with money and blood, and has to be redeemed from its present owners by purchase. Let it be done day after day, and year after year, now and henceforth till eighteen hundred and ninety-five (1895), which is the fulness of time in which year the temple must be raised before the sight of the most high God, that His spirit may dwell there, and rest within its walls in the fulness of signs, and gifts, and powers pertaining to the Gospel of Messiah.

Be not bigoted, nor narrow minded and cold hearted, and filled with any covetous spirit of hunger and thirst after gain and ambition, because the work of God is contrary to all such doings; but seek the truth only for truth's sake, and ye shall not lose your reward, nor be sorry in the end of your days for the course which you will have pursued.

Be not bitter one against another, nor shall you condemn as we did when we lived upon the earth, because our hearts are now rebuked, and are filled with sorrow because of our past lives. Therefore, take one another by the hand, as brotherly love shall cover the sins of your imperfections, as the water does the bottom of the sea.

Be not proud in your hearts, as the Lord has found you wanting as He found us wanting on our arrival here, and it has brought our faith into the humiliation of profound knowledge about ourselves, and we say to you : " Have the mind and spirit of Messiah, and you will not despise the dissenter and drive him from you, nor will you oppose the sons of Joseph and their followers, as they are honest before God, and doing a work which has borne fruit on earth and in heaven." Amen.

MESSAGE FROM JESHUAH, THE MESSIAH.

ON DECEPTION.

OAKLAND POINT, CAL., May 8, 1884.

Deception does not consist in being itself, but in consequence of being something else.

Deception is not in being what it really is, but in being what it imagines itself to be.

Be not deceived, as there are a great many deceptions in the world, and the world itself is a deception to all those who are of the world—not in the sense that the world is not, but in the sense that the world is not what the multitude thinks it is, or imagine it to be. The apostle said once in olden time: "That which is in the world is of the flesh and shall perish." In other words: "The world in a sensual conception is a deception," because the senses are only transient attributes, that in a few years shall vanish, and they are not the representatives of the eternal principles of the interior of man, who shall last forever.

Deception is not that God has spoken to man, but that man

does not perceive that God continually speaks, as His revelations are continuous and without end. Only a very little of the internal manifestations are written. In numerous instances they come to persons who are laboring hard for the necessaries of life, and are poor, and low down in this world's society, and when they come to such characters they are never written down; at the same time, as the sun's rays strike out through the universe with the same force and rapidity of light, it is only once in a while that they strike such a small globe as your planet, and give light, and force, and life by the infinite grace to your vegetable and animal life; but much more of the sun's energy and power of light is lost to the earth for some higher or greater purpose in the immense space of the universe, so it is not the written word which by any means represents the highest out-poured energy of the divine principle of truth and power. In like manner, but in a greater degree, there are thousands passing into the spirit world daily, who carry with them their own individual convictions which are not based on man, nor on the wisdom of man, but are born of the eternal life-giving inspirations out-pouring from my Father, and from the spirits who are in heaven, and the heaven of heavens sings together in one echo of harmonies and praise that it is so, and not otherwise.

Deception is not because God gives light to man, but because man chooses to remain in darkness, and not come to the light; but for their sakes who wish to come to the light, the scriptures are written, " that no soul shall perish, but have the light."

Blessed are those who stand alone in the spiritual faith and convictions, based on personal inspiration and interior knowledge, far above all written testimony of others; knowing in their inmost minds that there is no deception in the mathematics of the eternal world; knowing that this little abode on earth is the primary lesson of individual life, where the human mind stretches out its wings as young birds do in their first motions and efforts to fly. Be not disheartened when all kinds of deceptions are around you, and before you, and at the same time your knowledge about the truth is called deception. You are not the one who deceives, nor are you deceived; but those who cry out the loudest against you are deep in falsehood, and are the victims of their own darkness. Be never disheartened because the deceptions of the world are staring you in the face for they will all vanish, and there shall not be left one stone on another of those mighty churches or temples whose worshipers do not serve the eternal progression of truth to man. But as it went with Nineveh, and Babylon, and Egypt, and Rome, so shall it be with the great deceptions of christianity, the spiritual Babylon. Generation after generation shall shake their heads and say, "We thought she would never have perished;" but the word "deception" was written across her forehead, and as she was of deception she called the light-bearer to mankind to be as herself—drunken with her own wine, and filled with deception and cruelty.

You are not alone, nor shall you be left alone, but you shall have Him by you who has the tape-line in his hand to measure the heights and depths of the living words of God, even the holy Spirit of eternity. Let Him not depart from you lest your own lives should be a living evidence of the deception in your souls. By that light which never perishes, which gives light to every man, you shall see if you have eyes to see, and ye shall hear the hymns of paradise sung if ye have ears to hear, and a soul to comprehend, that you may know there is no deception in God, but that the world is filled with it, because the world is carnal, and shall perish as grass.

When your enemies bless you, then do not believe them, as they are in deception much more than when they curse you, and speak evil against you, but when they do all these things then rejoice, because you are not in deception, but in the truth with your relation to Jehovah.

When you are struggling onward seeking more truth, and rejoicing in light from above, then you shall not be counted in deception, though the world may call you a horde of deceivers; but when you are going into a spiritual sleep with your bounty from heaven, and peace reigns, and when prosperity crowns your efforts and works, and your barns are filled with the treasures of your hearts, then be careful, as deception is written on all of it, unless you keep awake day and night in the burning faith of Messiah, that the pleasure of my Father may fill your hearts, and you may be hidden within the palms of His hands, and baffle all the schemes of your enemies. Remember that only for a little while are you here, and again only a little while and I will greet you in the eternal mansions. Therefore be not disheartened, for the Son of man shall appear with power and glory before those who await Him in the truth of their aspirations, and those who are present shall know it, even if the world shall call it a deception.

When you, my messenger, write these words, and I am by you, it always appears that your hands are pierced, and the bloody cuts in both hands are before your spiritual sight, and your feet appear bloody and pierced, and a gaping wound in your left side. Now, I will ask you: "Are these things a deception to you?" If I am not individually the controling power the signs are not on your body, nor do you discover them at any time except when I am with you, and you see me face to face, and hear my voice, that you may know the Messiah and know his voice, and see upon your body the marks of my suffering and death. "Are the aches and the pains of the wounds that you feel a deception or a truth?" I have put this question before you as much for your own sake as for the sake of the world, and I say to you: "It is not a deception, neither to your physical condition, nor to your spiritual sight;" and as the signs have followed you, even from your childhood, then I ask you again: "Where is the deception?" That you are not the crucified is true enough, but that the crucified Messiah was by you personally from your childhood was made plain to your understanding by your dreams; and by the conceptions of your dreams it has been shown you from your early days, that you might be the messenger, concerning whom I will say: "The harvest is gathered into the barn, and is threshed on its floor;" and I will send my messenger to sift the seed, that my words may be understood, even the seed which comes out of my mouth.

It was said to you from the mouth of my Father, even from youth: "You shall be hated by many for my sake, and you shall be blessed of many for my sake, even so shall it be." I have been to you a shelter and a protection, even at that hour when in my wisdom I twice drove you out of Salt Lake City by the power of my arm, that you should live and do my work, and not be killed as my servants, the prophets, had been before you. When the world shall read your message from Messiah, even from the crucified Jesus, there shall be nothing known about you but that book; that monstrous book! These volumes of gigantic deception! Look up on that day and I will show you the woman sitting on the seven hills, and the minor power—the lamb with the two horns, which speaks as the lamb, but does the work of the dragon—even the Protestant churches in union with the political power of the world, as the Catholic church has been and is to-day; and across the forehead of both is written "deception," because I have sent out my servants on the highways, and called them to my nuptials, but they have not come, and when I have compelled them to be my guests they have refused to come. I have sounded the bassoon of the sixth seal, but they have not listened, nor have they accepted my warning; therefore is "deception" written across their foreheads, for their understanding is darkened by superstition and creeds with no profit any longer to mankind.

At my nuptials I have poured out a new wine, and whosoever drinketh that wine anew with me in my Father's kingdom, shall have his name written above the entrance to his dwelling in the city of the New Jerusalem, and his inheritance shall be forever with the angels, the archangels, and God's; but whosoever rejects the cup of my Father's house, even the new wine in the Gospel of Freedom, cannot eat the passover lamb with me in the heaven on earth.

The Son of man is not coming to judge the world, but to redeem it, even the world judges itself by its own judgment, and it is a "deception." Those who are not with me in the coming of Messiah are against me, or will, by the irresistible conflict, be drawn against me until peace is given to the earth for the long period of a thousand years. The battle is between the deception and the truth—the everlasting battle of eternal progression. Therefore, be ye careful, because as soon as you think that you have grasped all truth, then in that same moment you deceive yourselves; and at the moment when you say: "Now we have had all the prophets, and all things are restored, and all knowledge is given," even on that day I will visit you as a thief in your sleep, and I will expose your treasures, and on the sweet things in your heart, and on even that in which you placed all your confidence is written, "conception of vanity"—deception of man.

My servant, Joseph, did only his own work. Christianity

was fallen into the error of professing the name of God, and denying the power of God, and holiness, and angels; therefore, I called on my servants who were not my servants, and restored the power, and gifts, and blessings which were rejected, as the world cannot receive them, and the churches of christianity had become as the world in their working methods, and ambition, and aspirations, as the world within the world. The mission of christianity is done, and the world loves its own make ; but ye shall not fall into the same errors, for God has raised you up to be the children of Abraham, even as from the stones of the mountains, that the glory may be God's, and that you might remain in His glory whose name is one eternal hallelujah.

Therefore, greet the spirit of prophesy, and do not obstruct the pathway of the angels, as for that reason Babylon is fallen; for when you have received the testimony of even the meekest spirit, you have not grieved the Holy Spirit, nor have you made heaven to appear as a tent of brass without windows. The world is weak, but ye are growing strong. I will raise up prophets to try your strength, and I will make him you most despise my mouth-piece and my servant, not to be found at Rome, but as the president of the saints he shall know my voice whispering as from the dust to him for many generations ; he shall know my voice, and even babes shall prophesy, and I shall call on the lowly, and the humble among the saints, even as you are esteemed the outcasts of the world; and I will send my angels before them and after them to preach the hope of Israel, and the word of the living God in your midst, that ye may gather strength, as I have strengthened and comforted the lost tribes of the north whom my messenger has seen, and who are to come forth crowned with joy, and also those who are scattered afar off, that no flesh may glory, nor think to be something by itself ; but your glory may be in God, and your strength and your power may be the strength and power of God. Amen.

Now, I seal the benediction of Messiah on the church of the saints, even as my Father has sealed the power of Jehovah to be the power of Messiah. Amen.

My messenger is not my messenger because he called me, but because I called him, even before he was born, or conceived of his mother, and that he might be unknown I have cast him off away from you, and driven him from time to time, even out from city to city. I have tried him as in fire, and found him to be counted little enough in the eyes of the world for the use of heaven, and because the adversary called him "misery," and did not want him, therefore appointed I him eternally to follow after me in a peculiar work, even as I appointed you to be my servants.

Let my servant, George, read these words, but forward to him only that which I, from time to time, command you to send. Amen.

MESSAGE FROM DR. MARTIN LUTHER.

SAN ANTONIO, CAL., April 21, 1884.

I am Martin Luther: You are not of the conviction or persuasion that I was of when I arose and stigmatized the church of Rome. You are a prophet and have the spirit of inspiration. I was a reformer. Now comes the great point: "Whether you are to be a reformer in your effort or not." It appears to me that you are so to be; and also, it appears to me that you will break the ties that the inspired priesthood tied, and that were drawn tighter by their successors. Loosing these ties, we must all have the right to breathe, to think, to walk, and to move in freedom.

The Gospel of Freedom is a life and existence that we move and have our being in, as the water is the element for the fishes, and must be as natural to us as the air we breathe.

My dust is slumbering in the coffin down under the church floor at Wittenberg, but my spirit has been moving on. The church I gave rise to has remained faithful to what I taught them according to my earthly development, but in the progressive flight of my immortal spirit the Lutheran church did not follow me. I will visit you another time and give you an account of my spiritual experience, and present surroundings. I was a monk of the Augustinian order, and often saw such men as you in prison and misery, because they had visions, and were not acknowledged by the priesthood You are not able to testify to your writings but by your pen, and many will discard it, but it will be received by the saints at Zion, and will be given by them to the world. I say: "Live holy lives, and the marvelous power will never depart from earth."

By what you have received you see the curtain partly lifted between protestantism and the Gospel of Freedom in all its brightness and glory. The by-gone days are passed away, and the new era is at hand. Blessed be God to all eternity. Amen.

MESSAGE FROM PETER, THE APOSTLE.

BROOKLYN, CAL., April 7, 1884.

Blessed are those who die in the Lord, because they shall rest from their labors; and their deeds done in life shall follow them into the eternal habitations. Therefore, be of good cheer, and do good works before your God and Father who is in heaven, and shall pay you in the light for what you have done for the light, even unto those who were in darkness, and sitting in the shadow of death. "I have been young, but now I am old," said the psalmist; "but I have never seen the righteous deserted, nor his offspring begging for bread." Reprobation and compensation are everywhere, the power of God is everywhere, and heaven and hell will be found everywhere on earth as conditions are ripe for one or the other.

When you were at Terre Haute, and I spoke with you face to face, I said to you, "that you should be a witness of Messiah to his generation." I have not changed my words, neither has he changed his intentions, nor the means by which you shall carry out the mission. When you visit the Catholic church use your influence to harmonize it to the general work for humanity.

I have been honored as the supposed first bishop of Rome, but all honor belongs to our Master who is the only head of His true church, which consists of his true followers, both in heaven and on the earth. His password to those who believed in Him was "Follow after me, and I will grant you to sit on thrones in eternity." We have at times been rejoicing over certain persons on earth, and their progress toward the eternal habitations, but much more have we been filled with sorrow on account of the dark ages of superstition, and decay of true worship and knowledge about heaven and God. The fulness of time is, however, come for a new dispensation or restoration of the Gospel of Freedom, culminating in the coming of Messiah who shall bring the fulness of truth, which is himself, even the fulness of spiritual freedom down from heaven to the earth.

This is the Gospel of Freedom : " That ye know God, even as the Son knows the Father, so shall ye know Him, because you have known the Son, so also shall ye receive of His fulness in heaven, which is the Gospel of Freedom, in which there is no creed."

The Gospel of Grace, which was in its own time restored to earth with priesthoods, and ordinances, has not done away with the coming of Messiah, nor with his mission to earth in his second coming. No, much more has it been the harbinger of it to all mankind, and borne witness about it. The mission of the Gospel of Grace at its first coming was to overthrow the existing heathen worship, and plant the cross and the teaching about the crucified Savior everywhere, doing the best and the most humanity could receive of the truth under the existing circumstances. The Jews, having as a people rejected the news, and scattered as they are, have petrified their minds against new revelations. They did not receive the Gospel of Grace, but will be redeemed in their own land, in their own time, or in the fulness of the Mosaic dispensation, or the Gospel of righteousness. Only a little while from now will the entire old Assyria be restored to a Greek empire, and the Jews will be granted an unmolested return to their forefathers' home, and the soil will again be given to them, and belong to them forevermore. The Jewish spiritual redemption, however, will not be done by the Gospel of Grace which they rejected, but by the Gospel of Freedom, which has to come. The Messiah will receive the Latter Day Saints and the Jews alike, and also those of the christians who are scattered over all the world who believe in his second glorious appearance. This second appearance we have all partaken of by being with him in the eternal world; but that is not all, because, as He is in heaven, so shall He be revealed to earth, and to all the world, and to all those of his followers in the world who are anxiously awaiting his glorious advent.

I am Simeon Jonas' son, surnamed also, Peter, and I was on earth a rock, called so to be by our Master. It is with no little difficulty that I now control your earthly conditions, and remain with you for any length of time. Other intelligences or spirits will intrude and make their presence known; but as a seer of the Most High you perceive it all, and at once, but it only results in forming links of strength. You have seen Swedenborg and others by you during the reception of this message, and by me Brigham Young, Ezra T. Benson, Hiram Smith, Joseph Smith, and numerous Catholics, as Pope Pius Nino, and too many bishops, priests, and popes to mention; and some prominently known to the world, as Cardinal Antonelli, and Archbishop Hughes, of New York; also, Martin Luther, and many of later renown to mankind among the Protestants.

Perfection being in heaven, so it has to be on earth. The later work, even the perfection of creeds into the Gospel of Freedom, will gather in the saints in the fulness of their time, and build up Zion, and prepare the kingdom, even the kingdom of Messiah, where he shall govern in the gospel of spiritual truth and spiritual life manifested to the world, even as many as shall accept the glorious manifestations of His second coming.

The division fences between the churches shall be no more— creeds shall be no more. Rome shall sit on the seven hills; but the Pope shall no more dictate to humanity, and his council shall be silent. The Catholic church shall give up its pretensions and be simplified, even as Messiah is himself, and not by any external pressure, but by the internal divisions and conversion of the people and the priesthood when the redemption, which is at hand, shall come. Afterwards there shall be peace on earth for time and times to come, which is one thousand years, and the earth shall be matured to these events, even all creation alike with humanity.

When I spoke with you face to face at Terre Haute, you felt of me with your hands, that I was flesh and bone, even as you are a substance, and you touched me and wondered at my presence, and also the real presence of Messiah, even Jeshuah, the Redeemer. But this morning I am standing in the air above your left shoulder, with numbers of others surrounding me, and we are all beaming in a more beautiful light than the sun, and more calm to look on than the moon, and a light exceedingly soft, and filled with joy to the perception of your spirit. This is the light of our spirit home, or of the spirit sphere we have progressed into by gradual development, and our march onward following the Messiah. Why you perceive me shining with a stronger light, is because of the reflex action between me and the churches, including even the Catholic church. But Messiah will speak to you.

I will interrupt your conversation with Peter, as I wish to direct your attention, all of you, to one great fact: "That there will be no more churches;" there have been, but will not be any more. A kingdom has to come, but no church—the old has passed away, the new has to come. The last church went into the Rocky Mountains, but shall leave that country as the kingdom that has to come in all its preparatory features. When our friend and brother, Peter, the Master's faithful laborer, speaks about churches, he forgets what is to come.

Drink of the new wine, but don't pour it into old bottles lest it be spoiled, but put it in new and clean bottles, and cork it well up, and feast on it; and it shall last for years and years to come, until you shall drink of it with me in eternity. Freedom must come; not freedom to do evil, which is only mental slavery, but the freedom to live in God and God in us, without grieving the holy Spirit of truth and love. Amen.

I have taught mine apostles of olden time, those I elected in Judea, about the things to come on earth; but what I have told them has not yet ripened in their minds, as the time had not yet come, and they have continually been led away from my teaching of the Gospel of Freedom, by the influence of churches on earth, which are their only attachments to earth, being bound up in other and higher work in heaven. The adversary shall have no power from this time on to destroy my work—not until the thousand years are ended, when many nations shall be hardened one against another and give cause for war.

Spiritualism, in its gradual development, is one forerunner to the Gospel of Freedom to humanity. It is not the kingdom, but a mission, not in the kingdom, but in the world; but the kingdom shall hear about it and rejoice, because all things that are of the truth shall be united in me. Spiritualism, and Mormonism, Catholicism, and Protestantism shall all be united in me. I am the true light, which gives light to the world, even as I am the life of the world, and as the Father is the light of the heavens and of the worlds to come, so is the Son the life and the light of this world; and as many as come to Him shall abide in the life, and live forever. Amen. "God bless you," is the benediction of Messiah. Amen; yes, amen.

MESSAGE FROM JESHUAH, THE MESSIAH.

Concerning the Order of Messiah.

To Joseph Smith, at Lamoni.

Hyde's Park, Iowa, October 28, 1883.

My son, Joseph, I have been with you from your childhood, and I have been to you a shield and a protection, and I am now and shall continue to be all through your earth life. Be of good courage and never despair. When your mission is done you will be filled with joy by looking back on its days. Your father did the first work, and you have been working in his footsteps, and have preached the first principles of faith and salvation from evil to good, and from darkness to light. As you have done in the past, do also in the future; and your work shall not lose its reward, nor the fruit be cast to the ground as not ripe, but new events and new missions stand at the door, and my servants shall bring the Gospel of Freedom to all mankind, and deliverance shall come from spiritual and mental thraldom into the perfection of my Father's kingdom, which is the Gospel of Freedom anew to man at the coming of the Son of man. Be not astonished when I say to you, "that the kingdom of my Father has to come on earth as it is in heaven;" and the Son of man shall be revealed, before all things are restored of that which is in heaven, to those things which are on earth.

My glory is not mine, but my Father's, as my throne is not mine, but His throne who is in heaven. And to that end, labor and work in unity with the spirit of truth, until all things are finished, as it was by my individual mission on the cross, and your life shall be finished into that glory which I had with the Father from eternity, and you have in me, and by Him also. Not that I will preach another doctrine, but that I will add to, and add to, and develop your mind by the power of the Holy Ghost of truth until you see as I see, and hear as I hear, and understand on earth as you will be understood in heaven. Be, therefore, cheerful and rejoice, for your redemption is at hand. Not the redemption from what truth and good things you have received, but from the imperfect to the perfect. You have received me by faith, but you shall see me face to face, and your faith shall vanish into perfection of knowledge. You have hoped for the spiritual blessing, and your hope shall pass into perfection. You have loved me, even as I have loved you, because you were blessed of the Holy Spirit with that love by which I loved you, and with which the Father loved you when He sent me into the world, and as He loved the world. Therefore, listen to the voice of the Spirit, and as it teaches you so you should walk in its light and discern the truth, and do not make your heart of a narrow birth for the reception of it. As the lightning flashes through the air, so is the coming of the Son of man to you, with new ideas and new light—additional light, and truth, and heavenly conceptions that may at first be mysterious to you. But the feast is soon at hand, and a midnight cry to be heard, and the guests are to be invited, and the perfection of the Gospel of Freedom will give peace and confidence to all nations, and the priesthood shall have done its work ; because, when the supper has been eaten, the servants will be discharged, and the priesthood will no longer be needed, and there shall be none to teach in the perfection of my Father's kingdom who is in heaven, and shall come down on the earth. For until that day comes you shall go out into all the world and preach the gospel of truth in the name of Messiah ; and I will be by you, and my blessing shall rest on you, and my people shall receive the light as readily from a beggar as from an archangel, and receive the truth as willingly from your worst enemies as you do from your best friends, because it is the truth. Therefore, let your souls be as children's minds are—simple, and open, and full of confidence, thinking no evil, and ready to receive and not reject.

Do not love with a narrow mind, but with a heart broad, and full of tenderness to each other, and to all mankind. Do not sin against the Holy Spirit by rejecting the testimony of the Spirit, nor the gifts of the Spirit, nor by opposing the light which comes to you in ways and in a manner that you did not expect. Because, I tell you that it is manifested that the power of God can raise up a people of those who were not a people, and even He can raise up prophets of those who were not counted in your flock ; and, as it was in the days of Noah, so shall it be in the days of the coming of the Son of man; the work of the ark was going on by day and by night, but the multitude cared nothing about it.

MESSAGE FROM JESHUAH, THE MESSIAH.

TRUTH.

POINT CITY, CAL., February 25, 1885.

It must be evident to the world that I did not come with peace, but with the sword. I came in peace, and not in the power of the sword, as the angels predicted at my birth at Bethlehem: "Peace and good will to all men with good will." It was impossible for me, for the sake of pleasing men, not to be the truth—to destroy the ideal of heaven to make the road convenient. The object for which I was born and came into the world was, that I might bear witness about the truth, that all those who are born of the truth may hear my voice, and come to me, and follow after me, and be saved from their errors, and be made free in the truth from heaven as testified to by the spirit of truth. For that purpose I lived, and for that purpose I died, that the world might be saved by the truth—the truth that is found in me. To that end I was slain by sinners, who crucified me, as they wished to crucify the truth rather than receive it, and my innocent blood became the judgment, and the execution of the judgment came to that generation and their children at the destruction of Jerusalem. Neither in my coming did I bring peace to my people, but a sword; and when the christians took it for granted that they were saved by my blood, it could only be said, "that the Jews, as a nation, were destroyed by my blood." But, are the christians saved by my blood? Have they arrived at the fulness of heavenly truth by the blood from the cross, or to the fulness of peace from God, our Father? Is the Holy Ghost a spirit of blood, or the Father of your spirits a God of blood and murder? If not, then you have not entered into salvation with blood on your garments, or in your souls, but it was, for the time, the finish to my work on earth, for the truth had to suffer all contradiction, and I had to be killed as the prophets were before me, and enter into my glory eternally.

It also came to pass, according to the hate which the opposer, or the adversary of all progression, has planted in the human soul against all spirituality, that truth had to die bodily, in order to triumph spiritually and eternally. It was the consequence of being the harbinger of truth, and not only that, but the truth itself, that the Son of man had to be despised and crucified by his own people. Only by such a rejection of the truth became the word of truth to be the new covenant in my blood, as God's covenant with man sealed with my blood—a testimony against the world, but a saving power to all those who are of the truth, and enter into the salvation by the truth which I brought to man. Amen.

MESSAGE FROM JESHUAH, THE MESSIAH.

THE ATONEMENT.

SAN FRANCISCO BAY, February 21, 1885.

The world is not saved by blood, but it cost me my blood in the effort and work of saving and redeeming the world, and my life's blood was the finish and amen on what the world would call a failure, but in the council and wisdom of God, was a victory for the everlasting redemption in soul of all those who are of my flock, and see me, and know me, and follow after me in the work of God in their own regeneration. The mistake has continually been made, that the blood at Golgotha, by some external means, gave some conditions and relations by which salvation was attained, by leaning on the cross and adoring the wounds and blood inspired by faith, was salvation to be attained, instead of seeking redemption and salvation by the new birth, and by the spirit of truth which bears fruits of love and wisdom brought down from heaven to men? My blood was a calamity to my people because they rejected the truth of revelation, and the light went to the Gentiles, and they were blessed with the same blood which cursed my people; but the truth is, that there is no salvation in the blood of man more than in the blood of oxen and sheep.

As the blood of Abel cried unto heaven against Cain, so cried the blood of the Son of man against the chief rulers of the Jews; and for a second time were the commandments written on stone, broken asunder, for they were, in the spirit, dashed to pieces when I expired on the cross, and a new covenant in my blood was made, not written on stone, but with the finger of the Holy Ghost in the hearts and souls of all those who shall follow me in the regeneration, and be born by the Spirit out of all the nations of the earth wherever the blood of Israel, according to the Spirit, is drawing to me, that it may be fulfilled which was said to Abraham, "that in his seed should all the nations of the earth be blessed."

The peace from my Father be with you. Amen. That my blood may be a symbol of subjection to God's truth, and a lesson of obedience to all; that the sign of the cross may give healing to all the sons and daughters of the cross—those who are weeping and sinking to the ground under the burdens of the cross; and I will assure you that my burdens will not be heavy when I shall give you rest; even as I had rest by my Father when my life expired at His hands, as I hung on the tree crimsoned with blood. Amen.

MESSAGE FROM JESHUAH, THE MESSIAH.

On the First Principle.

Petershof, Cal., February 4, 1885.

Be not surprised when I tell you that the world does not know me, and be less surprised when I tell you that the christian world does not know me; nor have they seen me, nor have they seen my Father, nor have they, in the Spirit, communion with my angels, nor have they seen my world of angels. You have been listening most patiently to the fanaticism of religious excitement, or revivals of the order of the day, and you have put it on the scale of common sense and found it wanting, because common sense, which ought to inspire all mankind, is swept away by a thoughtless enthusiasm about nothing, as though my suffering on the cross could be a delight to my friends. This and all such excitements are kept up by spirit infusion from legions of corresponding spirits who are constantly yelling and shouting as the Indians at a war dance, and many, in such conditions of mind, are to be found in the spirit world.

It would be a loss of time and energy to convince such spirits and corresponding mortals who are influenced by such agencies, because thought has vanished into the background of the soul, and wild, frantic emotions, which such people call religion, are on the stampede; but I call it hypocrisy, because it does not radiate from the center of interior convictions of assimilated truths, which is religion. Such people do not know me, nor have they seen me, nor would they hear me; they call on my name all day and all night, but I am not the one they imagine me to be; because many shall shout, Lord, Lord! and shall preach long sermons and labor in my name, and many shall do great works and ascribe them to me; but the truth is, they went their own way, and did their own work, and the work of their own spirit, for they never knew me, nor my Father, nor did they ever follow after me. Therefore, be always awake, and if somebody says, "he is my disciple," and he has not seen me, that one is in deception; because I will show myself to all who follow after me; and also, show them my Father whom the world cannot see, because it has not seen me as the Messiah, nor has it known God as their Father. Therefore, do not cry out Lord, Lord ! nor claim to do mighty works in my name except ye know me, that I am, that I am by you, and with you, and in you, by the Holy Ghost and spirit of truth.

God is order, and more than that, He is thought; and in the highest term of that principle, He is wisdom. His love is not in confusion, as there is no confusion in His holy spirit of truth. There is no mental aberration in His holiness when He speaks in the silent whisper to the soul, and He never reveals His love to the souls of men in a hurricane of contests and arbitrary combats. To know me is to be me, in the same spirit power, and thought of living. Your father, and mother, and sister, and brother are known to you, and also your wife and children, but whosoever does not know me more than he knows these, cannot be my disciple; and whosoever is not willing to lose them all for my sake cannot be my disciple; and more, whosoever does not love me more than these, cannot be my disciple; and if a man or woman does not hate his or her life in the world, when it is in contradiction to me, he or she cannot be my disciple. When a person calls himself after my name, and his relations are not my disciples, but filled with contempt against the word of life, then his love to those who do not love me shall be as hate to me, and his love to me shall be as hate to them; and if he is not willing to be hated of father, and mother, and wife, and children, he cannot be my disciple.

How much more necessary will it be to know the one we love above all things on earth, that the love of the Father to the Son might be revealed in your souls. Therefore, be sure that you have seen Him, and that you know His voice, and that you see Him and follow after Him; because, every sheep knows the voice of the shepherd, that they all may follow after him— that wherever he goes they may also go. And the knowledge you have about the Son of man may be greater than that you have about your own wives and children. Whosoever knows me is also known of me, as those I have in the world; but whosoever does not know me, and has not seen me as I am, to them is neither I nor my Father revealed by the Holy Ghost, and they are not my disciples, nor are they my brethren in the kingdom of heaven, nor in the Gospel of Freedom.

To know the Son of man is to have the life, which is His life, within themselves, and it gives everlasting life in them, which is everlasting knowledge, which is everlasting love and wisdom, that the peace which is in heaven shall everlastingly abide with them; it is the true life—that power which made life permeate all things—that life first became of love the cause of all creation, which is the evolution of the world. Whosoever knows me shall know the first cause of that love which shall remain in them, by which all things in the creation are made ; for the Father loved the world with the same love wherewith He loved the Son. The world, however, is in darkness, and is a stranger to the love of God, and does not know the Son, nor the Father; but as many as receive the Son shall by Him also receive the Father, and receive the power from Him out of the high heaven, and shall not walk by faith, but by knowledge; because they have a testimony that they have seen the Messiah, and bear witness about the true light which was revealed before their eyes, that they may speak the word of life, that they saw, and heard, and felt with their hands, the Son of man who is the power and majesty of heaven. That is given as a testimony to the world before the midnight cry, which shall be heard all over the land when confusion shall reign supreme, and the Son of man shall come to reign among His saints.

Peace be with you; my peace follow you. Be of good courage, because my angels are at your right and left side, and they shall carry you on their hands, and you shall not hurt your feet against the stones of contention, which men are putting in your way. This is the last and the first that ye shall suffer the contentions of the world, but ye shall be exalted by me, and with me, and enter into my glory which I had with my Father before times and days were known on earth. Amen. Glory to God, the Father. Amen.

MESSAGE FROM MOSES, THE PROPHET.

CONCERNING PROPHESY.

PETERSHOF, CAL., February 15, 1885.

Woe to the inhabitants of the earth! Because the times and times are past, and the gathering of ancient Israel is at hand. As a man goes out into the field when the harvest is ripe and gathers in his wheat, so will the Lord go out among the nations of the earth and gather in the seed of Israel, His people—according to the promise He has given to His servants in all generations. All the nations have been blessed in the seed of Abraham; they have been permeated by the life and laws of Jehovah, but they have turned His blessing into a curse. Therefore shall Israel be gathered, and go out from the curses of the nations and into the land of Abraham, Isaac, and Jacob, and remain there forever.

As you see me standing here before you, also did the hosts of Israel see me when I, for the second time, descended from the mountain with both of the tables of stone, one resting at my foot to the right knee, and the other resting against the left knee; and I laid before all the congregation the blessings of the Lord, and also the curses which should come on the people if they departed from the path of life, and walked into the valley of death in union with the heathens, and forgot the voice which spoke to them in the wilderness, and God's wondrous ways by which they were redeemed from the power of the Egyptians. As I spoke to Israel so it came to pass, and also will it come to pass, because He who spoke it knows all things.

Live by the light, and you shall have the light as you see me standing in the light, and a stream of light is passing down on me from above, blessing the earth upon which I stood. The glorious light that you discover afar off and above is the light of Jehovah, with his hair more white than the whitest wool, and his face shining with the lustre of the sun. For your sake, that you may be able to receive this message, the light is reduced, for if you saw the vision in its full light, it would render you powerless, as it often has done before, and your mental faculties would be overpowered by the superior influence beaming directly upon your mind, in the celestial splendor which is too much for mortal man to endure, as Abraham said to the Lord: "I am only dust and ashes."

Palestine, as you call the land now, will soon be redeemed from the hands of its oppressors, and it will be given to my people as the land of promise, and the time will dawn upon the nations when the only beloved and begotten of the Father will be hailed: "blessed art thou that comest in the name of the Lord." Amen.

Look down on your enemies, but look up always to Jehovah, that your faith shall not falter when He asks you to dash the staff against the rock, in His promise that it shall give out streams of living water. Let your faith not stir from the line of His power, and you shall enter into the fulness of all His promises. Amen.

Long and weary has your pilgrimage been. Tortuous have your paths been over the grizzled and stony roads in your redemption; but you cannot fail to accomplish the work, nor to be victorious over all your enemies. Let it be as it may be; let it come as it may come, the ends of God will meet in spite of all human opposition, or the power of hell to frustrate. Before you, to the left, you are allowed to let your views descend into the lower regions of the spiritual world, where spirits are cast down on earth, and bound up in prisons, and conditions of their soul's appetite, and charmed with the desires of the world, which is the desire of the carnal mind to possess and attain to earthly things in possessions forever and forever, leaving out the love of God and His paradise of light and glory.

The Ancient of Days gave me this staff which I hold in my hand to lead Israel with, thousands of years ago He also showed you, seventeen years ago, all the localities, and departments, and societies which are among the spirits who are living in the earth, on the earth, and around the earth as far out as the third sphere; and He showed to you the celestial world, and you looked on its splendor and on its glory, which is a glory exceeding far the glory of the sun and fixed stars, and for which you can utter no words; for the human tongue cannot express it, nor can any natural man conceive it, neither can he enter into it and live; but Jehovah had to unclothe himself of His glory and descend to man, or man would be consumed in His presence. Therefore, He came to you in that degree of power and glory that you were able to endure, but you could not endure even that except at the point of death. He has preserved you, even in the midst of devils in the flesh and devils in the spirit world, for they were all harmless in His presence; nevertheless you did not enter the home of the Almighty, but He showed it to you as afar off, and His finger pointed to it; and a promise was given to you, that in the everlasting rest for the soul, after the work was done on earth, you should be gathered into the New Jerusalem, which shall come down from heaven and dwell with Zion on the new earth, made holy by the power of God and the baptism of His spirit in fire, as it was baptised in water in Noah's days. Neither did Jehovah allow me to enter.Canaan, but showed me the land and the mighty city afar off; and I lived by faith, and I died by faith, that He who gave the promises is mighty to keep them all, and fulfill them all in His own due time.

Blessed are Israel who accept all the Lord's sayings, but more than tenfold blessed shall they be if they continue in the good work, following after our Master and our God in all things; and your enemies shall vanish before you, as the fogs before the noonday's sun, even tho' they were thicker than midnight's darkest clouds.

Publish what you have received in volumes of two hundred pages each, and put the truth before the test of the world and the churches, and let the Lord take care of the balance, and what the verdict shall be. Do the work of Messiah until he comes to his people at Jerusalem, as well as to his people on this American continent. Push forward, as the time is short. My mission is to you, but not to the work at Zion; it pertains to another spiritual circle of friends, but your mission is a cosmopolitan work done by a single man, for a single purpose, to prepare and to be awake, as the herald who runs before the King's carriage and cries out aloud: "Prepare yourselves for the reception of the King, the King is coming."

Do not linger in taking up the mission that Daniel, the prophet, gave you, and go to your native land, for the Lord has given you Daniel to be a guide in the work of the union, and redemption of your people, who are the Scandinavian people; and the Lord will bless you in doing His work, for He is the ruling prince in all the political complications of the nations. Let that prophet be accursed who comes in the name of Jehovah, and prophesies a lie; let those prophets be accursed who come in the name of the Lord and Messiah, and prophesy a lie; let those prophets be withered who come in the name of the Holy Spirit, and prophesy a falsehood to the congregation. If any spirit return to the earth, he or she may be an angel from Jehovah or not, let he or she be accursed of it, if he or she tells a falsehood, or pretends to be a messenger from the most high God, and is no such thing, nor holds such an office, nor is endowed with such a power to officiate in the name of Jehovah ; let all creation know it, and all mankind, and all spirits that we have in the unity of eternity, nothing to do of ourselves, but all for God, and with God, and by God. Amen.

That man or spirit that goes his own errand is insane spiritually, as he has nothing to go for; and whosoever goes the errands of devils on earth, or in the spirit world, shall harvest by them, and get the wages of devils—so mote it be. Whosoever is a prophet, and is proud in his own mind, is a hypocrite, and will be destroyed by the logical development of his life on earth; but whosoever is a prophet, and is the very meekest among the entire congregation, shall live in accordance with the logical consequences of the laws which govern life. When a spirit wishes to control a prophet contrary to his own soul, that same spirit is a devil, and let him or her be accursed. Nothing but balance and harmony shall be accepted by any man of the living God, and if any spirit appears black as coal to your inner vision, then let that spirit be accursed to your soul, as that spirit will lead you a downward course into destruction and misery; do not listen to such a spirit, and do not follow after its counsel, as its name is death, and pain, and hell.

Many great men on earth have a narrow spirit, and are among the lowest after death; and many low and most despised men and women on earth are great and most glorious in the spirit world. Therefore, do not be deceived by great and little names and rank on earth, as it will amount to nothing when weighed on the scales of truth. There are devils who are kings, and counts, and barons, when in the flesh; and there are angels and archangels of God, who, when on earth, were of the lowest order of society, and in the most deplorable conditions of human life.

Any *commanding* spirit is not of God, but always of the devil; for there is only one commander in all the universe which is the harmony, and peace, and unity whispering to you by unspeakable joy in the holy glory of God. Therefore, let such a mentally sick, commanding spirit, who is a spiritual lunatic, be accursed, and do not listen to him, nor follow after him, or you shall be accursed as he is accursed, because you did not take the warning into your soul, and you ignored the salvation of your own soul. If any among you have the spirit of prophesy, I implore that person always to be the meekest among the meek in the midst of the congregation, or he will fall from grace and be condemned.

Nothing is more dangerous for a man or woman than to receive spiritual gifts, as they will stand up against them on the judgment day in their own souls, and condemn them, if they have not made the gifts profitable to others and themselves. But every one has to accord to his own spirit's dictation in God, and not walk after the dictation of strange spirits, nor of strange Gods, which is idolatry, and an abomination in the sight of the most high God. Amen. Let all the congregation say "Amen."

MESSAGE FROM JESHUAH, THE MESSIAH.

POINT CITY, CAL., August 11, 1884.

In regard to Joseph Morris' revelation about the keys of the priesthood: It is my will that you shall let it stand on its own merit, and by its own strength, and in its own spirit. Whatever I have given to him belongs to his dispensation, and not to your line of work for my name; and in all that I gave to my servant, Joseph Morris, I gave it to him as he was able to receive it from me. Let no corrections or comments be made on any revelation given to him, but in due time I will reflect more light on them all. The same can be said about the Old and the New Testament, the book of Mormon, and the revelations given to my servant, Joseph, the seer, and to his son, my servant, Joseph of Lamoni, and in numerous other instances when revelations were given to Joseph Thompson, and my servants, Lyman Wight, Sidney Rigdon, Strang, and Hendricks, and the Whitmers, and others too numerous to mention; some of them very little known, as Gladden Bishop, and Giles, and John Livingston, and whoever they may be, down to Joseph, my servant, of Lamoni. They are not to be corrected; because, what I revealed to them was according to their need, and the need of existing circumstances and conditions in the church, and in their personal conditions and surroundings. Therefore, as I gave it to my servants, so it has to be understood. The revelation pertaining to the keys of the priesthood that I revealed to my servant, Joseph Morris, I do not wish to be understood differently to what it reads; but I will, by and by, when it is necessary to do so, shed more light on what I told him to give to the people, that my words may be more fully understood by those who read them, and are seeking after the truth. Amen.

The introduction of that dispensation which I now represent, has nothing in common with other missions but the spirit in which they are conducted.

This is the new wine of my Father's kingdom. The wine, or inspiration that I poured into the Jewish nation, was most of it spilled on the ground; except that which the Gentiles have partaken of by adoption, that the seed of Abraham should be blessed, and gathered out from among all the nations of the earth. The wine poured out in the fulness of my gospel to the nations of the earth, by my servant, Joseph, the seer, was fermented in the bottles, or the inspiration got sour in the men I called upon; and the keys of heaven I bestowed upon the priesthood became rusty, and not any more fit in their hands to open the door to heaven on earth for the multitude who would have entered in, had it not been so. The church became identified with the world, and the inspiration of the church wine was given to Joseph, my servant, at Lamoni, and his little flock, to preserve my spiritual gifts until I shall meet the church in the Order of Messiah, and the saints shall know me, even as I am, and know my Father as He is, and not as many have supposed us to be. Amen. Then shall the kingdom come and not before; and when you sup with me in my Father's kingdom on earth, where the Son is His representative as king of kings, then ye shall know that I am, that I am, even as the Father is, so is the Son. Amen.

I have preserved my servant, Morris, for my work in the kingdom to come, that he may come forth in the power of prophecy, and prophesy to many people in the power of Messiah; for I will raise up a mighty tower in Zion, and I will put him as the watchman on that tower, and a guardian angel for my servant who shall preside over my church, even over the quorum of seventy times twelve who shall be my witnesses to all nations, and my servants over all the earth. Amen.

Do not despise prophecy, and do not reprove the spirit; for by so doing all the Protestant churches have been cut off from receiving light, and on their very birthday they were condemned to suffer death from a spiritual starvation. It is my will that all inspired writings given in my name shall be preserved for the reading of the saints first, and next, of the world. None can speak in the name of Messiah of his own accord, nor can any spirit utter his name and be saved in the eternal habitations except it be by His spirit which searches all things, even the spirit of the Holy Ghost; and by that you shall know the spirits of my Father's kingdom, that they confess the name of Messiah, even Jesus of Nazareth, to be born of the flesh, transfigured in the spirit, and who now is in the power, and might, and glory of heaven. By His spirit shall you know that a prophet comes from me, and speaks in my name, even as the spirit shall give the words to him.

My servant, Joseph Morris, rejoices over these words, and also that the time of his probation in the spirit is soon to come to an end, and he will pass on into the mission on earth which I have appointed for him in my Father's kingdom on earth. He also rejoices that I have accepted his offering by me to his people, that the words of truth which come through him may be preserved as among the holy writings of the kingdom. Neither shall my servant, James Strang, lose his reward when his time of probation in the spirit is ended, and he passes on into his mission at Independence, as a herald to open and close my meetings at that place; and not a hair of his head shall be lost to him, and much less, one letter of all his inspired writings in my name; even so with all my servants. I will gather them into the oneness and unity in me, as also I have pleasure in David Whitmer, my aged servant, and am pleased with his words; however they may be accepted of the church it matters not, as my grace is upon him, and that is all he needs, and is all sufficient to make his soul glorified with the joy he has in me.

I will break that spirit of hypocrisy asunder with the power of the Holy One that bears witness about me—that spirit of perdition which has crept into the church as a serpent moving under the dust—which says: " We are fortified ! We are circumscribed. Our church discipline is a brazen arm against the spirit of prophesy, and we will cry out and say ' devil;' although nobody accuses us, we will say it anyhow. If we can not say it by the spirit of truth, we will say it by the spirit of lies; and as sure as we are the saints of the most high God, we will use the word ' devil ' until our voices shall sound hoarse and tired with pain; and we will accuse each other, for want of strength to attack others, till we shall be like the devils ourselves. Those we accused for others to be, we found at last that we resembled—when we rebuked ourselves, and repented, and became redeemed into the spirit of peace." Therefore be tolerant, and stand in the freedom of the children of God, and you will not condemn my servants, nor shall you condemn one another, nor speak falsehood one against another; but you shall receive all the testimony given to my servants, the prophets, for the edification of my church and all my people. Amen.

When the time shall come, and my Father is presiding over the multitude assembled at Independence, Mo., and the minds of the people are matured into higher intelligence than at present prevails in the church of the saints, and the Order of Messiah is matured into the Gospel of Freedom in my Father's kingdom, then shall you, my messenger, and Joseph the seer, work together in a mutual work, and be seen as serving angels behind the throne of the Ancient of Days. Look and see and find out the interpretation of the vision. Joseph the seer, is standing at the right shoulder behind the Ancient of Days. The body of the seer, as he is approaching the throne, is as burning amber; he is bending his right knee as he stands behind the throne, between and behind the Son of man and the Ancient of Days. On his head he has a helmet, and it also is as burning amber. On the other side, or on the left side of the throne and behind the Ancient of Day's left shoulder, is the president of the church sitting. At the left side of the Ancient of Days is standing an angel who has a body of amber, like that of Joseph the seer. It is as burning amber to look upon, and over his shoulder hangs, as a shawl, a tiger's skin, and blood is dripping from it. That angel is you, my messenger. Where have you both been? You have returned from war. From what war? You have fought the battles of Jehovah, and conquered, and returned from the terrible scenes of blood, after which peace will govern the earth for one thousand years. Who shall understand the vision, and who can explain it? Only the Ancient of Days. He says: "These angels are the angels of wrath. The helmet on the head of the seer signifies 'intelligence, and the strength of the spirit by which he shall fight and conquer.' The tiger's skin dripping with blood thrown over your shoulder signifies the national hate by which the nations fought each other like tigers in the spirit of hate and revenge, and universal destruction, which is shown as a tiger's skin around your neck, dripping with blood until you shall atone or reconcile one nation with another into one brotherhood, subject to the arbitration of the kingdom.

Then the passions of men shall be satisfied and go to rest, and shall be as your bodies appear—burnt out, and as glowing amber, and as a dying fire."

The mission of the seer is an appeal to the intelligence of man. The mission of my messenger, who at that time will be in the spirit, will be an appeal to the common brotherhood of man until peace shall be restored, and the kingdom is the head of the nations, as I am King of Kings and Lord of Lords, and the kingdom is given to my Father, glorified on earth as he is in heaven, and from eternity to eternity. Amen. On that day shall Lucifer go to his own place and remain there, and there shall be no wars to trouble man with, and the Lord shall govern the nations in peace. The kingdom is represented by Messiah, and the church by a young man only sixteen years old; and the church and kingdom is united in one spirit under the government of my Father, and the church shall exist separately no more when the kingdom is perfected, and the Son of man shall call upon His Father to rule over it forevermore. Amen.

Who is that youth you discover? He is the son of the son of the son of the son of Joseph, the seer. The fourth link from Joseph, and the seventh of that family that shall preside in the church, or keep the priesthood in the direct line in the church. He shall not only be president from the tenth year of his age, but the spirit of prophecy shall rest upon him from his birth, and he shall be a mighty man in the Lord; and with two wise counsellors he shall preside over and lead the church. One of his counsellors shall be the son of his father's brother; and at his left hand shall sit the other counsellor, who is the third of the three first generals of the Order of Messiah, then affiliated with the church as the connecting link between the church and the kingdom which shall come in that day, when the Son of man shall put His feet again on the Mount of Olives from whence He departed when He vanished from His apostles. Where He departed from them, at the same place shall He come again, and bring with Him Moses, and Elias, and the council of the Sanhedrim shall receive Him; and from there John, the beloved, and the three Nephites shall prepare His way to be received on the American continent, where He shall descend at Zion with the twelve Nephite apostles whom He ordained at His first coming to the Nephite nation, and thus He shall come to His temple at Independence, Mo., and officiate there with the twelve Nephite apostles, even as He did with the twelve apostles of the Jews whom He shall, at that time, have left behind to regulate the affairs of that nation; and they shall sit on twelve thrones and preside over the twelve tribes of the house of Israel. Also shall the twelve Nephites sit on twelve thrones at Independence, and preside over the seed of Nephi and Laman. The twelve witnesses of the book of Mormon shall sit on twelve thrones and judge the churches, even as my servant, David Whitmer, has now in some measure done. It shall be done by each witness in his own degree, and it shall be done by the law, even the book of Mormon which went out from Zion as a law and a regulation for the church..

My servant, Joseph the seer, I have taken to myself to do his own peculiar work until his church mission is finished, when he shall bring back the lost ten tribes. At that time I shall take you to myself also to follow Joseph in your own political mission, which will be to make peace among all the nations on earth, and the kingdom shall govern supreme. Of the Order of Messiah shall on that day twenty-four generals march up in line twelve and twelve, or three times four, and three times four, signifying the fulness of the church on both continents when the inauguration and the restoration takes place. Those twelve generals shall be called by revelation and the spirit of prophecy when the fulness comes. In the establishment and progress of the order, some elders shall be found among the generals of the order; and I will put my strength around their loins and their lives, that they may do my work, and be glorified in me.

When the kingdom is perfected my mission will be finished on earth, and peace and prosperity universally shall reign, and as it was in the days of King Solomon, also shall it be the most happy time for all Israel, and my Father shall hold the reins in His hands, and it shall not be for me to say any more, as His government belongs to himself. The seven archangels who were in the commencement when the earth began, they shall preside as my Father's messengers, and be in power and dominion over the seven parts of the world, which position they now hold in heaven.

When the kingdom is matured for one thousand years in peace on earth, and the Order of Messiah remains as the advance guard in its connection with the kingdom, then the twenty-four generals shall in the kingdom increase to one hundred and forty-four generals, and they shall stand on Mount Zion near Independence, in glittering armour, sparkling as the polished silver, with helmets as of gold, and the triangle with the name of Jehovah within, shall sparkle as in diamonds across the front of their helmets. The order of king Solomon's temple, even the Masonic order, extending over all the earth, shall on that day work hand in hand with the kingdom, and all the orders of peace, and happiness, and regulation, and order, shall be in union with the kingdom. Amen; yes, amen and amen, which translated is, blessed be thou, and blessed be thy work, and blessed shall they be who receive it from God, to work in the name of God, and the Lord of Lords, and the King of Kings, blessed of man in all eternity.

Message from Jeshuah, the Messiah.

The Church.

Oakland Point, Cal., January 7, 1885.

That which is low down will I raise high up, and that which is despised will I glorify until the world will learn that the Lord governs. I am that I am, and shall not dispute with man forever, nor contend with his discordant nature and undeveloped propensities. From eternity to eternity my judgment is a just one. I know what is in the human heart, and I judge according to the measure of love which is in the heart. Therefore, be not confounded by pride, and prejudice, and haughtiness in your soul, as all these things will perish, and if you have cultivated nothing else, you may perish also, and sink to that sphere where love is not found. Amen.

When the clouds rise over the mountain ridges, you say there will be a storm; and when you see, in the signs of the times, the clouds which hang over this nation, why do you not know that a storm is coming? As a man's life is only a span in eternity, there are but few or none to observe it; but I tell you, that the fire of destruction will sweep over the graves of this generation, and over the graves of their children, and their children's children, and they will curse themselves when looking at the spectacle from the spirit world, because they did not lift a finger for the redemption of the race, and seek to prevent the calamities that are sure to come; but said "peace, peace," when there was no peace, and persecuted the saints who brought good news from above, and good will to all mankind. So shall it be, that only a little while, and a little while, and Zion shall be redeemed by the spirit of the most high God, the eternal Father. Amen.

The battle field is here, and right now is the contest going on, and it will not cease until the smouldering fire has broken out into a flame, and the brush and the rubbish of the wrath which is fermenting in the breasts of this generation is consumed, and the anger which God allows man to pour out upon himself has brought destruction, and made an end of his own wickedness. So shall it be. Therefore, let Zion rejoice, and do not lament, as thy redemption is at hand, and I will carry you on the wings of power out of all your trouble; and the hearts of the righteous will rejoice when peace again shall be restored. The contentions will continue until the measure of the Gentiles is filled, and the time is fulfilled for the new birth of the nations. When the time and times for the coming of Messiah is at hand, then it shall not be said: "Let the saints be accursed"; but it shall be said: "Blessed be God in the highest, and His saints on earth, because the adversary shall be bound for a long day of rest, even a thousand years; and men shall not lift up swords against each other, because the spirit of God has brought peace, and Zion shall stand redeemed and be always before their sight."

It is my will and desire that you shall send this message to my servant among the mountains, and to my servant, Joseph Smith, at Lamoni. They are not friends on earth, but I have known them to be friends in the spirit world, where I have seen them to be brethren in the eternal mansions of my Father who is in heaven. Tell them, whenever you see them personally, to be friends, even as they are the friends of Messiah. It is my will and command to the church and to all the saints after my name, that they build up Zion in peace, one with another, that the measure of time may be now come for my bodily appearance on earth, even as it was during the forty days after I rose from the tomb. Love one another, and do my work. Let not the policy of care and ambition of this world's fashion drive you estray from the council of the Holy Spirit. Thou, my messenger who writes this, I have set apart to do a peculiar work—a work for myself; mine own work for the church. I have hidden him among the Gentiles, as a bird within the hollow of my hand; and mine wounds from Golgotha are before him, and I am behind him, and on both sides of him, as a shelter from evil, that the adversary shall not consume him. Therefore, be ready, and listen to the voice of Messiah, and if you love me then do my work in the same love by which I loved the world, and laid down my life for the world. Amen.

Let not subordinate questions of lesser significance bring on contention and division among the saints. Let not the marriage question absorb all interest, and obstruct the light and spirit of the Holy Ghost, because it has been my will that man should live by all my commandments, and not be condemned by the words of redemption. Surely I say to Zion: "The Nephites were condemned by having several wives;" because it was not to life for them, but to death, for the entire nation became exterminated on earth and sent into eternity; therefore it was forbidden. Ancient Israel received no such command except for the high priest of Israel, that he should only have one wife, and to marry a virgin, and he should have none but her, as he was the representative of Jehovah on earth, and his mouth-piece in the holy temple and to the people. That as the Holy Spirit is one person in God, so also should the high priest have only one wife in the same holy of holiness by him and none else; but otherwise it was not forbidden, but commanded to Israel to enter into a plural marriage.

The order of marriage, written about by Moses, has never been condemned in the scriptures, nor by the prophets, nor by any spirit of prophecy coming from the God of Israel; but the abominations of David, and of Solomon, and of the kings and rulers of the Jews was condemned, even as the idolatry for which the people were led away captive was condemned, and because they married as the people did before the flood—without love; they went into sin, and cared about nothing, and lived with many concubines after the manner of the heathens, and did the works of the enemies of Israel; and it was all an abomination in the sight of God, and the Jews are now a by-word among the Gentiles. Therefore, condemn not what God makes clean, for whatever there is not is cleansed by the spirit of God in the spirit of love, that condemns itself. Therefore, my servant, Joseph, thou hast been working for the redemption of Israel, also continue in the same work, and the truth shall teach you the Gospel of Freedom, that you indeed may be free in the paradise of God.

It is my will and command to all my people, that they extend a brotherly hand one to another, and commence the work at Independence, to build me a house after the pattern given to my servant, Joseph the seer, at the time when the place was pointed out for its location. It shall be a house of peace and rest for the Holy Ghost to dwell in, and as my people in Utah have done a good work for the same purpose amongst themselves, it is my will that Joseph Smith, my servant, shall call on all the saints of my church scattered in the United States and in the world, to come or send their means of money or help to build me a house, and show their faith before the world by raising the temple in Jackson county, Mo. Also, I call upon my servants among the mountains, that you shall lay the same command before the people of the different states to assist in building the house, both by means and work, that it shall be redeemed by faith and work, even as the ground was purchased, and earned, and baptised in blood to be a resting place for the man from Golgotha. The time has now come, let the work be done, and let the nations of the earth contribute to the work according to their good will and desire to do the will of God, and to be the friends of His Zion. I want my servant, Joseph Smith, to push the work, that his life may be prolonged, and that I may add days upon days to his life upon earth, and bless him with all the blessings which I bestowed on the head of his father, and his father's father before him.

Let nothing be done in haste, but with order; and let my house be a house of order, and of peace, and of glory before all the nations on earth; and the seed of Joseph shall preside in my name at that house. I will raise up a righteous branch from him, and out from his loins shall go forth the law to Zion, even as it went out to all nations by the writings of Mormon, that my words may be fulfilled, and all the promises given to Zion may be bestowed upon her. Amen.

A spirit standing by you exclaims "glory," because he discerns the Messiah present in the spiritual sphere; but I say unto you: "The light which follows me now as your personal guide, is as the fame of a king who left his capitol and traveled incognito, or unknown to the people of many nations; and Messiah also is now in his preparatory work not seen except to those who know him to be the king, for humanity has to be educated to endure his presence, and the presence of his Father who is a consuming fire to those who hate Him, but an everlasting bliss to those who love Him in His love to mankind through His only begotten Son who is now speaking to you." This has to be said, and my words have to be read, and the minds of the people have to be prepared, and the work to be done in the redemption of Zion, even the building of the temple in Jackson county, Mo. My servant, Joseph, have faith and trust, for to that place shall the remnants of Utah come, and unite themselves with the remnants of Zion of the United States; and the glory of the Father, and of the Son, and of the Holy Ghost shall appear at that house with great power and strength of the spirit. It has been foreshadowed by the Spirit that the house would not be built by the church in Utah, and for that reason it would be built shortly before the Messiah came. Let therefore a cry be heard all over the land " to prepare," and let the Gentiles among all nations be called upon to contribute to the house of the Lord, and let the saints gather in the gold and silver, and bring the material and lay the foundation, even as it has been given to my servant, and let my congregation in Utah unite hands in brotherly love with the scattered saints of the reorganized church. I will have them do the work and finish my house, and invite the saints in Utah and in the territories to come and partake of my blessings in the house they refused to take part in building. Therefore, come all of the followers of truth and do my work; come ye, my people, from the ends of the earth and do the work of the Lord, that my measure of blessings may be filled up, which shall be poured out upon all Israel. Amen.

When I came to you, my messenger, last night in a dream, it was not to warn you, but to edify you. I have seen your toil, and your work, and your labor has been accepted of me, and of my Father; and I have one thing to tell you, and that is, "do not despair but be hopeful, because time shall be given to you, and I will release you from your present hard labor among the sick, and suffering, and those who are sinking down into the dust loaded with heavy burdens. Be hopeful; time shall be sufficiently given to you in which to do the work of Messiah." When I, in your dream, lifted the crucifix before your face, you saw written lengthwise these words: "Live rich among the rich;" and across it from one nailed hand to the other: "I was poor." It is no reproach to you, but given for your consideration, that you may know that you shall not be nailed hand to hand, as the poor among the poorest to a cross of poverty. But you shall be nailed to my work with your feet among the nations of the earth, even as the rich among the rich; even so shall it be. Amen.

It shall be a humiliation to you in the future, and you shall wish yourself poor without being able to be so, when you shall see with your mental vision written on my cross, "I was poor," for a servant should not be otherwise than his master, but when he is perfect he should be as his Master; but for your sake I have given it to you that you should sojourn in this world up to a very high old age, and not be in destitution and want in any place where I shall send you to do my work. Blessed are they who follow after me and do the work of the Messiah, which is the work of the Father and the Holy Spirit, and of the angels of heaven. Rest not from the work, my servant, till the temple at Independence is raised in all its splendor and glory before all the world, and I call on my servant, Joseph Smith, of Lamoni, to head the work. Amen.

Blessed are they who read these words, but more blessed are they who do as I have commanded; because it is not of me but of my Father, and He is the everlasting Prince, as the spirit of truth bears witness of Him. Amen.

As I have taught the spiritual church in Paradise, also I teach you, and as I have received of my Father in His eternal abode, so I teach you; and as I have spoken the words to my disciples, and to the quorums of the seventies and elders in my Father's mansions, even so do I teach you that heaven may be united with earth and earth with heaven, and peace be restored, and power regained, and unity be given to man in all spiritual affairs pertaining to his exaltation and his eternal salvation in my Father's kingdom. There are many ways to salvation, but there is only one way to the eternal salvation in my Father's kingdom, and that way I am. Whosoever follows after me shall not lose the way, because I shall constantly be before him, and he can always see my foot-prints; and such a person shall eternally be where I am, and partake of my glory, which is the glory of my Father. Therefore do not err and teach otherwise, as the way to my Father's house is narrow, and the darkness of the world makes it difficult to remain in it unless you are lighted by the light of the Holy Ghost—that lantern of peace and comfort which makes you know the way and see the road, even in the darkest hour of the world.

Blessed are they who read these words and receive them, that they may have a light on their road and a power in their life, for my words are the light and power which gives life, and the glory of the soul which never dies, and cannot perish with the external treasures of the world. The great unity of my church on earth is now at hand, for I have commanded the union of the saints by that love which is in me by which I love the world, and that I have given to live in the hearts of my followers on earth, even so I command you to love one another; and I have also commanded you to build my house at Independence, that it may be a house of love, where the spirit of love and truth may dwell. Do not persecute one another with foolish words, and fault-finding, and ill sayings one against the other, for all such things are not of God. Let every man and every woman be in meekness, and have an humble spirit within themselves, as God will exalt that which does not exalt itself in its own vanity. My servant, Moses, was the meekest man in Israel, but God exalted him before all his brethren.

Some have high positions in the church of the saints, and have lost the spirit of their callings; but whenever they repent and pray with an honest heart, confessing their shortcomings, and humbling themselves before God and their brethren, then the spirit of their calling shall descend upon them, and abide with them; but if they do not humble themselves, then God shall remove them from their places, and their names shall not be found there any more, but be hushed in death and oblivion. Therefore, many pass away into the spirit world at an early age, and the angel of death is among you, because you have not the blood of the Lamb painted on the entrance to your soul, that the Lord may protect you in going out and coming in everlastingly. I have seen Israel in the wilderness, and I have seen the saints in the mountains, and I have seen their rebellion against me, but I have not forgotten my promise to Abraham and his seed and his adopted seed scattered among all the nations; and for their sake have I blessed all the nations, and also will I gather the fruit which comes from his loins, and make it to be a great people in the midst of the earth, and give them the power to make peace on earth, that the nations shall obey them and keep peace one with another. But before that day, commotion shall arise over all the earth, and the working classes of society shall be very angry, and there shall be bloodshed and civil wars over all the earth; and Israel shall go out from among them and gather unto their own places of safety. Therefore, be not alarmed when you see and hear all these things coming; they are necessary for your redemption, and must take place that wickedness may lose its grasp on the reins of the nations, and evil designs and bloodshed may empty its own cup and be powerless.

You ask me what shall set the adversary free again, and I say, "nothing but contentions against the kingdom at the end of its reign;" for as there were contentions against heaven, so shall there be contentions at the end of the thousand years; but when the nations have marshalled themselves and march against the holy cities of Jerusalem and of Zion, the saints shall be taken from the earth, and there shall be an end to the present order of things, and mighty convulsions of the surface of the earth shall give place for a higher nature, and the New Jerusalem shall descend on the new earth more glorious than ever, and saints with materialized bodies, and immortal, as in heaven, shall live in God's paradise. So shall the earth be, and the spirits of those who rebelled against the holy cities and God's Israel and went up to battle against them, shall not enter into the paradise of the new earth for times and times to come. Man argues from the standpoint of himself, and his limited earthly career and experience. and he is right so far as his natural life is concerned and its conditions, but he is in error in a spiritual sense, as far as he makes his finite measurement to be the problem by which he will solve the infinite, and know the certainties by which the eternal worlds are understood. Man has to learn, if not before, then in the spirit world, that more than three-fourths of all his inventions and improvements accepted as the development and progression of the race were given to him by a direct inspiration, a truth there in fact is known by the great statesmen, inventors, and scientists of earth, because, were it not for this principle of inspiration, they could not have received the great truths which they have given to the world.

Humble and lowly of soul are the children of the light, and the children of the shadow and misery have harvested the benefit. These same light carriers have never been fully known, nor appreciated of their own generation, but only of the world of light above. When I tell you the truth and you do not believe it, then your mind is exactly in the state that you are ripe to believe a falsehood; because, when your souls are perverted away from the truth, whosoever speaks a falsehood gives utterance to that sound which shall echo in your own soul. As man is naturally sensual and carnal, he is only capable of misrepresenting and miscomprehending the spiritual truth, that there is ltttle capacity in the animal nature of his being to desire, or aspire, or grasp spiritual ideas of God; and even with a superior development of brain above the animal world, man cannot arrive at truths which are in the paths of his life except by the extraordinary quickening of the mental capacities by which his intuition is made to see, and know, and catch or perceive the spiritual glimpses which are shining on his road as starlight from above. Therefore, has inspiration to be studied into and understood by all mankind, and therefore have the saints to take another grand step onward in the general acceptance of a universal inspiration or infusion of light to man as a special dispensation by the Holy Ghost to the church. It is the personal work and power, and personal manifestation to the race and the church of Messiah by the Holy Ghost, and archangels, and of Jehovah or the Father who is in heaven, and the most high God to man. Although eighteen hundred years have passed away, the church of Messiah is yet in its infancy, as a baby wrapped in rags, and not able to walk and discern for itself. Therefore is now a schism in the church of the saints; therefore the truth is hidden within the wounds of my hands, and therefore do I now open them before all Israel; and therefore are the churches of men split up in divisions beyond all comprehension, that the world, by its own contradictions, might arrive at the recognition of the mind of Messiah.

As the principles of life are not yet taught you as a measure by which the whys are answered, it is not comprehended why God does not destroy the adversary, and why he has not as good a right to live in existing conditions as the Father has to live in His conditions. Exhaust the inferior, undeveloped conditions which make deviltry, and the devil is nowhere; but he has as much right to his world as you have to yours, so long as his world is to be found. "Whatever is, is right," has also been said, and beyond all doubt God has not excluded anything from His dominion, though the most of all spirits and angels cannot reach the glory of His personal presence. There are some persons in Zion who consider themselves good saints, and competent to conquer the devil of the flesh, and even to make the adversary of all the churches take flight. Such persons do not know that the church on earth has nothing to do with the archangel who opposed the establishment of the church on earth; that he is dealt with by higher powers, and by other means than the church can control, or than the saints have at their disposition; and it is the same with the devils in the flesh, or spirits, who connect themselves with the discord and the inharmonious conditions of mankind both in body and soul, and in homes and social relations, and keep up war, and strife, and sickness, and malice, and misery, and ill feelings one against another, which draws away the love, and turns away holy influences from holy angels and the harmonies of the Holy Ghost.

Therefore, do not go to war with evil influences, but overcome evil with good, or exhaust evil conditions by good works and harmonize discord. Let the desire both of soul and body be justified in all righteousness, and balance and happiness will be the result. You say we will stand up in the name of the Lord and put down evil. How will you do it? In the name of the Lord. Then you cannot be the Lord; or, in other words, as He was in the world so also must you be; the weapons He used you must also use, but His weapon was the cross, or to suffer, and to overcome evil by suffering; and by that He has drawn mankind to Him, after He was lifted up in heaven and above earth. All who follow after me belong to my family, and among such exist all my relations—those who listen to my commandments, and do my will because it becomes their own will, only such are my friends in my Father's kingdom, as the Lord does not govern of himself, but as the Father governs, so also does the Son. Therefore, are you not any longer subjects, but kings and rulers, for the kingdom of God the Father, is in the Gospel of Freedom, and he who embraces it is made to be a king and a ruler in righteousness of his own soul, and in its relations and surroundings. In such a manner is the Son of man the King of Kings and Lord of Lords. Some persons on earth are asking for their relations in the world to come, and not after their spiritual relations, but after their relations according to the flesh; and I have only one answer to give, and that is, whatever is of the flesh is carnal and will perish, and whatever is of the spirit is spirit, and will live in the eternal mansions of my Father. In the eternal worlds there is nothing to take away, and nothing to add to His glory, but if you are of His household you shall partake of His glory, and dwell in His house as His sons and daughters, because a servant is not of the family, but you shall be princes of the royal priesthood forever. Art thou a king? "I am a king," was my answer to Pilate, although all the earthly possessions of the kingdom at that time consisted of contempt and the cross, though I was a king. The least one in my Father's kingdom is a king among kings, and even on the cross of the world he is a king.

Although wives and children are a blessing, I say to you: "Be you married as though you were not married, and have wives and children as though you had none." It is not the external relations only that constitute marriage, but the external and internal wedded together in two persons, that they may not any longer be as two, but as one body and soul; and in such a union be parents to the fruit of the spirit of love, and elevate the world in the same love, and the fruit shall be found to be as the tree is. Your families on earth make up, in a measure, your happiness, and they may do the same in heaven; and as your families on earth often constitute a part of your misery, so they may do the same in the world to come. Therefore, marry what you are bound to in each other by the spirit of truth, as well as in the ties of the flesh. Marry the ideal of yourselves represented by the other sex, that you may be as one on earth, and as one in the celestial love of eternal worship, by grasping within your soul the divinity in a woman or a man; nothing else will be able to exalt you in the garden of paradise. Whatever is a matter of necessity has a right to be. Whatever is possible and constitutes itself as an unavoidable constituent of life has a right to be heard. Everything possible, it may be for good or bad, will, by the logical consequences of life, present itself.

Therefore be very patient in your judgment when the reaction comes in the nature of legitimate debts which humanity owes to the justice and light, and is the result of existing undeveloped conditions which will not be atoned for but by revolutions and blood; not because it was so ordained in heaven, but because it came to pass on earth because heaven was not heard, and its messengers were shot down in cold blood; therefore came the rebellion on this continent, and millions sank into premature graves, because the nations rejected the grace of God—that light from above, and that spirit of revelation by which the vexed question of slavery might have been settled. Also will this people be wanting when put on the scales of the future, and there will be strife, and fire, and murder, and misery, until that spirit which cries out for blood, and rejects the light which is beaming down from heaven shall be consumed in blood, for the multitudes are as mute people, and do not see, or hear, or understand to get wisdom, and peace with one another. That mind which serves the world as its ultimate treasure to be laid up for eternity, shall be deceived, because deception is its birthright, and it cannot be otherwise.

"Truth will prevail," has been the motto for centuries among men, and so shall it be; the ultimate result of that axiom cannot be frustrated; it will go on to victory over fallen cities and broken up nations, and march through the wilderness, and where princely palaces of kings were seen in splendor and glory, and where mighty nations have built their capitols, shall truth triumph, and the glory of the world shall be gone as a useless obstruction, and truth was the hurricane which, by the power of the eternal worlds, swept them all away. The world has defended the Roman Catholic institutions which, to a great extent, have been inherited from paganism and not from Israel. That church has defended the Roman and Greek monogamy as if it was a God-given institution by Moses to Israel, and not a fruit of Greek and Roman civilization. That which was the Jewish marriage was thrown aside and despised, and ridiculed, and treated with contempt; and the laws given to Israel were put aside, and so Israel was compelled to adopt the heathen custom of marriage, and so it came to pass that the christian world of to-day has not the remotest idea of its error.

Another state of affairs has to dawn upon this people before the redemption shall come. That which is in liberty shall not be confounded, but that which is bound up in slavery shall be confounded. That which is in liberty shall not perish, but that which is in bondage shall perish. That which is in freedom shall not fail to accomplish its work of redemption, but that which is bound up in thraldom shall cease to present its obstructions. If this nation was at liberty in the sense of progression, and in the spirit of its own constitution, then the views of the government would be as broad as the country is from the Atlantic to the Pacific. The Gospel of Freedom is the heavenly proclamation which will follow the opening of the sixth seal; that liberty shall be given to man to live in peace one with another, and the freedom of the sons and daughters of God shall be given to the church, that the freedom which is in the power of the Holy Ghost shall be the ruling power of the church, that neither man nor woman shall need any truer teaching; and teachers shall not find it necessary to walk from door to door among the saints except for edification, for the spirit shall teach both young and old to keep all the commandments of the will and mind of God, as the Spirit shall fall upon the soul and heart in one accord, and unite all into one harmony of unity and peace.

On that day shall no threats be heard from the pulpit in the congregation of the saints, nor shall one brother say to another, "I beseech you to do right and keep the law;" as the law shall be themselves hidden in God, and they will do right of necessity, because their will shall be born into a new nature, and they will no longer oppose the law—being the law themselves, but be in the freedom of heaven, even the Gospel of Freedom in the Order of Messiah in his second coming. Be not of little faith if you are living in the faith of your Master, but be perfected in His faith; for He has not counted on your faith, nor on your strength, nor have you relied on your own glory; but as His joint heirs He has given you the bread of eternity that you might eat and never hunger if you abide in His faith, laying your own faith on one side, and are living in His faith; for man's natural faith cannot sustain him on the raging billows and the storms of life. But if you pray that the faith by the spirit shall not vanish, then you shall remain in the faith of the sons of God, and you are indeed free, for the truth has made you free, as the children of God are free. Amen.

Force has never established the church on earth, and force has never made peace between God and the adversary, and force has not helped to build up Zion; because force has only been the weapon of the adversary, and not of God, who does not force or ameliorate convictions by force. That which is of the spirit has to be understood by the spirit, and that which is of mind has to be taught and corrected by mind; only brutal force which inflicts wounds and destruction on man will meet force, as those who use swords may expect to perish by swords. When the government of these United States is the representative of the people, then the people is the government, and the people are responsible for its acts, and will have to suffer the consequences; that is the reason destruction will come on this nation—on account of its government. Its action against the church is only another repetition of the Roman persecution in ancient times, and to conform to paganism at that time is to conform to paganism to-day. This conformation to the political creed of to-day would only be a strangulation of the life which is in the church if it should consent to be remodeled and controlled in its spiritual faith, and trust, a control against which the Almighty God is barrier. When the world's governments undertake to regulate spiritual faith, then they labor under a double mistake; first, because they can only act in governmental or state affairs, and not handle religious convictions; secondly, it is bound by its own tenets of the constitution to protect religious convictions, and not persecute them, as they have no weight in political life, and practically conflict with nobody, and should not be interfered with, for mankind must be free to enjoy religious convictions, or it would be better for it not to have any, but to have heaven locked up, and the prophets silenced.

This people of the American continent will be affected by the life of Zion, but it has to leave God's work alone; for in proportion as they will meddle with the work they will be affected by the notions and power of that people, and only Zion will gain in power; and the American nation will lose in proportion, and go down to a gloomy and contending end. The day that it marches up against Zion will be the darkest hour since the Boston revolution, and will be a short and bloody revival of New England's folly, when witches were drowned to atone the church, and appease God. When the Jews were scattered, after the destruction of Jerusalem, the head-center of Israel was broken to pieces, and wherever the Jews went also saints were scattered, and such the destruction became the leaven to penetrate humanity and rear progressive work in which the promise came to Abraham: "In thy seed shall all the nations of the earth be blessed." Now is the scattering reversed, and a contrary dispensation is on hand, even now commenced, in which is the restoration of Israel, and the gathering of that which was dispersed as a leaven among all nations, and a calling on those in the land of the north to come out of their hiding places, and go with songs of joy to the land of their fathers, which shall be restored to them as a gathering place for the Jews of the exile among the Gentiles. Therefore is now a voice heard which has been silent since the days of Moses, and since the days of Ezra, and Zerubabel, and since the first advent of Messiah. Come out, my people, from the places where you are dispersed, and come with joy and songs up to Jerusalem, for the things your fathers hoped for are now coming to pass, and Zion shall not stand deserted, but the King of Kings shall dwell on the holy mount, and shall be seen among Israel, for your people shall not forever be laid in dust and ashes, but when those who have slain you have filled their cup, shall Moriah again be redeemed, and the temple foremost among temples in Canaan shall be seen near by the Mosque of Omar.

When the world condemns the Church people, and denounces their faith and their social life, then remember that the world is not born in the love of God, nor regenerated, nor is the Holy Spirit revealed to them, and the truth is hidden from their eyes. And not alone from theirs, but from myriads of spirits also, who from their spheres do not know the light of love, which never shone through their prison walls of superstition to be absorbed of them as the flow of life from their Heavenly Father. Whatever is of flesh is flesh, and man's nature he has in common with all the animal creation, and from such a standpoint, when the judges of the world make an attempt to judge those who are born of the Spirit, there is not a more difficult task, because whatsoever there is of earth can be judged by those who are of earth, but whatsoever there is of heaven can only be judged by the Spirit, or the heavenly light of those who are born of the Spirit or of truth, and they will be true judges of the world, which is in a reflex opposition to the Spirit of God in the world, it breathing its own falsehoods about the spiritual conceptions which it cannot understand except by the acceptance of the inspired faith of God, repentance from the animal appetite and propensities, baptism to a new birth, and laying on of hands for the spiritual baptism and guidance into a new life, which is to be born of the Spirit.

The companionship of heaven is not like the prostitution of the world, no more than the earth is the sun, or the sun is the earth, and it is much further removed in conditions and conceptions. Also, when the world rises up against the marriage of Moses and Jacob, it wars not against its own evil doings, and its own misconceptions, and it cannot fight against spiritual issues which it has never conceived nor known anything about. It may fight external relations, but cannot fix the internal manifestations in the hearts of those who believe the truth and live it.

Therefore are marriage unions made by man, and not by God. They are social relations in the spirit of the world, with more duties to the flesh than to the Spirit, and also are some children born with more curses than blessings upon them. God blessed marriage, but many unions are not perpetuated in the blessings of God, nor are the contracts made and sustained by the Holy Ghost, and God never united that which never came together in truth and happiness, but was contracted by the folly of men and women. To be a saint is to live saintly lives in the holy Spirit of God, and be blessed by that Spirit in all marriage on earth, that it may be as the companionship of heaven is. Therefore do not confound the heavenly unions with the marriages of the world, which are carnal, and of the flesh.

All God's people should be fathers and mothers under the law of heavenly love, and not be living in all kind of contention and jealousy, which is of the flesh and not of the Spirit. It matters not what you are sealed to, or ordained to, if it is of the truth. If the vows you take upon yourselves are in the truth, then keep sacred such obligations, and live, and breathe and exist in the spirit of such ordinances. Only live in the truth and remain in it, and it shall be the freedom of Zion, and you shall have the freedom to the city of the New Jerusalem, and go out and in there in freedom everlasting.

Remain in truth for the truth's sake, and because you love it, and do not forsake its banner, and I will gather you in Zion as on the wings of my power. Swiftly shall mine elect come from the islands afar off, and from the continents shall they sing together in my name. I will give them my spirit within their hearts, and give them my mind within their brain, and they will accomplish my work, and I will exalt Zion as the city of Elohim which cannot be hid, and I will make distant nations send their sons to thee and wonder at thy glory.

Rejoice, thou fallen tribe of Nephi, and the sons of Lehi be glad! Thy seed was not slain without hope, nor were thy men exterminated without cause, but on their tombs is flowering the hope of all Israel.

Therefore, my people, obey the laws of the country in which you are living, and in all social relations be subject to the regulations of the council of the nation among which you are living, even as the Jews have been for centuries.

The messengers of God have obligations belonging to a greater work, and their missions are in a greater sacrifice to God than in the church, therefore when they are married they shall be as they were not married, and if a messenger's wife, that he is living with in the spirit of God, departs from earth-life, and she is also a messenger in the order of Messiah, and she leaves children born to him in the spirit of the Lord, then he shall not marry again, as I will allow her to be by him as a guide in the spirit of his being, and he shall not take a second wife, as the spirit of the first wife shall not be grieved by the presence of the second wife, except it be commanded by the spirit of prophecy as the will of the Lord, and as the will of the spirit of the departed first wife. This has so to be, because very often a first departed wife is grieved in the spirit by the choice a husband makes in the selection of his second wife, who afterwards becomes the stepmother and guardian for the departed mother's children. Such unions are sins, if contracted in discord, and a cruelty against heaven, as much as to marry into polygamy, in unholy and discordant unions of strife and jealousy.

It is also true that a man who marries a second time, when the departed wife clings to him as a guide in the spirit, is in polygamy by taking a second wife on earth. He is in polygamy in the spirit of his soul, though he is not so in the world, and if he clings to the second wife in a discord to that love in which the first wife meets his spirit in the Spirit of God, he is living in a falsified relation in himself towards his second wife, and the union is not of God, but of the world, and his soul shall be in discord on earth, and he shall meet both of his wives in a discordant spirit in the spirit world after his departure from earth-life. Upon this principle of marrying several wives on earth there is polygamy in the spirit, when you step over from one world to the other, until the condition in the flesh which gave cause for it is outgrown by the children into the Spirit, and freedom comes which is in my Father's kingdom, where they shall not marry, nor be given into marriage, but be in freedom as the angels are in freedom of the holy and heavenly law of companionship, belonging to the eternal worlds, and therefore is eternal, of one man with one woman, two in one and one in two, into the perfection of my Father with the Holy Ghost, into the same unity of peace and glory. In such eternal unions, one in two, men and women live in divine worship of love to each other, beyond the boundaries of the spirit of this solar system's spirit-world, and into the eternal realms of endless development in the perfection of my Father, or as gods and not as spirits.

This may be sufficient for man to know, that upon the pedestal of these unholy unions, and sorrows, and pains, and discord, and curses, where the spirit of murder and hate is rampant with violence, does love realize also its sweetest dream, and is built for eternity and in eternity the pavilions of Gods. Amen.

MESSAGE FROM JESHUAH, THE MESSIAH.

THE CHURCH PRIESTCRAFT.

LINCOLN, NEBRASKA, October 6, 1882.

I have called you to light and not to darkness. The Gospel of Messiah has only one meaning, and it is a grand message, full of news, and great joy and good will to all mankind.

There is nothing in the Gospel of Messiah which gives the right to one person to rule with force or to tyrannize over another person under the prestige of superior authority from God. Such conduct is abominable in the sight of God, but it has been done ever since the servitude of a priesthood has been established on earth. The blind have led the blind; the dumb and deaf have guided the dumb and deaf, and so on, and all fell into the ditch. That inspiration which justified itself in establishing God's priesthood in harmony with heavenly messengers was soon lost, and men without the gift of being seers, and without hearing voices of angels, and without the prophetic gifts and power of God, were called upon of men to do the work of heaven and its spirit world on earth. The result could be nothing more or less than a fallacy, and the great melodrama has been played and taken for good by the credulous multitude, not knowing, nor stopping for a moment to inquire into the real value of such a claim. Where is the blame to be found for such a state of affairs? I did not send them, nor did I give them authority to act in my name, nor did I call them with my voice as I did Samuel, nor did I call them by visions or by dreams, nor by prophets, nor by laying on of hands for the Holy Ghost, nor by any ambassador from heaven, but they spoke in my name and said it was my voice, and they commanded and officiated in my name, as if I had given them authority, forgetting that heaven has no authority on earth to act in the name of heaven, except it comes from heaven. Whatever dealings my Father has with the earth and man outside of the Gospel of Messiah, is as a Ruler and an Emperor, and not as a Father, and He deals with the world accordingly, and by the iron hand of truth and justice and destiny by the Spirit of Nature, but with those who are living under the law of the Gospel he deals with according to the law which is in the love of the Gospel.

The priesthood in Utah has beyond all comparison been a deception and an imposition to the church, and with few exceptions has been divested of all inspiration, and it has even contested the Spirit of God and His work, and been aspiring after self-rule and that despotism in spiritual things which characterized the dark middle ages of the Catholic church. If you do not seek the gifts of the spirit of prophecy, and have no wish to possess it and live in it as a branch lives in a tree, you cannot know God's will. To be a branch of a rotten tree does not benefit the branch, and to be a member of a decayed church, without gifts or strength, does not benefit any person; therefore be not deceived, but be members of the living prophetic church, and the signs shall follow you, as they live and are possessed in heaven. Do not worship the letter, but live in the spirit of the letter, or ye shall be guilty of idolatry. My favor follows many saints now in bondage to the church in Utah, but I am not one with the church, nor can it as a church fulfill its destiny, nor can it as a church ever enter Independence, because the prophetic spirit is departed from it as an organization, but I have my saints whom I will deliver from bondage. Therefore you can only individually receive me at Independence. I have rejected you as a church, even as you were at Far West, on the day that you were driven away from the very temple ground pointed out by the finger of my Father at that spot. You followed after other gods, and your offering was an offering of the world and to the world, and it was rejected, and you were rejected by heaven. Therefore, thus saith the Lord your God: Your priesthood has been taken away from you as an organization, and been given to another people, where the gifts and the power, and the dwelling of the Holy Spirit on earth can be cherished and enjoyed, and whosoever rejects one of those who walk in the spirit and gifts of my Father, rejects me, and whosoever receives them receives me, as though they were ordained by my own hand in the eternal worlds, and ye shall know them by my power and my gifts being possessed by them, even as my Father endowed me with them when I was upon earth.

You have ordained in my name, but I did not send you to do my work, and my hands were not present, nor my spirit, nor my consent, nor my approbation, nor the gift of prophesy, by which all calling has to be executed, and subsequently sealed.

You have made it a mockery to be a saint, and a farce to be called into the priesthood, but as this imposition on humanity has fulfilled its measure, it has only to be revealed to mankind in all its nakedness, as it has refused repentance and exceeded all shame.

Heaven has taken measures against a second apostasy, such as took place in the early days after my presence on earth, and it shall not be done—the priesthood of power and inspiration shall not vanish away from earth before it is finished in my Father's kingdom, when I shall be with you. I will remove it from place to place, and from person to person, even as I called Saul from among mine enemies to be an apostle, and a great witness to the generation in which he lived, and I will retain the priesthood in spirit and in truth, but not as an organization of this world, nor as any lifeless corpse, prostituting the name of spirit-life and Christ-life, and I will do my own work on earth in spite of all false priests, and all snares laid for mine elect, that the falsehood in man shall not retain power, nor be victorious. Amen.

To be confirmed by laying on of hands after baptism is an affirmation in the right and principles promised by faith and obedience, and signifies the birthright, or the affirmation of the birthright of Christ in man—to be in the world as he was, and possess in the world all the gifts and power pertaining to this dispensation in the world, but those who lay on hands for such an exalted state in man must be themselves in possession of it, or it is a fraudulent act, and an imposition on the intelligence of their fellow men.

The same by ordination. It is first a calling forth of a person who is the choice of God and of the spiritual church of Messiah in heaven, as it may also next be the choice of the church on earth. In other words—it is in the first instance the calling by the voice of God, which is the voice of heaven, or the spirit of prophecy, next it is an acceptation of the congregation to confide in that choice, and that it is a confirmation of the elders, who are called by the same spirit of calling, even as Moses and Aaron were. Therefore, when any person is needed in the priesthood, be ye silent before God in your meetings, and for a length of time until the Holy Spirit of truth breaks forth from the fountain of your souls, and it will be given to some one whom the spirit may choose to speak through to designate the person who is the choice of heaven. Being in such a manner called by inspiration of God, the calling may be confirmed and the person ordained by the elders who were called in the same way, and by the same spirit of truth resting upon them, and being in possession of the gifts and power of Christ's promises to man.

That is the order of any ordination in the church ; therefore do not officiate in the place of the Holy Spirit, nor put the spirit under your own guardianship, or the Messiah will, as a church, cut you off from all communion with him and the church in heaven, even as you have done on earth against the Holy Spirit, so shall it be done unto you.

The church in Utah has as a church fallen from its eminence for want of faith in the spiritual promises and in its own destiny. Now it is working in the spirit of this world, and fighting the world because it became of the world, as in the world as a people, in the state and government of the world, and if it does not repent, it will perish with the world, and all of its self-made apostles and presidents and elders, because I did not call them, will perish with the world. The priesthood lost its own sphere, given by heaven in conformity with the sphere of angels, and made a new sphere, in the spirit of this world, to live and prosper in, and be accursed in, as they are to-day and will continue to be, unless they repent from the defence of a false claim and accept the laws and privileges guaranteed by heaven to the church of Saints on earth. Amen.

MESSAGE FROM THE APOSTLE PAUL.

INDEPENDENCE, Mo., April 9, 1882.

I am with you to-day. Our conference is well attended. I am one of the apostles of olden time. My name was Saulus, or in Greek, Paul. I have been with you several times without being noticed. The Church of the Latter-Day Saints is in a muddle and will not recover from it before new light is infused into it by the Holy Spirit. Tell Joseph Smith from me, that he may as well as not pull the church up on the Rocky Mountains if he does not go on and give a new and superior life to the church by an infusion of the higher light. Humanity at present needs additional light which is given to the world by Spiritualism. A move in that direction would be much better than standing still and becoming petrified around old by-gone dogmas.

We are all well aware of what I said and what I did when upon the earth, but Paul then and Paul now are two very different personalities, or would be so to your comprehension. At the same time the fundamental principles are all good enough for the world to obey, but not to live on. The church must be liberal and leave all prejudices out, and be as a child, open and willing to receive new truths and more light, and they will get it, but not before they become petrified as stones, as a great many shall be hardened in their souls about the perfection of their own saintship, and say as of old; "We have Moses and the prophets," and we have Christ in the faith of Jesus of Nazareth, but it will help you nothing when you get over here. Now is the great sifting of your souls, and it is all that I want to say in this direction.

I do not look on the church as I did when on earth. Then everything was new, but now it shall be as we expected it in the coming of Messiah. He shall come with a new infusion of spiritual light for the church. I became at first a persecutor, but by the light o' heaven I became a spiritual and earthly mouthpiece for the Gospel of Jesus. Now is this gospel truth known, if not digested, as far as the doctrine is concerned, but at the same time, only very few of the present generation read and understand the scriptures.

It was the design of the religious circle of the spirit world, over which the Ancient of Days presides, to have the Gospel restored in its simplicity and fulness by Joseph, as it was in my time on earth, and have it presented in its original form to all mankind, and not throw any part or parts of Christianity overboard, and in such a manner as to form a link or union with the universal principles revealed in Spiritualism. This object has had its serious obstructions, and has materially failed in nearly every respect, on account of the leader's short-sightedness and disposition to gain the riches of this world. Now all that can be done, is to do our best and gradually to combine both wings of the church on a spiritual basis of eternal and universal freedom of the principles of cosmopolitan truth, and that will be the Gospel of Freedom, or, in the sight of the world, the religion of a Christian or bible Spiritualism. Now you see the direction in which we work, for we must put on the tape line further and further as the demand of the civilized world asks for it. The doctrine is, "Ask, and it shall be given to you."

I would personally like that you could devote your life entirely to the preaching of these principles, for which I suffered death when on earth. They are the principles of progressive truth and endless development. You will soon be bound over to a more extensive work than hitherto, and we will meet again and very often. Before long you will travel and work according to opportunity, and the dictation of your guide, Joseph the seer, who also suffered death for the success of his testimony. May the angels bless you, and the Father of heaven give you that eternal peace and happiness which is in His Spirit, and was given to earth that heaven might abide in you as in His beloved Son, our Lord. Amen.

MESSAGE FROM JESHUAH, THE MESSIAH.

THE SPIRITUAL CHURCH.

INDEPENDENCE, Mo., April 10, 1882.

I am with you this morning, and want to give you an idea of your position in regard to the church in Utah. There is no particular or especial reason why you should pay any more attention to that branch of Christianity than any other. The Christian churches are not one branch, or one body, but a portion of the spiritual church is found in them all, and the Spirit will designate that which is of me, and where it is. All over the world are my sheep, and they all hear my voice, and know the calling of the Spirit of God. The Gospel of Freedom is freedom to all and slavery to none. It is extended to Mormonism, but is no especial mission to that church more than to any other church; it contains within itself the elements by which the church in Utah will be delivered from errors and gain the spirit of truth to be the truth, but it is not specially a calling upon them any more than it is on the Catholic, Lutheran, Methodist or Baptist churches. The Gospel of Freedom will recognize no particular party or sect, nor do the errand of any especial clique of ministers, nor serve any ring or any ring-leaders of men. It will extend its hand alike to Protestants and Catholics, and will even invite the Jews, the Spiritualists, the Mohammedans, the Buddhists, the Freethinkers and the Materialists, to come and sup with Abraham, Isaac and Jacob in the kingdom of my Father to come upon the earth.

On that broad wing of liberality is the new-born message to earth to bring good will to all men, and honor and glory to God the Father, and to that Spirit of eternity who is the embodied spiritual principle to all persons both in heaven and on the earth. The Godhead is nowhere else to be found representing the Alpha and Omega, the commencement and the end of all things on this earth; it is the commencement of this present epoch of nature on earth, and also its end. It is for the benefit of the whole world that the present circle of archangels are working steadily for the development of the human intellect and brain.

Now you understand me that the Gospel of Freedom is a cosmopolitan measure, and cannot be confined to any special church, or it would cease at once to be what it is, and lose its claim of being the Gospel of Freedom. Looking out from that pinnacle of mental elevation, it will be evident that light has a general diffusion throughout the universe, and does not belong to a special kingdom or empire, so let it be with the Gospel of Freedom, and as *you* do not belong especially to any church, so let it be with all members of the Gospel of Freedom, let them be in the world, but not of the world, and let them be found in the churches, but not of the churches, as it is written : "I will gather mine elect from the utmost corners of the world, and from among all the nations of the earth." In the general acceptation, it is an inner or spiritual calling as the very first and most important one, that they may become the sons and daughters of God in their hearts, or in the sincerity of their affections. This calling has to precede all other callings, and is a gathering into the fold of the Spirit of God which prelude and precede all other gatherings, or you might just as well gather in wolves and present them to God the Father as his sheep, and do it in the name of the Lamb, or the bleeding and crucified Messiah in his humiliation, when he was torn to death by the wolves of the world. Be called and gathered in your souls, each and every one of you, and you shall be gathered to places of refreshment, to temples and societies, and the Order of Messiah, where your united spirits shall bring down great power and strength from above. Let the first be done, and the second promise shall follow after.

You see me at present by you, praying constantly, and you wonder how it can be. I say to you, be not astonished, as I have to pray for you by night and by day, that the adverse power and death shall not swallow you up, and my work be frustrated. As I prayed for Peter when on earth, so I pray for you in the spirit world, that you shall abide in the work in spite of all possible hindrances, as the work of the Gospel of Freedom is to give and not to take, is to bless and not to curse, is to liberate and not to enslave, is to build up the church of God, and not to tear any truth down. God's church is his spiritual church.

The Church of Christ, or the Church of God, or the Church of Zion and Saints, or of the Holy One, is entirely synonymous. It matters not what the name is, if it signifies or conveys the idea, as it matters not the color of the horses which draw the vehicle, so long as the work is done, and the destination is arrived at in safety. A great many nicknames have been given to religious bodies engaged in my name for the worship of God. Some are called Catholics, Protestants, Quakers, Baptists, Adventists and Calvinists, Lutherans, Mormons, Campbellites, etc. All this is only the custom of the world. In heaven there is only one worship, that in the spirit and of truth, and all other worship is of men and will perish, as the flesh loses its organization when decomposition sets in. That which is of God cannot perish, or that which is born of the Spirit to live eternally in the heavens; but that which is of man is only made for duration of flesh and blood, and will all perish as the flesh of man will perish. Therefore never let churchmen confound your souls, when they present to your minds nothing but the record of a name conveyed to the human mind as a type of an internal organization.

The Church of God is the church of souls gathered in an interior sense of the word to heaven. Its members are found in all churches of the world or Christianity. No church by any full membership represents the Church of Christ, and much less the Church of God in heaven. Some churches have been in possession of the priesthood of the living God, and some have lost it and retained the teaching and part of the ethics after the inspiration or the power of the priesthood had become partially or entirely lost. The priesthood does not necessarily constitute the church, as the saints may live and breathe and be accepted of heaven without a living, authorized priesthood existing among them. The priesthood is a missionary body of men, who have very little to do with the saints, but much more to do with the world. The priesthood builds up the church by material converted from the world, and in building up the church the priesthood performs its mission. The local priesthood which presides in the congregation has done immensely more harm than good, when it forgot its missionary work and made custom-house officials of themselves, mixing themselves in all individual movements, and much worse, when they acted as spies in the sacred private affairs of the saints' families and members of the congregation.

The world may be depending on the priesthood for its salvation from darkness to light, but the church is hidden up in the wounds of the Lamb who was slain, and do not need any shelter but that which is in his love, and is not the servant of a priesthood. It most assuredly has been a great blessing to the world in building up the church, but it has been a great curse to the church in persecuting and destroying that freedom of the spirit which is in the Order of Messiah. The finite mind of the saints has always reverenced the priesthood on earth, and the political power of the world was ever ready to captivate it, and the priesthood became the formidable enemy to the spirit of the Church of the Lamb, who was slain for the sake of the truth which the priesthood in its depraved spirit sold for coin and with the kiss of the betrayer, and for the gain and aggrandizement of titles and power borrowed from kings and rulers upon earth.

Whenever the priesthood monopolized the ordinances of the church as a world's institution for gain's sake, then the priesthood fell as low as Lucifer ever fell, and it became only a rattle, sounding its own shame of imposition played on the credulity of man. Such has been the fact all through the dark ages of non-inspired Christianity with a non-inspired priesthood.

Man is mainly positive to the world of senses, and negative to the world of spiritual intuition. The senses are mistaken for the real conductors to the interior life, and that which is the real life—the interior of man's soul—is mistaken for something next to nothing; because the external life of nature makes man less intuitive to his real life—his real power of spirit-life. As long as a man moves in certain conditions, this reality is very difficult to convince him of, as it manifests itself to his interior life, but in a contradiction to the world of his senses, or to the external conditions which his sensual life teaches him is the reality of existence. For this reason the inspired priesthood has always failed to remain inspired, and mistaken the exterior life for the interior identity, and thus has humanity been swindled out of the true life—that which gives light to every man, and is the pearl of all spiritual knowledge. My children, pray always in your soul, and let your life be a continued flow of prayers in the spirit of truth, that you may abide in God and God in you. Amen.

Message from Jeshuah, the Messiah.

Sin, Sickness and Riches.

Hyde's Park, Iowa, May 25, 1883.

There is sickness for which thou shalt pray, and sickness for which thou shalt not pray. There are sicknesses of disorganization and dissolution of those who are marked by the finger of God, by the eternal law of destination to depart from earth-life, and you shall not pray for those, as your prayers shall not be heard. There are sins for which you shall not pray, as your prayers will not be heard, because remission of sins is simultaneous with repentance from sins, or convictions about sins in the conception of the spirit of God. Sins are not the collision with a code of commandments outside of yourselves, or only written on tables of stone. Such, however, was to a great extent the idea concerning sin among ancient Israel, but sin is the antagonizing force of your soul's welfare, your body's well-being, and in your own perception of right and wrong in the code of your brains' highest conceptions about truth and true living, and in its relations to your fellow-beings. Sin is the violation in your soul's judgment, and against the spirit of God, and against the voice of the spirit of truth within yourselves, and the collision in your lives with His spirit of love toward yourselves, and toward others of your neighbors.

In the letter the law was written in stone, in the spirit it is written by the spirit of God in your hearts and souls. If a man or a woman is aware of that fact, then it is my will that you shall pray for any such man or woman, that strength and power may be given to overcome evil by, and your spiritual guides and guardian angels will step in and support such persons, and you shall with the united strength from above, pray for them, and my spirit shall bear testimony to every such person, and what I have made clean shall no person make sin, or call unclean, because I am the Lord thy God, and will justify sinners by the spirit of my judgment, and not according to the letter, for the everlasting life shall be found in the spirit, and not in the letter of my commandment; therefore be not confounded when you read the Scripture which bears testimony about the Spirit, but believe in me and believe in God, and come to the fountain of life and inspiration, and the Spirit of truth shall teach you all things and make you read the mind of God your Father, who can give you only and alone the power to keep all his commandments, being justified not by works of your own doing, but by His grace, who gives you the power and wrought the marvelous happiness in your soul, by him who sends you the greetings of the Father and does the wondrous work, even Jesus the Messiah, the mediator and your eternal friend; therefore serve God first in the spirit of your souls, mated with the Holy Spirit, and you shall do the works of the Holy Ghost, and when you see my disciples hungry, and thirsty, and naked, and forsaken, and lonely and despised, and in prison and an outcast among men, and persecuted and on the gallows, and spoken evil against of all men, then recollect that even a drop of water, and a word of comfort, or money given or lent or forwarded in my name shall I repay to you over and over in the eternal worlds, when done in my name and on my account, and charged to me because he or she was my disciple. Do even so good to an infidel and a hater of all truth, because also such a person is a human soul, and your fellow-being, and you may charge any of such service done in my name, to my account, and you shall certainly never lose your reward, neither in this world nor in the world to come. Be therefore filled with charity, as by that have angels followed many funerals, and been seen by the righteous' graves, and by that has honor been paid to thousands when in glory they entered the eternal habitations of friends in heaven. Be in hope; remain in the faith of the faithful, but live in the spirit of charity, which is the spirit of love, which is in the spirit of God, not only that to be justified by, but to be made rich by, even the richest among the rich in the spirit to possess the wealth of God. Amen.

MESSAGE FROM MOHAMMED, THE PROPHET.

INDEPENDENCE, Mo., August 24, 1882.

Be not moved by the external things, but by the internal. Let the external things come as they can or will come, but obey the Spirit, and it will guide you, and tell you of all danger, and give you a victory over the external affairs in life.

You are all safe—there is no danger. All will come to you in obedience to your control who has the power to reorganize society, even among the Arabs. I am in prayer for you, that Allah will protect you, and you must go on and not be afraid, nor grieved over any want of success, as it is God's work and not the work of man. Strife has commenced among my people; they have been fighting, not knowing their right hand from their left, and not seeing the consequences, as they are in poverty, and may be overpowered by the modern mode of warfare.

Peace be with you—I loved the day when you approached the earth. Peace be with you, and Allah bless your soul once in paradise. Amen.

MESSAGE FROM JESHUAH, THE MESSIAH.

TRUTH.

TERRE HAUTE, INDIANA, June 15, 1882.

To be the truth is not to be in prostitution of your own selfhood, but to be yourself harmonious in your interior consciousness or inner life, exactly as you are wedded with an eagerness to know yourselves, and progress in the spirit of that knowledge. That is a spirit of prostitution of yourselves, or a prostitution of your own soul-life, when it is exposed before the public, before other men and women, as a prostitute exposes to all who pay her for the fountain of her life, and makes the truth of her being to be a living falsehood—not as much for the man who embraces her, as she makes her own life to be a falsehood. Even so in the prostitution of our soul-life—it makes a person no better, but worse. It promotes no progression, but retrogression, as the world is moving in darkness, or on the bottom of an interior hell of discord, which comes from lack of desire for spiritual progression, and in spite of all social development keeps the bulk of the race in mental and spiritual falsehoods, which is nothing else in the sight of the hosts of heaven and its angels and progressive spirits; therefore truth, and that to be the truth, is not to be a confession made to priests, or man, or woman, nor to performing a penance, as truth does no penance, nor is in any penance, but is only the mathematical, most intense, earnest conception of that consequence, which is your life, and is the deep conviction and honest perception of its ultimate result; that interior and deep-founded desire to solve the problem or knot of life into a more elevated condition, and to be what you are to yourself in the sight of the eternal worlds without fear for your inner consciousness, that is, to be reconciled with yourself and the God principle, TRUTH. That to be the truth in one's life and conduct is the perfect assimilation of our mind's highest conception of truth, and the spirit of truth manifested into the world, and personified in flesh and blood, or in men and women in the intensity of their affections. It matters not whether you are a fool or a sage, a boy or a girl, ignorant or filled with knowledge, you are all embodied in the world, representing the same principle in various degrees, pursuing and seeking to attain harmony in your most interior conscience, which is the highest conception, if not perception, of truth or God, who is the truth in the intensity of love. This conception is more clear, or distinct, or perfect, in the perception of one individual than in another, but the principle is omnipresent, whether it be in the acute perception of an archangel, or in the blunt stupor of a Hottentot's mind, either can only conceive or perceive that much about God and truth which his brain capacity allows him to, as he has been prepared to receive by spirit guide or control, or by the guardian angels' impressions, and his own capability of receiving it by reflection and perception of mind. It will invariably express itself in the external life, but truth lives and breathes in an interior condition of the soul, which emanates from the interior fountain of God, and is not derived nor lived only from any exterior circumstance or thing.

Mathematics is the order of the universe and the attribute of the invisible force and intelligence which permeates all creation. The divine Architect expresses the exact science of truth of His own mind in the principle of evolution with the most mathematical accuracy, as it is revealed in astronomy, and the same truth manifests itself in the smallest microcosm. When we speak about the divine intelligence in the highest sense, where he ceases to be comprehensible to the human brain, or to be understood in any personal conception of the human mind; then you can only bow down your souls in reverence to the eternal governing principle, or what you call the eternal.

MESSAGES.

At Temple Block, Independence, Mo., December 29, 1882, 12 m.

I have overshadowed this spot with my glory.

Jesus.

Thou shalt not desire any more messages here before the Lord comes in his glory. This spot is holy, where sinners tremble and depart, and here shall be salvation from bondage to freedom, being the Gospel of Freedom to all nations.

Moroni.

When Shiloh comes, he will draw all nations to this spot.

Simon Peter, the Apostle.

You have not yet seen me in the glory with which I shall appear at this mountain of the Most High in Zion.

Michael.

Tell my son Joseph, that I am with him in my heart and soul. Tell John Taylor, in Utah, my fellow-prisoner at Carthage, that I am sorry that he does not stand by you as a partaker in the same union, peace and freedom. Amen.

JOSEPH SMITH.

The law of love shall issue from Independence, Mo., or Zion. Look, and be never more firm. You see with your natural eyes that landscape before you, which you saw with your spiritual eyes in 1868.

MORONI.

I am by you. God bless you! Harald, your brother, wants to see you before he dies. Go to Paola, Kansas.

OLE FAGERSTJERNA.

We will greet you here in the future as the Prophet of the Lord.

YOUR MOTHER.

Let your inheritance be here in the neighborhood, and buy a residence as soon as possible.

YOUR SISTER OLINE.

I am now the last, who was once the first. My tears are your guides, that you may not succumb to the world's artful foe, but be victorious. The Lord be your strength forever, and He cannot fail if you remain in Him and He in you. Amen.

BRIGHAM YOUNG.

Words from Joseph the Seer.

OAKLAND, CAL., July 28, 1886, 9 A. M.

Please tell my son Joseph, that I am by you in harmony, and I shall never forget his own mother's words to me when I saw her in the spirit world. She said: "Joseph is taking your place on earth," but I answered, yes, he has atoned with my enemies, and it is all right. He will some day know that the world is an angry friend, and a church in the world is no safe treasure. This is all. Send him my message I gave you long ago.

JOSEPH SMITH.

From Michael the Archangel.

CONCERNING LOVE.

HYDE'S PARK, IOWA, March 16, 1882.

Not because you do God a service have you received the commandments from Sinai, and in keeping these you have not honored him, but yourselves. They are given for your benefit and not His, as He is not affected by your misfortunes, nor can He get in debt to man, because man benefits himself by doing His will.

I am with you this morning. What you receive is from Michael, or the presiding Archangel. I have to tell you something, and it is, remain in God, and God in you, or remain in His love, which is in God, and let that love, which is His Holy Spirit guide you, and that is the keeping of all the commandments. You will, in other words, be guided step by step to obey the laws of health, or right living of life, for sin is the fruit of discord, and not of harmony. Sin can only be defined by the Spirit of God, which has in the commandments defined the outlines, but not its exceptions, nor its spiritual application to the code of existence. Every one of you that is born once out of water by your natural birth, and is born of the spirit by your spiritual birth, shall have the power to understand the mysteries of the spirit of heaven.

This is for your consideration and salvation, as to be saved is to be set free from thraldom or slavery and destruction which comes from humiliation or degradation of the human dignity, which is being in the image of Jehovah. The Gospel of Freedom will be understood by a few people of this generation, and they will carry it to all people and tongues, or nations and kindreds on the earth. It is: that ye are born of Love, and that ye remain in the Holy Spirit of Truth, and if you live it, you are controlled by that Spirit, and your guardian spirit shall be a messenger of truth, which shall abide with you, and your life is not in the spirit of sin.

In that you understand your mental sphere and moral code of existence, and in that consists our love to Him, or in other words His love burning in our spirit that we keep His commandments, and that it is His greatest and the fulness of all commandments that we love one another in His love. Therefore be of good cheer and be not discouraged, but be perfect as your Heavenly Father is perfect, by having His spirit of perfection resting upon you in the holiness of His love, in which there is no sin, that you may be holy as He is holy, and remain His messengers in the glittering armour of heaven. Amen.

MESSAGE FROM JESHUAH, THE MESSIAH.

THE MESSENGERS.

INDEPENDENCE, Mo., April 1, 1882.

Do not believe that those whom I have called to the local priesthood are the men whom I will send to preach new truths or progressive ideas to the people, for I say to you that they are not the humble instruments for my voice; if it please me to do so, I will raise up a virgin to do my work, and you shall listen to her as to Deborah, and I will raise up a man from among you as I did Habakkuk, and as I did Jeremiah and Zachariah, and as I did Amos, and I will call a David the shepherd from his work, and a Saul from his plowing, and I will work with instruments attuned to my spirit, and not according to the wisdom of men, nor according to the desires of flesh and blood, but according to the will of my Father who is in heaven. Therefore wonder not, but lift up your heads and rejoice, because the time of redemption from error to truth is at hand. Amen.

I will confound the wise men on earth with those they counted to be fools, but who became wise in my Spirit. I will sustain them on the battlefields as I sustained David and Cromwell, and as I sustained Joshua and Washington, when they fought in the darkest hours of their nations the battle for light, liberty and progression. My ways are not the ways of man, nor can man know my wisdom, but my Spirit will break down the barricades made by man, and I shall walk as the cyclone does over all its obstructions. Amen.

MESSAGE FROM JESHUAH, THE MESSIAH.

CONCERNING BAPTISM.

HYDE'S PARK, IOWA, December 14, 1882.

Baptism is only one baptism, and cannot be otherwise than one act, done once and for life, and only to be counted one, as Messiah is one. When a person is baptised into the covenant he makes with God by that act, then God's promises stand forever, as He is faithful and cannot fail in His grace given to the person, and his baptism is forever and lasts eternally. If it was of man it would need to be repeated as man fails, but it is of God, and He does not fail, so what He does is done forever and lasts eternally. For that reason there shall be no re-baptism, as such an act is a weakness in man, and is not of God, but has hitherto been allowed on account of the weakness of man, but it is not of the Lord, nor because He is not faithful in his promises. If it was not because man had lost the fullness of his faith in the everlasting work of God, baptism should only have been executed but once in any person's life and never repeated.

Anointings, and salvings, and spongings, and washing of feet are all symbols belonging to the temple, and will be repeated. They are not baptism, but only signs of purity before me, says the Lord.

Therefore the Saints shall not repeat the ordinance of baptism. When once done in the Lord, it shall be considered done, as any repetition of baptism in the church shall henceforth be as a blasphemy in my sight, says the Lord. Persons who are guilty of such an act shall be weak both in body and soul, because they have no faith to live on, nor faith in the promises of God to keep them from evil. The password for all such persons is : repent and return to your first love, and stand in your first place, and have not little faith, or the light which is in you shall go out, and you shall be in darkness ; and if you live in the first love you will be doing the work of that love, which you have always to return to, and remain in, that you may go forth and follow after me, and the Spirit of my Father shall dwell by you. Amen.

When the world speaks about baptism, it considers it to be an immersion in water or a sprinkling by water for the purpose of giving a name to a person, as though it required some church ceremony to give a name to a child. Baptism, however, is a symbolic emblem, and as old as the world, for water has always been an element necessary for cleanliness; even the lowest among animals love it and bathe in it with delight. Therefore wonder not that it was used as a symbol of a new birth, or of a new phase of life, as to be born from the water in the womb of the mother. The Greek and Latin nations, as the Jews, baptised new-born children by immersion and named them. Also was the same act done by the Scandinavian, Teutonic, Frankic and Slavonic nations. In fact it was a universal custom among the heathen to baptise the new-born child. Why was it?

The Greek, the Roman, the Frank, the Briton, the Teuton, and the Scandinavian, in common with the Jews, sprinkled or baptised children by immersion, because all sprang from the same origin, and lived by a perverted gospel. * It was a heathen and not a christian custom. It was a family celebration, and when the Christian sprinkling or immersion of children took the same method of naming the children, the symbol became a heathen usage of paganism restored in the church under the christian name. There was no difference, and perversion permeated the ancient church.

It is written in the scriptures that I said, "Suffer little children to come unto me," as the spirit of a child is in the spirit of the Holy Ghost, but such do not need baptism before that spirit of the child is lost by sin, as the Gospel baptism is for sinners and not to name children by. Baptism would not, and could not, make children better than they are, holy from nature's womb and in the spirit of nature, until the love of my Father shall draw them to me, for no one can come to me, except it is given him from above. When the Hindoo, the Brahmin or the Chinese immerse the child and call it by name, they do not suppose that they have performed any miracle, or wrought any wonderful change in the child, nor do they combine any such idea with the act. It is only a family custom of religious ethics. Otherwise with Christianity which believes in the baptism of children, it retains the pagan spirit and mode of performance, but calls it a sacrament, and attaches to it the most wonderful manifestations of the Spirit to be wrought in the interior soul-life of the child, where, however, no condition exists for the supposed change to be based upon, as the child is undeveloped in its nature, with only possibilities to receive by, and has not arrived at any conscious conception about sin, or the differences between good and evil, which has to prelude all baptism in the Holy Ghost.

Another essential point belonging to the blood of Israel is, that baptism does not belong as an ordinance to the world, but to the promises given to Abraham, or to mine elect in his seed, or in the spirit of his blood, and the spiritual truth must be a fruit of the Spirit and the conscious life in man and woman, or it can be attached to nothing in earth-life as a gift of God's grace from above, and it would be no improvement in the spirit of human progression simply to make a change of name, as has been done by calling paganism Christianity, and ancient heathen customs a sacred observance by sprinkling children by the millions, and by such an act suppose to convert the world to me, when man is not drawn individually to me by the Spirit of my Father, as the only means by which redemption can come to man. Therefore with the four hundred millions of professed Christians on the earth, the Son of Man is looking on the multitude and the Spirit bears testimony in Him about the fallen condition of Christianity, when from His elevated position He can only have reason to repeat what He once said while in the vicinity of Jerusalem : " Shall the Son of Man find faith on the earth in His second coming?" He may find a belief in many, as the acceptance of His mission, but the faith in God is the life of God in man, and the Spirit of God in the unity with the spirit of man, and constitute a life of an actual existence in God and God in man, which cannot be cemented together by a simple acceptance following a belief, but is wrought in man by the intensity of God's love to man, and to the law above all laws, or the new commandment, manifested to the world in the Messiah

To be baptised into that life is the engagement of the soul with God as a bride with a bridegroom, and as it is no child's work to be married on earth, also it is no child's work to be engaged with heaven. Blessed are those who hear the truth and receive it, and blessed are those who in the living faith of God come to me, because they are drawn to me by the Spirit of my Father, and in His love. For such is baptism by immersion into the water in my name, that they may be born of the Spirit, in which there is no evil, and understand the goodness of God, and live it in His love forever and forever. Amen.

MESSAGE FROM JESHUAH, THE MESSIAH.

CONCERNING JOSEPH SMITH, OF LAMONI.

SALT LAKE CITY, UTAH, Sept. 25, 1882, 12 M.

Concerning Joseph Smith, of Lamoni : I have given him power to go out into the world and preach the Gospel of life and salvation from error to truth, and from darkness to light for all people. In doing that he shall fulfil my words to him. For that purpose I have called on him.

I have called on you for another purpose, that of receiving the introductory principles of the Gospel of Heaven in its perfection into the Gospel of Freedom on earth. Do the work and be blessed. Call on my servants in that work that you are about to publish, and make them understand that my presence is now at hand, when I shall eat the Easter supper with them in my Father's kingdom on earth, and it shall be said in glory what I exclaimed in pain and agony and death on the cross ; "It is finished !" Amen.

I speak to you concerning my servant Joseph Smith, of Lamoni. I have given him the power to go forth and preach the Gospel, but I have not given him the power to conquer the church in Utah. In that he has failed. He has prayed that he might prevail against my people among the Rocky Mountains, but I will give him the final victory for his father's sake. I will bless his sons in many generations, and his people shall go forth and build up Zion, for the sayings of the prophets must be fulfilled. And I will bless those who bless him, and I will curse those who curse him, and I will not allow his enemies to prevail against him.

A great many people shall come together under the Gospel of Freedom, and build up the Temple structure at Independence, not because I need it for heaven's sake, but because it is needed on earth and for earthly purposes and considerations, by which heaven shall have its connecting links with mankind on earth. At that time shall the different churches belonging to Mormonism, and many others joining in with them, work on the Temple, and the Utah branch of the great coming movement shall not be too proud, but more than willing to send its working men's legation and deputation of the priesthood, and they shall go with joy on their heads, and with everlasting songs, and walk into the city of Independence. It is only a little while and priestcraft, and bigotry, and stubborn ignorance shall be taken away from earth, and that which was considered very wise in conduct and manners shall reveal its own interior rottenness, and the High Priesthood shall be low and humble in its own estimation, and be the servant's servant, and not any longer obstruct or barricade the ways of God. They have done much wrong, and are doing evil to-day, and will not understand what they are doing, until their stubborn course and the consequences of their obstinate proceedings compel them to understand.

You have asked me about the singing at the Tabernacle, and I will answer you. Let it be as it is in Salt Lake City. The people who assemble there do not know any better, nor do their minds aspire any higher; but let it not be a rule for my people to follow their example in singing as it is conducted at their religious services. There is no blame in having a good organ, and a good choir, and a good stand, and artistic singing, and instruments of music and other means by which song can be made impressive ; but when such service takes the song away from the congregation and makes the hymn books useless, and deprives the worshipers of their devotion, and makes them more of listening statues than partakers of the singing, then the Spirit of God departs from such heartless proceedings, and it becomes more or less idolatry in song. The people need less art and more truth ; less art because the Spirit which has been resting on them is more than art, and the lack of the Spirit has made their supplications to be like a sounding bell or a tinkling cymbal. The heart and the soul must follow the song, and the meaning of the song, or it will amount to nothing, and will be of no benefit to yourselves or to others, as you cannot be inspired by the instrument, but by the spirit of its tunes and in the spirit of God you rejoice in God.

There is a power in using a musical instrument, a power in poetical beauty and sentiment. There is also a power in the studied sermon, and art of rhetoric and logic in speaking, a power in ethics and moral persuasion, but it is not yet that spirit in which God the Almighty can be communed with. One grand step further on in the realms of that infinite love which moves men's hearts into the intensity of sincere attachment, that commences the religious development in men, which is not of the world, nor by the world, but by the inspiration of God in man and from heaven, and that most sincere Spirit of truth is God in truth, as it is written, thou shalt love God with all thy heart, and with all thy strength, because the Lord thy God is a jealous God, and thou shalt not have any other gods before Him, neither in heaven nor on the earth ; therefore your song is of no vital benefit, nor evidence of sincerity in praise except as you truly worship in singing in your heart's praises before Jehovah your God. So let everywhere and always the congregation keep their hymn books before them, and follow word by word with their own voices the music and the choir, and let it be done as an offering and a pleasant incense ascending before the holy angels by you, and before the throne of God, that the spirit of prophecy may rest on you, and the gift of tongues and interpretations may burst upon you, and the gifts of angels, and seeing and hearing, and discerning of spirits may be given to you, followed by the unutterable peace from your Father who is in heaven.

Surely I say unto you, if you do not obey the laws by which

blessings can be obtained and reach you, how can you complain that you are poor and deserted by angels and gifts and God, and be justified in your complaint, for I was poor and you gave me no bread, says a brother, but it is far better to learn the law of prosperity and say, I became rich and I fed and clothed the beggar. Therefore do not depart from the laws of life in your religious service, let the tongue be married to the spirit of inspiration, whether it be in preaching or in singing or in conversation, and you shall have abundance of life and life-giving power, by which to convert the world ; otherwise you shall work in vain, and your religion and your hope shall be in vain ; therefore rejoice if you understand my words, and follow after me in living the words and laws of eternal life. Amen.

MESSAGE FROM THE HOLY GHOST.

SAN FRANCISCO, CAL., March 11, 1884, 10-11 A. M.

Even so, says the Spirit to you—the Holy Spirit of God—the Spirit of the Church of God—the witness about the Father and the Son to all mankind—the true witness left in the church to govern by the power and gifts of God, and in harmony with legions of holy angels to work in the Spirit to bless and instruct man, and do the work of the Father and the Son, blessed in all eternity in one unity with the Spirit. Amen.

Be diligent. Do your work, and receive the pillar of light, which descends from heaven above, to give light to the saints, and by them to all mankind on earth. Amen. I am not He who comes to you and is by you, who hang on the tree at Golgotha. I was in eternity, and am of heaven in eternity, and before this solar system came out from its nebular condition and I was before the worlds you know about, and even before your sun moved on as an immense ball of gases, and was seen from the stars of eternity as a center-moving nebulæ. I am not the Father, but I was even before the Father, and was with Him and by Him in eternity. Here is wisdom, but as heaven is superior to earth, also is the knowledge of the Spirit superior to that of man.

I am the one who was before the beginning, and from the beginning, and am one with Him who was the beginning of life in its organization on this earth. He was the life, whom you slew and hung on a cross. I am not He, but I was with Him in that life He had from the beginning or from eternity. He was born of the Father in eternity, and by me, who was by his eternal conception in heaven and upon earth. He was born of a woman on earth, and of the Father in eternity, and conceived of both by the Holy Ghost, or the Spirit of eternity, whom I am. The Father is, that He is, and the Son is I am that I am, or in His mission to earth, also the Father and the Spirit combined in the person of Messiah. I am that I am, even as the Father is the Jehovah, and the Ruler of the nations in the capacity of being the Ancient of Days, He is also the Patriarch of heaven, and by the Spirit the expounder of the wisdom in heaven and on the earth.

The seraphims and archangels worship the eternal principle of truth before His face, saying: Holy, holy, holy art thou who governs supremely, through all eternity, thou Spirit filling the depths of all eternity, and when the Father worships, then the seraphs hide their faces from the intense glory of light which surrounds Him. The Elohims praise His name who governs from generation to generation, and when the Elohims, who are holy angels raised into glory of the celestial worlds, form rings or circles of worship, they dance and sing praises together, and the archangels sing, Amen! Glory, glory and glory forever and forever, because the Most High God has revealed Himself from the eternal depths with the eternal wisdom and given to you His testimony by the Spirit of truth, even that which burns in your bosoms as the fire of His love, so that testimoney may be sealed which the eternal witness, the Spirit of truth, has given to earth by his messengers, that we are of the truth even as we are born of the truth. Amen.

This truth which lasts forever was made flesh, and rejected of man on earth, but is borne witness of by me to all the generations on earth, even as it is known in heaven. This is the last witness coming that you have now amongst you before the prophet comes, the messenger who shall dash the earth, and there shall be none to stand on it without fear, but those who are willing to accept the testimony of God, and they shall live by the Spirit of truth, when pestilence, and wars, and earthquakes shall bring death and consternation upon earth; and the air you breathe shall be changed, and human bodies shall turn black, and shrink up, and die off, and be cast into graves by the hundreds and thousands, on account of chemical changes in the air, and in the water you drink, and in the food you eat. Only those who have the Spirit of God shall be strong to live through all that misery, and the Holy Spirit shall preserve them, and the holy messengers of truth shall guide them, and they shall have the power to overcome sickness and death, and be saved at appointed homes dedicated and prepared for their redemption. The spirit of man must be in truth, and in a sincere honesty and love for the truth, that he may be wedded to the truth. He must be truth itself manifested in flesh to be received by the Holy Ghost, who is the spiritual redeemer from the world, and in the church, and the true witness in the soul of every saint. Therefore was Jesus the redeemer manifested in the flesh, that the spiritual redeemer could be manifested in the spirit, and redemption could come to mankind from the day his work on earth was finished, when he was lifted above the earth in his triumph over death. From that moment has the Spirit or Holy Ghost been the personage which has wielded the governing power in the church, so that those who took upon themselves the name of Christ should not be left alone, but they should by me be one with God, as I am one with him, and one with the Messiah.

The Catholic Church has in the mother of Jesus, or "the Mother of God," found a kind of substitute for a bodily representative on earth of the Holy Ghost. However, the church has failed by making her the spokesman before the Father, for the Holy Ghost speaks from the hearts of all the saints, and he cannot be represented or substituted by any other person, or by any other power but his own, nor is any other power necessary to perfect the government of the Godhead. He is the Ruler in the Spirit, and the infusion of the Spirit. You have read about Jesus being born in eternity of the Father, and on earth by a woman as the Father's only begotten son, and by his birth in eternity called the Son of Man, and as such he was seen in the clouds of heaven coming with the host of hosts of the angels in heaven. The Father was perfected by the Spirit until he became an eternal being of eternity, or man in man, equally blended in soul and body into the great spiritual unity of two in one, and one in two, which is the perfection of love. Therefore be ye perfect even as your Father in Heaven is perfect, which is the perfection of God perfected in man, by which perfection he possesses and exercises both natures into one spiritual power of perfection, which is man in nature of God. The Father was perfected in eternity by the Holy Spirit, and the Holy Spirit was perfected by the Father into the feminine element of the Godhead, and the Father unto his masculine power and perfection, until the Father in eternity gave birth by will to the son, which was before the beginning of the earth, and He was born before your days were on earth, also before time, and in eternity. He thus became the redeemer of the creation before it existed except in chaos, and before it moved into evolution by His eternal power. As He was the beginning, also is it His mission to be the first and the last, and the Father has given all things into His hands, because all things were made by Him, He being the cause of the creation by which all evolution was put into motion in eternity before the days existed on earth. His birth in eternity was the cause of the life, and the heat and motion, and the eternal wisdom was born in matter, or embodied in Him, and He became the motive power in the immense solar nebulæ, and caused the existence and development, one after the other, of all the planets that emanated from the sun, and the moons again from the planets by the same process, and balance of the masses and distance in the solar system. This process became a necessity by His birth in eternity of the Father and by the Spirit, being the contrary condition to that on earth, where He was born in the flesh of a woman, and manifested in the spirit as the Messiah. God became manifested in flesh and blood of sinful man, and the Savior is the link between heaven and earth. This is the great mystery of the creation, that the birth of the Son of Man in eternity precluded the necessity of the creation, and evolution or emanation of the entire solar system from the immense nebulæ of the eastern hemisphere of the universe, and that one by one the planets were circled in rings and broken into existence, and rolled forth as from a process from yesterday. When your young globe, the earth, came into light, it was hailed by myriads of angels.

A nebulæ is not the fundamental stof of matter. It is emanated from mind in several hundred processes of atoms before a nebulæ becomes visible, or is observed on the retina of a human eye. When the divine intelligence by the laws of chemical condensation, friction and heat, moved the center of the large nebulæ, from which your centre solar system sprang into existence, the radius from center to circumference was five thousand times longer than from the present center of the sun and to its most remote planet, or it extended to the outer planet which encircles the sun Sirius. Man has not yet discovered the microscopic development from pictures taken of the heavens by photography. The telescope will not be able even in its most profound development to answer the questions of science to astronomy There is a *modus operandi* by which the smallest object on a fixed star can be found, observed as retained on the negative, and seen by adapted microscopes sufficiently intensified for the discovery.

The world of thousands of suns, which can be caught a glimpse of by its rays of light on the human retina, is only transitory developments in its evolution, and not to be compared in beauty and grandeur to the invisible worlds of spiritualized matter not intelligible to be observed on the retina, but only known to the perception of the seer. All the suns and planets derived or born from the universal centre sun, have been created by the same process of evolution from nebular atoms by an endless process of changes constantly emanating from the active principle of that love which fills all eternity with its intelligence and spirit power. As space and time is infinite, neither of them exist except for the finite human misconception, as nothing of that which is of eternity can be measured, but in a finite sense of acceptation both time and space exist as a measurement of man and according to this comprehension. Therefore is the term eternity used as a more exact equivalent for both time and space in its eternal sense where the Ancient of Days rules, as for him one thousand years are as one day, and with no difference to him, and the earth shakes for the spirit of his presence and power when he enters the air, and with the touch of His finger Sinai smoked in a constant fire and thunder, and His voice was heard of the Jewish congregation speaking from the cloud.

The wisdom of God acts upon the elements emanated from his love, and the evolution of things is the consequence. There is only one process, and one God, and one principle throughout the entire universe. Every globe has its cause or Spirit of the Godhead, its wisdom or organizer, and spirit infusion from the infinite principle of eternity and its redeemer, who was. the organiser by the eternal wisdom, and became the savior by the infusion of spirit-light from the heavens into a personal manifestation of God in the flesh and blood of man. The second epoch of the Messiah principle is the second personal and materialized appearance of the first suffering, but now spiritually triumphant Savior.

The mission of the Holy Ghost in the world is in the world of Spirits as on earth on an intellectual plane, and he is united with the intelligences from the other planets as with those living upon this planet, and he is the vital infusion throughout nature in harmony one with the spirit of nature, mentioned or discerned as such by the scientists and materialists of the world. When man discovers the laws and discerns the active principle in matter, the spirit is the operating force manifesting to science, as the spirit from which all is emanated, and the love from which all elements sprang in eternity.

The spirit subscribes to his own laws as a part of his being and in unity with the Godhead as one with the power of eternity always manifested as such, and only comprehensible to few of the spirit world, and few on earth. The Holy Ghost is the central power of the spiritual sun and its interior divine principle of wisdom and light, as of power and intelligence manifested to the worlds interior consciousness. To the church of Messiah his gifts are manifested, as to the order of Messiah leading into his kingdom in heaven and upon earth.

The Father is masculine in his first nature, and is a man in his duality, also is he perfected in his second nature in eternity by the feminine principle in the Godhead, or the Holy Ghost, until he became a man in a man, as a man by a woman equally blended, two in one and one in two into his duality of being a man, and he became I am that I am, I am, which is the perfection of man, or the spiritual bloom of the heavenly love of eternity, emerged into the baptism of the supreme spirit of eternity, or the principle and power of the universe. Also is the Holy Spirit perfected by the Father into the same oneness of a woman's purity, which is in his love, and by which the spirit loves him as a woman loves a man until the spirit became manifested in eternity like him, or become him, became a woman in a woman and manifested as a man to the world, symbolized in the purity of his love, as a dove descending with peace to the human mind. Therefore has the Holy Spirit a unity of nature, power and action with the Father from eternity, or before the entire solar system sprang from his love as the essence for its atoms. God's days are counted each a thousand of years on earth, and his year is fifty thousand of his days, and one rotation of the sun Kolob around his nearest fixed star or twenty thousand times larger sun, is done in fifty millions of years on earth.

In the hands of eternity is your sun as a snowball in the hands of a boy, and the entire earth is as a speck of dust floating in space, but be of good cheer, because even the animalcules in a drop of your water are counted, and there is nothing small and nothing great, and no life too small nor too great not to be accounted for of eternity from whence it came.

The Holy Spirit being a woman in his first nature was perfected in eternity, and before the world was in what you call loves interior creation, which is a formation or manifestation in the Spirit, and the Holy Ghost was perfected by the masculine element of love in the Father and into the feminine power of the duality of being a woman in fulness.

The perfection of the spirit into the Godhead is the perfection of a woman into her dual nature as woman, and in having conquered in the love of the father the masculine element in her nature, which by her love has been alienated in the masculine perfection of the Father and God. The Messiah is in the fulness of the Spirit resting upon him, but he is the father, and perfected as the Father is perfected in the duality of man in both natures, with the feminine element alienated in the bride, and with the fulness of the spirit resting upon her. In the union with the Father and the Son, the spirit is seen and recognized, and rendered worship in heaven as He will be on earth. This is the perfection of the eternal development, where the spirit as a woman is perfected by a man's love in the duality of being a woman, or into the Godhead as a feminine developed man, where the spiritual companionship is finished and outgrown into the perfection of individual intelligence. The duality in a man's nature of the father and mother principle, in the duality of both man and woman, is in the perfection emerged into one union of individuality of man in man. The duality becomes all man or all woman, but with no difference of nature in eternity, where the unity in the Spirit leaves behind as outgrown and lost sight of all sexual differences. Woman is perfected in her nature as woman, and man as man, but in the eternal world they are as God far above all the sexual differences, and therefore in their revelation to earth appear either as a masculine or feminine developed man, and can only be revealed as man. This is a higher law, where that sex principle of life, which governs the entire visible world and its interior spirit world, is outgrown with the human conception about marriage, and the spiritual perception about companionship. This knowledge is the last spiritual truth the spirit can convey to be meditated upon by the human brain, as in the eternal realms where the footprint of God is only seen no man can follow him.

Much has been said to mankind, and only very little has been understood, and for that reason have the churches reverenced the doctrine of the trinity of God as a great mystery, and refused any sensible explanation of it.

The Holy Spirit is the wisdom and power of the masculine element in the Godhead, alienated into a woman's love and affectionate nature, and perfected in her feminine development. The spirit's appearance is a woman's development in love, and in all the beauty of love, and spiritually a woman in a woman, or a feminine man, representing in every respect a man to earth, with much resemblance to the spiritual body of Jesus in the eternal worlds.

The son of the morning, or the ambitious and bright Lucifer, the archangel, was the first-born of the spirit by the will of the father, born of the Holy Spirit in the eternal realms, and as such not a person of the Godhead, but the first-born of the children of the light or the child of the morning glory. However he did not remain in the truth of love and wisdom, and in obedience to those principles of government by which the worlds are ruled, and he fell into self-love of his own beauty and greatness of offspring, and persuaded many spiritual brethren and sisters also to adopt another plan of government than laid down by the eternal father, on which exaltation and salvation should come to man on earth, and he fell into his own estate of egotism and worship of his own folly, and heaven wept and was shut up from his presence, and he became a world to himself in his own estate fallen away from the light of paradise. Lucifer and his hosts rebelled against the light, and in their ambition and self-love they denied the power of the light, and submission to it, for to be a power to themselves, such they fell into their own darkness of the perversion of principles and divine government and pride, and Lucifer was on earth in the freedom and power of his own individuality, and independence of the allegiance to the wisdom and love of the father, and it was early in the perfection of the development in the creation, when the earth rotated more perpendicular on its axis, and the climate was mild and serene, and as a garden of beauty from north to south. And there were men on earth in those days as giants, and the Mongolian race lived from pole to pole, and there was peace on earth.

Jehovah said, let us make man and woman after our own image, and engraft upon mankind a spiritual development that they may know God, and see him and walk with him, and be spiritual as the angels of heaven and man can walk with them. Jehovah made a trance come upon Adam and upon Eve, and the Holy Spirit rested upon them in its fulness when they awoke, and they saw Jehovah, and they praised him and offered him worship with the peace of paradise burning in their souls, and Adam recognized Eve in the love of the spirit as his companion, and he called her by Eve, or the new name as the mother of the life in his spirit, and Eve loved her mate in the love of the heavenly companionship, and she called him Adam, or the man of God. Therefore was the offspring of them called the children of God. Man lived in paradise, and lived by the fruit of their love and obedience to God's laws. In the garden of their happiness was also conditions by which they could collide with the glory of their life in committing sin, or emblematically eat of the tree of knowledge and transgress the divine code of their existence, and they became tempted in themselves to disobey the laws for their happiness in God's paradise.

When Adam and Eve were conceived in the image of God, their bodies became in a measure transfigured or spiritualized, and their yellow Hindoo skin became nearly white, and on condition of obedience they were promised immortality on earth, and an immortal offspring. The condition was to remain faithful to God and faithful to each other in humility to truth, love and wisdom. Lucifer appeared before Eve one morning in all his sparkling beauty, and tempted her to join the hosts of his angels or help him to establish his government on earth, based on an individual intelligence and independence of Jehovah, and not be led by the infusion of the Holy Spirit, or a new birth in the spirit. This last measure the archangel had opposed in heaven, and defended that man should never enter the spiritual presence of God before after death in the flesh, and his gradual development in the spirit world, and Lucifer had gained much power on earth.

The age of man on earth is about five hundred thousands of years, and during the earthly paradisiac estate of the globe, he lived from pole to pole because the climate was about equal all over the earth, and man corresponded in physical development to the present types of Negroes, Tartars and the Hindoo race. The antediluvian man suffered two trials to his existence. The first was the glacier periods, when the earth deviated from the perpendicular to the plane nearly thirty-six degrees, and ice covered northern and middle Europe and Asia, and much of North America, and men and animals suffered nearly extermination alike, and were either driven up north or south. The next epoch, fatal to man living in the belt south of the northern and melting glacier, especially in Mesopotamia and Minor Asia was the flood, coming as the consequence of the receding and fast passing off masses of ice, where an ocean of water had been bound up solid and floated with moisture the atmosphere.

The history about the creation, and the first man, and the fall of man, is as a tale to the children of Israel reported by

Moses and according to tradition, but it contains, taken as such, the truth.

Even as God raised up spiritual men on the continent of Asia, also did he raise up spiritual men on the continent of America, and the man of God, Adam, came to this continent and blessed his spiritual sons and daughters and their children in the valley of Adam ondi Ahman on the American continent. When the glaciers came all over the United States present territory, the people had a refuge in the present Mexico.

Lucifer had the most control of the races belonging to earth, as man lived according to his spirit and the spirit of the flesh, and without love, and in self-love, ambition, strife, revenge, anger, law-suits and warfare. There was no peace on earth except where regenerated and spiritual man was born by the Holy Spirit to be conscious about sin and repentance, and about righteousness and God's love, and judgment and God's will or displeasure with man. The birth of spiritual man by the spirit was the only light from paradise on earth, and when Adam fell from the glory of God the priesthood came as a compensation for paradise lost and not to be regained, except in the city of the New Jerusalem.

The animal nature of man is not in the image of God any more than the animal world can boast of being like God. Natural man cannot do the will of God before he has been quickened in himself about sin, and his entire being has been included under sin, that God may be able to justify man in himself according to his spirit. When God made man in his image, He gave him the Holy Ghost in proportion to the fulness man could receive, and man became born anew, or as it is said in Genesis, God blew the life into his nostrils, which were natural and of earth, but then became spiritual and of heaven. In such a manner is man to be redeemed, and return to the first cause of his being or to the redeemer, and the earth in her forsaken gloomy condition has to be redeemed into the glory of the sun from whence she came; also shall she be received of the sun, as he again shall be received by the sun Sirius, and he again of other suns of much greater magnitude. Upon the same principle shall the moon be received of the earth in her perfection, and follow her into the glory of the heavens and to a magnitude of splendor many times exceeding that of the sun. As men are greater than many suns, also shall your glory be in the presence of the Almighty God, as redemption is the ultimate result of all God's work.

In the new dispensation of the new light on earth were the first men and women born by the Spirit, and of the will of the Almighty, it became the mission of Lucifer to quench the spirit and blow out the light, which became blinded in the souls of men and women, and what he did on one continent he did on the other continents, until paradise was shut up and man was fallen away from living in its bliss, and the priesthood was the only glimpse of heaven retained, and when it also fell man was left in the dark and shed innocent blood, and killed the prophets and crucified the redeemer; but ye are confined to the history about the first spiritual parents in Asia.

By perversion of the truth did Lucifer succeed in destroying the inspirational element in man or the fruit of love between God and man, a life he lived in peace and harmony nourished from the tree of life, that he walked in the spirit with God in the garden at sunset, and spoke with him face to face.

God was Lucifer's eternal harmony, but he declared his independence of him personally to be an harmony to himself, which is impossible, as it was by God alone he could have carried out his harmony, and the consequence of his rebellion against his own greatest good was that he entered into discord and disharmony forever and forever.

This is the sin against the Holy Ghost and the spirit of murder came from Abel to Christ, and through all ages has the innocent blood of the saints crimsoned the earth by that spirit of perdition. However, so did God love the world, which is made by the essence of His love and emanated from His spirit, that He did not spare His only begotten Son, but gave him up for the salvation of the world, that as many as believed in him shall not be lost in perdition, but have the life eternally. The visible universe came into existence as the negative fruit of God's positive love, and as the love made the evolution of all things from that love, even so did His wisdom organize and redeem the world by love.

The lives of Adam and Eve were filled with the fruit of life, and God's love and light in the garden of paradise. This heirship to the household of God in the spirit of His love was not approved of by the adversary, and he acted upon woman's self-love and personal ambition to be of the world, and to be independent, and themselves sufficiently proud even as other men and women were, and not to be in degradation to their own selfhood or to be called imbecile and lunatic. He showed them also the practical knowledge about good and evil. She was delighted as she spoke to Lucifer in a vision, and as he could not any longer enter paradise, or the presence of the Holy Ghost, he lowered woman's mind down to his own estate, and came incognito and approached her in the likeness and cunningness of a serpent. Eve pondered on the words said by the serpent, and she spoke to Adam about her vision, and they rebelled both against the Holy Spirit of God, and imagined how much greater they would be both by being subject to their own personal knowledge and experience about good and evil, and how necessary it was to try the evil to be developed into the good fruit of life. Lucifer discarded the Spirit of God for the practical experience of life and its most demonstrative laws of existence, and he assured Eve that the plain ladder to reach perfection by was to be as God, and they declared themselves independent of God's guidance and wanted knowledge and experience, and they perverted their lives and lived contrary to the laws of the Spirit, and gave up to the passions and angers of the flesh and adulterated the freedom of the spirit to live innocent by, and they became jealous and bitter one against another, and they feared Jehovah as slaves, and they hid their presence before him, because the Spirit of His love was lost in their souls, and they became as devils full of accusations one against another, and Jehovah sealed the curse upon them even as they had put it upon themselves, and at Adam's control Michael the archangel appeared before them with a flaming sword in his hand by which he fought the serpent.

The spirit of paradise became lost to earth, and man became blessed by the priesthood, and ordinances, and dreams, and visions, and seership was given to Abel, but for that he suffered death because it did not come to Cain according to his birthright. The offspring of Cain became as other men and women, carnal and wilful, and selfish, and full of malice.

Jehovah sealed the curse upon Lucifer, even as he had brought it upon himself, and paradise was not any more on earth, when the fulness of the spirit had already departed from man. A curse was put upon the earth from that day, and it deviated much more rapidly from its perpendicular axis, and it became a cold and inhospitable globe, with many convulsions of nature, and ice covered the poles, and gradually the principal part of the known world became wintry, and ice covered all central Europe and all central United States, and only the equatorial belt of the earth was not covered with ice and snow, that the cradle of man should not be destroyed, nor the race be exterminated.

God bestowed the baptism and Messaic priesthood on Adam and his sons, and the redeemer spoke to them from a cloud and they were filled with fear, when he showed woman His hands and feet pierced and bleeding, and they saw Him in the likeness of a man. When Messiah laid the priesthood of the son of God upon Adam, he offered Him worship, and Messiah blessed him when He saw his humiliation, and spoke about His coming in the flesh in the fulness of time, and to woman He said : " Even as the serpent Lucifer has wounded thy heel, and taken away thy spiritual strength and freedom in God, also shall thou crush his head and power on earth, when the son of man shall in the flesh be born of a woman." On that day Adam built an altar and he and his sons commenced to pray verbally to God, and worship Him, and offered up sacrifices of burnt meat and fruit, as they did not any longer eat only fruit, and berries, and eggs, but they butchered animals and roasted the meat, and served it at their meals, and ate it at their feasts, and they became like other men and women subject to diseases, decay, and dissolution, and death. Also the sons of God married the daughters of men, and they led their men astray. When Abel was slain by the bloody hands of his brother, peace was taken away from Cain, because he converted his birthright to the priesthood into a curse, and he said trembling, " now every man who meets me from now will kill me," but the Lord told Cain to depart from the presence of his parents and never return again, but travel towards the east, and be received there of a great nation, and the Lord put a mark on Cain of horror and discord in his eyes and features, and the impress of his murdered brother's finger as he touched him in the death struggle, was seen as a bloody mark on the forehead, and the Lord said to him, whosoever kills Cain shall suffer seven fold for it. Also he went to Nod, the nation of the east, and married one of the king's daughters, and became a mighty man among that people, and built a city which was named after his son, the city of Enoch.

Adam and Eve had now no sons, but seven daughters, who married the sons of men, and some of them lost the true worship of God, and became wicked as the tribes of men were.

Therefore God blessed Adam and Eve in their old age, and Eve gave birth to Seth, and the Spirit of God rested upon him from birth, and he became the father of many sons and many daughters, and the offspring through Seth were called the children of God.

The light of paradisiac man vanished gradually into an interior consciousness of faith and knowledge about the paradise lost to the soul, and being shut off from the personal daily interview with Jehovah they became a world for themselves as the balance of humanity, except they were constantly drawn of the Spirit, because they were of the light and had rebelled against it, and fell back into their natural darkness and perversion of mind about the principles of the divine government on earth.

The seraphs wept over Lucifer when he departed from the spirit of truth, and the archangels wept over spiritual man when he departed from the tree of life and lost the light of heaven, because the angels had rejoiced over his spiritual birth on the central continent, which were in those days not two, but one country, as Asia and America were one land together. The sea was in those days confined to both poles, more than to the center of the earth, and land was a broad belt which surrounded the earth, and man could walk with dry feet all around the globe. The appearance of the earth was similar to that of Jupiter, only less in size and with belts around its equator. Adam preached the doctrine of light, and also did Seth and all who carried the Order of Messiah after him, and God raised up spiritual man all over earth, but many did not remain in the truth of the light. Eve humbled herself before the Lord when Seth was born, and she called him the precious gift of God, because he was born in the love of the holy companionship with the spirit resting upon him, and Adam said, " Now shall the Lord not take away entirely the light from the earth," because he saw a pillar of light descend and rest upon the head of Seth. Adam lived

meek hundreds of years on earth, and up to a very old age of
one of the Lord's days, or nearly a thousand years, and he visited
all parts of earth and ordained Seth with a holy power to be a
messenger of light after the Order of Messiah, or the order of the
son of God, and Adam visited the spiritual men all over earth, and
he called on the sons of God everywhere, and he visited a mighty
people living between the present China and California, where the
Pacific Ocean now is, and they received him, and he blessed them
with the order of the light. Millions of people lived there in
harmony and peace, and in high civilization and industry.
The country was low meadows and rolling land, very fertile, and
extended as far north as present Japan, and south nearly to a
line from Panama west, parallel with the equator. The inhabitants were nearly white, and very intellectual, and fine built
people. Adam visited twice that nation, and once on the present
American continent, where he built an altar and worshipped
with the sons and daughters of the light at Adam ondi Ahman,
in the present Missouri, and embraced the spiritual people on
the continent, and also Adamiahel and Ahmanah the prophets,
and they burnt offerings together, and kneeled and sung praises
together for the Almighty God. Then Adam arose and in the
spirit he prophesied about Zion on this land, and he blessed
them all, and they wept for joy when the spirit attended his
words, and fell upon the congregation with great power. Adam
was at that time over eight hundred years old, and as he blessed the
people he stood leaning on his staff, and his white silvery hair
fell over his shoulders and nearly to his waist. In the spirit he
foretold the rise and fall of the people that from time to time
should inhabit this American country, and the rise and fall of the
church of Messiah, or as he called it, "The church of the
Lamb," which Abel who was slain represented—the names Abel
and Agnes signifies symbolically "The Lamb,"—and second by
birth, he represented the church priesthood on earth. Also did
Adam speak about the restoration of the Order of Messiah or of
the sons of God in the fulness of the churches before the kingdom
of the son of man in his second coming. He also preached and
pictured the humiliation of Jesus on earth, and death on the cross
at his first advent, and said the Order of Messiah should surely be
taken away from earth when the light should be consumed by
darkness, and man should not walk by the sight of the spirit

any more, but by the faith of God given to earth and by the substituted priesthood after the order of the son of God. In the last days the Holy Spirit should visit the earth again, and the light of the Order, and power, and gifts could be spread amongst men, so the plans of Lucifer should be frustrated, and in the place of destroying the greater light in Adam and his posterity, they became the light-carriers to all the nations, with a holy spirit infusion to mankind. So Adam prophesied about the Order of the messengers of the Messiah as it was bestowed on him by the angels, when he and Eve were weeping together at the closed gate of paradise. The Order was only bestowed on the prophets among the sons and daughters of God. He spoke about the priesthood after the Son of God that had been given with the introductory principles to the message of light to all the earth, and how it gathered in the congregation of God upon earth. He said: "In the last days, and before the kingdom of the Most High God comes to govern on earth, shall the Order of Messiah be again amongst men, and the messengers of the most high shall visit all people. It shall be in the days when the church is restored by the priesthood called after the order of Messiah, although they are not the messengers of the order of Messiah." And Adam wept for joy and blessed all the people.

The Lord God put a division between the condition of life in the spirit of Adam and Eve and paradise, because the cherubims were not any longer serving angels from heaven to man, but were seen between paradise and the fallen condition of man, with flaming swords extending across the heavens, and such became the mission of the cherubim to man, that he should not inherit immortality in the flesh any more, but die in the body as the balance of humanity. Although death came upon man, immortality had been engrafted in the mortality of the bodies of both, and Adam and his offspring became very old. Adam lived to nine hundred and thirty years, and Eve to five hundred and forty years, and Cain to nine hundred years, and Seth to nine hundred and eighteen years, and so in proportion were their ages, because the gift of God vanished from their flesh only slowly through many generations, until the children of God became amalgamated with the children of men, and the average age became as that of all flesh, seven times ten, and very seldom more. Immortality of the flesh is therefore a possibility for man to reach into by the law of regeneration, and spiritually to have the blood changed to vita into a union with the immortal flesh in the Spirit of God which can never see corruption. That vitalizing influence is the infusion of vita or the fluid of God. It supplies waste and supports life, and makes disorganization an impossibility to occur in the body. Hence the body lasts forever, as much as the soul or the spiritual body does, because the spiritual body and the immortal flesh becomes one unity, and exactly the same thing in which there is no difference and no diversion to take place. This vita is the life of God in its essence of immortality and in communion with spiritualized matter, sustained as the negative substance in its oneness, with the positive force of the will of God or life everlasting.

Man could eat and be supported in his spiritual estate from the fruit of life, or vita from all of the trees, and all life served and sustained him in harmony with the laws of God for continued life upon the same principles as the angels live forever in God's paradise, but man could not sustain the passion of the flesh and blood, because the spirit was in the serum, and he could not in the passion of the blood remain in the society of angels. Adam and Eve could progress forever in paradise by the law of vita, but they could not be father and mother in the mortal blood and retain heaven and immortality, as the new birth was a heavenly birth, which they could preach of to all mankind, and gather into paradise their offspring who were born of them in the spirit into the same immortality of the flesh on earth.

Therefore the knowledge of good and evil came to them by the passion and knowledge of their sex, as by the desire of the blood the contention commenced, and they fell from their spiritual estate and became earthly, that they might continue their generations as other men and women on earth.

When they became transfigured from natural man, or from the dust of the earth into a spiritual estate in the image of God, then both forgot their sex, and they lived as the angels in heaven, and did not know that they were naked, as only guilt and not innocence knows of any shame. It was the beautiful and shining Lucifer that fascinated Eve's passion in a vision, and as he could not enter paradise personally nor pass the cherubims as an angel of the light, he possessed a Boa-serpent, and spoke to Eve as from out of the body of the serpent, and when he had convinced her by the truthfulness of the speech, she would be as God perfected by the law he is perfected by, and know good and evil in his wisdom, the woman believed him more than God. Lucifer omitted that the wisdom of God comes by obedience and in the love of God, and not from knowing good from evil, but he got power over her understanding and he materialized by the power of the vita in her, and he beguiled her and embraced her, and she became one in her passion with the spirit of Lucifer. Eve rejoiced in eating of the fruit, and thought it was a delightful fruit to get a knowledge which had been hidden from her, and she was filled with the joy of the passion and ran to Adam and persuaded him also to eat of it. The passion of Eve burning in the spirit of Lucifer called out the desire of the flesh in Adam, and he embraced Eve in the passion of the same spirit, and both ate together of the fruit of knowledge. Then it fell as a veil from their eyes, and they discovered that they were naked, and Eve was ashamed, and did not know how to cover up her nakedness.

The programme of heaven to engraft immortality in the flesh was lost. Man had descended back on the ladder into earth. The perfection of the heavenly love and law of companionship was broken asunder, and Adam and Eve returned into dust, or to natural man from whence they came. They became not perfected in love as the angels are, to become as God in the innocence and purity of embrace in His love, and by the will of the Holy Spirit, but they fell by the will of Lucifer into the passion of the flesh, and lost their estate in paradise, and harvested the promise given them to know about sin, and the understanding about good and evil. The ladder to heaven was broken asunder, but the generations of the sons and daughters of God in the flesh became a possibility.

The second spiritual man is the Messiah, and He bruised Lucifer's head, when he bruised the heel of the Messiah, and the ladder Jacob saw in his dream is by Israel restored to earth in the redemption of man. Amen.

The law of vita, or the fruit of the tree of life, became lost to man, and as he lost paradise he could not eat of that fruit any more, but became old by degrees and mortal. This law, which lays in all departments of existence, shall be given to earth again in the kingdom of Messiah, as you cannot enter the city of the

New Jerusalem in the Father's kingdom on earth except by that law.

The spirit world is as the world of man, not in harmony to the dealings of God with man personally, but only as a principle and in a cosmopolitan manner, and it is an obscurity to millions of spirits as to millions of men and women on earth, that such a personal condition really exists outside of their own condition and experience. As the Holy Spirit searches all things, also does the Spirit know all things, and what the spirit knows even that he bears witness about, and His testimony is true. Lift up your eyes, ye messengers of God, and look at the nations on earth, and look where the spirit of God can find a resting place to be known and accepted in the love of God, and your eyes will be filled with tears when you are driven from door to door, and from city to city, and you have no place where the love of God in man receives you, nor gives you a shelter, but I say to you as the Holy Spirit which is in God, and of God, and is God, even so it shall be known to you as being the condition in principalities, and localities, and societies, and organizations, and empires, among spirits in the spiritual world, as far as God's personal dealings with man and spirit is concerned, but the children in the wisdom of God's love are justified by Him, who is the head-light of their lives. Amen.

Lucifer became the representative of the spirit of antagonism to the Father's work, or the Father of the perverted spirit of the world to be something else but God, and the life in God. A great truth is often received well after being said over again, and by a repetition it will be seen from different sides.

The Holy Spirit is a man to the world, but a duality of a woman to the heavens. In His harmony He is a woman, but in His masculine discord, He is a man towards the earth-life.

The Father is a man in a man, or a man perfected in His feminine discord of love to the world, but in the spirit He is man to man in His duality, or God.

The Spirit became perfected by His discord in the feminine principle, the discord being the masculinity of his own nature, until the Spirit became a woman in His duality to be a woman, or a God in the heavenly world without any discord in His perfection, except in His relation to the earth, where He is revealed as man, not because the rapport to earth-life is a discord to the Spirit, but because earth-life cannot receive the duality of perfection of woman in the feminine principle of the Godhead, and therefore the Spirit can only reveal himself to earth-life as a man with the principle of a woman's love.

This principle is good all through earth-life, and ought to be studied and known as every person on earth has the dual principle in them, inherited from their parents, the father and mother principle, and can be perfected into oneness in man as in woman by a marriage full of love and truth.

When a woman is governed by the feminine brain principle of love, she is truly in love. Then the duality of both the external and internal principle is manifested as a true woman, and as such captivates man, and keeps his affection. On the contrary, where the masculine principle rules in woman, she is in discord, and in the spirit of jealousy, because she does not love as a woman with resignation, but as a man and full of pretension, being masculine and at the same time a woman is a contradiction, by which man is repulsed as with a chill, and murder is in her inner nature, and the serpent whisper in her soul. Her relation to a husband or to a lover is contrary to the law of her own nature, and she is in perversion or in pain. Therefore beware how you are living, and how you conduct your lives, that the discord shall not govern your lives all nights and days.

The same principle is good with man. He has to be developed with that same principle that is discord in woman, or the masculine principle in woman, that which makes her so very wicked, perfects him into the duality of being a man until he becomes a man in a man, in his own as in her nature. The masculine and feminine characters of the sexes are well known on earth, and a man has to be loved by a woman until his feminine principle leaves him to perfect her in the duality of her nature, as she shall be loved of him until her masculine element becomes a duality in the union and perfection of his nature. A man with a feminine brain principle is not a man any more in true love than a woman with a masculine brain principle; both are by perversion into abnormal mental conditions, which are difficult to balance in discord, but may be rectified by truly mating excess to excess in a possible love, and phases of excellen⁻ mediumship in the spirit are often developed, and is an indi vidual blessing even when men and woman live earth life, and do not outgrow their opposite dual nature. A woman who is a woman cannot live happy with a man of feminine brain principle, unless she is able by her feminine excellence of love to absorb it, neither can a man live happily with a woman who has a masculine brain principle or control in the spirit, unless he is able by the principle of love to win her and absorb it. Life makes it a problem for one woman and one man to live together and be perfected in the love of the spirit.

A man who is a woman in his spirit is an imposition and a falsehood to his sex, and is a perversion from the beginning, and a falsehood in society to all true women. He is in the contrary relation to all truth, which by the reflex relation of spirit life to earth life, is a contradiction in itself, but by a masculine developed woman becomes a truth in the exterior of marriage, but not in the interior of life.

Neither can a woman in the spirit life capture and control the brain-life of a man, and remain to him on any interior basis of truth. Natural man's undeveloped condition may defend contrary relations on the basis of mediumship, but even there much allowance must be made, because feminine control is a hindrance to his happiness on earth, and to his true union with her sex. He might have loved, but the feminine spirit control prevented him from loving, and prevents him from being mated during earth-life by her self-love, or revenge on him. His earth-life is consequently out of the truth, and has left the plane of his natural development. The brain principle of his life being conducted by a woman's interest prevents him for life from being developed as dual man. During the earth-life, she is spiritually an imposition and a perversion, and does not come as a spirit on the principle of truth, or in woman's love, which a man can only be reconciled with in a spiritual as tangible relation to him. Therefore in the undeveloped condition of a man controlled mentally by a spirit woman, man stagnates into a perverted condition where his strength may support the brain-life and save him from actual insanity ; but she can never balance the brain principle by a feminine influence, and derangement of the organ is always possible. She can never be an angel by her control, but always a discord, because falsehood and perversion brings not harmony. Man's true relation to woman in his exterior life is by marrying where he finds in the love of the spirit, a woman controlled in her brain-life by a woman, and a woman's great happiness is also in the spirit to find a man controlled in his brain-life by the masculine principle of a man's power and not of a woman's control, who in such a case will be a curse to the man, as she will also be a curse to the woman he may marry, for she will pervert and destroy the soul of happiness and love of that marriage. The same or *vice versa*, to be said about a woman with a masculine brain.

The principle of exchange advocated by many spirits is a dangerous experiment, but there is no truth in it. I am the Spirit of Truth, and I know what I am saying, and if any spirit knows better than I do, then all that is necessary is for him to prove the truth of his assertion, and it will be accepted in the eternal world. The principle of exchanging guardian spirits is an impossibility in itself, and is an unnecessary and complicated machinery in the spirit, without working capacity or practical value. A spirit who has been the guide or control of one person for years, cannot with any hope of success leave that person and serve another, and besides there is no need of it when truth governs, and degradation is not put on a man by making his masculine principle a fugitive by putting the discord on the throne, where the divinity of man is dethroned and put into the chains of pain by making a masculine woman in the spirit govern him as his brain or mental principle. A woman's position to any man is in his physical or earth sphere, and not in his mental or spirit sphere, where a man has to be a man in man, and a woman has to be a woman with a woman's principle of control.

The contrary mixture of man and woman in the control or principle of brain-life, makes mental discord both in heaven and upon the earth, and all jealousy and crime, and revenge, and murder, comes from such an abnormal condition in the mental sphere, and all the spirit can do is to command and obtain the rule to appoint guides in the Holy Spirit of the same orders as those who are united on earth.

Human conception is contrary to spiritual perception, therefore it is very difficult to convey spiritual ideas to man, except he is born in the spirit, or born anew, which entirely changes his mundane conception of things into a spiritual understanding and perception of truth and spirit life, where the testimony of the Spirit is not to the world; for it only makes the world angry not to be able to comprehend the spiritual things, and it is also foolishness to every fool in the spirit, but it is a fountain of wisdom to the wise to be born of the Spirit, and to understand that which is of the spirit, and of the kingdom that is to come.

That principle of man in his interior principle of life becomes in woman her interior principle of poetry by conversion from one nature to another. Upon the same law the interior principle of woman, or the feminine principle in her which is the masculine to man, is her true brain-life and mental sphere without perversion, and is the perfection in man by the love of the spirit, that woman's interior feminine sphere of life and love is manifested in his nature by the wisdom in the spirit by which the true life is revealed to him, that the spirit of the priesthood or spiritual gifts may find a root in the human soul, and remain on earth.

Beware of the perversion in the spirit, as you should beware of the perversion of the flesh, for all perversion is adultery.

Perversion in the spirit is a woman with an interior mental principle of man. It is an abnormal condition, and makes her life a pain on earth and in the spirit. Perversion in the spirit is also a man with an interior brain principle of a woman, because it makes him a hell on earth and in the spirit. This perversion is often caused by a man having mental feminine control, and by woman having mental masculine control, which is a perversion in the spirit and breeds the nature of devils, and makes pain on earth. Man should remain man, and woman should remain woman until both are perfected.

The sexes are never mixed in a person in the heavens as they are in the hells, but are perfected by harmony which comes from *wisdom* and *love*, and not from passions which breed perversion, or develop in a contrary manner, and not by the spirit but by the flesh, and into the contrary principle of a person's own sex, which is the element of discord, inharmony and hell.

It has already been said, that the Father is nothing but man and that the Messiah is nothing but man, harmoniously the son of man balanced in the union of both natures in the Father and in the spirit. Also is the Holy Ghost nothing but woman, perfected and individualized as a woman into the unity of the Godhead, where emblematically all differences of sex cease to be, because companionship ceases to be by being swallowed up by a higher law of the divine perfection, into I am that I am, or carrying the principle of God not being any longer an indivdual belonging to sex, but perfected above it into the principle of the supreme power of the universe, far above the creative force working by the law of evolution through matter, by being the intellectual and intelligent soul life of the worlds and stars, and tendered worship as such.

The perfection of man is in being a man, and the perfection of woman is in being a woman, and the perfection of being an archangel is in being an archangel, and not to assume to be the representative of the eternal principle, or to rule as a God.

In the condition of being masculine in brain principle, is a woman perverted and condemned, and cannot be perfected except by correction through the fires of discord. Upon the same principle is a man condemned and perverted in his own nature by being feminine in his brain principle of being a man, and he cannot be perfected by woman unless corrected by the truth of God, through the fires of discord.

God is the representative of the great positive harmony of universal intelligence, or of eternity, and in his highest personal ambition man is struggling to reach a glimpse of God's glory, but the shadows and sorrows are not excluded from his dominions, as God is as much the God of the devils as He is the God of the archangels, and as much the God of Lucifer as He is the God of the Messiah.

The apparent conflict does not exist in an external sense of understanding. The worlds are as legions, but all are supported by the life and strength of Providence, and Lucifer is born as much the child of God as Absalom was a son of David, and Cain was a son of Adam. Absalom represented a discontented element among Israel, and it existed there with Absalom or without him, also does Lucifer only represent an element of the dissatisfaction in the Spirit, and it exists there as the shadow of God's glory, either if Lucifer existed there connected with it or not.

The omnipotent power of God reaches as much down to the lowest hell as to the most glorious heaven. The universe is one great equilibrium of peace to God, as He is in peace with all of

His work, because He is perfected by it as it is perfected by Him, and He is not at war with Lucifer or He could have subdued him long ago. Far from being at war with God is Lucifer carrying out the great mission of contest by which millions of minds are developed, which the truth could not reach, but the falsehood was accepted by, and they harvest the spirit of perversion and pain, and were ripened through much suffering to enter the heavens. The spirits and angels of the different worlds do not converse with each other except through mediums or by prophets, and as the earth sphere is locked up from the lower and higher conditions, also are the other worlds locked up from each other, but God is in them all, and the Holy Spirit searches all things which are in God, even as the spirit of man searches the things of the human soul.

Eternity is everywhere, and time is nowhere except as a measurement for man, and the internal life is everywhere except in conception of man, when he speaks about external things. It is the internal thoughts of man which build up cities, and inspires history as monuments for the intelligence of mind. The external world is a term applied to the senses of man and animals, but in reality it exists nowhere except as a deception true to the senses, and in no reality but to mind, which is the only operator on the stage of life, and the only motor power through all the universe, and what you call external things is mind in its manifestations to the senses, and nothing but mind, and this mind is God or the principle of eternity.

Who is Lucifer? Is he prince of this world? The Messiah said, "now comes the prince of this world, but he has no power or part in me." Being the first-born of the spirit or the son of the morning splendor, it became Lucifer's duty to represent the principle he does, as sure as it became the duty of the Messiah to fill His position in the Godhead as the redeemer of the world. Lucifer's work is with discord to consume discord in the battle with the work of the Messiah, who is the heavenly harmony, which through suffering conquers the consuming fires of the hells of discord, and redeems the suffering soul by the suffering love of God.

Lucifer loves God in an adverse spirit or in a perverted soul filled with all kinds of suppositions against Him. He professes to love Him in his own way, but not in the intensity of God's spirit, which is the only true love of God and accepted by Him. The adversary is not in that unlimited submission of a contrite heart and an humble soul. In the perfection of God he sees deviations, and in approaching him he is trembling with fear. He professes to love the Father above all things, if the Father would comprehend things as he does, and would harmonize his ways, and the words of Absalom about David are always on his tongue : "If I governed it should be very different from what it is now." This spirit of accusation is the spirit of devils, and is so from eternity, the spirit of traitors and betrayers of the saints, and the spirit of murder and persecutions of the church, and the spirit of sin against the Holy Ghost for which there shall be no forgiveness in their souls, because they knew the light and saw it, and they hated it, and they blew it out of existence among men wherever they had the power to do so. Adam and Eve could have reached into the perfection of immortality in the body, and as such regained the consciousness of sex in their perfection in God, and been father and mother to an immortal offspring, even as children now are born on the exterior and more perfected planets, belonging to the same solar system as the earth does. Paradise would have been peopled on earth with an immortal race that could materialize or de-materialize at will, in similarity to the body of Messiah in his resurrection, and Adam and his offspring would have been the light-carriers from paradise, and all over earth to their less developed brethren living on the plane of natural life.

The heavenly transfiguration did not take place with Adam and Eve because they knew the light and sinned against it, and both died in the flesh, but Seth was transfigured and taken away at an age of nine hundred and eighteen years, also Enoch and his friends were transfigured, and many of his disciples, and they were taken away in the presence of many people. Adam lived and blessed Méthuseleh and he died, and he materialized after death with Eve his mate, and with Abel his son. Adam appeared in the glory of Michael, the archangel, who was his incarnation, and Michael appeared tangible at their side.

When Adam was about two hundred years old, he went on his first mission to the west to the great Atlantis empire, and it suffered much from a tidal wave, and a great many people perished, and many cities were destroyed by the ocean, but Adam visiting there prayed to God, and the wave receded, but he prophesied about the destruction of the belt which surrounded all the earth, and called on the Lord's people who repented to seek God, and emigrate into the mountains to the west and to worship there.

Adam was four hundred years old when the great Atlantis sunk beneath the waves of the ocean, and a great earthquake extended over all Asia, and shook the western part of Europe, which until that time was one land with America, and the tidal wave destroyed the valley of Enoch, where the present Mexican Gulf is, and the islands of the West Indies are the remnants of that beautiful country.

Where the empire of Atlantis had its capital cities, is now only a large field of sea grass in the way of the ships between Europe and America, which cover the gigantic ruins of grand temples, and a city where luxury and civilization had reached its climax in art and literature, and where the capital city contained over one million of people. More than five millions of inhabitants perished, when the Atlantis sunk, and about three millions in the valley of Enoch, where islands now are the melancholy landmarks of the once beautiful and tropically rich and fertile country. During that great destruction were Enoch and his wife and a son, and many of his disciples transfigured and were taken away, as Enoch walked with God, and God took him and his household to be with the angels in paradise.

The Jewish chronology is in some measure correct pertaining to ages of persons, but it needs sifting in regard to the ages of periods and times. Man's age on earth as stated before, will be nearly five hundred thousand years, if his age is reckoned from the remotest period, when man formed the first link with the most prominent species of apes, and you accept the Hottentot, and the Bushman, and the father and mother of "Krayo" to be counted as human beings, a claim which eternity does not dispute, and to the end of man. He advanced slowly to be developed intellectually above other animals, but the construction and perfection by evolution of nature made the human brain superior to any other animals, as in that structure laid the promise of what man has achieved during countless generations. It consumed a period of one hundred and fifty thousand years, before man had advanced in his physical and mental nature by the untiring law of evolution of mind upon physical structures, until he had become a nation on earth beyond the Negro, Mongolian and Tartar, and culminated into the Hindoo race, where spiritual man could be circumscribed to be developed and retained on earth in the flesh of man.

Adam and Eve were born in the period three hundred and sixty-five thousand, before nature's end. They were born of parents living far apart, and were brought together apparently as by a chance of circumstances, and both belonged to the young and finely developed Hindoo type of man. Adam being some years older than Eve, was an incarnation of Michael the archangel, and his extraordinary spiritual experience made him to be a lonely and forsaken youth, and when after a deep and long trance he saw Eve extending her hands to him, he was overpowered with joy by her beauty and spirituality, and eminent development, exceeding all other women, that he exclaimed " She is flesh of my flesh and bone of my bone, she is my spiritual mate," and he fell around her neck and kissed her, and she followed him and shared her joys and sorrows with him. The angel " Agnes," the incarnation by Eve, is the eternal companion of Michael the archangel, and she guided the steps of Eve by visions into the society of Adam. They were taken away together by the spirit of God and guided into Mesopotamia, and there they were placed together in a garden of paradise. Adam was aged forty nine years, when they came with each other into the Garden of Eden, and he was one hundred when they were driven out from the presence of God in His paradise. Eve gave birth to Cain when she was one hundred and ten years, and to Abel when she was one hundred and thirty years, and to Seth when she was one hundred and seventy-five years old. When Adam was two hundred years old, he commenced his mission and made travels all over the earth, and was active in his work till he was past the nine hundred years, when he ceased to travel abroad but remained at home, and slept away, dust to dust, in peace, at an age of nine hundred and thirty-six years, and was buried at the same place where Eve's remains were laid at rest several hundred years before

Adam had established the true worship of God, and Seth became the presiding general for God's people, and followed in his father's path, and in the spirit of the Order of the Messiah. The earth had been in a paradisiac state for not much over fifty thousand years, but after the return of heavenly man into the natural state again, and death came upon them and their offspring, the change in nature was greatly perceptible. Intense heat and cold alternated more, and with a gradual intensity into great irregularity of the climate.

The poles became barren and covered with snow and ice, and more rapidly as man degenerated became the change of the earth, until the glacier period came suddenly upon the nations on the earth, and covered with ice the globe north and as far down south as to 39 degrees, and from the south pole as far north as to 41 degrees, and men and animals perished by the millions, and immigration on a large scale went to the warmer belts of the earth. In another message shall the spirit give to the world the periods in length according to the years of man, and nothing shall be withheld that can give light to man from the remotest history of the earth.

Adam and Eve lived their old age in the commencement of the change, and before the glacier came, and you of the present generation are living in the receding glacier period of to-day, as your icebergs are only broken off glaciers, and the north and south polar regions are covered with glaciers, and even the Alps in Central Europe are covered with immense fields of glaciers in this very year you are writing in now. The glaciers commenced to form at the earth's deviation of sixteen degrees dropping off from the perpendicular axis, and the Lord God made it drop suddenly to thirty-six degrees from eighteen degrees, after the transition of Enoch, when it again commenced to rise slowly towards its former position, and the earth stands now at an inclination of 23 degrees. It depends on the grace of God and the intelligence and spirituality of man, whether this globe shall suddenly be converted into a paradisiac state, or be thrown back into another glacier belt to cover all the civilized world. The convulsions of nature stand in a reciprocal relation to the emanations of mind, which proceed from the spiritual state of mankind, the crown of all creation, which is perfected by mind in the evolution in nature. The destiny of your globe lays in the spirituality, and humiliation, and truth, and love of God's nature in man, and how that shall be able to generate in the human mind, as the only true and eternal happiness that can reflect back on the destiny of the earth, and the promise lays there for a perfect redemption from the glaciers into its former clothing of a paradisiac bliss. Like Sodom and Gomorrah, sunk in the curse the cities had sealed upon their soil by the judgment of God the Almighty, also the earth dropped its head by the same curse man had sealed upon it, to be barren and an inhospitable globe, because man is not made for this globe's sake, but the globe is made for man's sake, and even as man is accursed also shall the earth be accursed. Amen.

The great and glorious country called the "Oceania," located as the last remaining belt between Asia and America, had a population of eighty millions of people, whom Adam twice visited and preached to, sunk entirely in the days of Peleg—or as the scripture says, "In the days of Peleg was the earth divided." A tidal wave from the south united with a great earthquake and turned to the north, and swept Oceania, and raised mountains high over the glaciers of the closed up Behring Strait, and receded with an immense power, leaving the entire country on the bottom of the sea of the Pacific. As Adam preached to the people of the old Atlantis, and warned them before the general destruction of their country, but they did not hearken to his voice, except a few of the elect, who went into the mountains of Georgia and were saved, so did Seth preach to the people of "Oceania" for several generations, and called upon them to repent, and so did Enoch on his way from Asia to his settlement in the valley of Enoch. The highly civilized people of the belt scorned the idea, and said "There is not sufficient water on earth to submerge our country," and they lived in luxury and ease, and served their own comfort and learning of mathematics, astronomy and art, of music, sculpture, painting and the drama. Their houses and gardens were perfection in architecture and beauty, and their temples were dedicated to the worship of the sun and the star Sirius around which they could count the years and days of the sun's journey. They offered thanksgiving every year to the sun. A few accepted the teachings of Enoch and Seth, and served God the Almighty, and they emigrated in flocks to California, Mexico or China, and when the destruction came they were saved. The inhabitants of the Otaheite and of the Hawaiian Islands will tell you to-day by tradition how the great country they once belonged to was submerged under the sea and completely destroyed.

One civilization after another has been destroyed, because the people did not serve God, but served themselves and idolatry, and the spiritual emanation from their brain-life was a mental stink into the spiritual worlds, and they became only fit for a wholesale destruction, until a race would come on earth by continued mental evolution in the spirit, to serve the only true God, and his Messiah to man. As the Greek and the Roman civilization went down and its seed was scattered among the barbarians, so shall the Anglo-Saxon civilization on American soil go down for its want of spirituality to live on.

As the chronology will be given in another message it will not be read here, but suffice it to say, that the bible is in error in regard to time and periods up to Abraham, and is not correct before Moses. In the coming book of Adam will be given correct time and dates, and in the book of Enoch a complete history, and in the book of Noah a correct narrative of the flood, and the bible will give man the needed corrections. The great floods came principally in the Silurian period, and one great flood in the tertiary period, but after man came the earth raised and sunk, and after the break of the great Atlantic part of the belt, all floods became only local occurrences, as the flood in which Noah was concerned. It came down from the melting Asiatic and European glaciers, and Mesopotamia was submerged entirely, and the ark landed in the foot-hills which surrounded the low-land on a hill called Arat, and not on the high mountain peak called Ararat, or the chief among the mountains.

In the days of Peleg occurred the last great calamity to the earth. Six great civilizations have entirely disappeared from the earth on account of the want of spirituality among the people to live by and their disbelief, and they went down into oblivion, even as the people at the tower of Babel were confused and scattered because they tried to obstruct the ways of God, and did not seek into the fountain of their life for the inspirational gifts from heaven, the real guaranty for their perpetual happiness, harmony and prosperity.

The adversary loves God with his own love, but not with the love of God in him. He is in antagonism to the work of the Messiah on earth, but he is not in antagonism to God in eternity, although he is eternally opposed to the work of redemption by Messiah. Jesus wants to redeem the elect that His father has given to Him in the world, into the glorious light of His kingdom, but Lucifer wants to redeem the entire human family into his light of intellectual freedom of that intelligence which is the natural light in man.

On the ground plane of natural evolution, there is no contradiction between God and Lucifer in a cosmopolitan acceptance of nature or the animal plane of man, because the spirit of the flesh and blood is the spirit of the world and of natural man, and it is discord and selfishness, in union with the spirit of the adversary. It was in eternity the spirit of the Almighty God loved the world, and did not spare the only begotten son, as the spirit of the world cannot please God, and cannot receive that love except by the mediator. The word of God is not in that world except by the Savior, and in that is the salvation from darkness to light into the glory of God's love, which is in the Messiah, and by which he reconciled man to God, and did not save himself, but gave his blood to carry out his mission, which is the salvation of man. Because God loved the world He sent his only begotten Son into the world.

In a general acceptation of the term, there is no war between darkness and light, but peace in God as he is in peace with the fallen spirit of the world, and in the eternal life, God is in the most intense harmony with the universe, as its dissolution is not in antagonism to the eternal principle of life and its law which would otherwise go to war against God.

The world pretends to love God, but the spirit of Cain is in union with the world, and the love of God can only be tested by the suffering and willingness of man to sacrifice all things for God, in that love as Messiah laid down His own life in the flesh. On that test does the love of the world to God utterly fail, for it is the love of man and not the love of the spirit. Lucifer may promise to do great things, but it is only in the love of God by the infusion of the Holy Spirit in man, that man can overcome the spirit of the world and perform the works which are most pleasing before God in his spirit, as it is wrought of God in man by faith and sight. Man may be very fashionable in the spirit of the world, and in the spirit of progression, and intelligence and in learning on the intellectual or cosmopolitan plan of existence, but he has not the love of God naturally within his soul, nor has the world the love of God in its spirit, because God's love is a gift of God on condition of humiliation, suffering and sacrifice, by which man becomes engrafted into the nature of God, and into unity with his spirit.

In that measure the world comes short, and also Lucifer and his hosts of angels. With all their claims they are short of attaining the gifts of that love which is in God. The world has painted Lucifer as a very hideous being, with horns and hoofs, and a tail like an animal, but the fact is, that Lucifer is the prince of the world in the spirit of the fallen condition of man in his natural selfish propensities of grabbing and monopolizing all power for his own selfish aggrandizement of purpose. As true as the animal nature of man belongs to earth, so true is it that man's selfish propensities induce him to get the best of everybody else, and to get the most gain in the spirit of unrighteousness and perversion, and not of the love of God, but of the glory of the world and his own individuality. In that has man failed to please God, and in that failed the archangel Lucifer, when he started out from his father's house on his own resources, and through good and bad experiences moved his soul from that love which is in the Father. He became his own headlight to look out for himself, even as the spirit of his philosophy has taught men to live and breathe by, as a power of that spirit in the world. That domain of philosophy and intelligence without the love of God, is the perversion in the human mind.

Persons of the world take the horse shoe as an emblem of good luck, and the Christian takes the cross for the emblem of prosperity on earth, but when the spirit of the world pretends to love God, be assured that it is in deception, as the spirit of the world with the logical consequences of its own philosophy can only love itself and not God, because its spirit is selfishness, and its motto is self-approbation, and you will be the more in deception if you with the love of God in your heart, embrace the lifeless statues of the world's idols in a fancy to be in the love of God.

It is better for a man to have one foot or one eye, and with such a deficiency walk into the mansions of the Father, than to be cast into the fires of his own soul, and it is better for a man to lose goods, and wife, and children, and his own life, to save the love of God in his heart, than to have all the things of the world and lose in his own soul the love of God.

Therefore, fight the good battle in the armour of the Holy Spirit of God, and recollect that the battle is not with firearms, but the spirit of God shall fight within you and conquer the world. Be steadfast in the spirit of God's words to you, and your power shall be strong in His love. It sustains you in the world when you are as strangers, and pilgrims, and persecuted by the spirit of bloodshed, and in God you shall have peace, that peace which is in the Holy Spirit, and in the hearts of the Father and the Messiah.

Do not love the world, nor the things which perish and are of the world, and the desire of men's hearts, because the spirit of the world is not in the love of God. Whosoever loves the world has the spirit of self-love, and has the spirit of the adversary within him, and the love of God is not within him. Amen.

You read that in the commencement Adam was alone and had no society. It was in the days of his development from earth or natural man, and into spiritual man, because he came from the dust and went back to dust again, or to the natural condition of man. When the fulness of the Spirit of God came on him, he was alone in paradise, alone in his development, alone in his incarnation of Michael the archangel, who was his control, and God caused him to go into a deep trance, and He brought spiritual Eve to be Adam's eternal mate and companion in paradise, and led her to him by the spirit. When Adam observed her, he said: "She is as I am myself, and flesh of my flesh, and bone of my bone, she is not as a natural woman." Eve became heavenly and an incarnation as Adam was.

About the heavenly and spiritual man speaks the prophet Jeremiah: Thus says the Lord, "I will put my law in their mind and write it in their heart, and they shall not teach any more one another saying, know ye Jehovah, because who are in me shall know me from the least to the greatest, they shall have the mind of the Lord their God, and know the thought of Jehovah." This intensity in the love of the spirit is the truth, and the fountain of all life, and all creation, and evolution in that life, or the wisdom which comes from the truth.

Therefore the hate of the natural man against the spiritual man is in-born, and the natural man takes delight in that hate and rejoices in it, because the spirit of the adversary bears testimony in him to do it, and man will obey that voice of perversion until he becomes accursed in his soul and the light from heaven is withdrawn from his intellect, and man becomes a murderer in himself, and he cannot repent from his weakness and folly. Jesus said: "If ye do that with the green tree which bears fruit of the life in God, what shall become of the dry tree." It shall be cut off and destroyed.

Man hates by nature the revelations of God, and whenever prophets spoke they were killed, and man never regretted the deed, but rejoiced in it and justified himself, saying: "These men deserved to die, because they were the worst of all men living on earth, and the multitude thanked God when the crimson blood of the prophets was smoking from the ground. This is the true character of natural man in his fallen condition, and in the spirit of Lucifer.

Prophets and apostles have been tried, both in ancient and modern times, and never convicted of any crime, but were all the same condemned to death by natural man. Jesus came to His own and in the image of His Father, as the heavenly man from above, and was persecuted and crucified. The apostle Paul was in prison and was tried by forty courts and never convicted, but at last executed for no other crime than that he lived, and breathed and spoke in the spirit of God. Joseph Smith, the modern prophet, was tried in as many courts as Paul and never convicted of any crime, but at last murdered savagely of brutal men, and the mob rejoiced exceedingly.

Only a short time ago elders were killed in Georgia, but natural man did not repent nor show any sorrow for the deed, but rejoiced, and even the press of the American people rejoiced, but God did not rejoice, and in that element which rejoiced is the bloody power, which will bring down the retribution on the nation says the most high God in the power of His Holy Spirit. Amen.

Spiritualism has done a noble work, and connected with the spiritual congress in the spirit world are some of the most noble characters the world has ever produced, such as Shakespeare, Goethe, Newton, Schiller, Socrates, Swedenborg, Cromwell, Washington, Lincoln, John Brown and others, so many illustrious names that it would fill pages to mention them all. Suffice it to say, that by enlisting the spirit force of the powerful Indian element in the spirit, *that congress* has succeeded in breaking the ice for reform on earth, and its members have not shrunk from any sacrifice or labor that their efforts might meet with success.

The spiritualistic movement is an intermediate movement between earth and heaven. It moves the spirit-plane of life on the earth-plane by moving its spirit life. It uses the elements of soul force in the spirit sphere of the earth-life to open the rapport with earth-life. It moves the earth towards heaven, and not as the celestial or gospel movement moves heaven down to the earth.

Spiritualism is the discord of the lower realms of spirit life by the assistance of the intelligences of the higher spheres, to work out earth life's own salvation by harmonizing discord into accord, and disharmony into harmony. It cures discord by discord of corresponding souls. It harmonizes corresponding affections and ailments of the sick upon healthy, to restore health and transfer corresponding pains from one organism to another to benefit all, and restore harmony.

Spiritualism grasps the most subtle strings of the human soul, and brings out the usefulness of man for its purpose wherever it finds the law and adaptation to the application of its purpose. Spiritualism makes the platform as broad as possible to unite every class of spirit-power upon, and it does not interfere with any individual faith, or church organization, or religion, but adopts universal principles which are recognized by all, leaving to each spirit to work out his own individual salvation, as he may be best able to do it, putting forth as the proposition and only tenet, that God is the eternal principle of life, and that immortality is everywhere, and man has an immortal soul.

All the effort of spiritualism has been to establish immortality based upon spiritual demonstrations, or facts delivered as tests to man by various developments of mediumship now very well known to the intelligent classes of society, and has given to all the churches a new impulse of light from above. The mission of spiritualism is a most necessary one, and a most absolute advance for the second advent of Messiah. As the Order of the Messiah is the advance guard of the kingdom, so is spiritualism hand in hand with the churches the advance guard for the Order of the Messiah, but spiritualism had to come to make the churches sufficiently liberal for the preparation in the movement for the advent of the Messiah.

The consequence of the adversary movement in the spirit perverted the spirit of man in the obscurity of his inner vision and capacity for perceiving God, and conversing with the spiritual world. Therefore is heaven locked up by that spirit of contest, and natural man was left to work out his own way, filled with deception and pride.

The philosophy of man argued that God would not allow discord and deviltry, but upon the same principle God would not support the existence of the hurricane or darkness, but He supports the light, and He supports the bodies which obstruct the light, and consequently He must also support the shade and be the God of the shadows in nature as in social life.

Beware of ignorance and superstition, because from the lower stratas of life man comes forth to reach the seat among the lords of the creation and archangels, and all contentions are negative radiations from the positive light, or in other words all darkness is only negative light, and the sunlight is positive darkness. God revealed himself in the positive heavenly light for the heavenly man until he fell from that light or condition into the negative darkness or sin. Even so did God love the world, that He granted to man the grace of his redemption, and not that of Lucifer or his angels, because they loved the darkness and fought the harmony of God, and preferred the darkness to the light, and do not wish to come to the light, but want to remain in the negative darkness of the soul, and the law of progression cannot be revealed to any except through the probation and humiliation into the recognition of the harmony of God, a condition they refuse to enter into, and for that reason they remain in ignorance and superstition, and not in the freedom but in the thraldom by which they obstruct the heavenly harmony of light. God allows the devils to live as much as the angels, but not found in the same sphere, as they operate in a contrary direction. Therefore does the power of God not annihilate the devils, but they work out their own dissolution in individual progression by perversion in their nature contrary to the laws of God to live on.

The perversion is a discord in God's negative power or passive government of the world and to His positive perfection. No disharmony is prevented by him from working its evil design in discord, and being in open rebellion to His harmony. Such a condition will surely exhaust itself by consuming the fountain of its discord into the light of the cause or consume itself.

By consequent reasoning in humiliation before God, will men arrive before the light of the corresponding harmony, which caused all their misery in their error and perversion to the harmony, because God is in the reflex action the harmony, and counterbalances all the hells by the truths of heaven, but hell is the love of perversion. God allows the discord on earth as in the hells to live in its perversion, as the passive element of offenses to come for to work through pains into accord, which is in the harmony of God. where the cause and reason for the permission of discord to exist is to be sought for. From the discord in God's love sprung the evolution of all the planets from the solar nebulæ, and the positive force of the center was over-balanced by the circumference, which became a feminine, passive condition, controlled by the love of God and evolved one sixtieth part of the volume as the fruits of that love, or the planets and their satellites. All life is in God, but all life is not progressed into the positive harmony which is in God, nor are all men conscious of having their individual life buried in that life, which is harmoniously the spirit of God's personality. The discord of the hells is as a refiner's furnace, purifying the metals from the refuge, and so does God work through discord and pain to perfect men and women.

The earth is a comparatively very young globe, and sprung into the evolution of its present life as from yesterday, but it counted millions of years before organic life settled and became developed on the surface.

Through organic based on inorganic life, mind is working its way by the rivers of life and spiritual material thrown into the unseen world, and every fifty years you may count more than one thousand millions of souls to enter the spirit world and are disembodied from the earth. When the earth is perfected its spirit sphere will be on its surface and death will be no where, but all translation will be a sweet sleep by which the soul is passing from a lower and into a higher condition. If the earth is perfected for the celestial sphere, that condition will be on the surface, and the earth will be surrounded with the spiritual magnetic light of that sphere. The moon became the abode for a spiritual evolution of that life it had reared and for its own spirit sphere, when the grosser part of its organic life found its root and prosperity in the moisture and soil belonging to earth. The moon rotated originally with a great velocity at times of about six hours for one revolution. The spherical shape of that globe accounts for this rapidity, when it moved perpendicularly on its plane.

As the earth cooled down and contracted the moon became also contracted, and when its water and atmosphere was absorbed into its interior, then the velocity became beyond the capacity to revolve with, and on account of the changed proportion of the distance to the masses of the satellite to the earth, the moon dropped suddenly as from exhaustion nearly five degrees from its plane, with the south pole pointing towards earth, and is now sliding with only one rotation around its axis and the earth in twenty-nine days. When the south pole projects towards earth, so does the north pole project in same proportion from the earth, and the theory that the moon is flat, or nearly so on the side turning away from earth is not true. Around its equator the moon is about circular, as it presents itself in a view to man from the earth.

During the period of 100,000 years, when man on earth was very little above an animal, the moon was perfected into a spiritual state, and when the earth deviated from its perpendicular axis beyond 18 to 36 degrees, the moon moved into its present position. Intellectual and intelligent pre-adamitic man lived on earth thirty-five thousand years. During part of that period, the moon revolved with great velocity on its axis, and the motion would have been quite perceptible for man, if he suddenly could have been transferred to the moon. The history of organic life on the moon will be the history of the same life upon earth, and time will be the only distance of difference, which to eternity amounts to nothing, but the earth is not half matured, and far from death of its present nature.

On the moon is now an intense light and heat of a fortnight long day, and alternating with the same night cold as space, but this condition, which would be death to organic life on earth, is perfectly adapted to the semi-spiritual life and evolution of the nature now existing on the surface of the moon, where no moisture can be found, but the oceans are bound up in the moon's interior, and breathe a gentle dew on the semi-spiritual vegetation scarcely visible except as a mist, for the naked natural eye of man. Upon the same principle is fire bound up in the interior of the earth, and it exhales a gentle heat on its crust. The moon was perfected as the cream of the earth when that moved only in a chaos of steam and fire. In course of time the earth will consume its oceans, half is absorbed, and also its atmosphere after equally as long a time, and live in semi-spiritual nature for another long period. The earth is progressing slowly and cooling into maturity, and it takes about two hundred thousand years to diminish one degree of heat, at a depth of 2,000 feet below the surface.

The measure man uses is, his relation to the physical universe of his own organism, even as to good and evil is his measure of conditions and circumstances related to his mental capacity and conscious intuition about his own individuality. Nature makes its developments known by the same law, and Mercury freezes at about 32 degrees below zero, and is melting below such a temperature. Water is melting as any other metaloid, and becomes solid at 28 degrees. Alcohol does not freeze before at 150 degrees below zero, a too cold a wave for organic life on earth to endure. It must be evident to man, that matured life in its perfection lays only in an embryotic condition for another world, and all maturity is only relative relations from the organic or inorganic soul life and to its correspondence. Good and evil is not to be found in the perfect harmony of God, but by the slightest swing of not being conscious in the mind about what to do or not is the soul thrown into the eclipse to know good and evil, from which experience there is no escape before he is balanced again in the perfection of peace in God's love. If it could be possible that a seraph harmonized in the spirit of God should doubt what to do, he would by that same law of endless progression be thrown out from his sphere with the velocity of mental lightning, and evolve in the spirit of this doubt about good and evil into a higher perfection of mental experience, in which he will return again in God, and be balanced in the peace of His presence, and the divine evidence of Almighty God's eternal wisdom.

Man makes always a great error in judging about other globes and their spiritual things, by laying down his own condition of life, which is his own nature of existence, for a rule by which he draws his conclusions for other conditions he knows nothing about, but as man is situated and undeveloped, and ignorant as an intelligent animal can be, he cannot do otherwise and will remain in darkness till he comes to the light, that there may be light in his soul.

The times or years now existing en earth makes it very difficult for the spirit to make corrections, because if a year is one rotation of the earth around the sun in 365 days, then this length of time has greatly differed at periods, and the years on earth have been shorter or longer than they are now. Pre-adamite man had four years to one of the present years, as the earth nearly perpendicular on its axis revolved around the sun in 90 days. The intensity of that motion in connection with contracttion and density made the earth to be thrown away from its vertical position to the plane, by which it reduced its velocity to one-fourth of its former speed. The historical age on earth is as from yesterday. Very little is gained by records from the Chinese and Egyptian astronomers, but the most exact calculations and observations were made by the ancient Chinese, who knew the orbit of the sun, and gave to man the valuable information that it rotated, but during the entire historical time from the remotest period, the sun's orbit is with a radius which shows only a fraction of one second during 12,000 years. It is the perplexity for man, when the life of his organism on earth is compared with such immensities, but the triumph of the spirit over matter or his immortality gives to him the only equivalent. When the moon, by the same law which increased the speed of the earth, revolved with a velocity from 12 hours in its chaotic condition, and 6 hours during its organic life, increased the speed of its revolution to three hours, then its oceans sunk into its interior, and it turned to 5° from the vertical position, and nearly all rotation around its axis ceased to be. It was when the earth iucreased its velocity to less than 18 hours for one rotation, that it turned to sixteen degrees from the perpendicular, and when it further deviated from 18 to 36 degrees the day and night were 36 hours for a period of two thousand years, after which it recovered some of its former balance, and at its present inclination rotates around its artificial axis in 24 hours. When man looks on these figures it will be evident to him, that time is not any infallible measure, but related to conditions and circumstances The immensity of the worlds and the diversity of the globes, makes it very difficult to draw conclusions from one to another, especially if they belong to different solar systems, something man is at present in no danger of doing, as he does not know of any planet by his means of observation except those belonging to his own sun, but conclusions can be drawn from a satellite to her planet, as the satellite lives the life, and passes through the history on a shorter scale of what will be in store for the planet. In years to come the geological condition on the moon will be studied closely by man on earth, and the rocks will speak, and man will draw most valuable conclusions by which the future history of the earth will be understood.

The scriptures say, there are many Gods and many Lords, but ye have one God, the Father, and one Lord, Jeshuah the Messiah. Therefore recollect every sphere and every society, and every degree of intelligence has its climax reached of development and mental strength, and spiritual salvation, according to the attachment to the truth and the light of the love inherited from God in the life of the soul. It matters not where you are and who you are, if you are found in that life which is in the Messiah, as it permeates all things and moves all things through the suns and the planets, but blessed are you if you are found to be a citizen in his individual sphere, and you are conscious to be received of him in his father's home.

The light contains all the colors found on earth. They are all in the white dazzling sunlight, and as it represents all colors in itself, even so God represents the universe and His spirit worlds, but the diversities of mind exist, and diversities in colors exist, and each nation has its own battle flag with its own color for a standard, and throughout all the spirit world exists the same deviations in societies and principalities through each sphere, but those who are gathered in the spirit to be with the Messiah shall be where He is, and partake of His glory, which He had in the spirit, and in the Father before the nebulæ existed from which your world came. Therefore rejoice and let your harmony be in God, and take delight in speaking the truth and doing good deeds by the spirit of God working in you, because devils and men who serve the adversary take delight in speaking evil and all kinds of blasphemies, so do angels take delight in speaking good, and to bless rather than curse, because when Moses walked into the mountains alone when he was one hundred and twenty years old, he did not eat nor drink for many days, and the adversary came to him and used all kinds of blasphemies and accursed him, but Moses did not answer him with any other words than " The Lord my God shall deal with thee." At the moment of Moses' translation when his body became transfigured in the presence of a circle of angels, and he looked transparent and shone with the glory of the sun, then Lucifer accursed Moses, and called him a murderer and a thief. Michael the prince, who had Moses by his right hand, did not curse again but said to the adversary, " The Lord thy God the Almighty shall punish thee, Amen." Therefore if possible do not curse, but let that which is accursed be accursed in itself. Suffer for God's victory in your spirits, and rejoice with angels, and do not rejoice in revenge or hate, but keep away from those who are perverted beyond redemption in the flesh, or are accursed in their own souls, and God shall deal with such and you shall not, because you are not of that spirit which is in them, nor are they born of the spirit of God. The difference between good and evil is as that between heat and cold. Good is as heat positive and active, and evil is as cold, negative and inactive, except in consuming heat. Evil is as the seven lean cows, who swallowed up the seven fat cows, but did not become fat themselves, also evil may consume ever so many good people and will remain evil, as cold will swallow up much heat, and remain cold. The measure of good and evil is adapted to earthy conditions, as heat and cold is related to the human blood of 100 degrees F., even so is good and evil related to the human spirit. There is more evil than good in a human life, but good is intermixed with it, and the soul is matured by good in a continued conflict with evil until it becomes balanced and individualized sufficient not to be afflicted of evil, but has overcome evil with good.

Man is a most perfected microcosm of the development represented through the universe by the spirit of the earth. He suffers the agony and pain in common with the globe, which is represented by his own nature, and as the chemical pressure is intense in the earth, also is the spiritual pressure intense in the human soul, and as the cooled crust which envelopes the earth is not much thicker in comparison than the peel of an orange is in proportion to the meat, so is the human soul living on a thin crust, which is keeping it from sinking mentally into an eight thousand mile chaos of red hot fire. The interior of the earth is symbolic of the sea spoken about as a lake burning with fire and brimstone, or the chaos of the earth, into which the refuse of all things will be cast, when the world and that which is in the world shall perish by fire, and in many places destroy entire civilizations, even as often before has been done by floods. Charity at last will overcome evil, and that turbulent element will be no more, but all will work into one grand harmony; so will the earth absorb the raging waves of the oceans, when they sink into its bosom, and the hurricane will drop into the silence of a summer's night, and peace will once more reign supreme on the surface of the earth in the semi-spiritual condition of a summer day. It will be the new heaven and the new earth, not alone in the human heart, but in the reality of an exterior creation of a progressive interior life on the earth.

The cooling process will go on for an indefinite period of time, and also will the passions of the human soul be cooled down by degrees, by the development of the race. The period of purification by fire is the earth now moving into, when the crust has assumed such a thickness that the interior electricity becomes in less correspondence to the atmosphere than to the spiritual magnetic condition of the life on the surface, and severe convulsions and revolutions in the mental sphere of man downwards into the degradation of his divine nature will withdraw the Almighty's support of balance, and render the crust in numerous places and destroy large cities and entire nations.

Look at the height of the mountains in the moon in comparison with which rocks on the earth amount to little. They were thrown up to that height in a latter period of that globe, later than the present maturity of the earth. That period has to come on earth, and will remodel and destroy most of its surface before the water shall entirely be swallowed up and disappear.

The end of the present creation is spoken about in the scriptures to be preceded with signs in the sun and moon to be visible before all people. The electrical storms in the sun's light atmosphere will increase in proportion to the perfection of his planets, and more than half of the sun will show a large black surface, and it will lose three-fourths of its light. The vegetation on earth will turn yellow and pale and not be green any more, as on the new semi-spiritual earth the vegetation will be of a more briliant white than present sunlight. The moon will reflect a crimson red light, and the blue sky will not be any more, but heaven will appear black as cloth, and there will be seen written signs and ciphers on the firmanent, by which the spirit world will report with earth, and there shall be great consternation among all nations living on earth. One epoch after another shall pass over this globe with several thousands of years apart, until the last one shall come, and finish up the entire system of planets, when the life of all planets and satellites have outgrown and perfected its degrees of development into a celestial sphere of spirit life. Then the satellites will rush into the planets, and these again into the sun, and all united shall make one spiritual globe or sun, shining with lustre and brilliancy of the divine magnetic spirit light of eternity, where all the remaining spirits from all the planets and satellites will unite, and be gathered in union of peace and harmony together, and enter upon the sphere of eternity with the celestial world, uniting with the spirits from other suns mingling in the heavens along the milky way, and on the spirit belt of thousands of billions of miles encircling the sun Sirius, and from there into larger spirit belts around suns after suns and planets without end.

All the planets were once a nebulæ in common with their sun, as all planets were once a ring of gases and heat in common with their moons, and upon the same principle they belong together, and will once have to recede again in the same order together, when the law of centripetal force has exhausted the motion of the centrifugal power, and they again meet each other. That epoch is however at such a distance in eternity, that all time man can count must dwindle into nothing, and the event can only take place when the organic life is lived out into spirit through all the solar system, and more than that, when the spirit spheres of all the globes are perfected as far as the present creation can do it, based upon the emanation of life germs sent from the suns Sirius and Kolob, which impregnated the nebulæ brought into existence by the evolution founded on the creative principle of the divine will and the divine love of the supreme mind.

The first sphere of the spirit life belonging to a planet lays directly around that planet, and in and with the life of man on that planet as two hands are clasping fingers together. The spirits are living the interior life of men and women, as man in a developed estate of soul is living the revealed life of the first spirit sphere through mediumships and dreams, and impressions, etc.

The spirit sphere around a planet is there by necessity and not alone by choice. On the exterior or outer planets is no violent death by sickness or accidents, and not any chemical change such as men on earth call death. The semi-spiritual nature gives birth to a semi-spiritual vegetation and life is similar in some respects to that existing on the moon, and man is born there never to die, but to be changed by growth and spiritual development from one condition to another, and to join the spirit sphere of the planet by trance or transition, and the lower chemical parts of the body are secreted by degrees, and no physical death of a chemical body is left behind, as the body is perfected without death into one spiritual body in heaven immortal and lasting forever. The planet Mars is rapidly absorbing its oceans, and its atmosphere is growing very light, as on the highest of your mountains, and its first spirit sphere will soon unite with the spheres of its moons or enter into harmony with them.

Man on earth suffers in most instances a violent death by diseases in the vital economy of the flesh, as all diseases are an inharmonious estate of the living soul, and at a certain point of that discord the condition becomes mortal, and the rupture which you call death, takes place between the interior soul, or real spiritual body of man, and its medium the physical body, or that shell left behind you look at as the exterior clothing of the soul. The body corresponds always to the nature on which it is living, although the interior or real body may be perfected to mingle after death with spirits from higher spheres. Upon that principle most of the spirits who enter spirit life from the earth-sphere are undeveloped and cannot move beyond their mental condition of development, and sink back by the law of mental gravitation into the life they lived before death. The differences between earth life and spirit life is therefore so very slight to many spirits, that they have a difficulty to realize that any change has taken place of their real soul life aside from the external cutting away from earth's nature, which they however live again by mediumships and as guides, and guardian spirits for friends or relations on earth. Therefore the spirits live earth life as much for their own necessity of support and education into higher conditions by the law of progression or mental evolution, as for the benefit of those they love and have left behind on earth. There are a thousand millions of human beings on earth, and for every hundred years there are three thousand millions of souls entering the spirit world, and officiate as guardians for mankind, during the next hundred years. You can count one hundred thousand millions of spirits are busy day by day in a direct work with the soul-sphere of man on earth, and more than five hundred thousand spirits are incarnations in each generation, of which three are counted to each hundred years. Where are the hells? They are in persons' souls on earth, in homes of contest and discord, and misery, filled with anger and revenge, and murder. They are in the spirit world upon the same principle, but the earthly rudimental conditions get sifted at death, that good and evil are passing to their own places of comfort or discomfort, as the inclination has been before death, and societies of hell are diversified as the societies of heaven are diversified. Spirits gravitate to spirits of their own condition. Lazarus lifted up his eyes, and found himself meeting with Abraham in the eternal mansions of God in paradise, and the rich man lifted up his eyes in hell and in pain, because Lazarus gained everything by death, and the rich man lost everything by the same process. He had not his soul's treasure by him, it was all left behind, all his costly linen, all his velvet, and silk, and purple garments. His mansion of white marble, and his gold and silver were all lost to him, and his soul knew of nothing else. Therefore was he indeed poor and Lazarus was rich, and he was in hell after death and Lazarus was in heaven. Charity shall cover a multitude of sins, but the rich man had not charity, and had not done the works of charity, and there was none to receive his soul after death, not one to invite him to a mansion of rest. He remained alone, in a solitude of recollections about a life as a slate on which nothing was written of him but reproaches, but he recollected the poor Lazarus and his conduct towards him, and he saw him far off, and he begged Abraham to show him a favor, and relieve the pain as his soul was burning in the interior fires of his consciousness. That fire had to burn out, and convert his pride, and arrogance, and covetous spirit into ashes to gain humiliation and truth, and worship, before charity in the spirit of God could convert him to take the first step on the ladder of progression across the deep and dreadful ravine which parted him from the poor Lazarus, that despised beggar. Spiritualism and the gospel of Messiah teaches man this first principle of truth in faith, but if he will not believe Moses and the prophets, neither will he believe in spiritualism, nor that a spirit returns after death. Such was the answer of Abraham, and he would neither allow Lazarus to go to the brethren of the rich man, nor relieve his agony with the comfort of a drop of water. Other persons on earth persecute the harmony of God as Paul did in his ignorance, when Jesus exclaimed, " Saul, Saul, why persecutest thou me." This dreadful sin is done every day on earth by thousands of people, as at the moment when Saul rejoiced in the murder of Stephen, and took care of the clothes belonging to the men who stoned the saint to death. Some of such men repent in deep and honest humiliation, and become great instruments in the hands of God, and atone for their sins during earth life, as when the great apostle suffered every privation for the sake of him he once persecuted, and at last laid down his head on the executioner's block as a willing sacrifice in death to glorify his master, the Messiah, by.

There is another sin for which there is no forgiveness on earth, and it is the wilful crime against the Holy Spirit, which is mentioned so often in the bible ; that which Judas, the apostle, committed, and caused him as well as Pilate to commit suicide. When a man or woman commits that sin, then the guidance of the holy angels are withdrawn from them, and the light from the heavens is shut off from their souls, and they are left to themselves in the utter darkness of their own condition, and their life on earth becomes intolerable, and they are thrown into despair and insanity, and often commit suicide, but all suicides are not from that cause, for it is written, "I will punish the second and third generation of those that hate me, but bless those in many generations who love me;" and again, "neither has he sinned nor his parents," who was born blind, but it came upon him in the third and fourth generation, and God was glorified in taking away the curse.

When that wilful pleasure enters a human soul to fight against the light, he is not any longer in indolence but moves on as an active member to the inferior hells, and such a person is in the darkness of that sphere, and guided by devils. Such a person cannot speak the truth; when he speaks falsehoods he speaks of himself and of his own guardian spirit, for he is a liar, and is in union with the father of lies. Such a person is filled with accusations and bitterness, and without love and gratitude he assails those who do him good, hating his parents and persecuting the light carrier from heaven. In that spirit is no repentance, and no reconciliation with the spirit of God, and he hates the Messiah, because he has the spirit of that hate within him. That is the spirit of murder by which Cain killed Abel, by which Jesus was crucified and the prophets were slain, and it is the mission of Lucifer to blow out the light, that there may be no light of inspiration from the third heaven to reach into the human soul. The hells are divided into numerous societies. You have no fight with flesh and blood, but with societies and principalities, and the unseen powers in the air. On the surface of rivers and lakes, and on the sea-shores, in cities and groves, on graveyards, and in dwellings formerly occupied with the spirits as their homes, dwell some in comfort, and others in hell's societies of spirits. Hell is a condition of mind in corresponding society. Thus you find saloons and houses of ill fame the gathering places of many spirits, who suffer from bad habits and do not repent, and are attracted by the force of inherited dispositions to corresponding places as during their earth life all the same in spirit life, where they indulge in the spirit of intoxication and uncircumscribed passions the same as before. Some spirits do not for a long time leave the graveyards where their bodies or earthly remains are laid. Others roam at sea, and on board vessels, and even descend to the bottom of the ocean, and travel in the interior of the earth, and its chaos.

All location is only an exterior fiction to the spirit, as the truth is that the condition of the soul-life is in accordance with the spirits living, because the locations are to be found in a correspondence to the disposition of mind, and its inclination and development, so all external location is only a secondary circumstance to the reality of soul and the intensity of its affections in which the spirit is moved, or attaches itself to exterior relations belonging to earth-life.

The second sphere extends in a broad ring or belt of spiritualized matter, emanated from the first sphere and the earth sphere combined, and all things in the mental and physical atmosphere in these spheres, and also from the moon's semi-spiritual sphere and spirit-sphere, which unite in a unity with the earth's second sphere. This belt extends beyond the moon in a circular belt 250,000 miles broad, in between the orbit of the moon and the planet Mars, twenty millions of miles from earth. The zodiacal light is nothing else but an illumination of reflected light from that sphere, revolving in the same plane as the planets. The semi-spiritual emanations in the first sphere around the earth extend as far as 200,000 miles out in the space not far from the moon, and consist of four stratas with 40,000 miles apart. The first commences about 5,000 miles from the earth. They are not visible to the natural eyes any more than the semi-spiritual nature is, but may be discerned as a scarcely perceptible mist, except to the spiritual perception or clairvoyance. The four stratas of spiritual matter are only parts of one belt moving along with the earth, but revolving contrary to the earth, or is moving from east to west. These stratas are only departments of spiritualized matter. The natural eye of man is adapted to observe objects corresponding to nature's camera, which his physical body reports with, and things are photographed on the retina by the modification of the light and its law in passing through the lens.

The natural law of seeing pertains only to negative objects, as life on earth is manifested in crude or negative formations of which the globes are composed. Semi-spiritual magnetic materials, as that comets are feeding the light atmosphere of suns by, are transparent, and even stars can be observed with ease through a comet's tail of several millions of miles density all through space. On your streets you are passing through crowds of spirits nearly every minute without inconvenience to either parties, and the spirits are not observed by the natural sense of seeing. Upon the same principle is the belt with its stratas between the earth and the moon not visible to the eyes adapted for negative seeing of matter, corresponding to its own material in the physical universe, and it can only be discerned by positive spirit sight of beings corresponding to that condition of a world as their own. By spiritual impressions from the above, you are able to see and discern the spiritual things and know the worlds in which spirits and angels dwell, and for that reason is that faculty in man known by the name of second sight.

When men and women possessing the superior faculty of seeing, have told the world about houses, cities, fields and multitudes of people in the moon, then the astronomers at once denounced it, because the moon is dead to the nature and conditions now existing on earth. However, it is not dead to a semi-spiritual nature, which in the future will be observed by new and improved instruments, not known at present by the astronomers.

Spirits that are disembodied cannot report with this earth or the physical universe, except through the negative condition of matter of which men's bodies are composed. Hence mediumship and materialization, or the physical universe, do not exist to them any more than the spiritual universe exists as a reality to man. Of that reason can man not report with the spirit world, except on a spiritual plane of its positive existence, as long as man has a negative living in his natural life on earth, and does not enter upon a positive spirit life except by inspiration, or seership, or mediumship in various manners. Like spirits report through man with earth-life, so does man report through spirits with spirit-life. It may be evident from these facts, that the belt between the earth and the moon cannot be observed by natural sight, any more than the earth can be visible to the perception of positive spirit sight.

When the zodiacal light reflects to earth from the celestial sphere, it is because of the abundance of asteroid matter which compose the lower strata of that immense belt, encircling the moon and earth from the lofty latitude of twenty millions of English miles from earth, or nearly half way to Mars. This heaven contains many societies and principalities, and has a beautiful spirit light forty times stronger than the disc of the moon appears on a serene moonlight night, and is dazzling white, and substantial, and cream-like in appearance.

The terrestrial world of spirits has a dim spirit light, which is graded in strength according to the different societies and their intelligence from a starlight of seventh magnitude, to the starlight of the first magnitude in brilliancy.

The light of the lower worlds is yellow or pale grayish, where little intelligence prevails, and in the hells the light is of a brick red color, and indicates the spirit of hate, and revenge, and murder. The domains of Lucifer and his hosts have a pale, whitish yellow light, and are of a polished metallic brightness, when the archangel appears in his royal estate of splendor.

The lower hells or the utter darkness, where there is wailing and gnashing of teeth, are deprived of all light, except that of red hot fire. It is a spiritual condition more corresponding to the wild, hot and consuming passions of hate and revenge, and the insanity of perversion, and is not balanced in passions but in a craving of diverted or abnormal appetites for satisfaction.

In second or terrestrial sphere the developments of the earths and moons and their heavens' intelligence are mingled together on a belt as broad as 250,000 miles, and twenty millions of miles from earth, with the zodiacal formation as its basis, and revolves around the sun in the same plane as the planets from west to east, and is seen in the tropical regions with a brilliancy, and in the northern latitudes during the spring in the east after sunset, and in the fall months in the western hemisphere after sundown.

The celestial sphere, or the third heaven, is located five billions of miles from earth. This belt is broad, about five millions of geographical miles, or twenty-five millions of English miles, or one-fourth as broad as the distance between the earth and the sun. It shines with the brilliancy of the spiritual sun.

This third sphere or the celestial heaven is a spiritual illuminated belt beyond all the planets and along the milky way in between the sun Sirius's planets, and the earth's planets, and encircles the entire solar system. From all the planets and the sun spirits are associated there, and it represents to those highly developed intelligences the entire solar system of spiritual evolution. The third heaven is an emanation of spiritualized matter from the sun, and the second sphere, and from all the planets and their satellites. It is the most tangible and real world of the spirit spheres which belongs to the solar system, and the spiritual cream of the intellect and power of the orbs. The intelligence of mental and divine evolution and thought is treasured up there. Being the spirit sphere of the entire solar system, it is shining with the lustre forty times brighter than that of the sun or with the perfection of God's mansions, and is called the heavenly world. There are numerous societies as in every other sphere of the spirit world.

All globes in a solar system are derived from the same center nebulæ or sun, and they belong to a corresponding nature and corresponding spirit worlds in all of them, with the same variation matter present in regard to density and volume. The sun orb being the center, is the most dense body, as heavy as platina.

The vulcan and mercury have less density, but as quicksilver and as lead, and so on less and less, and the moon has in proportion much less density than the earth, and Mars less again until you arrive at Jupiter, with a density of only one-fourth of that on earth, and in each is the density continually growing less, and the last planet omega is of a half semi-spiritual density. Such a composition is also the bright magnetic light atmosphere around the sun, moving opposite to the exterior shell, but in the same direction as the second or interior shell or ring, and opposite to the main orb of the sun, which generates the great magnetic light by chemical pressure and the electric friction during the intense velocity of the shells in a contrary rotation of the interior and exterior ring or shell. The main globe of the sun and the light atmosphere is moving in the same direction. If the exterior shell of the sun should evolve in fragments and form a globe, then the sun would lose more than half of its light. This shell revolves around the axis of the sun in 29 days, and is seen as black spots on the sun's disk during the severe electric storms and hurricanes of the light atmosphere. The sunlight is the vitalizing element for the organic principle of life, through which the organic life on the planets has been conceived and received their vigor and support. All planets have passed through the baptism by that light. It has encircled them all together at long periods before they rolled into existence and became independent globes. The sun is contracting all the time by throwing off material for planets. The similarity, and again the dissimilarity pertaining to matter and life on all planets is corresponding to the differences of the organic life upon their surface as to their spirit world.

When science starts out with the idea that the earth is the normal type for all the worlds, it arrives at one of the greatest possible mistakes. For instance, a man living on the belts of Jupiter is commonly eight feet and six inches, and a man on earth is five feet and six inches or six feet, but his gravitation to the center or weight is 175 pounds, when the man of nearly double that size does not gravitate to the center of Jupiter, with a greater weight than a few pounds, which he can diminish again by control of the atmosphere on which he glides, and with great ease can walk on water, providing he is not subject to the pressure of the earth's atmospheric conditions. You can draw, step by step, safe conclusions from matter to the spirit generated from it, and the future generations will learn wisdom in the spirit by such calculations. The body of the man from Jupiter would appear as a condensed air bag, when the body of a man on earth would appear as a bag filled with condensed muddy water, and thence the differences.

When a planet has only one-fourth or one-sixth of the density which is on earth, then nature's organisms are correspondingly different in density. The main body or orb of the sun is largely composed of magnetic iron, and is very compact, but not hot, as some scientists have imagined and been convinced about by the spectrum analysis, which teaches that in the sun's rays are the metals and metaloids to be found atomatic, but by the corresponding process of analysis can they be found in the atmosphere on earth, or on any other planet, where the air can be tested. The atmosphere represents the globe. It is a fact that the sun's rays pass through a cold space without generating heat, and it can only be done by the action of two factors combined, the perpendicular fall of the magnetic ray, and the density of the atmosphere.

It is well known that the rays of the sunlight come directly cold down on the equatorial belt, where snow covers the mountains of the Andes in Peru, as in the equatorial mountains in Asia and Africa, on account of the height and not sufficient density of the atmosphere. The north pole has a sufficient density of air, but during spring and fall months not sufficient vertical fall of the winter sun's rays to develop heat, and those regions are in a perpetual glacial period. The sun's rays generate heat and life, but it is no heating furnace by any means. When its rays come vertical enough to produce the electric friction or influx of heat, then the heat waves become developed, and they are only a further development of the light wave, and as the light which is a cool magnetic wave can only develop the electric heat wave in proportion to the vertical ray, then strong heat can be generated in dense air by an absolute vertical position of the sun's rays, to reach air to be electrified, and in proportion heat is developed from the light in the atmosphere; so there is no truth in a white hot body for the sun, when science admits the sun to have a black body, which is a black exterior shell. There is an interval of ten thousand miles between the interior ring or shell, which moves opposite to the exterior shell which generates vital solar electricity. The light atmosphere is ten thousand miles away from the sun, and is floating more than a hundred thousand of miles away to the center. Between the exterior shell of the sun and the light atmosphere is a protecting photo-atmosphere. Between the exterior and interior shell is a very mild and pleasant atmosphere, which in grand perfection and beauty surrounds the interior globe of the sun, and generates streams of magnetic rays from that body which pass through the openings in the rings or shells into the photo-atmosphere, and feeds the light atmosphere. The difference to earth is that the light wave is only of five-eighths in the summer to three-eighths in the winter, when the difference in the heat wave from summer to winter is as from four-fifths to one-fourth. Hence the extreme small density of the volume of the sun's circumference, although the sun's orb is as heavy as platina. Following this conclusion and evidence, we find also that the ray from a reflected intense sunlight on the moon does not develop any heat on earth. The atmosphere on the moon is extremely rarified, but sufficient to receive and reflect sunlight, which spirit belts do not do, but coming in contact with the upper regions of the earth's atmosphere, about seventy miles from the surface, it electrifies the atmosphere by the light wave, and absorbs moisture by the correspondence of the heat wave in the ethereal atmosphere of the moon, with the upper atmosphere surrounding the earth, which clears the sky, and makes those beautiful moonlight nights on earth.

The inhabitants on the sun are not troubled from heat, nor from any excessive light, as the double shell rings moving in opposite directions leaves only sufficient light to penetrate the openings, and make the perpetual day pleasant and comfortable to the people. The scientific views are, that the sun is one molten mass of fire. This is erroneous, as science disproves that argument itself by seeing the dark spots of the exterior shell which the astronomers take for the body of the sun revolving with great velocity, independent of the light atmosphere which actually is drifting with its mighty waves of magnetic light in the opposite direction, and sending out tongues of light far as five hundred thousand miles.

The inhabitants in the sun are very intelligent and correspond to those living on Mars, and the largest moon belonging to Saturn, in scientific attainment and elegance of physical structure and civilized refinement. They are much like the Hindoo race, but nearer white, with finely developed heads and large brains, and very compact bodies, but not as coffee brown as the inhabitants on the sun Sirius.

The astronomers' calculations about the density of the sun is not correct, as the globe is very dense, and for the balance is thousands of miles between the shells, with atmospheres they know nothing about.

Man has difficulty in comprehending spiritual substance, but when he considers a comet with 150,000 miles diameter, he can see with the naked eye contains a sublimated matter so refined that it does not reflect the light, and stars are seen with all their brightness shining through that substance without obstructing the rays of their light, then he gazes at it with wonder how it can be. If that substance was gas, or smoke, or fog, or clouds, or anything known to the earthly conception of things, then the 150,000 miles diameter of any visible substance of that nature, or meteors, would certainly obstruct the delicate ray of a star of the seventh magnitude.

The distance of the globe Eve, or the spiritual earth, is nine hundred billions of miles from the earth's sun, and societies of former citizens from the earth are living in the spirit on that globe, adapted to the life in an intermediate state between the second and third heaven, and for some spirits meeting there from both heavens. The planet Eve belongs to the exterior group of planets which encircles a sun to the spiritual sun Kolob. Eve is twenty thousand miles in diameter, and has four moons, which are from two to five thousand miles in diameter.

During the time Israel lived in Egypt, and the great pyramids were built by Pharoah, Rameses the Second, the architecture was so arranged that the great hallway in the king's chamber ran directly north and south, so a person from the interior looking north would in the middle of the entrance discover the sun Thuban, the north star four thousand years ago. Abraham was well versed in the Egyptian and Chaldean astronomy, and mentions the great sun Thuban as Kolob, the sacred orb amongst the Egyptians, and as the symbol for the corresponding invisible dwelling place of the Most High God, the Almighty. The sun Thuban can be observed a short distance from Polaris, the present north star, and in between the two Dippers. The pyramids were built in strict conformity to that great sun, which at that time was considered not movable in its position to earth, and the pyramids are there after a lapse of four thousand years, but the earth has changed its position to Thuban, and that is not any longer the north star. God, the Almighty, was offered worship by the patriarchs, and the light of Thuban was to them as the light which descended from His throne, or from the invisible heavenly spirit sun of the same name, Kolob. This mighty central sun for the eastern hemisphere of the invisible universe will be described in full in other places.

Another great sun is Luto, in the constellation of Ursa Minor, in the Dipper, near the handle. It is a central sun of another order than Thuban, and for a group of suns and their planets, and its people are corresponding in intellectual development and intelligence to the summer land or the second heaven. Luto means "the light in the soul." Kolob means "God's mansion," a name the Egyptians gave to Thuban, but in a more true sense belongs to its spiritual globe, the great central suns of the eastern hemisphere of the universe, the spiritual Kolob.

To Thuban belongs a large, magnificent group of planets, which are all shining suns, and encircling Thuban in all the brilliancy of light and beauty, and the heavens are illuminated for millions of miles in one perpetual light. The spiritual light for the invisible central sun Kolob, is wisdom shining in the glorious beauty of God's love, and with the intense power of the Holy Ghost, moving in the spirit of eternity. No spirit from this solar system has ever attempted to approach that globe nearer than its exterior suns, which move in allegiance to its light and millions of miles from the central sun, and with one hundred millions of miles apart, where the spirits have been received by the Messiah and entertained with his love and harmony. Spirits and angels can not approach the suns of Kolob, except they are from the third heaven of the solar system they belong to. The Kingdom of the Messiah is in the celestial sphere, and His mission is to bring the principles of it down on earth, that He may govern there in His Father's name, that His will may be done on earth as it is done in heaven. This work is not granted by the world nor by the spirits out of the world, but by His elect from out of the world, and by His elect in the world, and they belonged to Him and His redemption from eternity, and in this movement from the third heaven is the entire race saved in their own orders to their own spheres.

The spirit sun Kolob is one hundred and five trillions of miles from the earth's sun. Such distances may appear impossible to travel for any intelligence or spirit power, but the velocity of inorganic electricity is 60,000 geographical miles, or 300,000 English miles a second, and amounts to nothing in comparison with vital magnetism, which travels 250,000 geographical miles or 1,250,000 English miles a second, and that appears again nothing, when spirit magnetism travels 500,000 geographical miles or 2,500,000 English miles a second, and by the intellectual will force a spirit can use ordinarily to his own disposition, he will move through space with an intensity of two millions of geographical miles or one billion of English miles a second. That is the spiritual movement with the power of his will force to report by, although his spiritual body by another law of gliding on the spiritual magnetic highway of rays travels with a quickness of 200,000 English miles in a second, or as fast as the light does. Angels in the celestial heaven report instantly with their friends on earth through guardian spirits after guardian, and may communicate such by impressions to human brains on twelve different individuals, in the same interval of five minutes.

When a spirit has entered the second heaven, and visits the earth from that sphere, he has outgrown all obstacles which negative substance or matter can afford to him, as in fact such does not exist to him as any hindrance, and he moves with the same rapidity through mountains, and stone walls, and houses, as he would in space where they did not exist.

Spirits dwell where they belong, according to the law and disposition of gravitation of mind, and attraction of the soul. The sun Sirius and its planets are visited by many spirits from the earth's solar system, and by millions of spirits belonging to the second heaven, who find themselves in sympathy with that law of life.

The great sun Sirius exercises a powerful influence on the earth's sun, although their distance from each other is about one hundred billions of miles, and the diameter of Sirius is about twenty times greater, or fifteen millions of miles. It moves onwards in space with a speed of nine hundred miles a minute, and contains in its photosphere, sodium, magnesium, iron and hydrogen, and has a more white light than the earth sun, on account of its greater perfection, and less proportion of iron in its central body, and more of calcium. The earth sun and Sirius are moving around and with each other in a gigantic eclipse, and one is towing the other at present with a fearful speed to the conception of man towards the constellation of Hercules in a journey of two hundred millions of miles a year, which in space amounts next to nothing, and would in ten thousand years not make the difference of one thousandth part of a second of the position of the sun's radius around the universal center. Such in an endless labyrinth to man, swings those immense suns with worlds upon worlds of planets attached to them in every possible manner, more complicated than the wheels in any machine, but exactly as uniform and correct in the mathematical relation to each other. When man looks upon Sirius, that sun appears as a star of the first magnitude, but when the earth sun is viewed from Sirius it would appear as a star of the seventh magnitude, as the proportion in the diameter is between eight hundred thousand miles, and the Sirius diameter of fifteen million miles.

The sun Thuban is fourteen trillions of miles away, and the center suns of the Pleiades headed by Alcyone are moving in affinity to it. The diameter of Luto is forty millions of miles, or one-third of the distance between the earth and the sun. The diameter of Thuban is one thousand times thousand hundred miles, or one hundred millions of miles, and one rotation takes a thousand years. The present north star, the sun Polaris, is of a corresponding size.

Thuban or visible Kolob is located between the little and the big Dipper. The sun Polaris is the old Greek star Cynosure, known as such to the Egyptians. In about 12,000 years more it will pass out of its focus in the north by a general movement of the universe, and the sun Lyra, with its dazzling light, will fill the office as Polar star.

The law of rotation and revolution which follow as a general rule the planets in the solar system which the earth belongs to, deviate in regard to the satellites, in proportion to their deviation of relation to masses and distance, and makes one of the moons of Mars move around that planet three times, in the same time Mars makes only one rotation. This difference is also more observed in regard to the rotation and revolutions of the suns, and makes it an utter impossibility for man to account for it all by this present system of astronomical calculations, because the suns are independent of the general laws for the planets as the comets are, and the semi-spiritual belts and globes and worlds are, and the entire unseen universe, which affects the seen universe most powerfully and constantly, but cannot be seen nor accounted for by man. Suns are moving by mutual attraction of affinity to each others' spheres of intelligence. Some come into such a close attraction of that condition, that they become double suns moving around each other, or triple suns moving in a triple manner, one always between the two suns in a constant revolution and rotation, sparkling in all colors and light of brilliancy, independent of common laws known to science on earth. There are suns more than five hundred million times larger than the earth's sun, illuminated with the most dazzling spiritual magnetic light swinging in eclipse around each other and very close.

Adam and Eve were children in development corresponding to the life in the second heaven. Enoch and Elias, Seth and Moses, went into that heaven, and on the mount was Jesus transfigured with Moses and Elias in the light of the summer land, and Peter said, "Here it is well to be, let us build our pavilions in this place." It was in the second heaven the thief on the cross met Jesus, as He said to him, "To-day thou shalt be with me in paradise."

Paradise is in the second heaven of spirit life, and is also called the summer land. The effort to supplant it on earth failed by the effort of the adversary principle, and the spirit of man and his earthly persuasions. The effort of spiritualism is to establish its mission from the first sphere, and to the rudimental spirit conditions of earth-life, and to work from there into the summer land, and bring the spirit of that sphere again to recoil down on earth.

The mission of the Messiah is the effort to redeem man as far and much as conditions will allow, and bring many of the elect in the celestial heaven to dwell on earth in the city of the new Jerusalem, and the coming with thousands of angels. The third heaven is the place where Jesus prepared a place for His elect, from there He shall appear with them again on earth. The third heaven contains the order of Messiah and the kingdom, and numerous other societies of art, philosophy, learning, theosophy intelligence, dramatical achievements, and department of sciences not known to man on earth, but all recognize the Ancient of Days as the supreme Ruler of that heaven, and all spirits in that sphere are members of the Order of Messiah, and there are many military organizations fighting for the principles of liberty and truth, and in a spiritual sense they are all united in recognizing the guidance of the Lord in the spirit of their doings, and they are willing to do all that humanity calls out for in its spiritual need. Messiah is ever active, silent and retired, but powerful and strong, and mighty through all the lower and upper worlds. Many of his dearest friends and most devoted apostles and prophets are members of the spiritual congress, which heads the movement of spiritualism. For the worlds He has no ambition, nor is the honor of man or spirits of any value to Him, as there is one that honors Him, the Eternal Father.

The Messiah mansion is of eternity, which is beyond the celestial sphere. Eternity is another development and emanation of spiritualized matter by evolution of supreme divinity. It is worlds without end throughout the eternal life, or the spirit of His home. He was before the world and its spirit spheres. The battle between darkness and light is, in whom shall man trust. Darkness says in everything you can get hold on, your capacity, strength, money, property, friends, the world's patronage, standing in society and your own success, but light says, trust in nothing of all of it, as it will prove to be a deception, trust in God, and in Him alone, because they who have struggled through all the spheres of life, and arrived at the celestial world or third heaven, have all and every one that same philosophy in which they found the power of progressional strength, that in God we have everything, we possess everything, and the only true life is that in His spirit of love and truth. Nobody can enter the third heaven except by that conviction, and with that life within him so he may be who he is, or what he was on earth, and when Lucifer fell from that conviction in his entire soul, he fell into the idolatry of his soul's selfishness, and fell from the presence of that love which is in the eternal Father. There is not a person in the third sphere who has anything of himself, but the continual prayer in his soul is, that all power is God's, and that his life is strong when it is swallowed up in God, so that he lives not in himself but in the spirit of God, and He is man's daily bread of life, and man's only true nature.

Therefore are the spirits of the celestial sphere all messengers of the Order of Messiah to those of the second and first heaven, and when that order shall come down on earth it has to be organized in accordance with the Masonic order on account of the wickedness of man, who will blow out the light if possibly it could be done, and destroy the life of the messengers of the Most High God.

Spirits from a superior sphere can travel in all spheres below them, but those of the lower heavens cannot raise to the higher sphere except by the interior evolution of light in their mind by the law of eternal progression into the unity and oneness with God, and in the most unconditional submission to the authority of that love which is in the spirit.

For to raise the lower spheres and mankind in allegiance to that standard is all mission done, that the hearts of the redeemed may beat within the heart of God. Therefore have all spirits in the celestial sphere been passing through the baptism of love, and been suffering the humiliation of the fire which is in that love, as man is not in the Lord without woman, nor is woman in the Lord without man, and man is perfected by woman even as woman is perfected by man through suffering in his love. That suffering in love which redeems a woman to a man, and a man to a woman from the lower nature into the glorious light of the element of love emanating from their souls, and commanding their spirits, is singing in their souls about a new world of happiness reached by suffering. Wisdom is the light of such a love by which man can enter the presence of God in the glorious light of His supreme love, that man may be perfected in that, even as he receives strength by that love between man and woman to overcome the world and its humiliations, and be in unity with God and not strong in himself any more, but have his strength hidden up in the life of God as his only life and his only victory.

Some amongst the spiritualists count seven spheres, and it is correct if they count the rudimental earth sphere with its hells as one, and the four belts of the first heaven as four spheres, then the summer land makes up the sixth heaven, and the celestial sphere makes the seventh heaven.

Beyond the seventh sphere is the eternity or the eternal worlds, and the abode for the eternal Father and His hosts of archangels, seraphims, cherubs and Lithyllys, or spirits from other worlds and other planets than the solar system to which the earth belongs.

Besides the different spheres mentioned are there numerous globes or planets destined of the eternal Father as abodes for different spirit nationalities. The Chinese have with some exceptions their spirit globe, where the great majority of the

Chinese spirits gravitate to and enjoy the happiness and peace wished for. The ancient Egyptians have their own spirit globe. Also those earth spirits so developed and disposed who wish with a preference the life on the spiritual earths, of which there are seven, and the largest is the planet Eve, and all are corresponding to the different spheres or belts, so all the difference consists in the degree of mental and spiritual evolution. The Chinese globe corresponds to the third strata of the first heaven in spiritual development, and Chinese spirits enter there after much probation in the lower earth sphere into their happy home. The spirits on the planet Eve correspond to the second belt of the first heaven. Spirits on that strata correspond directly with the spirits on Juno and Confucius. It is not any very high degree of development to live there, but the spirits are satisfied for themselves, and live their highest conception in amusements of art, and music, and literature, and away from the brutish hells always pervading the atmosphere around the rudimental earth sphere, until the adversary gets bound, and peace is restored to earth by the effort of the Order and kingdom of Messiah and for a thousand years. The Negroes and Hindoos have for each race their own spirit globe. The Negro globe is shining with a star-like spirit light, and belongs to the second strata of the first heaven, and when the spirits progress higher they enter the spirit belts. The Hindoo globe is a most beautiful world corresponding to the summer land in beauty and light, and is shining at times with a celestial splendor. It is the home for the followers of Buddha. The Arabs inhabit a small globe east of Juno, and dwell there in a luxury of home-like habits, until they have outgrown their ideas and pursuits of happiness by earthly aspiration, and progress onward and mingle with the Arabs on the spirit belts and higher conditions of spirit life.

Hades is a spirit globe for the inferior world of spirits. To Hades Jesus descended after the death on the cross, and preached to the spirits who were kept captive there for more than two thousand years, or from the days of the flood, and many believed him and received the Holy Spirit of progressive light and true philosophy and freedom. There are four spirit globes for the inferior conditions of men's and women's souls, devoid of the higher spirit life to progress on. These planets are Hades, Merijam, Baal and Gehenna. Hades and Merijam revolve around each other at about one thousand miles apart, and each one has a diameter of five and four thousand miles. These measures are given according to the conception of man.

Both are grayish looking orbs with a light of a newly polished stove, and they are densely populated. The planet Hades appears mountainous, and looks as a barren country with low bushes and shrubbery, and scanty grass. The people are mostly spirits of a lower order than society on earth. The expression of their features denotes wrath, brutality, and hate, and they excel in ignorance and superstition more than in any real wilful, evil intentions. They are living in peace with each other, and not as on Gehenna, in one continual war. A useful spirit animal is coming from the soul of the Tapir of South America. It gravitates after death amongst those people, and does the spiritual use for them, as man on earth has from the horse and the cow. These animals live for a long period of a hundred years amongst the people as domestic friends and servants, and are gradually transformed into a nomad, or spirit germ for higher spiritual conditions, according to the law of spiritual evolution from planet to planet.

Merijam is about of the same material and consistency, and crude, refuse substances of sublimated matter emanating from the earth and other rudimental planets congregates into abodes for inferior conditions and intelligences from those planets. The race on Merijam looks as Tartars on earth, and spirits who assume or are of corresponding type of development. They are fine, stately looking people, with regular features, black hair and beards, and not without ambition and aspiration for a higher life, and are living in peace with each other, and trying to excel each other in the manly art of wrestling, and sparring, and gymnastics, making it a point to have the most perfect developed form of the body, and beauty, and elegance. The spirit light on Merijam is brighter than on Hades, and the planet is more smooth, not so mountainous, and more fertile, but inhospitable as Mantchuria and Tartary are on earth. The people on Hades have the rugged Mongolian stature and features, and resemble spiritually a low class of people from a very remote, ancient period. Spirits from the earth and the other interior planets are constantly coming in. Only few arrive from

Mars and Jupiter, but numerous from Venus and from the earth. Every planet in the solar system has its hells and heavens, and for that reason the spirits do not generally mingle except in the highest heaven and the lowest hell, but in all conditions of spirit life are transient travelers, which by the law of force in the will push their way in a constant uneasiness, and are conquering the most formidable hindrances to reach there, and are true spiritual pilgrims, and for some interior satisfaction are as comets which come, move around their center of attraction and exhaust their strength, and are charged with the spirit of the world they visit and go again.

Numerous obcessions on earth come from such spirits, and they make themselves accursed by causing epilepsy, disease and insanity, by imitating higher objects and aims of life, without having the corresponding development of mind to push their design and ambition with. There could be written many books on the inferior worlds, but only a few hints can be given, that men may know the first lesson and ask for more light, and the gifts from the light of the Messiah shall be given to them.

The globe in utter darkness is Gehenna. This spirit globe is black, and the spiritual sun radiates a reddish light in its atmosphere as a furnace, when in the atmosphere of the two former planets just described the spiritual sun radiates a pale yellow, slight orange light.

The Gehenna is the lowest spirit globe belonging to earth. It is called the utter darkness, where there is wailing and gnashing of teeth. Jesus did not descend there, but He will banish in the spirit of their own judgment those who have cursed their souls to gravitate there.

On Gehenna are numerous societies, which are in constant war with each other about right and wrong. All claim to be right, and all accuse others to be wrong, and there is no peace except in exhausting each other's condition into a mental paralysis, from which they revive to commence a new warfare, without ever being satisfied of gaining justice for their assumed self-righteousness of mind. On Merijam the spirits are fighting for the poetry of beauty and bodily perfection, and on Hades spirits are working and toiling for comfort and goods very much as on earth, but in the lowest hell on Gehenna, the spirits are fighting for righteousness very much as when a woman calls a man an adulterer, because he has not the spirit of satisfying her wishes, or a thief calls a man a robber, because he failed to steal his gold watch. Every spirit tells immediately who he is by his accusations of another, which is the eternal seal and password of all deviltry. There, has perversion reached its climax, and spirits from earth and other planets, who are so utterly perverted by doing evil as a second nature to their mind, are sinking down as in a dark pit, where they find themselves at home in that same misery which they so studiously prepared for others during their earth life. They wished nothing but destruction and were without charity, filled in their souls with selfishness, and charged in their minds with demands without any pleasure in their hearts to help or assist, self assuming to be more righteous than others, taking the exterior goods for the interior wealth of the soul, and perverting the interior light, denying God, despising the Messiah, worshipping themselves, and preferring darkness to light, they are left to depravity according to their own pleasure to be chastised in pain by the same spirit, which is in Lucifer to make war upon light, by calling darkness for light, and light for darkness, and by fighting for wrong and perversion, hating truth and despising angels from the heavens.

Around Gehenna is a spirit belt, or ring, as around Saturn, where the spirit-sun generates a light less than that on Hades. To that belt emigrate spirits, who are getting the slightest sympathy into their souls and wishing for a better home. The light commences there to give them a faint hope of life and its aspirations, which is the first symptom of progression. The life on Gehenna is without hope, without faith, without charity, without any aspiration. It is the actual spiritual death, and nothing else but a living death, as their spirits shall not die nor the worm of their consciousness perish, nor shall the fire in their souls be extinguished, because they love perversion and hate the truth. The spirits from Hades and Merijam visit the belt of Gehenna, and help spirits from there across to them, but nobody visits the planet, as in the utter darkness no spirits can see to move except those who are perverted into the same degree of spiritual ignorance and hate.

There is a great difference between undeveloped spirits, as some are without any malice or dark intentions, and only ignorant and perverted without wishing to do harm. All such spirits are redeemed, and so are the elementary spirits and monads. Only those spirits which cannot receive light because they are opposed to it, and love ignorance and dark intentions as the most natural element for their souls to live in, are not to be reached with any missionary work man or angels have at their disposition.

All who come to the Messiah are drawn by the Eternal Father and given to the Messiah by Him. The Messiac mission is not as much a propaganda as a gathering out from all nations, and all classes of spirits, who belong to Him from eternity. This view makes tolerance through the spirit spheres. The Messiah travels through all the spheres and visits all the societies, and most of the time is not known except to His elect. It makes often a sensation in the first heaven and the earth's spirit sphere, when Jesus is passing through without being observed of the spirits, and thousands of them are visiting his mediums to get a glimpse of Him, which however cannot be had except it pleases Him to reveal Himself to them.

The movement of spiritualism has met with the most hearty endorsement and co-operation of Jesus with the spiritual congress now presiding in the summer land. Although His individual mission is all through the heavens, it is especially confined to the third heaven and earth, as far as this solar system is concerned, but His mission is to every one of the planets in accordance to that it is to earth, and he visits all the heavens on the different planets in conformity with that he does to the heavens around the earth. Besides, He connects the spirit sphere of the sun with the celestial world, and as the Prince of the eternal world, His abode is at His father's right hand in the eternal heavens, and far above all human conception. In all this various work for the race of man, He has been active personally in the work of spiritualism, which is done by a class of spirits and men to whom His celestial work does not reach, but they are reached in the effort of spiritualism. He visits spiritual seances and controls and inspires mediums, and has materialized repeatedly at Terra Haute, Indiana, and other places known well to the history of spiritualism, and His ancient apostles, as Simon, Peter and John, and others, have enlisted in the work of spiritualism, by that means to convince man and spirits about the spiritualism in the scriptures.

Spirits enter the spirit world at all ages, and arrive even before the natural birth, by accident to mothers, such as miscarriage of the foetus. Another class of angels mentioned as disembodied intelligences, have missions to earth from the second and third heavens, and are directed there for man's benefit, but there are other spirits of an astral nature, or astral spirits, from the stars, who enter this solar system as embassadors from other governments and other suns, as every globe has its governor, or God's representative of the eternal principle, or patriarch, which all corresponds in the grand harmony together and in the same unity. It must be remembered that harmony and intelligence are not the same principle except they are united in one person, because Lucifer is a very intelligent personage, but he is all discord, and harmony is not found in his nature, because intelligence is an individual development, but there can be no harmony except in God. He is the only harmony through all the universe, and every man or angel not found in Him cannot be in His harmony, but is cast away from His presence and is under a curse, whosoever he may be, and however intelligent he may be. In the summer land intelligence is matured by charity, knowledge and love, but in the celestial heaven is wisdom matured into harmony with that love, and intelligence in unity with God and His celestial harmony. A woman may be very intelligent, and at the same time wicked as the demons in the inferior hells. Another may also be found to have very little intelligence, but is blessed with the harmony in the Holy Spirit of the third heaven. After death she will enter paradise, and in the spirit of her soul gather up the light of intelligence, and enter the celestial world and be in the presence of the Messiah, when the first one, with much intelligence and being without charity, and without love, except that of passion, which is self-love, will descend to Hades with all her knowledge, because there is no redemption in it except the affectations in her soul are in God, and cling to God in His love, which has to govern her entire being in His harmony, or she will never come out from Hades before she has paid every penny she owes to His eternal harmony. That is the redemption for which the Messiah works in strict accordance to the will of the Eternal Father.

There are other astral spirit germs born on the suns and in the eternal world, which swarms space, and these spirits are sent to men and women and to generations to come. Every person has not been an astral spirit germ, born in the eternal realm, because those intelligences are made flesh and blood as they are heirs to their father's home, and they are by birthright the elect from heaven, which the Messiah gathers in again to His kingdom. There are two other classes of spirits which enter the human organism after conception. One class are astral devils, fallen down on this planet through rebellion against the eternal harmony. These spirits never enter into harmony, however intelligent they may be. As men or women they will persecute the harmony of the third heaven and the eternal harmony from which they fell, with all the joy of bitterness and gall in their souls inherited in the flesh by their prior fallen estate in the spirit. Such intelligences on earth in human form crucified Jesus of Nazareth, and killed the apostles and prophets, and are the persons who build their graves and raise the monuments and gigantic churches and temples, but invariably will kill again when prophecy shall appear on earth. They can never enter the harmony of God, and they know that there is no salvation for them in His presence or in His kingdom, because they will never enter into His harmony, which they will fight again eternally except when they are compelled by the force of God's harmony to keep peace, and the adversary is bound to peace, and they will progress on the general principles of intelligence in worlds after worlds, in their own way and their own places.

The third heaven and the eternal worlds in that line of development in God's harmony, is closed up forever for that class of astral spirits which are cast off from the progression in the flesh, but enter by adoption, or familiar incarnation, and will always be very righteous, and speak about the commandments eternally, and never keep nor correspond to the spirit of them, but say it well, and do it not. The earth is swarming with those intelligences ready to persecute the harmony of the eternal Father. They can never become the savor of the world, and their spirits are cast out after death into their own place. Some can become very learned and intelligent, but they remain all the same totally blind for the salvation into the harmony of God.

The next class of spirit germs are monads moving into the sphere of the planets by the aid of odd-force from the animal world. Monads are small sparks of spirit life living by the life of God, and sustained in it by the odd-force as its fundamental principle. Monads come by mental evolution from the intelligence of the soul in the most developed spirit animals. By the dissolution of earth life, animals' souls can live for a long time and enter into a new state by losing all form and leaving all shape formerly had as outgrown, and by a sufficient intelligence enter a new scale of existence, which they support in their aspiration as sparks of spirit life or spirit germs, called monads. These monads are neither angels or devils, nor are they astral spirits, but they are the fruits of the evolution of soul-life through the nature of the animal world below man. He has only his immortality as far as flesh and blood are concerned in common with all nature and animals on earth. Everything is immortal before it comes down on earth, also shall it remain immortal after it again leaves earth, and the earth shall drop its fruit in the spirit of eternal progression, and the fruit will be diversified and correspond to the tree from which it comes. Monads are spirit germs of intelligence which enter the lower department of human life, next to the animal plane of living. There are entire families in tribes amongst the Negroes and Hottentots, and native Australians or Bushmen, who are spirit incarnations from monads. In such a view there exists a transmigration of souls through the universe from the very highest to the very lowest form of life, if only one point is remembered, that no animal becomes a man, as no man becomes an archangel in the quality of being a spirit from earth. A monad has no recollection of its former estate. It moves by the power of intelligence and will, and with the assistance of the odd-force seeking something it does not know as a spirit germ before it enters into it, and regains consciousness after being born again in the flesh.

Astral spirit germs are children of the stars or of eternity, and are born of spiritual parents, and regain their consciousness about their former state after death in the flesh on earth, which recollections the monads after death in the flesh very rarely attain to, except in a dreamy perception, which their spirit cannot account for.

The astral spirit germs proceed from the spiritual suns, which govern the spiritual planets to which the earthly solar system belongs. They unite themselves with the monads wherever the affinity strikes in harmoniously, and form a nucleus, which unites itself with a familiar spirit sphere around women and men, and especially congenially attached to a family circle, according to customs by the inherited law of civilized life, and the astral spirit germ is acting consciously to the moment of the union with the monad, when he gradually enters on the earth-plane and at the union after conception with the foetus forgets his former existence, and is living earth-life without being able to account from whence he came except in dreamy suggestions. The monad and the astral spirit germ get developed together into the same unity of one soul, that they cannot account for themselves, but that they are one after death in the flesh. Monads exist in the greatest variation, and are the transition or stepping stone in the soul-life to another state, until they are perfected and reach man. Where they enter without any astral union in the lowest types of humanity, they become after death sustained in societies and worlds belonging to such monads in the spirit, but they do not arrive to the individual soul-life, and retain a monad's inclination, without possibility for individual progression, but to recline into the union with astral assistance for a higher development through new life in the flesh.

Astral spirit germs are often incarnated without any union with monads, exactly as monads enter lower races of man without astral help, but monad races are cruel, brutal and bloodthirsty people, without spirituality, living in the passions of the flesh, and in strife and battles, and hate and murder, without individual immortality, and are found amongst cannibals and barbarian tribes in Africa. These people's souls remain only a short while after death before they, like animals, again are in a monadic state.

The life of Jeshuah, the Messiah, in the flesh was dual and an astral spirit-life on earth. His being was the Father in a pure incarnation, and the lower animal nature had no part in Him. Therefore had His body of a dual reason a feminine development, with a very loose attachment to earth, as the short endurance of His physical strength on the cross also bears witness. Many of the prophets were astral spirits without any union with monads, but with earthly father and mother, and not as in the case of Jesus with only an earthly mother, and the fulness of the spirit of the Godhead resting upon Him. Whenever the hosts of Lucifer disperse on earth they unite with monads in some instances, where the religious element is sufficiently depraved in families to be in a rebellion against holiness, and comes forth in men and women as their souls' delight, but such persons are hostile to the light, and when you look into their eyes a serpent expression is staring at you. They will persecute every astral developed intelligence with any show of success into blood, murder and death, caring nothing about their own lives for revenge. Hence they are not allowed to enter humanity, but when the conditions become sufficiently low, and depraved, and void of spirituality and worship, they will enter the flesh by that law, and emigrate to earth from their spirit planet, Baal, beneath the south pole of the earth, and about 500,000 miles from this globe. Before the millenium commences, will the great opposer of the light be bound over into his own place or home, and the earth will be purified from his spirits to intrude on humanity, and they will remain in their own place on the planet Baal, and peace will reign one thousand years on earth.

The spirit planet Baal is located south of the earth, between Gehenna and Merijam. Lucifer is the lord and master there, and is rendered worship by his hosts as the god of the spiritual sun. Baal is a dark globe, some resembling Merijam in light, but is more rugged, mountainous and desert looking. The spirits are living in peace with each other, and are not in war with themselves as on Gehenna, where the government of Lucifer cannot establish order out of the existing anarchy. The spiritual sun throws a yellow, brownish light into the atmosphere of Baal, which gives to the globe a reddish, faint light, not any stronger than a starlight night on earth. When spirits travel to the heavens or spirit belts, they go north, and exit into the earth atmosphere at the north pole, and above and between the earth's axis and its inclination of $23°$, and directly above its vertical axis is seen the spiritual sun Kolob. When spirits descend to the lower regions their exit is at the south pole to the inferior dark planets, and to Baal and the spirit belt around Gehenna. The earth is the place which serves in many instances as the refuge and the restraint for the spirits on Baal, until Messiah has commenced His reign on the earth, when such a migration will be strictly and entirely prevented. Therefore is the earth a disputed ground between good and evil, until the spirit of truth shall prevail forever.

Individual immortality is not given to monads, as they after incarnation and death sink back into monadic life, except they unite with astral spirit germs into the union of the human flesh and blood, and unite element with spirit, and they get redeemed in man.

Harmony is the flower of God's love. Intelligence is the flower of knowing good from evil and truth from falsehood, but it is not necessarily applied to the love of the truth, because it may be the contrary to the acceptance of truth, in living a deception. This perversion exists on the planet Baal, and the inferior planets, and on Gehenna perversion becomes complete in departing from the light into utter darkness, which breeds aberration from perversion and impossibility to be harmonized into the love of God's spirit of truth and its perfection. Therefore are the spirits on Gehenna deformed in features and build of body, because as their minds are in relation to truth also they appear. The cardinal sin on Merijam is self-love, and ambition and worship of their own dignity and self-esteem, which leaves out the light and love of God's harmony from eternity.

On the spirit belt which surrounds Gehenna, are spirits saved from the utter darkness by the awakened symptoms in their souls of self-esteem, and they rise up in an interior dignity and escape to the spirit belt, where missionaries from Merijam are proselyting, and taking them across to the planet. This proselyting effort is going on from globe to globe, and missionaries, and messengers, and priesthoods are working all through the spheres and earths, and all the heavens, and in fact every society but the Order of the Messiah has its propaganda by which to gain strength and multiply its hosts.

The Order of Messiah and His kingdom is a gathering in of His troops, and calling from parole all of His army to which His elect belong from eternity, and not by subscribing to a creed or a certain propaganda of a society, but by being in the freedom of God's spirit and found in His harmony of love, peace, holiness and truth, not of themselves, but by being one with Him, as in His own perfection, which is not of the world, but by the Father and in Messiah to His elect. On the planet Baal heavy burdens are laid upon the shoulders of all the spirits, and they work out their own vanity filled with deception and pride, but they cannot come to the light nor to the acceptance of the truth in God, and the truth in themselves is only vanity and deception, because the light of the spiritual sun bears witness against them, that they are in a deception, and are filled with malice against heaven as they are barricaded from progression and have not the laws and principles which are in God's harmony, and revealed to the world by the Messiah. These spirits rebelled against the eternity, and were cut off from the progression, on the planets. Baal is a hundred thousand miles in diameter, and is a hundred thousand millions of miles from the center of the earth. Baal and Merijam are moving around each other, and Baal encircles Gehenna's belt, and is moving in a spiral between Merijam and Hades, contrary to the plane in which the earth's solar system and its heavens move. Baal's serpent-like revolution runs around Gehenna and Hades, and makes them points in the eclipse.

The inferior world moves according to the plans of Lucifer. Spirits from these planets cannot enter harmony with the flesh and blood of man, as some are fallen astral spirit germs, mixed up with inharmonious spirits from Hades, called demons, on Baal and Merijam, and devils on Gehenna, and they bring along only discord to the planets, and they are under a curse, when they obcess animals and people for pleasure and by will, and produce discord and insanity, which their perverted minds breed to the calamity of the human organism. They are not allowed by human guardian spirits to enter persons' bodies, and cannot do it when guardian angels protect their client, and do not leave on account of the person's perversion. Devils obcess the body as they did with Judas, and made him commit a sin against the Holy Ghost by betraying Jesus to His enemies. Spirit control works from discord into harmony. Demons and devils work contrary from harmony and health into dark discord and disease. Guardian spirits build up and heal. Demons break down the organism and destroy the body and soul by harmonizing their evil nature to man, and bring him down to their own fallen condition, which is death to the flesh and a curse by perversion in the spirit.

The mission of guardian angels and disembodied familiar spirits is upon the principle of charity, love and affinity to do well and conquer evil, and disease, and discord, in elevating the human nature and soul above the infirmities, and fallacies, and deceptions of this world, into a better hope and more grand harmonial philosophy in recognizing the truth of life, and disbanding the falsehoods of the world. It has been the elevating effort of the second and third heaven to save the human race, and to lift man up in the love of eternity. Therefore came the Messiah, therefore suffered His messengers and preached among men and women on earth.

Man is apt to mix up the service to the world with the service to demons, and make it the same thing of serving the world and Lucifer. This is a great mistake, because God loves the world in his spirit of redemption, and He sent the Messiah into the world, but He did not send Him further than to Hades, where Jesus preached two days. After His victory over death and His ascension, the Father sent Him to other sheep on the American continent to preach to them the same gospel He promulgated on Hades. These people were Nephites, and were not of the flock gathered in at Judea and Jerusalem.

Man has to serve in the world, and in serving his fellow men he is serving the principle of God to do good and bring forth happiness, but wheresoever the elect, of God are moving on in that line, they meet the spirit of Lucifer exercising control against the spirit of God, and there the fierce battle is going on of demons against light. Ignorance, superstition and hate is modified among men by converting them into knowledge of the truth, but demons do not get converted by the divine power vested in man, and are dealt with by higher powers and by archangels in the eternal world, and by the Messiah in the power of the Father, as their designs are evil and filled with malice.

It is by the positive will of positive light in the eternal wisdom, moved by the eternal love, that the eternal principle of God governs supremely the universe, and on the inferior spirit planets is darkness accumulated from the solar system, and subject in its negative conditions to His decision. Darkness may serve its end, but the positive light is sure to disperse its negative condition, as positive wickedness is only negative goodness, and positive blasphemy is only negative holiness, and positive opposition to the Messiah is only negative force before the power of the Almighty, and the hells will be consumed by His light.

The principles of life are eight, four times " you are" from earth to spirit life, and four times " you are not" from spirit to earth life. The four " you are" sounds positive from earth, but are negative in the spirit. The four " you are not" are negative to earth, but positive in the spirit. During earth life man uses them in the spirit unconsciously. The guardian angels use them continually, and keep all to their disposition to act upon. In these principles rests the key and the power to the word of God. The animal world cannot reach farther than to the first principle " you are." The mineral world utters the principle as a low moaning. The vegetable world reaches to the affectionate Oh! The brute, angry, selfish and revengeful nature in animals as in savage man, says " thou" or " you." " You" expressed of two persons against each other is enemity, or warfare, or intense anger. The common greeting: " How are you," or "you are," is friendship. The horse, the dog, the cat and the bird, amongst our domestic animals, can express that harmony as well as man. " You are" is the intellectual development which animal nature can reach into in common with natural man in the common plane of physical life. Civilization developes man's intelligence, and humanity moves into a more impressional life where art, philosophy and luxury makes life more beautiful and rich, and man in his cultured state of existence says " you are." It is the grand achievement of the human mind, which he reaches to by mental culture, energy and perseverance. Civilized man without revelation worships God corresponding to his development as the power and spirit of nature, and from that comes the frequent instances, that entire nations in ancient times rendered worship to the sun, and intelligent people of to-day look into the sun for the visible fountain of life, and render it admiration because the sunlight gives to nature the two harmonies, which are the divine love expressed in nature on earth, or two times " you are." Life is balanced between accord and discord, or harmonies and disharmonies, upon the same principle as the art of music. The full harmony of earth life is four accords and four discords, and the discord sounds in every harmony, and makes harmonies, or there would be no music, and there would be no heavens without the hells, and no angels except there were demons. Neither would there be good without evil existed, nor any light except for darkness. The discords are the shaded sides of the harmonies, and they are the brilliant, shining part of the disharmonies.

It may be evident to all observers, that life and death, or organization and disorganization, are two points in the eclipse of earth life, around which every individuality moves in the accord and discord of his existence. Disharmonies are expressed by "not," added to the harmony, and " you are" is the harmony, but " you are not" is the disharmony. When it is said of woman to a man in her harmony to him, " you are, you are not," it indicates love, and she uses the principle in her spirit always. When she loves and admires a man, unconsciously she speaks the principle in her soul to her guardian. She says it in the silence of her spirit, in the bottom of her soul, and whispers it by the eternal law of God. " You are, you are not," she says, " I love you, but you are not my husband." By the same law he answers her "you are not, you are," which is, "I love you and wish you were my wife." Thousands of unions on earth are made by this law, whenever the correspondence exists in two persons who meet each other. If a man greets a woman with " you are," which is the positive harmony of friendship, and she says in the spirit "you," that man is warned that she cherishes no friendly feeling towards him. If he for goods or money in his ignorance marries her, she will be sure to act more or less hateful to him and her children.

Woman is feminine by birthright, and she is the receptant of that life which is in man, and in sustaining it she becomes the negative principle of man, as he is the positive principle of woman, and she becomes a mother to coming generations. Her harmonies are negative expressions, and to be womanly is to be in accordance to her principle of " not," as that of man is " are."

The world comes in perversion often in its conscious life, because life in humanity is related transverse to instinct in animals; upon the same principle the nerves from the brain cross by entering the spinal cord, and the right side of the body corresponds to the left side of the brain, and the optic nerve receives an opposite reflection on the retina as a picture shows on a negative in a photographic camera, so has the consciousness of man's intellectual life to correct the transverse appearance on earth, to the transverse principles of the spirit, as in all civilized conduct and rational conclusions.

When woman is masculine and says "you are," she is by the logical consequence of her own sex at war with man, because she repulses man from her by her similarity, as the same poles repulse each other, and the opposite attract. Heaven is built upon the law of corresponding conditions, when hell is at war by its law of love-lorn similarities. When a woman requests to be loved, she is perverted into a masculine condition. The passive condition of a woman's love makes the active principle in man corresponding to her nature in that love, to be attracted to her and approach her. If she plays her part of earth life to appear as a man, she is perverted under the masculine principle, and in her activity to attain the imaginary impossibility to command love, she becomes a demon in the battle with the contrary principle to her own existence of harmony and peace.

A woman's affectionate attachment is expressed by "you are not," or in her negative attachment to the other sex. Man has to overcome that negative retired condition by the positive manly love of "you are, you are." Such unions are very happy if woman responds with "you are not, you are not." The perfection of the poetry of love is another step in the direction of paradise, and woman expresses it by the three times expressed, "you are not." She gathers all her soul up in a devotion full of affection and says, "you are not, you are not, you are not." It is the despair of love in the most intense devotion, and the most unconditional submission in the spirit to his personality. Such a love is like indelible ink, which will never die out, and a man and woman can only love with that devotion few times of their earth life, nor can a person ever forget such a love. It will follow a woman during life, and she owes it every sacrifice and development in the spirit. She must not sin against that principle of truth in her soul, because it is next to the divine worship she only can express in the celestial world, or a three times misery will come as a burden upon the woman as upon the man, who confesses in his soul towards a woman a three times "you are," and sins against it by rejecting her love, and she by rejecting his love for worldly considerations.

Guardian spirits in harmonious union with men or women make the most happy marriages, but they do not always succeed in their efforts. Incarnation is upon the principle of "you are, you are, you are, you are," and obcession or hate is the contrary principle, and is "you" four times, or the full repulsion. Incarnation is upon the principle of the full love. Jehovah was the incarnation of Jesus of Nazareth, and the Father was in Him even as He was in the Father, and they were one in the same body, manifested in the flesh to the world. Even so did God love the world.

Incarnation is the union of spirit with spirit in the same affinity, and love, and unity, as Jehovah with Jesus, as Moses with Elias, as Elias with John the Baptist, as Michael with Adam. Some spirits incarnate many times, and incarnation exists in every generation. Socrates' demon was his incarnation, and his teacher, and told him about his death. Every sincere love on earth with a full accord sounding in the full harmony of the corresponding discord is an incarnation of soul to soul, which is made manifest after death by the soul gravitating into the other soul in the same unity of oneness continued in the spirit world by a matter of necessity, after dissolution of the physical body. It is no effort, as there is no effort in love: it moves by a divine necessity. In God's dealing with humanity, incarnation has a missionary design by inspiration and new revelation to elevate and comfort, and teach the human mind.

Incarnation does also another individual service to develop man on earth to woman in the spirit world, or contrary woman to man, but severe mental conflict comes in at times and makes the development a keen suffering in many instances, as numerous spiritual mediums can bear testimony. Because the parties are not together in the same sphere of existence, and the conditions are always broken, as a stick half-way in the water appears broken on account of the more dense medium the light is reflected by. Such conditions are not the most preferable to work under, but the most of all mediums in spiritualism do their mission to earth in the conflicts and pains into the perfection and harmony of such conditions.

The battle-field is between a four times "you are not" in

the spirit, and two times "you are" in the earth sphere. The two missing "you are" constitute the deficiency in earth life and corresponding discord, which cannot be harmonized except by the unity of the two spheres, into one in two souls, or the mediumship perfected in the earth sphere as it is towards the spirit sphere. Woman is positive in her interior soul life by "not," which is to be negative in the exterior life. Hence women control men's affections. The earth sphere and the first heaven are not perfected into the general application of the harmonies of existence, because they are not revealed into the perfection of love before in the summer land, nor in wisdom before in the celestial sphere. The earth sphere is called the rudimental life, but existence is not much better in the earth's spirit sphere, when the principles of life are not studied and practiced in the spirit of love, and not in that of only selfishness. Most people are engaged in the truth of soul to some person on earth of the other sex, and take that love along with them into the spirit world as their soul's attachment, and enter the spirit life as upon a new field of pioneering.

However it may be, all have guides, and they have homes, and have prepared a place for the new comers, where they are introduced to their friends and relations in the spirit of their attachment and love, and enter there upon their new vocation, where truth is the basis of every sincere movement of their souls. If a spirit continues to aspire in that direction, and does not love perversion in preference to truth, he will by the irresistible law of progression be moved towards his affinity in the spirit realm or on earth. The vacuum of a person's want must exist before it can be filled. No person can ever enter the summer land except by love in the principles of "you are" three times, and have found the subject for his perfection in the other sex in that love, which flowers in wisdom by the fourth principle "you are." She will know him at sight, and greet him with a three times "you are not." It makes such unions absolutely not dissoluble, because in the celestial sphere sounds the fourth "you are" to the fourth "you are not," which is perfection in wisdom between a man and woman. The most marriages on earth are "you," or "get behind me." It is a miserable way of living, and death to either of the contracting parties, as there is no life or happiness in their ways, and but a minority of marriages sounds "you are," the kindly exchange of mutual friendship. Jesus of Nazareth did not recognize the marriage of earth as binding for longer than the earth life, neither did the apostles, as in the resurrection they do not marry nor enter into marriage, but are free as the angels in heaven are free, in the freedom of the heavenly companionship. The basis for social life on earth is the family circle, and the continuation of the race, therefore, is marriage of earth, and flesh of flesh, and will cease to be, but the spirit of it goes on into new phases of development until it is perfected in the eternal world, where individuality is perfected in the parties, and differences of sexes ceases to be, because man is perfected by woman even as she is by man. This love cannot be sundered, but that which man put together in the flesh, and was never joined in the spirit, shall also be apart in death. As the light crosses the lens of the eye as in a camera, so does the principles cross the division of existence between the earth life, and the spirit world. Whatever appears positive to the earth " you are," is negative to the spirit world, and that which is negative in the earth life " you are not," is positive in the spirit. "Are" exercises its power over matter or negative spirit, but " not" exercises the mental control over positive spirit, and by four times " not" does the spirit world control the conditions existing in the heavens of mind. Because a woman's life is based on " not," she is negative in the external life, but controling in the positive sphere of mind, or the interior spirit world. A man being positive by " are" in that earth life, is by that same " are" negative in the spirit, or becomes negative to woman's positive spirit control of " not," which he overcomes on earth, but cannot control in the spirit. Man approaches in love woman on earth in her love to him, so approaches woman by her positive spirit principle of " not" that man she loves in his love or in the spirit of his being, and balances her deficiencies of the negative exterior condition of existence. The rudimental relation between the sexes called marriage on earth, exists not much in reality, and more or less in the spirit, until it vanishes in a broken up condition, or appears new into a higher spiritual companionship. No spirit is bound to exterior relations, but only to the interior realities of truth. It goes with marriage as with the churches of earth life, they are broken up by degrees to exist in the mind of spirits for higher and more perfected ideas corresponding to more elevated conditions than earth life. During the Kingdom of Messiah, spirit rules the rudimental earth sphere with four times "you are not," which contains in itself the divine worship embodied in wisdom. It matters not who a spirit is, or from whence he came, if he is embodied in the interior of the spirit of the heavenly love, by which he enters directly the summer land. However, it cannot be done except by a woman he has loved heavenly on earth or in the spirit. The woman may be where she is—it makes no difference, either she is on earth or in heaven, or if he ever spoke with her, if he is developed by her interior principle of three times "you are not," he has the key to the summer land in his hand, and can enter the second heaven by that, or he will never enter there.

Monogamy, as it is, or polygamy and priestly celibacy is all of the world, and will perish by death as institutions belonging to the world, but the interior truth of love which is in it, will live. A man loves a woman in the embodiment of his interior soul-life as its exterior personality. He loves himself, his ideality, his soul's highest conception, and he worships in that love the representative of it in the other sex. That person may not be absolutely defined, but if once found and attached to, he or she becomes the one, and on his or her progressive road onwards in the spirit are the two spell bound in the soul of that love into the dual individuality. When a man on earth loves a woman with a two times "you are," he is considered to have given up his being in love, but he cannot enter the summer land hand in hand with his bride, except by three times "you are." Love has no intention to make idiots of men and women, because man shall always recognize the beauty and greatness in other women, and render such the homage of sincere admiration, whenever he discovers representation of the heavenly truth in the dreams of his soul, and his own highest conception of beauty. This development is neither balanced nor perfected except by wisdom of love, which comes by a four times "you are" of interior attachment in the soul, which is the divine worship in the celestial world. The love of God in the Messiah is four times "you are," in the corresponding development "you are," and united in the same soul-life of divine worship. "Blessed are the pure of heart, because they shall see God," is the embodiment of that development. For to attain to such a love in God, man must be developed into it by woman, and woman by man, in the interior secret of soul's attachment to soul. Man is striving into the negative sphere on earth of " not" seeking the attachment to its positive spirit, for the continuation of his nature as he in the spirit world, is fighting the battle for filling the vacuum of his soul with the principles woman says he has " not" attained to, and in his negative condition in the spirit there he greets her with three times "you are," and a four times "you are" in his celestial perfection, where she greets him in the same perfection by a four times "you are not," which is rendering half of divine worship in woman's assimilation of man's " you are," or the celestial dawn, and blessed are those who attain to it, because they are not any more spirits but angels. That is to be born of love and to wisdom of the soul in four times " you are," answered by a four times " you are not," or facing the gate to the celestial world. Intelligence attains in love its climax of truth. Your eternal love will be your soul's celestial mate in the heavenly law of eternal companionship, and can only be engaged into with one man and one woman. Before they were two, but now they are one in spirit, and the life in the flesh is as a long ago faded away, troublesome dream. Marriage on earth is entirely null and void for such relations except it contains that love which reveals interior truths. The rudimental spirit sphere around the earth is much about as on earth. Only by degree does the great mass of human souls progress into the interior truths from an external perception of things, but nothing elevates a human soul as quick as the true devotion in love. Man on earth or man in spirit has nothing else, but that love he has in his nature and of God, and belongs to God. In that love man and woman develop to each other in their souls, and gain treasures by the grace of God.

For to live happy in a marriage on earth, man and woman must love with a two times " you are," and in two " you are not." A marriage in " you are" is only a fraternal relation, and is not above earth or the physical nature. " You are not, you are," responded to in woman's soul by " you are, you are not," is an intellectual marriage, and " you are not, you are," said of woman to the response of man, " you are, you are not," is a marriage of poetry and intelligence. Love commences with two " you are" and answered by woman with two "you are not." Perversion of the sexes comes in when a man approaches a woman with two " you are not," as it makes him a woman in his soul, even if he may be a man in his physical nature, and a woman who answers him " you are, you are," responds to him as a man in her love to him, and although physically a woman, she loves him with a masculine principle, or as a man. Such perversions are very common, and result in many instances in the decline of the man, and cannot always be rectified by the aid of spirit guides. Man sinks rapidly into an extreme negative condition, and death is caused from paralysis, morbid insanity and phthisis. Man being mentally woman, and woman the man, brings childless marriages, and enervate man, until he becomes idiotic and sickly, and unfit to live, or too feeble minded any more to conduct business. "A hen-pecked man" says the world, is of no value to practical life. His calculation is destroyed, his perception is blunted, his energy is wasted, and he hates his own life in its gradual decline, and if he has not the strength to leave forever, he has to face death, or suicide becomes his angel of relief.

Man must not greet a woman as if she were a man. Woman loses her womanhood by such a relation, and becomes perverted in her affections and fails in her own sphere of life. She enters upon man's work and puts her own work in the shade, and makes him unfit to live in his own sphere of business. Man cannot flourish in a woman's qualities and in her opinions of what to do; she makes man indolent and a vagabond, and crowns her deed in saying "he is good for nothing." When such a woman at the same time is of a nervous temperament, she becomes a terror for neighbors by her assumed position to rule, and regardlessly will she insult them. Man must decline such unions, or capitate better judgment. When a man captures a woman with "you are not, you are not," he is a weak and mentally feeble person, and without manhood to be discovered in his appearance, with a wandering soul, and the melody of his harmony is, if he only had some one to care for him and support him for love, which he has not, as perversion is out of all harmony. He has a mission first to perform, and it is to repent or vanish from the earth, or he must rise up in the manhood of being himself and redeem his lost self-esteem in the spirit. Progression is not possible eternally except the graded principle of self-esteem is living in man, as the redemption to self-esteem is necessary in all harmonious balance of the human mind.

The anger in animals when they are fighting is based upon the principle of I. It does not belong to the harmonies, but to the melodies of life, and belongs to the category of self. The cannibal says I, I, I. The tiger says I, I, I. The Indian on the warpath says I, I. People quarreling and fighting say I, or I, I. Murder is always I, I, I.

Melodies of life belong to the romantic, poetical sphere in the summer land, and are perfected in the melodious harmonies of the pure soul love in a sincere and affectionate attachment. Therefore are the spirit belts around the earth beaming in the light of unspeakable melodious hymns, which cannot be expressed in notes on earth. The songs in women's souls is the romance and poetry of a better land than the rudimental earth sphere, with its swarming elementary spirits and complicated causes for missing hopes and sad failures. The harmonies on earth are grand expectations with graded inquiries, but the melodies take form and action in the courage of an unfaltering hope in life's reality.

Melodies are the songs of what love is longing for, when the harmonies of the soul have the possession of the treasure. Harmony is the victory and the balance of love into the flower of wisdom. That must precede the arrival at the celestial heaven, even as the songs of love in unspeakable melodies shall perfect men and women to enter the summer land.

Some persons may think that the love of God would be all omnipotent without any man or woman to enter the heaven single handed by, but such are mistaken, as man is not in the Lord without woman, neither is woman in the Lord without man, nor can man be perfected without woman, nor woman without man, and no man or woman can reach into that love which is in God, and have received it from Him except it is given to them by the development in their souls in the most deep and sincere attachment to the other sex or to one representative of it. If you do not love the visible image of God, how can you receive the love from his invisible image? Every possible grade of marriage contracted on earth vanishes into nothingness by the affectionate companionship of "you are, you are," and its corresponding answer, but it must be lived as a reality of existence and enter into the harmony of souls. The dreadful cruelty of mankind's undeveloped condition, is the present fashionable customs of society, that persons who are not introduced together, cannot exchange words together, and some of the sweetest melodies are sung in the air and lost to the social soul life, because young men and young women were so related, that they had no occasion to enter each other's society in the harsh education of the society on earth; but nothing is lost after all, and it is often necessary through suffering to unfold the wings of the soul, and after much tribulation to enter the glory of God. When you consider a man who lived richly in money and palaces, but was poor as a Lazarus in his melodious relations on earth, and all his poetry was expressed in tears, and in the bondage of the soul he prayed for sympathy, as a Lazarus prayed for bread, but he got nothing, and he died, and his remains were wrapped in costly linen and laid in a marble tomb, and when he lifted up his eyes in the spirit world, he discovered his guardian angel standing by his side and sang the dearest melodies his soul ever dreamed about. It became then evident to him that his desolate condition through earth life, and the lonely and longing melodies expressed in his soul, were from his guardian angel, and she waited faithfully for his arrival and was his ideal perfected in the dreams of his soul, and she prepared his development, and as the poor Lazarus, he was educated to enter the summer land by her side. Men and women are through much suffering and desolation in the spirit educated to that glorious appearance to be associated with the sons and daughters of God, and enter through the love between souls into the love of God, which is the perfection of the second heaven in a three times "you are not," said of the bride.

This state of development is always only one man with one woman. Therefore was Adam and Eve only two, and the perfection of the melodies are one in two and two in one. In the lower departments of the rudimental earth and spirit spheres, are imperfect and promiscuous relations, as nothing is definitely settled, and souls of both sexes are floating in the question about who or whom. Prostitution on earth is a degree of that unsettled condition, which demands a love not arrived at, and although the mind is rational on ordinary questions, it is an aberration in the sexual life, as hurricanes and winter storms in the melodies. If these conditions are not to rest at death, they will continue after death and in the spirit, as drunkenness does, and other discordant conditions rule, until they are counterbalanced by true relations, and are conquered by philosophy and love, and become outgrown.

Polygamy and harem life, after the pattern of the world belongs to the same category, and are all sifted and balanced on the way through the lower spheres and the first heaven. Some of the worst crimes ever committed on earth, as murders done in cold blood, are where male spirit guides get into love with female spirit guides, and indifference exists between the parties on earth, where the woman does not like the man nor man the woman, who does not by any means assimilate or return the tendered affections existing between the guardians.

Fortunately, higher powers will generally interfere in time, as every spirit has again his guardian, and the link continues so all through the heavens as the method by which God governs humanity, the spirit world and the heavens. However, there exist laws on which crimes are permitted to exist by Providence, without removing responsibility from the offending parties, as there are laws by which the cyclone is permitted to do its depredations, and the earthquake to destroy cities and thousands of human lives, but it is all counterbalanced in reasons existing in mental and spiritual conditions affecting the intelligence by which man and the world is ruled. Humanity, and especially the selfish element in women, has to be counterbalanced so not to ruin or destroy harmonious melodies, nor permit any development in love to sink as prey for inferior or low spirit intrigues. This is the infernal work from the lower hells to pirate on persons' affections as a traffic in the spirit sphere around the earth, and make men and women haunted and killed by pretended lovers, filled with jealousy to persons they cherish no true affection for nor attachment to. Soul unions in marriage can be haunted by demons, so the guardian must call for help or be compelled to leave, or be a prey for the persecutors. Human death from disease or murder is the melancholy result of the work which demons from Baal and Hades do to mankind. Female guardian angels, as said before, are often haunted by such unprincipled male spirits, with the spirit of Lucifer and blood in their souls.

The Holy Spirit, which is God, conquers the animal part in the souls of spirits to disappear in proportion as the globe is perfected, and new and better social conditions will exist on earth. When you analyze the spirit sphere around earth, it is about a fac simile of earth life. Monogamy is not outgrown, nor its evils, nor its prostitution because of death, as the spirit of it will last for a long time in many souls. Monogamy is strictly in accordance with the progressive views of modern civilization, and is the most liberal and free mode of tieing both sexes together, and gives the best facilities to family life with its natural love and protection for offspring, and for that reason are all true unions after death continued in the freedom of the heavenly companionship through the heavens, based upon the corresponding full accord of the principles of life.

Mankind has its dual life in the father and mother, or positive and negative principle, as also in the union of the soul with the negative monad from elementary spirit, and the positive astral spirit germ.

The spirit is developed by the affection in the negative love and positive principle of wisdom moved by the will of God in man. The language is perfected in the same evolution beyond all expression in words, and whatever is unspeakable cannot be conveyed by words, as Paul the apostle said, he heard and saw in the third heaven things which could not be spoken out with the human tongue. All nature has a language, and it is expressed from the souls of animals as vibrations in the principles of life, and human language has to be perfected by degree and the progress of civilization, but words cannot exhaust the full sound of the affection which beats in the human heart, nor can words convey the exact modulation of thoughts beaming on the human brain, and civilized man knows the imperfection of his situation, and that he can only be understood approximately, and not in any absolute sense or with any distinct comprehension.

Spirits with a language on their tongues labor under that same difficulty, but most have mastered the higher law for conveying thoughts in condensed cycles, or a multiplied short-hand system of breathing thoughts by, or in hyperboles and concentration of truth. Guardian spirits use that method daily in conversing with men and women on earth, by impressing the brain as the negative receive its impressions of the landscape with its beauties and sceneries. By direct conversation spirits must adapt themselves to the infirmities of man, and convey thoughts by a language without being able to give man in his present development any better substitute for it. Hence when the Ancient of Days does not accept prayers by words, but only those which come to him in the spirit, and are the united concentration of wishes in the human mind bound together in one cycle, as the force of a bomb is concentrated in a little shell, because the force of the human desire and application before God shall be united into one focus of the soul, and thrown upon eternity before the consideration of the Almighty in heaven. All spirits pray and worship such, and in cycles and hyperboles, and converse with each other in the same manner, never using words, but ideas, except in conversation with man on earth.

By the principle "you are, you are, you are," or expressed in the intensity of the love, which admits the spirit to the second heaven, thoughts are gone directly to that heaven in a prayer cycle, and any audiant can hear its departure from the brain with a continued sound in vibration repeating itself, moving onwards in steam like ring with intense velocity, and disappears. After a silence of a few seconds it returns from its destiny if accepted in the divine mind, and it will be heard at a distance repeating the spirit of its content, and with a velocity stronger than two millions of miles a second drop with power of the full spirit on the applicant, and fill his entire being with the assurance of the will of God to the fulfillment of his application. Should no harmony in the heaven respond to such a grant from the supreme power, then the prayer does not return, because the conditions to realize it do not exist, and the application is not granted. Man may try to apply this method in praying, and it will never fail to reach its aim, if it is done in the honesty of spirit and truth, and will return to the applicant in the most convincing manner with the power of acceptance if received in the love of God. This law belongs to the first heaven in the common prayer of man, with the principles of two " you are." The second heaven is reached with the intensity of the love which is in the three principles of life. No prayer can reach the celestial world, or third heaven, except by the intensity of God's love revealed in his harmony of wisdom to man developed into that wisdom from His glorious presence by the Holy Spirit of Eternity, and expressed to earth by the four harmonies " you are," sounding in one accord with the four discords of " you are not."

If men and women in the flesh on earth can offer up such prayers, or be taken by the spirit into the third heaven, the same persons belong there, or wheresoever their prayers can reach into, but it is only given to those by the grace of God, who are matured in love to wisdom by the incarnation of holy angels from the Holy Ghost, and with the power as tongues of fire.

Man must be wide awake in his soul, not to enter into misery in his conjugal life. The sexual relation amongst animals is a passing by moment, but the conjugal relation between men and women leaves a lasting recollection, and wedded in love, never to be forgotten. Therefore it is one of the most sad experiences to be disappointed in love by the inner exchange of guardian spirits, as the ultimate result of mental conflict and mutual interior misunderstanding. A woman with a male guardian angel must a man have courage to marry, except he is feminine as a woman in the spirit, and play willingly the contrary role of life. There are instances where a woman is dual woman, or woman in woman with a two times " you are not," and a man with feminine guardian spirit becomes her lover, and greets her with a " you are not, you are." Then she says "you are, you are not," and when he rebels in his soul against such an outrage in the spirit, she says " you are," and he says " you are," then the woman's female control will leave for a male control by being compelled to by circumstances. It commenced in harmony and love, and gradually the woman aspired to be man, and with male guardian angel she can only say " you are not, you are," or the guardians " you are," and in the open war for the supremacy she says " you," and he says ultimately " you, that is you, you," or be condemned.

The difficulty comes as an evolution from the feminine guide by the man, which was a misconception to the woman guide in being three females to one male in the flesh, and could have been corrected if the man had exercised control in the spirit as man in man, which however he will be compelled to assume, when she is established masculine in development with a male guide for control, after her female angel has stepped out of power, then she cannot assume any other part in life than that of command or extreme perversion, by playing the male character on the stage of life in the part of Othello's jealousy, or Jago's malice. She does not aspire to Paradise any longer, but to Hades or Gehenna. The female guardian will by the same necessity be compelled to give up control to a male guide for her, and the war is declared in the spirit sphere as on earth, and it will be fought by all the repulsive hate of two times " you," drenched in jealousy, accusations, bitterness and cold-blooded murder, as sure as two of the same poles never unite, but will by the inherited power of nature always repulse each other. Such a life is insanity in the spirit, as there is no reason why marriage could make two be one in the union of souls, because priests for a few dollars fee have pronounced them to be one, when God never united them together. This exchange of guardian angels is a dreadful delusion to that man who believed honestly to marry a woman with woman's soul, and woman's guide, there answer him in the spirit of his interior consciousness with two " you are not," and then on account of weakness in a man's feminine guide incite the woman to assume control in earth life, and is supported by a male guide to a masculine control contrary to her eternal salvation and happiness. She is by her female guide betrayed into the hands of male control, which is the most contemptible high treason, which ought not to exist in the spirit sphere around earth. A woman with masculine development is kept back in her progression, and becomes a by-word in heaven and earth, and the man is equally lost to be of any value or capacity for earth life, so the only salvation will be in rebellion against the usurpation of playing his own part, and if he has not lost all self-hood of being a man, he cannot assume the contrary play which restricts his soul's advancement, but he must retreat in good order and be himself once more.

This condition during earth life is however not confined to the deficiencies just described, because man, who is man in man, cannot be thrown into contrary control in the spirit, and the same phenomena in the spirit occurs only opposite to that described, when it is man who plays the part of feminine jealousy and vile accusation, and shows a hateful disposition, haunting the soul of a woman with untold bitterness. By a true conception and full understanding of the principles of life, can crimes be diminished and entirely prevented in numerous instances. Mind has storms through the human nature and spiritual observations knows them more violent and tempestuous than the hurricane on the high sea, and all this disappointment and suffering serves to man's perfection in heaven, as to give men and women's guardian angels the light and truth of the sphere they belong to.

The harmonies of man in their correspondence to the principles of life does not reach far, and the evolution of his mental life is very low in comparison with the intelligences on other planets, but in consideration that the earth is a very young globe he has not progressed as slow as he might have done, but slow enough to keep the evolution of nature below him in a check, because that is in pain by the stagnation of the human mind, and every animal, and tree, and flower, and stone, is aspiring to the redemption in the spirit from the bondage it is laid under by the negative manifestation of its life through matter into the positive freedom in the spirit of its liberator.

The language of nature sounds in the human soul with an unspeakable longing and songs of poetry and romance, and the harmonies from nature strike the human body in some correspondence. The mineral world touches the feet, the vegetation the calf of the leg, the insects below the knee, the fishes the knee, the birds above the knee, the reptiles the lower thigh, the whales the upper thigh. The harmony from the types of elephants, tapirs and rhinoceros reach the human pelvis. The cats, tigers and lions' harmonies are below the hips. The domestic dog comes with his affectionate harmony around the human loins, and is the conductor in many families by his magnetism for monads.

The tame elephant and horse reach the affectionate part of man with an harmony across the chest of "you are," and the cow and sheep strike man with a harmony above the loins. The elementary spirits and monads are personified in man in the most distinct manner according to the monads' former existence, which accounts for the peculiar similarity in outlines that man resembles a cow, a dog, a pig, a horse, in his external appearance by features, walk, building and characteristic peculiarities. Also does the former estate of the astral spirit germ give to man his mental inclination to be a poet, a preacher, an inventor, an orator, and dispose him in the choice of his vocation and in making life a success. The heavenly image of the divine is impressed on the dignity of man, where the astral spirit power is merged in his nature from the fountain of God's harmony to man with a four times "you are," responded in a four times "you are not." The absolute choice for an eternal companion is not made on earth, nor in the conditions strictly belonging to earth and the spirit sphere around earth, but it is made in the first heaven and in spirit conditions reaching to men and women from the first heaven. All exterior forms of marriage will be outgrown as from chains of bondage and remnants of barbarism, when a spirit ascends the lofty attitude to unite in the absolute oneness with another spirit, not as man and woman on earth to be made one in the flesh, but to be made one in the spirit. That love by which spirits enter the second heaven can only be lived, and blessed are those who attain to it, but it cannot be described. All words to exhaust that idea by, would sound as blasphemies.

That is not a demand to be loved, as there is no demand in love, and there is not any compulsion to keep love together, as there is no compulsion in love, but it is the spirit power of the necessity in two souls to be one in the same purpose and motive of life. It is that intensity of the mutual affections which have found the sublimity and ideality of spiritual correspondence in two natures, expressed by the transverse principle of three times "you are not" in woman, who is negative in the flesh, but the positive spirit principle in heaven. Also man's "you are" three times is positive according to earth, but in the spirit is the negative attachment in his love to the bride, for which he gives up everything, even his own life.

This love is in a silent condition of trance, in which two spirits remain for a long period as in an insensible condition and experience that which no eye has seen, nor ear has heard, nor has it been conceived in the human heart. When it is permitted to be observed by the seer, the two appear enveloped in a special element more tangible than the spirit atmosphere, and encircling them in an oval, egg-shaped eclipse. It is the element of love, and is more clear and transparent than refined crystal, and more aromatic than any perfume made by mankind.

The two worlds of souls emerge into one, and move and exist in each other. This love is the focus for the new transition of the souls, in which man cannot be perfected without woman, nor woman without man. After being conscious in that love, do spirits enter their new homes in the summer land, or the second heaven.

To the first and second strata of the first heaven are several spirit globes attached, where certain races go and sustain for a long time their life and institutions from earth. Such have the Jews the spirit planet Canaan, where they have their spiritual temple, and a cultus corresponding to that on Mount Moriah, at Jerusalem. They are at liberty on their own planet to follow the law of Moses to its full extent, and are not in report with the personality of the Messiah before new light comes by degrees of development to earth, and transition takes place individually to the second and third heaven.

The Mohammedans are passing over from earth in large number to Ismael, the bright spirit globe shining with the light of the crescent moon. There they continue a spiritual harem life with the black-eyed, beautiful houris. Like the Jews they sustain spiritually the polygamy from the days of David and Solomon, and according to the law of Moses.

This condition comes also necessarily in as a part of the social life on the stratas of the first heaven in its numerous societies where men have been married and related to, or in love with, or had children by several women on earth, and of that reason men are attached to several wives as women are attached to several men, and during the first conditions of spirit life are the sexes related to each other in a complex attachment, which gradually clears up into higher and more true relations of companionship, which however breaks up in numerous instances as engagements on earth, and new acquaintances are made until stability comes in by more experience, and stronger unions, and general development.

The unions from earth life have very little to do with the final engagement of soul to soul, where the only scaling there will be valid forever is in man's highest conception of the sublime ideality of his nature he is to be represented by in the other sex.

On the spirit planet Brahma, where the Hindoos have their spiritual river Ganges flowing, is no attempt made to reform marriage relations from earth, and for that reason they do not progress into the second and third heaven of the spirit belt, except in numerous select instances, but are spreading from their spiritual condition relating to the first heaven into new spirit planets and suns, where polygamy and caste system is recognized, and accepted in the spirit of the institutions governing the globes.

The spirit planets Canaan, Ismael, Orises, Brahma, Thesis, Confucius, Eve, Freia, Kalmus and Pan, are of that group, which is moving around the exterior sun in affinity to Kolob, and directly above the north pole. They are rotating one hundred millions of miles apart.

Freia belongs to the Scandinavians, Thesis to the Germans, Pan to the Sclavonians, Oresis to the Egyptians, and Confucius is the Chinese globe, etc., because the different nationalities do not assimilate into the same unity, and there would be no heaven for them in that conflict except by having separate spirit homes. Only the elect in the Messiah gathers out from all the nations under His guidance into a cosmopolitan brotherhood of love in the Holy Spirit of eternity.

Ormus is the spiritual globe for the negroes. It has four spirit belts and two moons, and is in a line with the equatorial radius from earth, about forty-five billions of miles. Negroes who do not enter the second and third heaven emigrate to Ormus from the third strata of the first heaven around earth. There are the negroes developed into their own peculiar civilization, not any more to assimilate with the Anglo-Saxon life, than the Indians on the American continent. The Indian spirit globes are Zuni, the bright, and Zuma. Zini for the war-like tribes on the big hunting ground, who enter there from the second strata of the first heaven, and Zuma the sun-like, for the more peace-loving Aztecs and Pueblo Indians, and Nephites.

The Lamanites on Zuni have done some to pacify the wild and turbulent war spirit, and to civilize and move into progressive order. On Zuma is a highly developed civilized life by the effort of inhabitants from ancient Atlantis. There are magnificent temples and universities, and science and philosophy is cultivated with much vigor.

When two persons in the eternal companionship enter the summer land, they are living in the actual embodiment of their interior love, realized in a substantial identity. By attaining to that degree of intelligence the life in the summer land is continued for any indefinite period, and a multitude of spirits who progress in allegiance to the divine harmony but do not enter into it, are moving towards the spirit suns, which are encircling Luto, the central spirit sun in the little Dipper near the handle, which again is in affinity to Hercules, and that again with its myriads of suns to the Pleiades, headed with the great central sun Alcyone, there is moving in affinity to a gigantic eclipse, in which Thuban, Polaris, Lyra and five hundred suns of equal size, are the center, and representing the invisible solar suns with Kolob, the central spirit sun for eastern hemisphere, or the milky way of the universe.

The third heaven for all the planets is alike, as also the lower hells are alike, but the intermediate states on all the planets differ. Those on the summer land who enter into the third heaven, or into the glory of God, cannot do it except in God's love. Man and woman were perfected to each other in the element of their ideal individual love to be one in two, and two in one, after thousands of mistakes on earth and in the lower sphere, have now after a multitude of failures to give up their own strength and their own resources, to progress on, and their own love to be sustained by, for in the love which is in God to be thought wisdom.

Such they arrive before the portal of the third heaven as

little children, and as such they are gaining admission to their Father's house in His love, by which He loved them when their spirits as astral children of life, and sparks of his glory descended into the flesh and blood on earth.

To love with the love of God is superior to the love between man and women, and superior to the conjugal love, as that is superior to the sexual, or animal love. That strength by which man progressed from earth onwards is vested of God in him as the commandment says, "thou shalt love the Lord thy God with all thy strength, and with all thy heart, and all thy soul;" but now God says, "I will give thee a new name after the Order of Messiah, and I will give thee a new heart according to that love which is in me, and I will give thee a new law, according to the freedom of my own house, even the Gospel of Freedom, and I will take away thy fear, that thou shall know there is no fear in the children of my love. That love shall be as light before thy feet, that thou shalt not stumble, nor shalt thou know of darkness any more, and I will put my light in each one of thy eyes, as the fire of my love, and that you look at on earth shall be blessed, and that you turn your back to shall be accursed, because thou art a messenger of light and wisdom from the high heaven." Such is the introduction. These are the words which come to the candidate for the celestial sphere. Woman's love is the spiritual element of man's mind. She is negative to earth, but positive in spirit life, and able to move the affections of man within her until the perfection in the summer land. There she exhausts her strength in his behalf, and as he by her love was growing into understanding of the causes of things and their effects, so he aspires to wisdom, and in that effort he gives woman compensation for all her toil. The same law is active below man, where nature gives to humanity its elementary spirits and monads, and she exhausts all her strength in that culmination, when rescue comes by the masculine principle in astral spirit germs, or the sons and daughters of the light which unite with nature, and man leads woman onward all through earth life. Woman's positive sphere is the heaven of love or the summer land, but from there man is the leading spirit wherever he moves on, and woman follows him by the same law of affinity and mutual attraction, as they are not two any more but one, and it is through new steps of progression the individual harmony shall teach them wisdom, and the eternal life shall mature their souls in the light of the third heaven to be as God in having known good and evil, accord and discord, pain and joy, darkness and light.

The four harmonies " you are," correspond in harmony to four links or guardian angels between the earth and that sphere called the third heaven. If a man or woman on earth says " you are," she corresponds only with her own guide in the earth's spirit sphere, and she is not developed much further than some animal who corresponds in " you are " with his master, to whom it tenders its affections.

When a man says " you are, you are," in his development he expresses the harmony with his guide's guide in unity with his spirit, or that the first heaven is in correspondence with his soul, and light of that Spirit is able to teach him the truth belonging to that heaven. When man says, " you are, you are," he must by necessity be in a correspondence of development from " you are not, you are not " in some object for his admiration of love and interior attachment. Woman makes the attainment in progress continually more difficult for man by telling him constantly what he has " not " attained to, and he answers her " you are," and is working to attain the treasure, which is a positive relation to her in earth life, but in the spirit he becomes negative and passive, where woman by her " not" points out the causes of existence, and in her love explains the effect of the discords in balancing the harmonies. The three times " you are not " in correspondence with a three times " you are," is the perfection of the third line of guardian angels from the earth sphere in a direct support of the second heaven. If a man and woman live earth life in the third harmony, and he and she are in a three times support, then they are in direct support from the guardian spirit in the summer land, and being developed themselves into that state of perfection, they are although in flesh on earth, living the spirit life of the summer land. They may walk the streets and till the fields like other men, but they are spiritual citizens of the second heaven in which their spirits move and exist.

Upon the same principle you move towards the celestial sphere by a four times " you are." The fourth " you are" in the correspondence with the fourth angel, or the angel of wisdom in the celestial world of the third heaven. The Apostle Paul said he was taken into that heaven, and he could not tell if he was in the body or not, but he saw and heard things not lawful to utter by a human tongue. This confession has been given of all men and women on earth, who ever approached the sphere, that it is too much for any person not incarnated with the fourth angel to endure the light of wisdom or the fourth " you are." Therefore approach the Messiah and the persons of the Godhead earth, in the lesser glory of the second and first heaven, because the third heaven is a consuming fire, and in that glory can nobody see God and live on natural principles.

When Moses saw the brush burning it was with the glory of the second heaven, or the light of love. When he descended from the mountain, and covered up his face, for the glory it shined with, it was the glory of the second heaven. But when Daniel was nearly consumed by the presence of the Ancient of Days, it was by the glory of the third heaven, or the light of wisdom. Therefore, Daniel fell to the ground before the Ancient of Days, and the power made him shake as a leaf, and his strength was gone. The messenger who brings this message from the Spirit endures the power of the second heaven, which his life is in contact with. The Ancient of Days showed him twenty years ago the heavens and spirit world belonging to earth, and the hells beneath the south pole, or the government of Lucifer below the earth, and also showed him the third heaven, and the kingdom in that heaven, and he entered that sphere by the grace of the Ancient of Days and the Messiah, with Daniel the prophet, and a multitude of angels for companions. The Ancient of Days, the patriarch of that heaven, showed them the rising of the spiritual sun Kolob, as it came above the horizon. No mortal can endure the glory of the spirit sun, which was below the horizon when the company arrived, and although night, it was serene and more pleasant and bright than any sunlight day on earth.

The spiritual sun Kolob is immense, with a several thousand times larger disc on heaven than the earth's sun, and fills much space on the northern horizon. The soft light is looked at with the spiritual eyes easy as man is looking at the moon. Kolob shines with a brilliant, blushing, orange, golden light, and throws no rays but an element of love and beauty over the celestial worlds. The Ancient of Days is the God, the Eternal Father on Kolob, and its hundred attending suns, and he is the patriarch of the third heaven as he is the Jehovah on earth. He said to the messenger, pointing at the rising sun: "There be thy home, when my work on earth is done." All the teachings and interviews between the Ancient of Days and the messenger will be written in a separate book, called "The Visions." It is not the intention of the Spirit to dwell by that severe experience to flesh and blood in the high heaven for light to earth, which will on some future day be related, and humanity will learn something from that heaven and receive knowledge of the truth. Amen."

The kingdom of heaven is four times "you are" to four times "you are not," or the sphere of wisdom. The messenger met his father according to the flesh in the celestial or third sphere, dressed in the glittering armour of a king in the high heaven. He had progressed rapidly through the spheres, and only been seventeen years at that time departed from earth life. On the brilliant suns moving around Kolob are the differences between the sexes perfected and wiped out, and the passion is dead, and the human nature perfected into equality of both sexes with a mutual four times "you are." There woman remains woman in man, and man remains man in woman, but perfected in both natures. Hence they have the same harmonies of four times "you are" perfected into the eternal life, which Jesus promised to all who believe in him and follow after him, that their inheritance should be that with him by his Father and of the eternal life in the eternal world. On earth the human understanding knows but little of God's wisdom, because the construction of the human brain is not able to argue on the principles of eternity. Seraphims and archangels with a superior organism and a further mental development understand eternity, but the spirit of man is not an archangel.

There are women filled with a masculine nature from birth, and approach the most of men as a man, but such are perverted in their womanly love, and are masculine in nature and passion.

They are jealous and commanding, filled with suspicion and self-love until murder, and are at war with the dignity of man, which they take a delight to destroy by intrigues and caprices, and lower his capacity of being useful into ruins before the world. The women in hell and on the lower planets are all perverted into that kind of development demanding all men to be women, and in subjection to them, that they may rule most absolutely. This is the culmination of the common prostitution. A class of men on earth are women more than men in their nature, and are seeking shelter and redemption by masculine women. Such men will never be developed to any maturity, but always die as dwarfs in their souls, and spiritually crippled, and will return into earthly conditions again for a long period as familiar spirits until the perversion is counterbalanced. The masculine developed woman will have to accept her true position of harmony or remain single in the spirit through the modification of her assumption by severe trials and mental difficulties, until she arrive at the truth and is made free in her work as a guardian spirit. The suffering and battle for deliverance from the chains of bondage socially and matrimonially, into harmony and happy and peaceable relations, is in the lyrical songs and romantic tales and the dramatical action of the poet on the stage, and as nature struggles to reach man, also does man struggle to reach angels, and in that struggle is the poetical " you are not, you are," and " you are, you are not."

During womanhood are monads harmonizing themselves to women, as astral spirit germs are to man during his manhood, but the space is full of fallen astral spirits, who fell before they were matured into the condition of germs for human nature, and for that reason cannot be heirs to the eternal world in any condition belonging to this dispensation known to angels. Those fallen spirits will in man's depraved condition enter human nature, and seek to destroy higher development if possible. Upon the same principle there exist elementary animal spirits not matured into monads, but are nearing humanity in such a degree that man is influenced by them and will personify them and take upon himself their animal force as much as they are living in his sphere until death, when his spirit becomes free, and the elementary spirits sink back into their perfection of maturity in being monads.

The new birth in the Holy Ghost is another celestial monadic estate of transmigration for the soul by being submerged into the divine love, and the soul forgets its own claim for that of God to be one with his life in the conscious adaptation of his love in the Spirit, that the soul may finish its long orbit, and in affinity to his love return into the eternal mansions. As man's life is before death, also he moves on into the same condition after death, and only by degrees the soul progresses in the spirit of the eternal life, which is the life of the Messiah in the eternal worlds. This life is beyond the third heaven, and into the harmony of God's eternal wisdom. Spirit love is perfected in the second heaven, and the eternal worlds of wisdom can not be reached from the summer land, which is the harmony of love and peace, and individual development, so is the third heaven the portal of God's love, where spiritual wisdom is perfected, by which the spirit wisdom can be reached in the harmony of God's wisdom.

That is eternal life to be a citizen of the fourth heaven beyond the earth sphere and inherit the eternal worlds. That is the redemption and the salvation into the kingdom of God, and the final triumph is that such a spiritual state of eternal life shall come down on earth in the Kingdom of Messiah.

In the present condition of man's development on earth could the power of the third heaven not be endured. Few of the race have been educated to receive the lower developments in the spirit by the movement of spiritualism, and only a few comparatively out of every nation will be able to grasp the ideas of the Messiah, and move into his life with their souls. The intelligence who receives these words, knows about the consuming power when he stood in the presence of the Ancient of Days and said to him "I shall perish before thy sight, if thou do not leave me," but he answered him: "Fear not. Thou art flesh and blood, and man cannot see me and live. Only few have heard and seen me, but thou shall live on earth. Write to the churches that you have looked into my eyes, and they are red as fire."

The reason why the spirit spheres are not known to man, is on account of his undeveloped condition in the spirit, and if the spheres would break the silence in discord as it cannot be done in harmony, it would result in general disarrangement of the human brain and insanity. All the departments of science have progressed during the last centuries, only theology in the churches of the world has been at a stand still, and mankind has remained spiritually in ignorance, superstition, indolence and bigotry, and one church has barricaded the way for the other, until they have all consented one with another to remain in darkness. Mankind read the scriptures and presume in them to have eternal life, but man does not move into the condition of mind, which is the mind of the Messiah in the eternal life. He observes time and seasons by his natural perception, but he does not observe eternity which is moving upon him in the spirit with an intense speed, and hurls him out of earth life, and into that, to him, unknown future, where he possesses nothing but that he has worked out during earth-life, either so his treasure is in heaven, or his interest in life is left behind on earth as a dug down treasure in the ground.

Some persons do not consider the blessing of having children, and some women look on children as the greatest abuse of their comfort, dignity and pride, and consider the trouble of taking care of babies too monstrous in comparison with the sweet joy gained from their company. Other women delight in abortion and infanticide, and have no compassion in their soul to endure the cries and smiles of little ones, but use all means to prevent conception. In the spirit world are children their earthly parents' representatives, as parents are the children's earthly representatives to the heavens. It matters not how depraved children are in the estimation of their parents, the links of harmony exist, and no child will prosper on earth by ill will and in opposition to its father and mother, because the promise is : "Honor thy father and mother, and thou shall prosper and live long on earth." Therefore says the spirit of the same words, "If thou dishonor thy parents, thou shall be accursed on earth, and thy days shall be very few." When persons build up happy homes and family relations in good hope, they must remember that within a short time they will be transferred to the spirit world, and there they will be re-united with the family in the same spirit of love. In the spirit world parents will have the pleasure of soul by progressive children in the fear and obedience of love to parents and memory from earth life.

The love for offspring does not last very long in animals. Exactly as the animal love is only a passing by passion, and the bull does not care for the calf, but as man becomes civilized the family life enlarges in importance to his well being and happiness, and parents are attached to children, and children to parents, with a stronger link of affection than among savages. This love is illustrated by the Messiah in the parable about the prodigal son. He deserted his father's precepts of life, but he returned again by repentance, and humiliated himself in his father's presence. The harmony of parents to children is " you are, you are," and children to parents is " you are not, you are not." It is the strong attachment of an intense love in obedience and reverence, and in the spirit of the first heaven. Deviation is more or less discord. When a son says "you are" to his father or mother, he will compel parents to humble themselves for him by " you are not," or to rebuke him to show them reverence, or command him to leave their home, because " you are," on the lips of a child is rebellion and the spirit of disobedience. Man does not need to hate his own flesh and blood, because he demands children to obey the laws of existence on principles of interior truth, harmony and peace.

Obedience of a child is the negative spirit of his being, and by that relation will it progress in the soul into the positive power and strength of the heavens, where the paternal love is the basis for all love between man and woman, and that is the attachment for the love of God. You can read a child's future at a glance, when you discern how it approaches its parents, because to love them is the fundamental law for social greatness and prosperity. "Thou shall honor thy father and mother in all sincerity of thy affection and of a meek spirit, because thy mother gave birth to thee, and tender to thy father her affectionate obedience and reverence, and as thy father loves her in the affectionate spirit of protection and support for her need, also does he love thee, if thou meet him in truth and reverence." If a boy says " you are, you are," to his father, that son is a murderer in his heart, and the spirit of Lucifer is resting upon him, and he does not love his father, because he hates him in his soul. Such children are not conceived in love, and a fallen astral spirit from Baal has united with the monad in the mother nature, because the spiritual union between the father did not exist at the moment of conception, which has excluded higher astral spirit germ of life.

Such children are all mother nature, and are without spirit power, which they hate all their days as they hate their father, and the serpent look is in their eyes. The state prisons and dram shops are filled with such persons, and the gallows are peopled with them, because they were not conceived in the union of mutual love between their parents, and the ambition of their souls is to destroy the paternal authority vested in their father, and they go to war with him on " you are," which is his prestige to meet them with, and they have to be in submission to. It is better for a man to have no wife and no children, than to have a family on the contrary principles to truth. It is better to enter heaven with one eye or with one foot, than to lose the soul and body in the fires of hell.

A woman who calls her husband by bad names and hates his presence, is not his wife in the spirit of her calling, and cannot be mother to the astral spirit germs in his sphere, and if she conceives by him, she will give birth to demons incarnated in the flesh. It is the punishment eternity inflicts on loveless marriages.

Repentance is impossible for such, as it was impossible for the Jews who crucified Jesus to repent, because they had became the children of perdition, and spoke falsehoods in their souls, and were a perverted generation not to repent. God could raise up the spiritual children of Abraham better from stones, than He could convert the Jews to the spirit of Abraham, and to do his work; and for that reason did Jesus condemn Jewish marriages as fornication, because they had perverted the entire nation and made the people fit only to destruction. They were blinded by that spirit and they guided each other as blind are leading blind, until all plunge into the ditch of death.

Elias came in the spirit of John the Baptist as a defender of the sanctity of love in marriage, which Herod declared void by compelling his sister-in-law to be his wife, but John was cast into prison and beheaded. The spirit of Elias is working in the same mission to turn the hearts of the children to their parents and those hearts to the children, and construct the link of love between heaven and earth, that the judgment of eternity by departure of the holy angels shall not reach earth. Hence is instituted the baptism for the dead, or the act of the friends to officiate in the flesh for their departed friends and relations by a symbol of love in obedience to their faith, that parents may bind to them the spirits of their children, even as children may bind to their hearts the spirits of their parents, because they live all resurrected in the spirit, even as those in the flesh are to be with them again.

David loved Absalom with a woman's love of " you are not, you are not," which is extreme weakness in the character of a father, and developed in the soul of Absalom that independent principle " you are, you are," which is a son in rebellion against the father.

Lucifer fell with an eight times " you are" in his heart, or in the rebellion of an archangel, when his true position to God is eight times " you are not." He assumed the crown of the Almighty by eight times " you are." How he came to that is a mystery for man to know, but it was the eternal birth of the Messiah his love did not submit to in obedience, and his ambition became aroused into the rank heresy about birthright, succession and eternal position. Being the first born of the Holy Spirit he could have no pride, and no aspiration but that life he lived. When he aspired to succeed the Messiah in the Godhead for which there is no succession, then his pride became folly, because he assumed the position of equal rights as a claim in the love of God. There he stepped aside from that love, and lost his birthright, which he fell from with disobedience to God's holy spirit of his nature, and the hosts of spirits which belonged to him followed him in the same spirit of "you are" eight times, or in rebellion by accepting his claim to be a God and of the Godhead, which is the delusion of his pride, and of the pride of his followers into eternity.

Children cannot by " you are not" judge parents " you are," because their negative relation cannot with any right judge the positive claim parents have, neither can a woman judge her husband in her true relation of " you are not," to his " you are." When a woman judges her husband, or a child its parents, truth has ceased to govern their relationship, and rebellion is in their hearts, and they have assumed the position of perversion in relationship governing the harmonies by "are" dropping into that perdition, which is the spirit of Lucifer.

In the lower classes of society, some men live in perversion of the principles in their relation to women, as is done by prostitution, when a prostitute says "you are" to a man, and he answers her as a woman "you are not." This same perversion permeate a large number of marriages where men are brutes, gamblers and drunkards, which make them weak-minded, rude, dull-headed, and animals until idiocism. Woman has no duty to live such a life, which will pervert her own nature and the offspring of said unions, and leave an open avenue for judgment, accusations and mutual hate. Is a woman a prostitute with "you are" on her lips, then she is as bad as the lost dignity of manhood, which makes a man say to a woman "you are not." Both are unfit for marriage, as they are only able to build up dens of misery, but the pavilions of peace and heaven will not be found under their roof. No such unions should be contracted.

By the key to the principles of life in his hand, man must be fearless and serve the truth, knowing that it will eternally prevail, and it does not profit a man to gain the entire world if he lose his soul by the undertaking of adulterating his better knowledge, and crucifying the truth.

Man is in deception when he appeals to science about the real and not real things. Making the visible things real, and the invisible not real, and all this dropping back is on man's own observation by the senses. It is not by sight and hearing men live and exist, and above all in man's mental faculties is his interior sight and hearing, more strong, and most powerfully intensified whenever he is developed from the stupor and counterbalanced from the deficiencies in his nature by living in an exterior world. You say the sky is blue and the cloud is whitish gray, but it is all modifications of colors contained in the sunlight and depending on its diffusion through the different stratas of density in the atmosphere. Remember the metaloid which you call water is in a melted state filling the oceans on earth, and constituting more than three-fourths of the human body, but it is solid on the moon and many other planets.

What do the inhabitants on the largest moon belonging to Saturn say when they are observing the earth in huge telescopes?

They say " this earth is broiling hot all the time, and vapors are arising from the depth of its melted surface as steam from a kettle, and clouds are sweeping over the chaos, which moves in waves most of the time from storms and cyclones, driving the vapors with intense velocity suspended in the air with a terrible hot temperature of evaporation." The inhabitants on one planet cannot draw conclusions from its own development to the life existing on another globe, when the differences of age and position to the sun and the universe count billions of miles and years. The greatest mistake is to speak about the visible universe as a real existence, and call the invisible world for the not real existence, as if the retina of the human eye was the sole judge to decide upon such an important question. To give the eye of man a chance to observe things, then in a cloudy dark night the condition of light is so negative, that nothing but dim shades are reflected on the retina. When the night is clear and the stars are bright, man knows that the sun is shining on the other side of the globe, but it transmits not its light to the sky. Therefore the sunlight you see reflected from Venus, and Jupiter, and Saturn, is passing unseen through a dark space, and is passing the earth in the darkest night, in billions of rays, without giving a spark of light to the ether, before it strikes its affinity on a planet, where it in the most refined atmosphere will develop and reflect light. The sun's rays carry no light, but only conditions for it.

The invisible rays from suns are highways to travel on of spirits from one globe to another, and from and to the different heavens which spirits belong to, and are used for material for building purposes in the summer land.

Imagine a person to travel from the earth, and in the dark at midnight to ascend into the air. He will move into a dark space apparently lifted towards the stars. When he arises sufficiently he will discover dim rays from the sun and moon reflect a phosphoric shade into the upper stratas of the atmosphere. If he is then moving on, he will be able to discern himself as a body apart from the earth, which is moving with an independent velocity below his feet. About at one hundred geographical miles, or five hundred English miles, he will find himself in a silent Egyptian night of utter darkness to the retina. The bright sun is now a very dull, pale, faded away disc on a black ground, and without giving any rays to space, and the moon is as a dying out coal fire.

The stars are faded away, and the sparkling light is no more, and in the intense cold and dark space is no light generated, nor heat produced. Then follow the guide a thousand English miles further away from the earth, and the heavens and earth, that visible identity to man, has disappeared. The earth, moon, and sun and stars exist no where visible. The visible universe has disappeared, and light and heat has disappeared, and the visible world has perished to man as a fixed reality. In this dilemma let also the universe of the person's physical body discontinue its operations, and instantly his consciousness becomes transfigured by a new birth, and he breathes again in another world. Yet in the depths of the interior soul life appears a world more real and more tangible to man than the physical, visible universe, which so cruel to all expectation vanished into a nothing. Consider that the spirit and his traveler become now conscious about spirit life in the fourth strata of the first heaven, where instantly the intense dark space disappears for a beautiful landscape in the rosy and yellow golden colors of light from the spiritual sun. The transition takes place like a flash, and is nearly too much for the new comer. He gazes at the scenery in amazement for a moment, and he is overcome with joy. He sinks to the ground and blesses the soil as a deliberated prisoner who was in custody for life, but now is free in the glory of God's freedom. The world he left behind is only a dark shadow to this reality of his soul's most daring expectation. Now he hears a voice. It sounds as from the grave. It is the voice of his mother. He buried her body with many tears thirty years ago, and had only a faint hope ever to see her again. He counted her among the dead, but said to himself, blessed are the dead in the Lord. He believed that she lived, and hoped for a life laid up for her in God's glory. He can see nothing but his guide, but her voice sounded again as to prepare his mind for the dear embrace after the long absence, and at his side stands his mother in a shining, white garment. Her face beames with love, her eyes with tears of joy. It was too much for his emotion and he sinks speechless in her arms. Not a word was said, but he rested by her bosom again, he rested in heaven. He had explored the visible universe, and lost it to find the true realities of his soul's love. The chains of the dust existed no more, and he lifted his hands in the liberty of the spirit, thanking God. The next persons he received were his father and his sister, but behind him stood his spirit guide during earth life. It was his first love on earth. He married her, and she sickened and died, and his days on earth were one gloomy night from that moment, but he lived in the faith of the Messiah that she lived, because her life was in Him who said I am the life. He felt a touch on his shoulder, that touch he knew. During the gloom of his soul when toiling on earth this touch had convinced him that he was not alone, but an invisible power followed him, and in his dreams he saw her whom he loved so dearly. He turned around, and there she stood dressed as a bride, and shining in silvery garments of dazzling white, with a sparkling diadem on her head. For another time he was speechless, he rested in her arms, and there was silence in heaven for a long time.

Here the holy guide left the loving couple to themselves and breathed his peace to them, and the relations departed, but arm in arm the two ascended, and when they became conscious again, they were together in a beautiful mansion she had pre-prepared for him in the summer land.

He found himself dressed in the richness and beauty of love's garments, white as snow, and above his brow was pressed the crown of love. She spoke to him and he listened. It was her voice, but it rung as the music of melodious silver bells. His soul was lost in an ocean of happiness. At last he said, " it is beyond all human conception," but she answered " blessed are those who do not see but believe, and more blessed are those who shall see and know the truth." In the summer land they lived and enjoyed the bliss and love of the second heaven, and at last the spirit of untold prayers fell upon their souls, and they remained in the spirit of prophecy as unconscious to each other.

Such are spirits prepared for the third heaven. They forget themselves, they forget their own love, they forget their own lives for to be found in the life of God and in his love. In this intensity of their soul's affections they are bound in the unspeakable burning attachment of the Messiah to the eternal Father. The Holy Spirit draws man and woman together into the celestial world. In the adoration of worship they are moved apart from their individual love, but together in God's love. They are sinking in a trance of divine worship for a long period, and do not even know each other for to be known of God and to know Him. Their own love appears now as small to them, and their loving companionship appears only as a shadow in the love of God to each other. Nothing can compensate them for the love in God. This intensity of a spirit's affection is the eternal worship in love, and can only be lived and understood. It may appear an unspeakable folly to all who are foreign to that experience, which is to be found in God by the Messiah, as in Him they gained the ground for the admission to the third heaven. Blessed are those who attain it, because father and mother, sister and brother, wives and children, and the conjugal love from earth and all the spiritual bliss of companionship is only of secondary consideration, and of very little value to that which is revealed to man in the third heaven. All possessions in heaven and on earth are only as hate to a man or woman if it should hinder their salvation in the Messiah, who is the door to the third heaven.

The development of the third heaven in God's love is four times "you are," or the spirit of the fourth head guide from the life on earth. Every spirit guide corresponds to the sphere man reaches to with one more "you are," or by woman's one more "you are not."

The spiritual sun Kolob shines into the third sphere with a golden light of beauty and peace, and you associate there with the seraphims from the suns moving in affinity to Kolob. There you are in the daily society of the martyrs and saints, but they are nothing, because God is the Almighty and everything.

There is the passion in the human nature overcome and dead, because the divine nature has been victorious. They are all one in the Messiah, like He is one with God, and there is no jealousy, nor hate, nor anger, nor malice in the great brotherhood and sisterhood of the Messiah, and after His order and in the heavenly kingdom. All the societies in the celestial sphere are camps with a military organization and regulation of discipline, working under the direction of the spirit of prophecy and fighting for the establishment of truth, love and order, for as it is in heaven it may also be adopted in the different degrees through the lower spheres, and the will of the Father may be done on earth as it is done in heaven, so the kingdom from the third heaven may be received by His elect, and the Order of Messiah established on earth. The four times "you are" is the mystery of heaven to be explained by the wisdom of God to those who are perfected in the spirit of his love, and the fourth "you are not" is the feminine assertion, that perfection is "not" arrived at before the redemption of her negative condition is restored to individual freedom, which takes place speedily in the fourth sphere, or the eternal world, where woman says four times "you are," to man's four times "you are," which is the perfect individualization or the perfect exchange of soul power, knowledge, love and wisdom. Hence they are not any longer two in one, but one in two, or woman in man, and man in woman, and the heavenly companionship after the celestial law is outgrown in the perfect individual life aspiring to the seraphims and archangels in holy lives, where the eternal life commences.

That is the eternal life to know God, the only true God and the Messiah he sent into the world, that man might know God in His perfection. That knowledge is life, and in God's life is the light of His wisdom justified by the children of the wisdom and the light. Therefore are they not any longer spirits but angels and are in freedom, and the inferior love between men and women is outgrown, and they move between each other as the angels in the freedom of heaven. When the Ancient of Days enters the third heaven he is received as the Patriarch of that sphere, and in the eternal world beyond He is called the Eternal Father. The angels of the third heaven do not kneel in the presence of the Ancient of Days, but offer Him reverence and homage of worship in the spirit standing erect on their feet, or as Israel leaning on his staff, and the angels are singing and worshiping in the Holy Spirit the Eternal Power throughout the eternal world.

In the first heaven the light is white as on its spirit planets, and all the animals, and flowers, and trees, and vegetation are somewhat like on earth. That is spiritually supplanted there from the earth, as it came to earth from the sun, and in the perfection of the moon.

In the summer land is a rosy light as on the planet Mars, and many monads from hosts of animals in the first heaven are gravitating from there in union with astral spirit germs into the earth sphere. In the forests of the second heaven are multitudes of birds and spirit animals not known on earth. They enter the summer land from the spiritual spheres and planets above, and come originally from the spiritual suns. Also in the celestial sphere with its golden light, are myriads of flowers and the most luxurious vegetation, and birds with hundreds of colors and many wings, sing melodies of love and poetry. The countless spirit animals do not resemble those on earth, but are developed on spirit suns and in a different order to those on earth.

The light in the celestial sphere is as sparkling gold. Therefore are the members of the third degree after the Order of Messiah, called the Knights of the Golden Cross. In the summer land the light and vegetation is of a rosy pink color. Therefore are the members of the second degree of Messiah called the Knights of the Red Cross. The light from the spiritual sun appears cream white in the first heaven. Hence the members of the first degree of the Order of Messiah are called the Knights of the White Cross.

In the summer land the rosy pink predominates in different shades, but in the celestial sphere all colors are in golden variation, and the birds, and flowers, and vegetation are boundless in golden colors. The sparkling golden light gives to the sky a purple, rich glory, and a most serene beauty. The air is substantial as the element of love, and the angels move with great rapidity through it, passing as flashes of light. The atmosphere is loaded heavily with electric and spirit magnetic power, and it moves in perpetual waves of strong shocks sufficient to destroy any organism on earth.

The zephyrs in the summer land are singing very melodious, with loving, longing sounds and a thousand-tuned whispers.

In the celestial sphere the air is moving gently in the spiritual sun's magnetic light, the shocks sound as golden bells, and the vibrations in the light like many concerts distant and near by, playing beautiful hymns, accompanied and echoed as with thousands of harps. This music is modulated at will into sweet melodies in low rythms, according to the angel's wish to hear or not, at their own pleasure. Every sphere reports to the sphere above and below, exactly as people on earth do. The same law operates in the third heaven. It reports with the summer land and first heaven and earth, as it does with the eternity above in the fourth heaven, and the eternal worlds. However, man has nothing in his power to report with eternity by, except in the prayer of the spirit. Eternity is exclusively to be known in the heavenly wisdom, which emanates from God to the celestial sphere coming down in the light from Kolob. The spirit of man ascends into heaven high enough to be in the society and the presence of God, and archangels, and descends low as to obcess animals and descend to the inferior hells.

The eternal Father is harmony beyond all measure, and the Messiah is one in His harmony, but Lucifer is towards mankind a discord in eight times "not," without one trace of God's harmony to balance his disharmony by. Therefore are the multitude of spirits from Baal screaming demons. They howl for a long period and continue different sounds, as foxes when they bark, or hungry wolves, for to relieve the interior discord. Harmonious spirits have been perfected by discord and have been victorious by harmony and overcame discord, when disharmonious spirits have remained stagnated in discord, by ungratefulness in rejecting harmony and fighting goodness, and in perfecting themselves by mental madness. They have been victorious in perverting their own soul, calling hate, revenge and murder for goodness, praying always in the worship of their own righteousness. Branded by falsehoods with perdition in their own heart, and with a burning in self love and ungratefulness, they are planning by day and night how to ambush those who once did good to them for to delight in their destruction, and take pleasure in the persecution of those who love God. Such spirits hate the sight of harmony, and they are in a rage of interior violence against those whom they presume are living in happiness and peace.

The spirit of God is unspeakable peace, and He sends His messengers into the world, that His peace may rule the children of God. Some persons have lost all hope on account of the misery in the world, but the spirit says " hope again when the harbinger brings new hope to you, that none shall be lost who cling to the Messiah, the rock of the eternal inspiration, and lean on that hope sheltered in holy places, that your souls may be filled with the spirit of the Messiah and with His eternal glory in heaven.

" I will raise thee high up, thou down-trodden daughter of Zion," says the Holy Spirit, " and I will redeem thee from thy enemies," says the spirit, " and I will take thee by the hand thou fallen tribe of Judah." " Therefore come, Ephraim, thou who art speaking from the grave of thy Father, and from the dust shalt thou arise powerful with the holy scroll in hands, and I will make thee walk hand in hand with Judah. To him I will give the land of Canaan, and he shall build up my holy temple at Jerusalem, and he shall bring to light the lost records buried beneath the ruins from the days of Titus. My words shall sound to you, and you shall weep from joy, when you receive news from the Holy Spirit.

" The Gospel of Freedom shall open the door and ye shall come home again from your captivity, and my peace shall follow you as it did in the days of Moses. The world shall not any longer point fingers at you, and ye shall not any longer be a by-word amongst the nations, but glorious shall your days be when the Messiah shall appear in your midst.

" Your enemies shall on that day be bound within their own territory, and they shall not trespass on your ground, but you shall head the nations in the spirit of Jehovah, when the fear of the Lord's power shall again be in your midst. Amen."

When spirits enter eternity or the fourth heaven, beyond the intellectual sphere of this solar system, they are in the humility and love of soul to the supreme intelligence with the principles of five times " you are not." Man and woman enter individually eternity or the presence of God, perfected in the wisdom to each other of the third heaven in the perfection of four times " you are." The serving messenger angels and administering spirits before Jehovah hail Him with six times "you are not." The archangels with eight times " you are not," and the seraphims with twelve times " you are not," in divine worship and reverence. Elohim responds with the same numbers of " you are." These principles will be understood by those who shall receive the gift of God to comprehend by.

Man's relation to God is in the negative " not" to His positive " are." He is supremely alone, and you " are not." He is above all things, and fills all things, and you are His love united with the manifestation of his power, but you " are not" Him. Therefore is all worship, love and reverence tendered Him in His love's adoration, or in the negative principle to His almighty power, in what man is not, nor spirits, nor angels, but He alone. To approach God with what you " are" in the heart is blasphemy, because it is self righteousness. If man possess anything which is not God's but is his, that is mental perversion and rebellion against God's love, which says man has nothing. It is all God's and he is God's too, and he is "not" the owner of his own body, and "not" of his own life. This is worship and submission, and truth of humility, because what men " are" before God is only vanity, toil and vexation, as he is nothing in the presence of Him who " is " everything. Blessed are those who shall by the understanding of the principles of life receive the gift, which is the key to solve and comprehend the mysteries of life.

In consequence of the logical necessity of circumstances the liberated mind will offer its negative submission, and enter into the positive freedom after the departure from earth, perceiving itself in the beautiful interior of the real positive universe. The spirit will be gliding on the electric highways to the destination of its spiritual home. Like suns attract each other by affinity, also is light generated by affinity in a planet's atmosphere, and heat from the intensity of the electric friction many times multiplied by the density of the air to the vertical ray, and its reflection to the surface.

The unseen world is extended in beauty all through space, and the so-called visible universe is only a small nucleus in comparison with the interior reality and grandeur of spiritual things. Globes of majestic suns not seen by any picture on a human retina, are seen in the interior realms of life on the retina of the spiritual eye, and true to the interior life of perception, known to the seers on earth.

The different heavens are different conditions. The third heaven is the portal to eternity for those who lived out their own world of love in the summer land. Man and woman are living on earth aspiring to a much superior life than their own love life, in the harmony of God life, which is the love and the essence and the cause of wisdom. Man and woman do not comprehend during earth life their high rank and destination, nor the importance of knowing God's ways to eternal life, based upon the principles of existence.

The mission from heaven to earth comes from all the heavens and eternity, according to the want and desire of the human spirit. Some men and women report in their souls daily with the second and third heaven, and are wonderfully blessed of God in their interior soul life. Others are living in report with the first heaven, and others report by their guardian spirit with the rudimental condition of the earth sphere, and persons very depraved correspond in their soul with the inferior hells. When death in the flesh occurs no change takes place, but every soul departs to his own home or her own sphere, where the souls lived, and all during earth life reported with in their interior consciousness. Wherever your heart and its affections are there will also your soul's treasure be found, and it may be in the high heaven or in the lowest hell. The password for good or evil is "follow after me." It was said of Messiah with the divine authority of eternity, or God manifested in flesh, and with the greatest power presented to man in the principles of eight times "you are." Follow after me can also be said of a woman, when she steps in the light before a man and allows him to walk in her shadow, and she is greeting him continually "you are, you are," which is not the humility by which a woman aspires to the third heaven in the perfection of four times "you are not," but is the perversion of soul by which she conceals herself to her wrong claim and to the spirit of Hades, where she may be hailed with a great cry of "great is the Ephesus Diana." Nothing is so disastrous to the future happiness and development as a discordant marriage, because it disorganizes the very core of existence, and makes life a blank leaf upon which truth has left no record.

Try all persons and all spirits by the law of love and truth, which is the principle of life, and ye shall know who there is of God, and who is in allegiance to the adverse power, and who is of your own heart, and who is your enemy, but pray always silent in your heart that your interior life may have the light to know by, because those who pretended to know much by their own wisdom were only counted fools in heaven, but those who prayed always for wisdom as the thirsty traveler for water were granted to drink of the divine fountain which flows from beneath the throne of God. Avoid mistakes, and do not enter into those forsaken, lovelorn conditions in which some marriages are, but conquer errors and honor truth by the light of the Holy Spirit. Amen.

That love which I have in the Father, and He has in me and in the spirit, shall draw all mankind into one peaceful union. The work of the Holy Ghost is a work of love, and his spirit is a whispering of love in many human souls. His voice speaks to man in the silence of the night, as in the glory of the sunlight, and blessed are those who listen to the voice and receive Him, because they shall receive the Messiah, and it shall draw the hearts of the elect to the Son, who is in the presence of the heavenly Father. Therefore pray always, and let your souls be prepared for the light of the spirit by one continued prayer in your heart, that the spirit may permeate your entire being, and dwell there with the power of eternity. And the son shall come and abide with you, and redeem you into the light, that you may remain in the light where the Father dwells. Pray in the spirit, that you may live, and move, and exist in that spirit. Pray always in your heart's love, and it shall be received in the spirit, and the answer shall come to you in the spirit of the prayer. Worship in the spirit standing or walking, leaning or sitting, or in bed as David did, and let the spirit of prayer never depart from your soul. Then the spirit shall rest upon your spirit with the power of eternity. Ye shall know for yourselves the response upon your heads, if your prayers are accepted of God. Even as your prayer left for the Father, also shall it return to you with the power from the Father.

It shall come to pass what you ask in every upright prayer God shall fulfil it in your behalf. Lift up the palms of your hands turned to the eternal God, and in the spirit of His love He shall fill your hands with the harmony of your prayer. Ye shall know His wisdom manifested to the flesh to guide you and redeem you from darkness into light. This is the glorious knowledge of the Father, that He is the perfection of all things in heaven and on earth, and you have in Messiah the communion with Him and by Him with eternity. Rest in your prayer without doubt that it be fulfilled in the power of the spirit beyond all conception of man. Let every breath be worship in the Holy Spirit to the power of the eternal world beyond all personality, and by the eternal God shall you dwell forever. Amen.

Because Jehovah represents the spirit, therefore He is the eternal Father, but He did not show himself in any likeness to Moses that Moses should represent him by to the people. Nor was there any image, or picture, or sculpture work made of His person, by which he was represented in the holy chambers of the temple, as He is known by the incomprehensible and impersonal principle He represents as the Jehovah, or the great spirit of all things.

Even when Moses spoke to Him face to face, and the glory from the burning bush rested upon Moses, he discovered no likeness given to the voice, nor in the thundering cloud and voice from Sinai was no person seen, and even Moses saw only His back, when Jehovah was passing by, that Moses should not be able to lead the people astray by describing His face, and turn the people into the worship of an image, as when they tendered worship to the golden calf.

To all messengers on earth from God, in sending this message I am saying to you, that knowledge about the spiritual things shall come to earth, because men and women have desire to understand by themselves.

Alcyone, the sun of suns of the Pleiades, is in beauty the great, and it governs millions of suns with their billions of worlds, visible on the heavens, but greater is the invisible universe which is endless, and greater is Kolob than Aeterus, Myra, Thuban, Alcyone and Luto combined. Thus says the Holy Spirit : Blessed are those who seek the peace of God, and the knowledge from His spirit.

All men who love God in the love of His harmony shall call His messengers blessed, and all men and women who hate God in the spirit of self-love will not receive them, but shall hate them and call them accursed. Do not fear for thy enemies' weapon by day, nor the assassins' knife by night, nor fear the adversary who destroys body and soul in hell, because I have redeemed thee out of his hands, but fear God, and thou shall remain in His love and do His work, and the Holy Spirit shall abide with thee and rest upon thee, and upon all mankind who receive these words in their understanding. God is wisdom and His understanding is in the Order of Messiah. Amen.

Seraphims are serving angels before God, but they were never men or women on earth, nor in the earth's solar system. They are developed children of the eternal world, and perfected astral spirits in development, foreign to the earth and its heavens. They belong to the superior spiritual globes of eternity. The seraphim is the average stature of man and generally five feet and less. He is exceedingly fair, with skin white as snow, and hair white as the whitest wool. His face has a bird-like appearance, with a prominent, sharp eagle nose and angular features, and well formed mouth and chin. The pupils of his eyes are round, with a purple colored iris.

The seraphim has a peculiar, thoughtful, silent and staring look, which characterises all the high astral angels. They are standing looking for days on a person, as they were studying him through and through, without saying a word. He has broad shoulders and hips, and a small waist, hands and feet, and would not be considered beautiful according to man's ideas. The seraphim never speaks except he has a message to bring to man, or is appointed guide for prophets in special dispensations. The Messiah appears often as a seraphim in the mighty glory of beauty in heaven, and glittering with a light as of precious stones and diamonds sparkling in the colors of the rainbow. Seraphims do service as swift messengers before the Ancient of Days, and appear at times covered as with wings of beauty. They traverse the universe crosswise, and serve as guides and protectors for God's special messengers in distress and events of danger.

The Elohims were once seraphims, and in the eternal world they can appear as seraphims. Therefore saw John the Messiah riding a white horse with a sword extending from his mouth, and with hair as the whitest of wool. This appearance corresponds also with the appearance of the Holy Spirit, and the Ancient of Days as Daniel saw him in the vision, with hair as the whitest wool. All creation springs from germs in the lowest as in the highest type of life, descending from the sun. By the eternal law of evolution are they developed in earth life corresponding to the life of the planet from one epoch to another, forming link in link and the entire chain is the progressive representation of the different species.

Monads are the intermediate developments between the species from the rock to man, but astral monads or spirit germs do not connect with the creation on earth before in man. Without astral life is man only an animal, and will sink back into a monadic estate again after death. The astral germ in man secures him individual immortality, and on condition the eternal life, which is a new birth in the Holy Ghost and by allegiance to the eternal principle of God or eternity.

Therefore is the celestial heaven a sphere of kings, as all persons there are kings in the Kingdom of Messiah, and He is the King of Kings, and the Lord of Lords assembled in the heavenly house of peers of God's household.

It must be remembered that astral spirit germs come from the spiritual stars or suns, when they unite themselves with the monads from elementary spirits. It is also a fact that spirits of animals continue their identity in allegiance to their masters in earthly conditions for a long period of years, and the spirits of dogs and horses will continue their affectionate attachment to their masters for one hundred years after their arrival into the spirit sphere, and the same may be said in regard to canary birds, parrots and the tame elephant. Their spirit life continues until conditions cease to be that they are attached to, and in a spiritual sense they by degrees vanish into themselves as from age and become monads.

In eternity, and in an eternal meaning of that word man is nothing, the universe is nothing, and God is all things and everything, and there exists no other way into eternity. All other ideas about the supreme being is only approximatory efforts in that direction. He fills all things, and in Him all things move and exist, and without Him there is no existence. That is the truth, and blessed are those who remain in the truth, because it shall make them free even as the Father is free, also is the Son free and the Holy Spirit free, in the same freedom which is laid up for the sons and daughters of God. Therefore proclaim the gospel of freedom to all mankind. Preach it early and late, and prepare the minds for the Order of Messiah, and the kingdom of heaven to come down on earth. Amen and Amen.

MESSAGE FROM JESHUAH, THE MESSIAH.

JUDGEMENT.

PETERSHOF, January 1, 1885

Woe! Woe! Woe! is the cry which comes from the east, and sounds to the west. Woe to all the inhabitants of the earth because the day of judgment is at hand. Woe to those who are living in the valleys, and woe to those who are living in the high places, for the day of judgment of the Most High God is at hand. This is the cry on this first day of the year, and it sounds as the sound from a bassoon through the heavens. There shall be wars and there shall be pestilence, and much convulsions in nature as in the hour of a mother's pains, when she labors in giving birth to a child. Amen.

Such shall be the hour for the inhabitants of the earth when the son of man shall reveal himself to them; it shall be in an hour of pain until they shall hail me saying, " blessed art thou who comest in the name of Jehovah."

Therefore, my messenger rejoice, and all who read these words rejoice, and all who labor for my cause rejoice, and all who are called upon to enter into my father's labor rejoice, for I shall tread the wine press alone, and the new wine I shall prepare alone unfermented from grapes in my father's vineyard, and I shall give the new wine to those who love me. Amen.

I am the bright morning star. I am he who was slain and am living forever. The son of the glory of the morning fell to his own estate, which is his own glory, even as Judas, when he went to his own place. But ye shall be hidden up in the glory of my Father, even as I am in the Father, and all who love me and rejoice in the seeing of the bright star of the morning, which shone in the beginning of eternity. Amen.

MESSAGE FROM JESHUAH, THE MESSIAH.

Faith.

Hyde's Park, Ia., Nov. 15th, 1882.

Much has been said about faith, and the justification by faith, and of pleasing God by faith, and when you read the letters of Paul it seems strange how the Christian world could err as they have done on the question of faith. It is true that active faith which comes from the love of God is very pleasing to heaven, but it is not true that a simple acceptance of the existence of a God, a spirit world and immortality, has any value above.

What is born of the spirit without charity is according to the spirit dead to the world, and in that sense did my servant teach in the letter named after James, that faith is dead without the works of love from which all true faith receives root, and growth, and strength, and development into the faith that is pleasing to God.

It is not the works of man according to his own selfish nature that can be called the work of faith, but it is the work of God in man, that he may be born anew, born as a spiritual being in his interior life, and be developed by faith into the knowledge of God, the fountain of the works of love. To be justified by faith in peace with God is not to accept simply the existence of a principle of justice to punish and reward man for his acts, but to be justified is to be adjusted by the Spirit of God in man, to be one in the spirit with God. That is the secret of the holiness born of faith, or the justification by faith. Abraham believed God, and it was counted unto him for righteousness, and he was called the friend of God, even as I called my disciples friends when I was with them upon the earth, and one with my Father who is in heaven. Without faith from God " It is impossible to please God." Amen.

Message from Jeshuah, the Messiah.

Gospel of Freedom.

San Francisco, February 4, 1885, 11 a. m.

What is the Gospel of Freedom? It is to be Christ. It is to be in the world as Jesus was in the world—not to be exactly identified with His life, but with his spirit, and live as He lived in the world or would have lived in corresponding conditions to those that you are in. Christ is a principle of office bestowed on Jesus in all its fullness, and beyond all measure, and is to be given by Him, and of the Father, and with the Spirit, to all who become His brothers and His sisters by adoption into the same union of soul, and purpose, and work. They become what he was from eternity, given of the Father to be one with him in the Gospel of Freedom, which is in heaven. This is a law of progression into the life which is the life of the Father who was in the Son—the true life—that same life that gave life to all the evolution from the creation of the worlds, and all things that are in the worlds, which did not come from any external cause, but from the interior life, which is God. The external things are only manifestations from the interior source from which they were gradually created into the laws of development or evolution. In the same manner have the souls of mankind to gain growth from the life, and in the life which is the first cause of all life, and is life itself, even the supreme intelligence of eternity. The Messiah idea is with that power one principle far beyond all human comprehension. You have one God, the Father of your spirits, and one Redeemer before His presence, even Jesus the Christ at the Father's right hand, that you may be as He is, and approach the Father as He does, and be perfected in the Messiah principle even as your Father is perfect, and Jeshuah is by Him the Messiah. That is the Gospel of Freedom, and its motto is, I am that I am, that I am born of the spirit of God. Amen.

Therefore be not disheartened nor of desponding mind, but pray always in your souls that ye may be filled with the freedom and truth of God which is in the Holy Ghost, and even as I am, that I am, your Redeemer and Savior from darkness to light, so you should be in the world until you meet face to face in the Gospel of Freedom, where you shall not walk by the gift of faith only, but by the gift of sight and power, and by the manifestations of the Holy Spirit and prophecy. Amen.

Message from Jeshuah, the Messiah.

Fasting.

Point City, Cal., December 22, 1884.

Fasting is an ordinance in the church, the same as washing of feet, and others for the benefit of man, but not especially for the service of God, but to help the mind more fully to comprehend the mind of the Holy Spirit. Except the brain is kept clear from the embarrassment by a too active digestion, the spirit world as well as the Holy Angels have a difficulty in manifesting their intentions and messages to man.

Food is good for the body, but the brain and digestive powers do not work equally well together at the same time, and the vital strength gets divided; therefore has fasting been instituted because food to the stomach is the food of flesh and blood; but food to the mind is the spirit of God, and it does not benefit a man to nourish well his physical frame, when his soul is found starving in the hour of death. The food for the soul is the light from God, and in an eminent sense of the word, I am the light from God; therefore whosoever believes in me shall not starve in the hour of death. Amen.

Message from Jeshuah the Messiah.

Pre-Existence.

Fruitvale, February 21, 1885.

I am not able to reach you with the spirit of love, if you do not reach out after me in that spirit more than you do.

Read often my speeches recorded in the New Testament, and do not allow yourselves to become lukewarm in your spirit, for the love of the heart is the foundation for the Holy Spirit to work upon, and as you open your soul in love, even so shall love be meted out to you again ; therefore do not curse your enemies, as they do not get better by cursing them, but only further away from any reconciliation leading to their salvation in the Kingdom of Truth.

The curses from Sinai did not save nor redeem the fallen seed of Abraham according to the flesh, but they became a hindrance to the redemption of Israel according to the spirit of Abraham, and his son Isaac, and his son Jacob, and his son Joseph, who became the father to thraldom, and he shall be the deliverer from slavery

Pre, or before, is the question you have to solve about pre-existence. All organization has a pre-existence, all evolution has a pre-existence, only life has no pre-existence, as it existed always, but the manifestations of life have and always will have a pre-existence. Matter has a pre-existence in its organization and forms, but not in its molecular atom of the nebulæ, which is the negative element of life or mind, in fact its clothing, and always existed as a part of life itself. All that your senses behold are only evolved from a higher source called life, and existed with life as the negative element of life in the world, and existed forever.

Your soul is not outside of the universe, but only a spark of the life which permeates it, therefore your soul must have existed in some form of development co-existing with the universe.

Why do you say the Eternal God and not the eternal man, for the divinity in man is the God principle in man, or the eternity of his soul, only differing from God's in the degree of development ?

Worlds originate by the evolution of life upon matter, or in other words, circumflexion of both in one, and one in both encircling each other as two or more great powers in one principle, which caused eventually the birth of organic life to flourish on the barren surface of the earth. Organic life manifested itself on earth by the interception of light, for God is light, and there is no darkness in Him, but the negative principles of creation is in darkness and does not come to the light except when the light operates on it.

All organic life is wherever you find the cell born of the light from God individually, or from the God principle personally, and his wisdom is eternally wedded to matter organic, as to inorganic life, which is called into existence as manifestations to the senses first, and to the spirit afterwards.

Therefore the intelligence which permeates the universe and was in the life, and supremely is the life, is the wisdom, and is represented by personal intelligences born to play the active drama in the world, and manifested in the continued evolution from lower to higher steps of development of the life, which pre-exists in its various definitions, qualifications and expressions of degrees of intelligence moving into perfection on earth from the power invested in the light. This globe you live in will be perfected in its nature to be the spiritual abode for immortal beings, and the New Jerusalem shall dwell upon it, peopled with millions of angels who were perfected by a continued work of mission after mission, or transmigration and incarnation of life grafted on life, as branches on trees, until good fruits are grown by the will of the Father to live by eternally in His holy presence of holiness. Amen.

MESSAGE FROM JESHUAH, THE MESSIAH.

THE COMING KING.

TERRE HAUTE, INDIANA, April 30, 1882.

Heaven and earth may perish, but the spiritual truth will last forever. The present organization on earth is only a development from interior conditions, and it will all give way for higher and more developed, and spiritual growth. That is the reason that this world and what is of this world will perish, and its sphere and what is in it will perish, and man will continually enter into higher conditions and more spiritual growth.

At the same time there is nothing that will perish, but will be changed in its organization, and in a chemical, and dynamical, and spiritual change from one organization to another. This world is that which will perish by death, but the truth is that nothing is annihilated, for the elements of the body and spirit have existed forever, and all spirit is a portion of the divine intelligence you call God, so there cannot be said that anything perishes, for if anything perished the fountain of life would perish in the same degree, and at the same time. The atoms of matter are only inferior in development to the various forms of spirit life, and it is impossible for matter to perish, as the particles may change without end and exist fully as ever, only under other conditions, how much more can it be said about the spirit which exists always and is not subject to similar changes, or similar inferior conditions, that it will last forever.

There shall spiritually come a new heaven and a new earth in which the righteous shall live. This condition will come down on earth when the Messiah is revealed in the present organization of this earth, or this present generation or estate of things on earth.

He is revealed to-day to the messenger who writes these words, and He shall be revealed to many people before the end of this present century, and the present condition of things is the forerunner of a new era. Joseph Smith was truly a prophet sent by my Father to give the infusion of a new light to humanity, as true as Emanuel Swedenborg was my messenger, and I revealed myself to him and gave him light, but they were only the commencement, and not the end, and Joseph was taken away in the prime and strength of his life. My messengers I do not wish to perish as Joseph, but to live and give the next great movement a new and strong life, to be pushed on as a preparation for my second appearance on earth as witnesses to my people that I live and shall be seen as you see me now, in a tangible form shall I be seen by my friends. The physical organization of the earth shall not be changed at once, but gradually, until the final great overthrow of the present nature, and the same revolution shall be extended to all the planets, and to the sun and the satellites. But in my second appearance it shall be as in Noah's days. Not that a new flood shall come, but man shall eat, and drink, and be merry, and the new light of the gospel of freedom in my second appearance on earth shall be to the race as the flood which took all away, and man shall awake as out of a deep slumber and say, let us go to Independence, and Palestine, and we will see for ourselves if this thing is true, or are the prophets telling us falsehoods? And they will come as flocks of sheep and droves of cattle, and as clouds of birds of all kinds migrating in the spring. The nations will come and go and be satisfied, and the thirsty, and hungry, and the sorrowful, and the mourners, and the sick and forsaken, and crippled, and they will rejoice and be satisfied that Jehovah is living, and that the night is past, and the glorious morning star has been seen in the east, and is shining to the west. That is the new era of peace for one thousand years. The Messiah's second coming is to establish among you the gospel of Freedom—even my Father's government, that His kingdom might come, and His will be done on earth as it is done in heaven. Then is the New Jerusalem descending from heaven down on the earth to commence at Independence.

My people I will gather into that place to prepare my second appearance on earth, as I have told you in former revelations, that I will call mine elect among the Jews and gather them to Jerusalem, and reveal myself to those I love and make them gather in where I wish them to live and prosper, and be happy in the expectation of seeing the coming of the Son of Man. That is the introduction to the new heaven, and the new earth. On that day I shall raise up the fallen throne of the house of David and govern in peace the nations on earth. Amen.

Message from Gautama Buddha, the Prophet.

To the Messenger.

Omaha, Nebraska, July 12, 1882.

Brahma made the Ganges to be a holy river, because the people could concentrate their thoughts around it as their home. Heaven above cannot supply the want of the human soul, except it comes down on earth and becomes the life of existence or our daily bread, and a part of ourselves.

I am Buddha, but I was Gautama. Buddha was my mission. Now you will understand why I am by you. Look at my footprints in the sand of the Ganges, where my sandals have marked the road I walked—step by step are they seen, and the long line of steps are marked up to the spot where you stand now, or in other words, your feet are resting on the line of my footsteps. Go on! Go on! My life was a success, it was a triumph, and yours shall be so if you remain in my footprints, which shall be to you the footprints of Messiah.

Blessed be thou before all thy brethren, because the God of Brahma the meek has made thee meek, and caused thy soul to be ground in the dust, that it might be polished in its own suffering to be a shining star in the firmament. My feet were naked in their sandals, that my head might be clothed in the white of my garments among the yellow monks. Buddha stands by you as he once walked earth; he says, "suffer from evil men rather than do evil to men, and you shall be victorious in your death." It is "Blessed art thou if thou shalt keep thy feet clean of all men's blood, and earthly gains, and the accusers shall have no cause to curse thee." Blessed shalt thou be on earth, as Buddha was blessed amongst his people. I fought the battle of heaven and not that of man, and I became a conqueror over all my people. The truth echoed into the hearts of my countrymen and that gave me the victory.

My peace I give to you, the peace of God, and may the fragrance from the flowers of Paradise be always where you are. My peace follow thee, waving to thee a kiss of brotherly love from thy

Gautama Buddha.

MESSAGE FROM JESHUAH, THE MESSIAH.

VICTORY.

KANSAS CITY, Mo., April 5, 1882.

There is no reason why the church in Utah should not be in harmony with the church presided over by Joseph Smith, at Lamoni. All are united in the same faith, all are in one unity for the same purpose, all expect some time to be united with the same host of saints in heaven and on earth.

All I wish to say to you now is to go to Independence, and I will make you understand a new mode of thinking about the churches.

Your enemies are not many, but some of them are very crafty. You shall not be conquered by any of them, but you shall live and see the work finished for which you were sent into the world. The work is to build up Zion and prepare the way in the hearts of mankind for the second appearance of Jesus on earth. He is now by you as you see and hear him, and the one who gives this message and will continue the work until it is finished in his personal appearance before the eyes of all men who wish to know him. Be therefore of good cheer and go ahead, asking for no better work and not doubting, for the light is shining into the darkness of the world, and the world shall be judged by it, for the light shall shine into the darkness of the souls of men, and they will love the ignorance of creeds and superstitions more than the light and the truth which is derived from the light, and pain and death shall come on them as a silent messenger and make them weep, because they rejoiced in shutting up eyes and ears to the inspired voices of my servants. Men's riches shall die with them, and as the dung from cattle they shall be cast out with their faded glory of the world, and their lives shall be counted worthless, because these men were high and uplifted, and priest-ridden in their minds, and their ministers who deceived them shall perish with them, and they shall be hungry and thirsty in the spirit, and naked and in the prison of the spirit world, those who followed up the servants of God and said, "cursed be ye who bear the new tidings to men," and heaven shall answer them : " More cursed have you made yourselves, more so than your fellow beings, by having perverted your own blessing, and banished the peace of God, and the messengers of His truth ; therefore is your harvest already over and your reward is received. Therefore shall your hope be to you as a barren wilderness, and ye shall not find the place your imagination sought ; but for those who keep my commandments and loved to listen to the spirit of my Father's voice, will I raise up a standard as Moses did for Israel in the wilderness, and those who look at it shall be healed, and the holy ensign shall be to you an emblem of peace and salvation for the down-trodden and meek among men. I am the standard of heaven to all mankind, and in the church after my name cannot be raised any other. I am the truth, and as far as you are able, I say " follow after me." I am the light, and as far as you are able by the spirit of revelation to discern the light, I say look and be satisfied.

I am the way. Carry my cross on the road full of thorns and stones, and flowers are growing by every one of your footsteps, and you shall not miss the reward. My home is built on the heights in eternity, and from all nations the road shall be thronged as though heaven was to be taken by force, and in my Father's kingdom are your dwellings, as in the spirit world are many heavens and societies, but the road to my home shall not be any mystery to you.

MESSAGE FROM JESHUAH, THE MESSIAH.

THE LAW.

INDEPENDENCE, Mo., November 17, 1882.

The truth which I want to impart to earth, is not to endorse what you call capital punishment, or execution. It pertains to an eye for an eye, and a tooth for a tooth, and it was so among the Jews on account of their hardness of soul, and mental disposition. That people was a terror to the Canaanites, and so were they ruled by terror from above, or Israel would have gone far astray and scattered themselves among the idolatrous nomadic tribes which occupied the country. Jealousy is terror, and Jehovah was a jealous God. "Thou shalt not kill," was the commandment, and affixed to it was, whosoever kills shall be killed, but the love of God is in the perfection of man's relation to man. Thou shalt not take revenge; leave thine enemies, go out from them as Abraham did, and as Lot did, and as Joseph my guardian did when he took me, a babe, and fled to Egypt. Thou shalt not put thyself against evil, but leave it behind thee, and go out and away from it rather than do your brother an injury, and by doing him good you might lead his soul to salvation, and if he desire your coat, give it to him, and if he should not be satisfied with that, give him also other garments. Be bold and daring in all your controversy with men, and convince them by the sword which comes out of your mouth, but convince none by scorn, or blows, or ill sayings, or oaths, as all such things are blasphemies as compared with love and truth.

"Thou shalt not kill," was given supremely to all men, and includes thou shalt not execute, which is but an official killing, or judicial murder, and war is a legitimate killing of man among the nations on earth, but in the sight of heaven it is all cruelty, and as many people abhorred the killing of me, so they ought to abhor the killing of their fellow beings, as it is written: "Thou shalt not kill," and it is the perfection of the commandment and without any exception. "Pray for your enemies," and bless your friends, that you may overcome evil with good and conquer the deviltry by being the harbingers of the spirit of God, and leave the judgment to God.

The "law" condemns, but you shall be justified by the spirit of God, and live by the His spirit, even through the portal of the death in the flesh you shall live by the same spirit, which is not of the flesh nor of the law, but of the spirit, and in the spirit is the freedom of the spirit of God. Amen.

MESSAGE FROM JOHN TAYLOR.

WEST POINT, CAL., August 3, 1887.

I am very feeble; my strength is gone by the long imprisonment. We did not expect that such a combined warfare would be kept up against the plural system of marriage. "All is for the best" was our thought on earth, and in the spirit I have already seen enough to convince me that the eventual result will be the breaking up of our social life, at least as far as our practical life is concerned in the church on earth towards the civilization of christianity.

Theoretically we will not change our faith in any truth, but I am too weak to say much more. Only this much, we will retain our faith spiritually, and so will our brethren in the church on earth. They have suffered, and some have died for their testimony, and they will know how to appreciate it and fight for its spiritual understanding and practice. Somebody in the spirit says nonsense. I think it was your guide. who said so. Very well, let it be so to him and many others; if I am wrong I will get better knowledge by and by. At present I am too weak and debilitated for any controversy. The brethren help me to stand and walk around, which I could not do without their most kind assistance. You ask me if I have seen the Lord? Yes, I came here this morning and have seen Him by you, as I have seen him once before when I entered my circle of old friends, the apostles at Joseph's house. He took me graciously by the hand and said: "Welcome, be strong in my love, and be weak in your own soul until I shall build you up in the strength of Zion, which has to come down on earth, and in which I will designate you as a member;" and He gave me His blessing and departed. I am so terribly weak now that I have to come to an understanding that the love of the Lord within the church must have departed from it, and left the saints in such a spiritually debilitated condition.

Brigham tells me that the Lord teaches his friends by experiences, and symbols, and conclusions which he draws to our mind from cause and effect. Our first lesson is to be conscious of our own weakness, which I am now fully aware of, but that the church is in a corresponding condition I had no idea about before my departure from the earth. This weakness teaches us of our dependence, and what he says of our restoration and growth in the strength of God's love, until we stand in the midst of God's Paradise, eating of the tree of life in which is all the knowledge and wisdom of God, but the church on earth is not living by its fruit, or our enemies would not have triumphed over us, but we eat with them of the fruit of the serpent, which he gathered from the tree of knowledge about good and evil, in the self-love, and pride, and ambition of man, and therefore our shortcomings. Man never gets too old to learn, and the church will have to learn more, and know better how to remain steadfast in the truth which is in God's love, and get strength to arise and be powerful again.

I greet you my fellow servant and messenger to the people. Some will hate and some will love you, but either way does not concern you, as your work is in God and not in man. Only once do I remember to have spoken with you. We are as strangers to each other, but I remember our meeting; it was at a great fire in Salt Lake City, when the hotel burned down. We spoke together about the assassination of Joseph and Hyram at Carthage jail, and about my own suffering there, and the effect of carrying the bullets in the flesh, as they are now buried with, and will some day be found in my coffin among the bones. It was a great fire we were looking at in Salt Lake City, and speaking together as we did then, I did not even dream that I had to go through another great fire of severe trials, and come into the world of spirits as through a great fire escape.

Now I am meeting you in the spirit of a great fire, as the Lord by your writings from above is going to cast fire upon the earth, and it will burn as many prairie fires, to be seen from one end of the earth to the other. The church of Utah will receive it in part, and in part not, until you publish in full all that you got, and not before.

The Re-organized church has the president and the apostles as far as the men are concerned, but not as far as the truth is concerned, and the truth is more than the men, who will have to conform to the truth. Yielding will be necessary when the

Lord shall appear personally on earth again at Independence, and both churches will have to merge into one when they see their own nakedness, and prostitution, and need, and want, and they hunger and thirst after the righteousness which is the love of the Lord that we have spoken so much about, and known so little amongst ourselves.

Then shall the righteousness of the law, the garment we used on ourselves be thrown away, and we shall be clothed in the garments given to us free of cost, and made by his love for the purpose of saving our minds from the tenets and creeds of men, and bondage of dead doctrines, and the chains of traditions, and he shall lead our souls into the glory of peace which I have experienced in all my weakness, from the day I entered here to be tried in the needs of the church as well as in my own need, and by symbols from the Lord we learn to work without any self-love, in the truth and wisdom which is in His love. Amen.

Message from Jeshuah, the Messiah.

Salt Lake City, Utah, Sept. 25, 1882, 11 a. m.

I am not disposed to allow any spirits to express their opinions through your organism, especially now when your guardian is absent, and you are weak in your natural strength.

You listened yesterday to G. Q. Cannon, and I say to you that he has not yet comprehended the first law of the gospel, which is obedience to the government of the country in which he lives.

If polygamy is such a vital necessity for the life of the church, then conflict with nobody, but gather into Syria, or India, or any place in Asia, and nobody will hinder or dispute the right of plural wives, which is not worth fighting about, or to impose upon the people of the United States. Joseph Smith, of Lamoni, has taken a course which in many respects is approved by me. He has done a straight-forward work, and has succeeded in the main point, but he has not succeeded as well as he would have done if he had removed the office of the church from Nauvoo to Independence. Plano and Lamoni are small mistakes, but he will get the right method by and by. In locating at Independence, will he virtually conquer his enemies in the heart of their desire to banish and destroy him, and he will from that date commence my work, which is not gathering in numbers to Independence, but the building up of the temple at that place, a work which has to commence now, and to be built in this generation. Another reason why I wish him to remove to Independence, is that he will be in the head-center of the churches' aspirations, and in the capital on earth next in importance to Jerusalem in Asia. It will give a grand weight to his mission, and compel in time the church in Utah to affiliate with him. My work on earth is rolling on by degrees, but only as the minds of mankind are willing and developed to receive the truth.

The people of Utah profess to keep their hearts and souls close to me, but they do not walk in my ways, because I am the way, and they do not love my life and follow after me, for I am the life and the way of life, and they do not know where they are drifting when they quarrel and fight with the world, as the world would steal the bread of life out of their mouths. I have seen your trials and your misery, and your earnest desire to do my work; therefore be ready, and visit from time to time Independence, and it shall be given to you what you shall do, and where I wish you to work in my mission. I say to you many are called to my supper by baptism, but only a few will enter the Order and sup with me in my Father's kingdom, and none can enter but by me.

The work of Joseph Smith, of Lamoni, is not ripe yet, but it will be by and by, and the power will be given to him which is in me, and I will draw all the redeemed Israel to me, and gather the elect among men under my wings. Joseph will do my work, but his son who shall come after him shall do another work, and gather my elect before the coming of the Messiah to the temple at Jackson County. It shall be built, also the temple at Far West, but the one at Far West will be of less grandeur, and of less magnitude than the one at Independence.

My servants do not know yet my ways, but my messenger knows me and has seen me, and knows my voice, and has received the testimony of heaven by the voice of my Father, and he knows my Father because he has seen Him and heard His voice, with a body trembling in His presence, and was thrown into the dust as a worm at the roadside when the earth trembled and the leaves were shaken. The noon sun was shining as with an evening light, thus men know His power, and how terrible God's presence is. Therefore be awake, and lift up a warning voice to this generation. Be without fear, for the elect are protected against evil influences to harm or kill them. I have given you the marks of my sufferings in your hands and in your feet, and in your side, that the evil shall not take your life away from earth before it is finished in my Father's kingdom. Amen.

I am the life, and I have given mine the promise and power of life, and there is none who can stand in the road and change my hand nor put to naught my words. Some elders are at present persecuted by evil influence at Salt Lake City, but I have shown the spirits the marks in your hands, and in the hand you write with, and they have been humbled to profess my name, those who have not known me.

There are angels by mine elect as guards and protection, which you now see surrounding me, as Heber C. Kimball, Hiram Smith, Jedediah Grant, Parley P. Pratt, Orson Pratt, Brigham Young, Willard Richards, David Patten, Ezra S. Benson, and Joseph Smith the prophet, and many others whose faces you can discern, but have not known in the history of life. These men are now serving angels for the progression and development of truth. You will see them a little while, and then you will not see them, because they will scatter among friends when the time comes to push the gospel of freedom and deliverance ahead for the churches, and for the people of the world. You have only a small pencil, a very imperfect tool to write heaven down on earth with, but my work is done in the power of the spirit.

The Gospel of Freedom is not another gospel, and is not the fullness of the Gospel, but the perfection of the Gospel, as I have said at many other times and in many other places, and fully explained. Now I say to you do not fear, but send the message to John Taylor, and say to him from me that he has done my work according to his understanding, and that is all I shall expect of any of my servants, and as time rolls on shall this understanding become more ripe, and more full, and more broad, and more true, till the knowledge about God shall fill the earth. Amen.

MESSAGE FROM JESHUAH, THE MESSIAH.

CONCERNING CHURCH AUTHORITY.

KANESVILLE, August 7, 1883.

Have all things together; be one soul and one heart; let none be great and none be small, and let nobody call himself father, as one is your father, even my Father who is heaven, and one is your master, and your guide, and your shepherd, and your Lord, even Jeshuah the Messiah, but ye are all brethren and sisters of the common brother and sisterhood. This is the spirit of the church of Messiah, that if anybody is great among you in his own mind, that person is the smallest among you, and if any is small among you in his own mind, that same person is great among you and filled with brotherly and sisterly love. I have seen you as sheep among tearing wolves, when I commanded you to go out into the world to preach the message of Messiah, and I gave you no money, nor salary, nor position, nor rank, according to the pattern of the world's officials, but I gave you the promise of my heavenly Father that all things should follow you, and the promise has been fulfilled. When you went out the spirit of heaven followed you, and sanctified your words in the hearts of those who received you, and they called you blessed, and gave you plentifully of their means and supplies for this life, and the old adage became true, that the poor made others rich. In doing the work of heaven you are only doing the work of the spirit of the heavens, and if you abide in the path of heaven you cannot exercise any church authority which is not laid down in heaven, even before the foundations of this world was prepared for the habitation of man. There is no authority anywhere but the laws of the spirit of God, which permeate by the spirit all things, that is the only authority.

This universal God principle is not vested in man, nor in man's wilfulness or caprice. It is not of man, nor of earth, but of heaven; therefore pray, " Thy kingdom come."

To be an apostle is not to be a duke or a prince, but simply a messenger. There is no hierarchy in heaven. His grace, the Bishop, and his eminence, the Cardinal, or his holiness, the Pope, is not known there even by name. All these are external conditions and will perish by death, or with the world.

There shall also be no Rev. nor Right Rev. among you, because you are all brethren, and the ripe men among you shall form a priesthood of elders, as the aldermen of the church, and the elder sisters among you shall form a board of elderesses, and shall officiate even as the men do with counsel, preaching, prayer, exhortation, laying on of hands, baptism, and breaking of the bread and blessing of the wine at the supper of the Lord's table. Verily I say unto you, you shall be as one, and there shall be none high nor any low among you. The elder shall preside at home, and preach before the world where they may be located or may be able to go, but the young men shall go out into all the world after having received the priesthood of the elders by the laying on of hands, and preach the truth and light to the salvation of the race from ignorance and superstition, and gather them into the Order of the Messiah, prepared for the kingdom of heaven on earth. I have now given you a new order of things; not that I give you a new commandment, but that which is eternally new and will never grow old, that you shalt love your neighbor as yourself. Therefore love ye one another.

The priest is a spiritual servant at the temple. The priesthood is a band of servants, but the servant is not superior to the one he serves, nor is the servant more than his service. My servant Moses wrote, even that which I commanded him, and the service of the priest of Levi became the type of the servitude at the altar, after the pattern by which Levi served his brethren.

During the period of hundreds of years afterwards, the spirit of the Lord by which Moses wrote was gradually lost to the children of Levi, and they became carnal, worldly, idolatrous and wicked, and walked in their own ways, and led Israel to commit all manner of crimes after the pattern of the heathen nations which surrounded the land of Canaan, and the tribe of Levi became lost and scattered among the children of Israel, and is now dispersed as snowflakes, and hidden upon earth, to be a witness that the Lord is living.

The catholic priesthood has exalted itself, even more than the Jewish priesthood ever did. It has become a proverb to say great and infallible things about the Pontiff at Rome; but I did not make him, nor did I put him there. This has all been the product of vanity in by-gone ages.

Of what use is salt when its savor is gone? It would be of little consequence for the sun to be in the heavens if it should lose its light. Even so with church authority, when it has apostatized from the truth—even the spirit of truth—the heavenly power of God is lost which I have sent into the world, that the world should not be smitten with spiritual blindness, but those who are of the light could come to the light, as they are seen of the hosts of the angels in heaven. A fal'en priesthood is a priesthood according to this world, and according to this world's pattern, men who take praise and honor of each other for gain's sake, void of spirituality, which they stigmatize as of the devil. They are blind guides, and will eventually plunge into the grave alike with their congregations, and all find themselves in utter darkness of their own mental condition. "Such men ought not to live," says an angel; but according to the justice and mercy of God they are kept alive in the world, although many of those high dignitaries of the churches are spiritually dead to truth, yet they are allowed to preach, and advocate, and live. To that class belong thousands upon thousands of clergymen who say it well, but do it not ; who profess, but deny the power and gifts of God ; who stand in the door, but do not enter unto me, nor do they allow others to pass them and enter. These ministerial hypocrites are more poisonous to the truth than rattlesnakes are to your bare feet, because you can avoid a rattlesnake, and jump aside and be saved, but if you ever listen to these religious gamblers and thieves, or falsifiers of truth, and you are not aware of the danger, they will poison your soul in its innermost life, and condemn you with their own damnation of ignorance, superstition, blindness and bigotry. Woe unto those who say : " I know God, I see angels, I know the spiritual world and the life after this," and tell falsehoods to humanity ; for only by the spirit receive you gifts of a prophet, and know any of these things. Even so has the Messiah never been known to any man or woman, but by the spirit of prophecy.

Pray first for the spirit of prophecy, or spiritual development. Live forever in that spirit which has revealed these things to the world, which no eye has seen, nor ear heard, nor has entered into the human soul, except it be by the spirit of the Holy Ghost and by angels who have descended from the celestial into a minor glory, to teach man about the eternal worlds. Be not deceived, let nobody lead you astray. The time shall come when you shall seek and not find, if man persists in making war against the spiritual truth. Remember that only stagnant water decomposes, and when you are all in repose, and are gone to the rest of this world's ease and comfort, then death, dissention and dissolution shall creep upon man, and the day of the Lord shall be to Him as a thief who enters his chamber and finds him asleep. Therefore be always awake and ready to meet the Lord of the heavens. He made His glory, and now invites you to enter into His spirit, glorious in all eternity. Amen.

There shall be no church hierarchy, as there is none in heaven, and there shall be none on earth. Blessed are those who denounce the yoke of any priesthood, as it is not laid on man from above. Blessed be those days when you shall not say, " know the Lord," because in the new, glorious era, they all shall know Him, both young and old.

The fountain of truth is the spirit of truth, which conveys to the human mind the happiness, and glory, and love, and wisdom which is in God, and its spirit is far above all human conception; it impregnates your perceptions with as much of its intelligence as the mind of the individual can possibly receive and mentally digest. It calls the treasure of wisdom into active life as a part of yourselves, it revives your soul into a perception of lost knowledge, and gives you laws upon laws to unlock new truths. It brings the kingdom of heaven down on the earth, and the spirit from the fountain of God flows as a stream of living water which fertilizes the human soul, and makes the flowers of Paradise grow at your feet, and opens your hearing for the songs in the glory of heaven.

That supreme inspiration of heavenly intelligence is the priesthood, according to the order of the sons of God into the Order of Messiah, for which the priesthood of Melchisedek is a forerunner, as the Order is for the Kingdom of Messiah. But that which was high up has been laid low down, and that which was filled with light has fallen away into darkness, and dullness, and ignorance, and short sightedness of this world's care and love of ambition, and power, and misrule.

The priesthood whenever given to earth has always lost its savor, and always became an abomination to me, said the Lord of Hosts. It has done its own mission of gain, and grasping, and tyranny over souls, and enchained the spirit by the cruel inquisition which burned for heresy the innocent victims for the political pretense of appeasing God, who in the essence of His being is spirit, and has to be worshipped and served in the spirit and in the truth. I will wage a war, and I have opened a fire against church hierarchy, or priesthood exercising the power of this world, and I will continue the war against church authority, until the Father in heaven will put my enemies under my feet ; for of all enemies in heaven and on earth none are more dangerous, more subtle, more treacherous, and more poisonous to the church of Messiah than a fallen, perverted, egotistical and dark priesthood, devoid of all mental and spiritual inspiration or truth from heaven to teach the people.

Woe to those serpents in the garden of Paradise, because they say it well, but believe it not to be true, and they pervert the truth into evil purposes, and destroy souls to gain power; they persecute the Holy Ghost and His works, and they condemn inspiration and the gifts and powers of God. Woe unto all false teachers, because they adorn themselves with the cross of the crucifixion, and with garments of splendor adorned with gold and silver, and say high and solemn mass and long prayers, and do not discern that it is all their own handiwork, and that Messiah has long ago washed His hands and said, "I am not guilty of all that innocent blood. These men are deceiving and wasting lives according to the traditional customs of their fathers."

There is no church hierarchy except the truth. Whatever can be proven to be false cannot be the truth, nor any church authority. Creeds are always falsehoods. Theology is far off from mathematical truth. Ministers' claims appear as mathematics, but the most generally applied spiritual truth is only approximation, and adapted to the conception of the human brain, and is the highest truth in accordance with the highest human conception about truth. The spiritual mathematics is as much superior to human rudimental mathematics as a rose is a superior organization to a stone. In the realms of spirit, there truth can be measured with the exactness of a tape line, inch by inch, and all the laws of the most acute mathematics can be applied to truth, and it will not be found wanting. Therefore I am the truth, and blessed are those who follow after me in the love of truth. Amen.

MESSAGE FROM JESHUAH, THE MESSIAH.

CONCERNING REJECTION.

POINT CITY, CAL., April 28, 1884, 10-12 A. M.

You shall not write in my name or receive any message from me, except you see me and hear my voice and receive the marks from the cross in your hands and feet, and a crown of thorns on your head, and you see the thorns mixed with laurels. All these things shall be a sign to you that I am that I am, and I sent this message to you and mankind, and when the marks burn in your hands like my spirit burns in your heart, then pen down my words to you, with your hands on my cross, and with your feet bound up, fastened to the block. You shall remember me hanging on the cross, when your spiritual sight discovers blood flowing from your hands, and from your feet, then remember my blood which was shed on account of the sins of the human heart, because the Jews did not know what they were doing when they hung the Messiah, and the Lord, on a cross. Therefore are they rejected as a nation.

Now you perceive a bloody wound in your left side, as it was pierced with a spear. Remember my heart's wound, when Israel rejected God's love. It was with my heart beating in love to humanity that it silenced in death. Now your heart is aching as you feel the agony which I suffered, because you have the stigmas of my death on your body; it shall be an evidence to you that your life is redeemed to my Father to live in the spirit in which I died. Fear not because you are surrounded by angry enemies. You shall be hated of many, as you have been hated of your own relations for my name's sake. The world is building churches in my name, and it has become fashionable to be a christian, and the christian ministers of all denominations nearly agree in the opinion that my blood was shed as a sacrifice to my Father to appease His anger from inflicting terror of eternal destruction and damnation. Such doctrine is the spirit of their own understanding, and is not even in the spirit of common logic, and much less in the spirit of heaven or the spirit of my life, and my words, nor the words of mine apostles and disciples of the first centuries after my departure from earth.

Therefore let it be said to all in heaven and on earth, and listen ye eternal worlds, and harken ye archangels, my blood was shed as the logical consequence of my rejection as the Messiah. I did not come with legions of armed men to drive out the Roman soldiers from Judea, but I came with legions of holy angels more powerful, to give the nation common sense and redeem my people from the errors of the letter into the spiritual conception of God's message to Moses, and he knew that day when Israel should need the redemption and not seek it, when he said, "hear ye him;" however, they hardened their hearts against me, and rejected their Redeemer, and hung their Messiah on a cross, and in return they were rejected as a nation until this day. My blood came upon them and their children, but in a reverse relation to their salvation, for they came under rejection, and under the curse they made.

It was the teaching of mine apostles, but when the spirit was lost, then christianity kept crying out, a hallelujah : " By His blood are we saved," as though the rejected Israel had pleased the Father by hanging the only begotten Son to death on a cross.

Why do you shudder in your body when you are looking at the silver crucifix standing on the shelf beside you, because the Holy Spirit bears witness to you about the cruel deed, and you look at the cross with abhorrence, because my love is within you. Israel did not know what they were doing, and my prayer was, " Father forgive them," and as far as forgiveness was possible they were forgiven and are forgiven, but the blessing they rejected was sealed up to them in unbelief, and it went to the Gentiles, and the new covenant, not with Israel, for they as a nation entered into none with the Gentiles, and scattered sons of Abraham according to lineage and adoption, was made in my blood or it would not have come to them, for I was only sent to redeem the lost sheep of the house of Israel. Thus the covenant made in my blood went to mankind, and the Gentiles received the adoption to be the seed of Abraham and the heirs to the kingdom, by the rejection of Israel, and a new covenant made with the world in that blood which Israel spilt on Golgotha.

The christian ministers do not make that point clear, that in the rejection came salvation to the world, and that in my blood, or in my death, the turn was made to gather in spiritual Israel, because the nation rejected the Son and the heir to the kingdom.

The Jews have no reason to glory in my blood, neither have the christian churches, nor the world, for the redemption came by the rejection of my nation, because my blood will always be one eternal disgrace and stain, crimsoning the soil of this planet, and as it was a crime most detestable to eternity, there is no glory in it for my friends, and but a very small satisfaction in it to my enemies.

When the Jews of the present age proclaim my execution to be the work of Roman policy, and not a theocratical measure of the high priests and high council, then I can assure humanity to the contrary, for the Roman pro-consul opposed the crucifixion, but yielded to the pressure from the rulers in Israel, and that point is clear and settled as a fact in the heavens centuries ago.

Another reason that it had so to be, that the Son of man had to suffer the rejection of His people, was so ordained even before the foundation of the world as a circumstance not to be avoided, nor was it possible in accordance with the laws of predestination, and wisdom, and knowledge of the Almighty to avoid it.

It was impressed on my mother from the moment of her most holy conception; she saw me in a vision hanging on a cross, and did not know the meaning of it.

To me it was known forcibly as a part of myself in the interior perception of my earthly career, that I had to be crucified, and this knowledge from eternity was born with me in the flesh, as it was born with me in eternity.

When you discover in my presence and by you the crown of thorns interwoven with fresh laurel leaves, it signifies that I, who am by you, bore the crown of thorns in that supreme hour when Israel tendered me their unlimited rejection, and the Roman pro-consul verified my position by the crown of Israel, not of gold, but of thorns. It was the political symbol of degradation and madness shown to a pretender, or to the mockery of assuming a royal prestige.

It was the most tragical moment in the history of the Jews, but they were rejoicing in it, and Pilate wrote the epitaph of their kingdom: "This is the king of the Jews."

In the fresh laurel leaves intertwined among the thorns of the crown, you perceive symbolically the victory you will attain to on earth, by, in a spiritual source, being admitted into my presence in such a union of souls, that by the gift of heaven the unity becomes so complete that you appear to be at times myself in the hours of my suffering, with the signs of my suffering upon your soul and body.

As the events connected with my death always turn you away from the topic, it has been difficult to make you speak or write out the true meaning of my blood shed on the cross.

The atonement to mankind was in giving light to mankind, and redemption by the truth which is in the light given to the *world* by the rejection of Israel as a nation.

It was finished on the cross, that great center around which the history of Israel has been moving and is moving to-day.

It is finished. What was finished? The work of my mission in the reverse of its aim—that which I wanted to do for Israel in harmony to humanity was that the curtain between God and man should be rent, as the curtain was rent in the Holy of Holies of the temple in my death.

In fact the reverse of my mission to my nation was finished, but the Messiah in His humiliation and death faced the world, and God so loved the world that He did not spare His only begotten Son, but by His rejection of Israel made Him in His death the redeemer of mankind by being the light and the truth, and the way for man to His Father's mansions in the eternal heavens.

"By His blood are ye saved," cried out the apostle, and the meaning was, by His blood is redemption now within your reach, or made possible to be obtained.

If the Jews had been the spiritual children of Abraham as they were his literal children, then the Son of man would have been accepted, and the spiritual light had emanated to them as out of the heaven of heavens, and humanity had gone to the fountain and never thirsted, and ate of the spiritual manna and never been hungry any more, and I had appeared as you now see me dressed in the robes of the high priest's office, according to the order of Melchisedek, and officiated in the temple on Mount Moriah, offering dense clouds of incense before my people as their leader, and before my Father who is in heaven. The world would have known the Messiah, and not Israel's own degradation.

I had to be born into the world to convince the world of sin, of its own degradation and selfishness of purpose, and darkness of spirit in not knowing me, and of JUSTICE, because God did not spare His own people, and neither did He spare His own Son. In rejecting Israel and their circumcision, He took away the veil between heaven and earth, and opened the gates of Paradise from whence Adam was driven, that no curse should hinder man from entering the land of the spiritual Canaan and walk with God, and speak to Him face to face in Paradise, even as you have heard about in the beginning.

The symbolic sacrifice of the paschal lamb for which Cain in enviousness slew Abel, caused perversion in Cain's soul, and he fell in love to the spirit of Lucifer's inversion to the truth. God being the truth compelled Cain's sacrifice to be in truth, and of an upright heart to be accepted, because truth is the essence of God, and the principle which Jehovah represents and reveals to man.

The lamb, the most harmless being, without guile or guilt and almost defenceless, became the symbol of innocence, and as the guilty could not pay the debt by his guilt, neither could the law be satisfied with the law breaker, then God presented in man's place as a substitute the symbolic, innocent lamb, that by the grace of God man might be counted innocent of sin, as even the lamb which was substituted as a sacrifice, that man's sins might be dead as the lamb that died, and that his life might be preserved by the blood, even as the angel of death passed the houses of Israel in Egypt where the blood of the lamb was sprinkled on the door frame or seen at the entrance to the house, where the penalty of the divine law by substitute was satisfied by the death warrant execution on the substitute. The innocent and spilt blood was taken as the blood of man or woman, and of the nation, and as the symbolic sacrificed blood had been spilt on the ground, for the law said: "If you do not keep all things which I have commanded you to keep by my servant Moses, then I will come hastily upon you, for I am a jealous God, and I will destroy you in the first, the second, and the third generation."

Thus the law gave the conviction about sin, to keep the people in humiliation and obedience before their God.

The sacrifice represented the mercy and sacrifice of God to descend to man by His servants, the prophets, and in the consciousness of guilt and in conviction of sin, which begot humiliation in the spirit to raise the ladder between heaven and earth, on which the heavenly angels have ascended, and also descended to humanity.

I am the lamb that was slain, even as John bore witness about me, and as it was foreordained to be, before the world was, and foreshadowed in all the bloody sacrifices as a symbol to man.

Only by such means could man be reached and the redemption of the race take place, as man is naturally carnal. The temple service shows my rejection by the Jews, and was known in eternity. Therefore when the Jews shall be gathered into Palestine, heaven will restore the priesthood of Aaron and offer up burnt sacrifices, and they shall not know me before my wounds are revealed to them at that place where I disappeared from before the sight of mine apostles. When they have received me there shall be no more bloody sacrifices, but the smoke from the altar shall be a holy incense from herbs, of praises and thanksgiving to the holy name of the Almighty who has done all things well.

The temple service was the lesser light which should shine and preserve Israel, waiting for its spiritual fulfillment in the course of time.

I say spiritual fulfillment, because it was symbolic when the chief priest at the great feast of atonement laid the sins of the nation on the head of the lamb, and sealed the curses of the law upon its head, and then drove it into the wilderness. It was to teach the people that as often as they repented and got into the right position before the Lord their God, and loved his ways with all their soul and strength, then He would hide from before His sight their misdeeds, and would let all their sins be forgotten, as substituted into innocence and perished in the wilderness of the eternal forgiveness.

It was in this symbolic manner that the nation transmitted from generation to generation the faith, and hope, and longing for the advent of the Messiah.

John the Baptist, as a lineal descendent of Aaron, perceived the spiritual idea at once when he saw me walking lonely on the banks of the river, and said, "behold the Lamb of God, who taketh away the sins of the world." But to be the Son of God and at the same time to be the Lamb of God, included in itself, that I would have to suffer death, as also John the Baptist shortly after our last meeting had to suffer himself as a victim to the cruelty of the age in which we lived.

The entire temple service was the dim light given to the lesser priesthood. It was only the symbolic representation of the higher light of the Order of the Son of God which was lost, but had to be restored in the person of the Son of God.

This higher priesthood was sealed by election and revelation on Moses, who by that entered into my presence in the wilderness, and by the power of the higher prophetic priesthood led Israel out of Egypt. That was not in symbols, but in light and knowledge. By the same priesthood after the Order of the Son of God, or the priesthood of Messiah, did Joshua conquer, Deborah sing, Daniel govern, Elias and Elisha and all the prophets prophesy, David reign, and it gave Solomon wisdom, grace and power, and by grieving its holy spirit he brought desolation and suffering down on his old age.

To save Israel in the wilderness the lesser light was substituted, and the higher light aspiring to was kept before the people in the symbolic and bloody sacrifices, until the day of their wickedness was made manifest to the world by the passover or easter crucifixion of Him they rejected. Hardened in their souls and lost in their hearts, for the wisdom of God had deserted them as a people, their rulers were men of worldly ambition, and not according to God's pattern, but according to Roman pride, arrogance, luxury, deception and frauds of policy and purpose, forgetting and ignoring everything but their own shallow selfishness. Such was the world in which the love of God was revealed. God did not send His Son to collide with the world, but to call Israel to have everlasting life, and come to the light, even as the Father is the light of heaven so is the Son the light of the world, that the world should not remain in darkness but come to the light, that light which shines into the soul of every man or woman, that they may conceive the light and be born again by the holy spirit of truth. That is the wisdom to be born of God's love, or of the holy baptism of fire and power. Therefore is the baptism in water only a symbolic sign, or an interpreter of truth to the spiritual Order of the Son of God, even as the natural birth out of water into the world is a symbolic representation of the spiritual regeneration to the kingdom of God. According to the foregoing it is evident that man could not be saved by blood, nor by any external act, whatever it could be. God's work in man for his benefit is in a spiritual regeneration substituted symbolically in various manners.

In an external conception of that to be a savior, a great king may lay down his life on the battle-field, and the soldiers and officers in common with him, and gain the battle and save the country from invasion of the enemy, but the Son of man is not a king of the world fighting for some external gain or benefit. His kingdom is first and above every other consideration in the souls and hearts of men and women, and only as a secondary result will it be manifested into the world, even so in His second advent will He be manifested to the world.

In the cosmopolitan mission of the Gospel of Freedom His day will be heralded, and the churches will move into the perfection of the gospel of grace and salvation which went to the Gentiles, until perfection comes in the gathering and belief of the Jews.

The new testament was written with blood, and had thus to remain in force, as it was only from its rejection by Israel that the covenant made with Abraham became universal, and his children according to the spirit became the first, and more numerous than the stars of heaven.

The covenant was made with Israel, that the seed of Abraham by the Messiah should come to the light, truth, love and wisdom of God, which is the salvation that came into the world.

My words are life and power, and whosoever drinks my blood and eats my flesh follows after me, and becomes me as I am, shall have that life and that power which I received of my Father. Amen.

Therefore, although the new covenant was made in blood and by blood, and with blood, that you are saved, is into the spiritual regeneration of the new and everlasting covenant. It is surely not by blood that you are saved, but by my Father's spirit who is in heaven by THE HOLY SPIRIT OF TRUTH.

If my blood is taken in the way or manner of a sacrifice, it can only be done in a symbolic sense, as the blood of the lamb being substituted for the mercy of God.

The principal object of the work of Messiah and His mission was not to be sacrificed, but to bring light to the world; nevertheless His life became a sacrifice.

My mission to the Jews was the mission of a king, even the Messiah, and the Lord of the Glory became the lamb slain on Golgotha, and the cosmopolitan savior, for from that moment the redemption came not only to the lost sheep of Israel but to the nations of the earth.

Therefore when you are assembled together early or late and talking about me, then remember me by drinking of the symbolic cup, and you shall teach the world that the Son of Man had to suffer all these things, even the shedding of His blood on account of the darkness of Israel and the sins of the world, that the light in His humiliation might go to the world and humanity generally as the work of God's grace and forgiveness of sins, and redemption and regeneration to many. Even so shall ye take the bread and break it, and eat it, even as I did, and ye shall remember me, how ye are many, but one in me and of the same spiritual flock. Like my bodily temple of flesh and blood was broken down, also did I again rise up on the third day visible and substantial before my disciples. Therefore eat ye all of the bread, that ye may be one with me and with my Father, and with the Holy Spirit, and as my body hang upon the cross, also keep your bodies trained in obedience before God your Father, remembering that in the subjection for truth's sake is the coronation from God, and what ye lose of this world ye shall gain eternally.

The world loves its own, and so the Holy Spirit loves its own, and as the Jews got only the sign of the cross to their condemnation when they were craving for signs in their unbelief, so shall the world have the sign of the cross, not to salvation. The faith of the Son of God and the spiritual light shall not vanish from the earth until the Son of Man shall appear on earth again. Therefore you are not saved by flesh or by blood, but by the spirit of my Father who is in heaven, or the Jews would have done the eternal Father a pleasure by crucifying the Messiah, and the redemption would have been an external work, as the battle which armies fight in the world. I became the contrary to any deliverance for Jerusalem, and the word of life came to destruction of those who did not know their own welfare. Therefore, oh, Israel, do not remain in the faith of man, but in the faith of God, that His spirit may abide with you, and teach you His love in all wisdom. Amen.

When the Catholic church perverted the symbolic wine from the laity, it was only done in supposition that the hierarchy is the right wing of the church, and the cup is not any individual but a church claim, that the blood in the wine is retained in the clergy. That the catholic priest claims by confession in the power from God to forgive sins by that virtue invested only in the priesthood as the mediator between God and the laity. This theory is characteristic of the catholic church. The Gospel of Freedom is not a new church, but is the perfection of the churches into the unity of the Messiah, because I am the Gospel of Freedom. The fullness came in the restoration of the first principles of the gospel in all its simplicity, but the Gospel of Freedom is heralding my advent, and I am the herald myself, even as I am preparing the new wine myself in the freedom, and perfection, and union of my elect from out of all the churches to meet me when I shall come again on earth. Amen.

As the Jews fought Messiah in my first advent, also will some of the churches show fight in my second advent, as they would crush the truth out from earth, but I am the king of truth. To attempt to crush my elect in my second advent would be to revoke the power of God. His finger will mark my enemies, and they shall be no more. Blessed are those who receive the truth and keep it. Amen.

MESSAGE FROM JESHUAH, THE MESSIAH.

Concerning the Order of Messiah.

Peterhof, Cal., May 25, 1887.

The Gospel of Freedom is not a new dispensation, but the perfection of that which was given in the fullness of the first principles. It is not any anti-church movement, but a deliverance from church bondage into the freedom of the spirit of God, from the spirit of the world and priestcraft, and tyranny for gain's sake and political aggrandizement. The Gospel of Freedom is the gateway for all the churches, and all mankind to approach the Order of the Messiah in the great preparation for the kingdom of my Father who is in heaven. The invitation is in the tenth hour to enter the work and gather the grapes, ye my people, and cast your lot with those who have worked all day, and receive your reward with them. Therefore unite all, catholics and protestants, and Mohammedans, and Buddhists, and saints, under the broad banners of freedom from the slavery of creeds, as the Gospel of Freedom is written above the portal of the gateway which leads to the New Jerusalem. Rejoice in your soul early and late, rejoice always, because it has pleased the Father to give the kingdom to His elect, forever and forever. Amen.

Only a little while did I remain in the flesh on earth, and a little while did my friends not see me, and again in a little while did they see me never to be parted from me again.

As I said at that time, even so do I now: In a little while my friends shall see me again on earth. This a work of perfection in finishing up the old leaven and the old wine, for the new wine and the new supper I will eat with you in the twelfth hour. The Order of Messiah will be perfected to mankind in the eleventh hour, and in the twelfth hour I will sup with you again in my Father's kingdom on earth.

Blessed are those who do not get offended with me, but believe that the Son of man has the power to do his own work and fulfill all His promises if you remain in Him, even as He remains in His Father. From now onward shall the light flash from across the horizon as the lightning before my coming to earth, and many shall believe, but only few shall preserve the burning faith of God in their souls, and even among the elect shall many go asleep, and it shall be to the Son of man, as He should find no faith on earth any more. In the Gospel of Freedom my words were laid down in the perfection of God's fullness of hope and glad tidings, that it may come to pass even as it has been said to you. A preparation of perfection into holiness is necessary, before you can enter the advance guard of the Kingdom, or the Order of Messiah. When you have seen the Order you have seen the advance column of the great army of the hosts of the kingdom. Work for my reception in preparing the hearts of mankind for this great event of perfecting the spirit of the churches into the freedom, and love, and unity which is in God.

My servant Joseph Smith, at Lamoni, stands in his father's place by birthright as the president of the church, but he must consider his position is for the people, and that the people are not called for his sake. I have called upon him to preside over the people, and they are my people and not his people, and he is the servant of my people. To that end my spirit has been with him and borne testimony to him, and revealed my will to the church as to himself.

If he will understand his position, I will uphold him and sustain his life to very old age, but he must consider that tolerance is the first law in the kingdom of God in heaven, and will be the first law in His kingdom to come on earth, and tolerance should adorn and stamp the church with God's spirit of love.

The basis of the church built up by inspiration and revelation is I am, as taught in the first principle of I am that I am. Anything less than the first principles is less than Christ, and anything else is another foundation than Him. Therefore let it suffice and give freedom for the balance. Let the mind be free to expand as it is free in heaven, and the Son of man shall not come to a people in bounds or in high treason, but to a people who are moving in the freedom of the spirit of God.

As to the manner in which the dead shall appear again on earth, the saints know their own philosophy, but none shall know it except those who are present on that day.

Also in regard to the last supper, it is my will that it be done as I have commanded in all the houses of the saints after evening supper. When I am remembered in my suffering, let it be in the spirit, and these emblems of my death shall not be confined to the meeting houses only and alone. As I have said before even so do I now, that re-baptism is an abomination in the sight of God, and the reasons I have given at other places.

Also I wish to repeat that polygamy, or monogamy, or celibacy, or any social recognized manner of marriage, or nuns', or monks' ways of living, belong all to earthly conditions which are of the world. In the Order of Messiah which will prelude the kingdom, it is my will that the members can if they desire it, remain single according to my own pattern, and the pattern of some of the ancient apostles, and if they marry it shall be after the pattern of Peter with a sister of the Order of Messiah, and within the Gospel of Freedom.

A messenger shall have no more than one wife, and if she dies he is in freedom to like the high priest, after the line and order of Aaron, to remain single. The Order of Messiah is not an Order after the world's pattern, but after the mission of John the Baptist, that cried out to the multitude and defended the sanctity of marriage, saying, "prepare the way for the Lord."

Therefore Joseph receive the Order of Messiah from God. It will not substitute the church nor change the church, nor will it annihilate the mission of the church. Have no prejudice against the Order because Zion's counsellors shall be messengers of the Order. All are elders of the church organization, so nothing in the church will be interfered with, and they shall stand by the president's side and be messengers of the Order, and counsellors between the church and the Order, which shall havs its own degrees given to it. Having in itself both priesthoods, the Order shall act side by side with the church, and in unity with the church, and cultivate the fraternal relation with the church. Not any orders can be issued by the church to the Order of Messiah, but the Order receives it only by and through its own general, acting as church counsellor and third general of the Order. The president of the church may be a member of the Order, but it will not make him the head of the Order, in the capacity of being president of the church. Although he may be a general of the Order of

Messiah, he cannot preside over the church and over the Order at the same time. My will is that it shall forever remain two distinct and different offices.

Let the church not stumble, but be wise in God's love, as new power has to be given to man under a higher law, which is the Gospel of Freedom. Some persons will accept the truth and others will not, but the Order of Messiah will go out over all the earth as messengers of the Most High God, and preach the perfection of the gospel, and call into the church millions of men and women.

Only few in comparison with the multitude will embrace and pass through the three degrees, and subscribe to the discipline of the Order of the Messiah, as the healers, preachers and prophets, given in three departments, embodied the truth from the three heavens into the Order to give light to the world.

The Order is not secular in its life, but cosmopolitan, so its spirit is not confined in preaching only of the first principles before the world, but its mission is broad to Israel and all the Lord's elect, and to be brethren in bondage among the mountains. Some will become worthy members of the Order and subscribe and live the regulations of the Messiah as they shall be given from above.

The members of this Order are the forerunners which have to herald the coming of Messiah by a chosen work, and much sacrifice and humiliation, which has not and will not be required of the church, therefore shall marriage not be made a duty but tolerated by the Order, and the missions shall be severe, and those who are married shall be abroad as they were not. If the church objects and opposes the Order, then it matters not, as my work will go on until the church will be glad to unite with the Order.

The Order of Messiah is the Order of the Son of God, and not the priesthood after the Order of the Son of God, being the Order itself. It preludes the kingdom from above as "the King is coming," and that He is spiritually present within the Order. The general cry of the church to the world is, " the Lord comes," but in His coming the church will be the advance guard for the Order in the army of the kingdom. The Order's organization on earth consists of one general in chief to be called by revelation and by the spirit of prophecy. Next in rank is the second general, also called the general to the Jews. The general in chief is called the general to the world. The third general in rank is the church general. His position is as a counsellor to all the churches between the Order and the churches. These three constitute the first line, and are field marshals and commanders.

The second line is one Attorney General, Adjutant, and two Lieutenant Generals. The third line, six major generals. The fourth line, twelve brigadier generals. Those twenty-four generals belong all to the third degree of the Order of Messiah, and are Knights of the Golden Cross. There are twelve brigades, and each brigade consists of twelve regiments. Every major general commands a corps of two brigades, and each one of the two lieutenant generals commands a division of the army.

This is the symbolic organization of the first wing, or the advance guard of the kingdom, or the Order of Messiah.

Because the kingdom cannot be on earth, before the king is there personally to take command, therefore is the organization not called the kingdom, but the Order of Messiah. The perfect organization of the kingdom is seven armies, of which the Order of Messiah is one. The central army will be commanded by the Messiah in person, as the king and chief commander for all seven armies. This force can be increased to seven times seven, of exactly similar organizations.

A few remarks will now be given in regard to relation of the churches of christianity, and the church of the Messiah to the Gospel of Freedom, and the Order of Messiah.

The protestant churches are not in harmony with the doctrine of rejection and election, and they are not in harmony with their understanding of the atonement.

I did not make any distinction in the simple problem to be of the truth and nothing else but the truth, to live the life before the world as you are regenerated into it by your interior life. It is to live your life in the spirit, and according to the spirit, in harmony with the spirit of God. The protestant churches did not omit the problem of sin and a depraved condition of human nature, but they forgot the regeneration as the most necessary thing by which the human family in the church of Christ could be elevated above the depraved condition of the world.

The reformers were men who had to contend with the united power of the catholic worship, and their entire effort was centered in the problem to convince the existing and dominating church about sin, judgment, and the shortcomings of man by his own inherent nature to please God in his nature of superior spirituality ; therefore the reformers, always bordering on the point of imprisonment and death, declared that no man could by his own work be justified of God, who has included all man's doings except it was done in the holy spirit under the judgment of sin, and that God would show his mercy to all. In that effort the reformers arrived at the principle of justification by faith, not by the faith of men, but by the faith of God, or by the faith which is in God, or by the nature of God to perform the work as the only method to please God, and in such a manner they drifted into the justification by faith, and not by works. If the catholic church had compromised with the reformation, it would have been characterized by the heavenly wisdom from above and have shown a tendency to its great claim of infallibility of the Pope; but contrary to such a mediation the mother church was too arrogant, and with a too stubborn hierarchy to offer anything but a long continued warfare for about one hundred years, and suffered the consequent defeat from its haughty position towards mankind. However, the protestant churches soon became more divided and subdivided than in the days of the reformers, and at last they forgot their former persecutions by the catholics, and commenced persecution against each other, until at last bloodshed became a part of their faith and worship, and although they spoke as the lamb they did the works of the dragon as in the Spanish inquisition, the most cruel of all persecutions.

These extremists culminated in their evil work by burning men, women and children at the stake, or drowning them in the rivers, as the most holy method to serve God. Degeneration was everywhere, and truth was nowhere except in dilapidated fragments. The Lutheran church remained where Luther left it, and rather retrograded than advanced. The Presbyterian church never progressed beyond the pattern cut out for it by Calvin, and the same with all the churches and sub-churches that sprung into existence by and after the labor of the reformers. No church ever moved ahead or beyond the intellectual development of its founder, and in fact the ritual of the English Episcopal church has remained since the days of Henry the Eighth. The religious world was spell-bound in a straight-jacket of dogmatism when the restoration came in all its original simplicity, embodying the first principles of the gospel to humanity, and Joseph Smith did the best he knew how, and when his work was done he was taken to another field of labor in the spirit world to prepare the way for the kingdom to come on earth.

He was not perfection, nor was the church which originated by him, and which was started from the book of Mormon, or the law of Zion amongst the Nephites, and other revelations to embody in man an order of human progression much higher than the balance of the churches possessed.

Degeneration crept in everywhere, even during his earth life, and the law which was given to the Nephites as the law of Zion, did not become such to the restoration of the saints, but much more, it was ignored, and put aside, and counted for an inferior gift in comparison with the word of God which went out from Judea, as a line for regulation of life and conduct, and the law to the Nephite Zion sank entirely in the background in comparison with new and numerous commandments, doctrines, and covenants, which flowed profusely to the church from an inspired prophet. At last the social conflict became infiltrated with political mobocracy of the worst law-defying type. A class of men who were once of the church, and went out from it, took the reins of terror to destroy the church in the conflicting chaos of doctrinal contradictions in regard to marriage, and authority to direct the different quorums. It became every day a more desperate struggle between the protestant churches and the new light, and the accuser was never idle. Wild rumors permeated the entire nation, mingled with little or no truth in their flagrant assertions, until bloodshed became the result, and Joseph and Hyrum were killed, as the consequences of the immature effort made in building up the kingdom, which is not the mission of the church, and massing mental material on the saints for such purpose, which was devoid of all caution, as it was premature, and courage could not fill the demand of the mental uproar, and the constant cry of greatness among Baptists and Methodists, and great are all the churches, and great is the old and new Testament, and greater are we, the clergy, who have received it all. In this confusion of ideas it was the mission of the church to let the kingdom alone until its own time should come, and go out into the world and clear away the fogs, and work for the restoration of the Gospel of Christ, and leave the marriage problem and the political aspirations alone, for the single purpose of building up the church of God on earth.

This simplicity of aim and purpose did not lay in the heart of the high priesthood, but it laid in the charter of the church, given of God and signed with the blood of the Master, Jesus of Nazareth. This charter was broken asunder from the moment the church trespassed on a domain foreign to its mission, and the state charter of Illinois did not any longer give the promised protection in political capacity to Joseph and his company. In this moment of adverse fortune, there was no other result to be obtained except by reversing the wheel, backing the ship, and turning the rudder of the church, to save the lives of the saints, and to prevent blood from flowing in streams, by declaring the fallacy of the aspiring church in social and political complications, and to direct the energy, and every available mental and spiritual force to combat the protestant and catholic churches. If this great war had been waged as a crusade in the spirit all over the world, in the place of a too close gathering which promoted the conflict, which the revelations to Joseph from time to time had been heeded, then the combustive pressur would have exhausted itself by a general mission carried out to all and for one purpose, to redeem the world in the love to the world, and not for to establish Nauvoo in Illinois, or to quench a few men's thirst for earthly ambition, and the glory of men and this world.

That interior work to be done in the soul of mankind was the general outline of the church mission, and how should the restoration come except by the conversion of the churches into the unity of the restored church of Christ during the latter day work from heaven to earth. Now, when the Order of Messiah is restored to earth and is in working order, the church will be taught its duty and will be kept strictly to it. The Order will be a schoolmaster to the church, and the division will be known between the church and the kingdom to come, which the Order will herald to the church, but the church has to go out into the world and convert the churches, and prepare the way for the Order and the kingdom to come.

I will point out a few lines on which stress should be laid in all sermons delivered before the world, because as the church is to the world, so is the Order to the church, a mediator and a regulation against trespasses in the household of God. The church shall compare existing conditions with its teachings, and preach as the spirit does. It shall put the plumb on from the height to the depth on baptism, infant sprinkling, Baptist immersion, and all modes of heathen, and Jewish, or Hindoo baptism, and then put the line on the baptism to the saints. There is too much preaching without getting to the point of the mission, because the spirit controls subjects which the saints should always study and learn by heart, but they are in ignorance of. The spirit mission is to reveal the truth on subjects chosen to speak about. Church government, in comparison with the churches to the church of the saints, is a proper subject, also the last supper in the Catholic, Lutheran, Calvinistic, and other churches, compared with the scriptures, and how it was originally and is now in the church of the saints. Follow these lines of subjects into the spiritual gifts, continually comparing the light in the churches with the lesser or greater light into the fullness of all light, and into its perfection in the Gospel of Freedom.

The mission of the church is not done, and it will take one thousand years to do it in. The principal amusement of the church mission has been not to redeem the world, but like a child to turn summersaults before the world, and making the saints a laughing stock and ridicule before the world. This time will now be over. The church will in harmony with the Order of Messiah establish its manhood, and move on with steady steps of progressive life and strength in God, and the power of the Order of Messiah will move through its childhood into the maturity of the kingdom of heaven, and in that moving of manhood unite with the kingdom which is in heaven, and shall come down on earth. The Order of Messiah shall on that day be a full grown man in the strength and power of the kingdom of God, and constitute the advance guard before all the nations on earth. Like the church is related to the Order, so is the Order related to the kingdom, with the exception that the Order is eventually a part of the kingdom which the church is not, nor can it be except through the Order. When the kingdom is on earth the church will continue its mission among the nations. The nature of the Kingdom is not understood by the church, nor can it very well be comprehended before the Order of Messiah commences to preach the Gospel of Freedom and deliverance from the social, religious, and political bondage of all people by the progressive acceptance of truth.

Mankind is chained in falsehoods, ignorance, superstition and bloodshed.

The Order of Messiah is the Order of the anointed, or the body guard of the King at His personal appearance on earth.

To finish these remarks I have to impress upon the mind of humanity that the churches of protestantism as well as the different catholic churches, are all wandering away from the truth in their understanding about the sacraments, and about the gifts in the church, as well as the conception about the spirit of prophecy and the Holy Ghost.

They have all erred in their entire code of dogmatics, and in the construction of their theology there is not a resting place for truth to get a foothold. The primitive apostolic church suffered for its own apostacy and craft of the high priesthood. The spiritual death of the Levitical priesthood was complete at my advent on earth, when the high priest's office of the holy of holies in the temple was sold for coin by the Roman pro-consul. Hence the fanaticism of the nation, the burning of the temple, the destruction of Jerusalem, and the scattering and rejection of the Jews for centuries was only the logical consequences of the spiritual apostacy from the truth.

It may appear strange to some when I say there is not spirituality left in the churches sufficient to prevent a similar epoch of the world. Although the Holy Spirit has been working among mine elect there is not sufficient strength in any organization to secure its life beyond the light of Messiah, the bright morning star. Christianity is doomed in its present attitude, and its conception about God is not any better, nor any more free from bigotry and superstition than the same conception amongst the Mohammedans, or Hindoos, and Chinese. The churches have given up the battle against one another as a useless task, but truth is nowhere to be discerned except by the mathematics of natural science before which an infallible Pope becomes an absurdity.

In such a dilemma of the religious world was the church of Christ restored and reorganized on earth, but the christian pulpit, adorned with its ethics and poetry, and claimed morals, and much boasted charity, has not made a move towards the truth of the church, not any more than the Jews did in mine apostles, days, who walked the earth in my personal company.

The eternal world does not palliate falsehoods but rejects them ; therefore when natural science progressed, and humanity was adequate to receive the truth as far as it could be applied to that line of knowledge, the ethics of inspiration presented by spiritualism was attached to scientific progression, and it was in measure what the churches with their arrogance and haughty position from the pinnacle of centuries could not receive.

The clergy's most lofty claims to be divine, fell through their pretensions as the bible became a dead letter, like faith should not be found on earth in the coming of the Son of Man. Sermons were delivered in the cathedrals defying the spirit of God, as a staggering man defies to balance himself, and makes the declaration not to be intoxicated, and what is much more strange, gives a temperance lecture to the bystanders, declaring his own soberness, and that the balance of humanity is intemperate. Shall the Son of Man find the faith of God on earth?

To palliate such a condition by a reform, would be to put a new patch of spirituality on an old, homespun jacket, worn out by the wear and tear of the world.

Let the world keep its own make, for it does not alter the essence of the wine because it carries a false label, nor does a church of the world become the church of Paradise because " Jesus the Christ" is cut in marble above its portal. Therefore the restoration of the primitive apostolic preaching and power came into the world, but the world comprehended it not, and they persecuted the apostles. The premature death of

Joseph the seer, and the straying of the church of saints into the mountains, and the final rejection of its apostleship, and the loss of the spiritual gifts, was all caused from the fact that the spirit of the world captured the church from want of caution among the leaders, and the sagacity and shrewdness of the adversary, and his tactics in cornering the saints into the world and driving the remnants into the wilderness, and gaining as it appeared a complete victory over God's designs.

Finally the reorganization came by Joseph, the son of the seer, and the gifts returned among the reorganized saints, and the apostleship was restored by revelation, but it would not suffice to roll on the work, as the church lingers scattered in the world in a suffocating condition, unless a higher power steps in and takes the church by the hand and accomplishes its connection with the kingdom, a work which Joseph the seer should have done in time, but which he failed to do, and it was not bestowed upon his sons, but it was so arranged in the eternal worlds that a messenger should by birthright come forth in the power of the Order of Messiah, and give to the church the link, and in that work shall the redemption come to the churches, even the redemption from bondage. To the nations of the world shall a work be done by the Order of Messiah, even as I did when Israel was redeemed from the bondage of Pharaoh in Egypt, and I will give my people power to go out from thraldom. To every one of my servants is a work, and I will make them powerful in the spirit to do it.

Now I beseech you to be faithful in the spirit according to your election, even as my Father sealed that blessing upon you to go forth as a messenger to this generation, and I will raise up powerful messengers at your right, and your left side, and before you, and behind you, and I will not leave you alone, and they shall do their missions in the spirit of the Order and my words. You shall be strong as Moses and Elias, and many of the prophets, and I shall not leave you alone, nor shall I bend you down to the ground under the burden of my work, but I will be the strength to do it with, and I will raise up messengers to do my work. Even as my Father sealed the strength of Messiah to abide with you, so shall He seal it again upon others until the Order shall go forth in the same strength, and messengers shall work without getting tired, and fasting without getting hungry, and your bodies shall be built up in strength, and you shall live without sickness, and some without feeling dissolution of the physical body. Some shall be transfigured in the spirit, and others shall grow powerful in the spirit, and be powerful before all men in doing my work.

Therefore bathe your bodies daily, and sponge every morning with cold water in the name of Messiah, and put your feet into a basin of cold water, and wash all uncleanliness from your feet in the name of Messiah, that the spirit may bear testimony to you by your guardian angel that your ways on earth are clean before the sight of God.

Also shall you make a covenant daily with your God, and your bodies shall be preserved even as your souls shall be preserved, clean and powerful before the Lord your God. And you shall take oil from the fruit of the olive, and pour it from the bottle or cup into your left hand as much as an olive nut shell half full, or as much as half a tablespoonful, and in the name of Messiah you shall rub your hands together, filled with joy and praise God, and you shall anoint your head with the oil to give strength to your head and your hair, that you shall not grow bald, and remain powerful in your mind, and it shall give nourishment and vigor to your brain, that your memory shall not grow weak nor your senses grow dim, and old age shall not touch you, but you shall remain as you were in a youth all your days, and the burdens, and trouble, and worry of life shall not bend down your neck under the yokes of men or the world. When you have anointed your head all over, you shall put the palms of your hands the right upon the left on the top of your head and remain in a silent, prayerful mind in the spirit, remembering me when my hands were lifted above my head on the cross, and you shall say " King of Kings and Lord of Lords." When you have finished your invocation in the spirit, then the spirit shall bear testimony that you are salved with the prophetic ordinance to the apostolic office of a messenger in the spirit of the Order of Messiah to serve the king and lord on earth. Do not make slaves of yourselves, but remain in the freedom of the spirit, and as often as the spirit bears testimony to you do it every day, or may be every other day, the ordinance of the Order of

Messiah may be repeated, even as it was done when you entered the Order, when the presiding officer washed your feet in my name, as I washed mine apostle's feet.

Even as you have yourselves by the hands and power of the priesthood taken the symbolic sponge bath in similitude of your former baptism into the church, as the sponging belongs to the Order and is done with your own hands, so you shall stand free in the Gospel of Freedom and spotless in your God. This is to be done before the first degree, in that of being a messenger.

The Gospel of Freedom is the entrance to the Order, or to the degree of the Order called the White Cross. The Gospel of Freedom is the perfection of the fullness of the gospel for the gathering in of the elect from all the churches, and it has to be preached of the priesthood and of the messengers, before the end comes of the present regimen of the world. Those who enter into the Gospel of Freedom from the church have to be received by blessing and laying on of hands by a messenger, but members of the protestant or catholic churches, or Jews, or Gentiles, have to enter through the restored church, by the first principles of the gospel and baptism by immersion, and laying on of hands. Then they can be received in the Gospel of Freedom by laying on of hands by messengers, and become qualified to enter the Order.

The baptism into the church shall always be by immersion, and the sponging and bathing by the messenger shall be a symbolic sign done by himself, and to himself, according to commandment and regulation laid down in the general discipline of the Order and degrees of the Messiah.

The first degree is that of being a messenger and knight in the degree of the White Cross, and the breast-plate of Nephi is attached to that degree. The full proceeding will be given in the white book. When the messenger has been accepted into the Order by the spirit of prophecy in a meeting of the degree, and has himself taken the first degree by the holy sponge bath, and entered voluntarily into the midst of the barracks where the degree is assembled, then the presiding officer shall arise and approach him, extending to him the right hand of fellowship and say : " Blessed art thou who comest in the Lord's name."

The presiding officer invests him with the white cross on his left shoulder in the front, and with the breast-plate of Nephi hanging as a white star in a white silk ribbon around his neck. After this ceremony the messenger kisses the right hand of the presiding general who is officiating in the name of Messiah, the king.

Then the candidate is seated in a chair in the midst of the congregation of messengers, and puts his feet into a basin filled with water. The officer is kneeling down on his right knee and commences washing the left foot first, and then the right foot, and wipe them dry with the towel bound around his loins. Then he blesses the candidates' feet with strength. When the messenger arises and the officer has put away the towel, he greets the messenger with these words: " Blessed be you, if you keep your body clean from the sins of the world, and keep your feet clean on all your ways in the world, and so in all your dealings teach mankind." Then extending his right hand of fellowship the officer says, " All the gifts belong to you, and more abundantly the spirit of healing."

In the second degree, or the Knight of the Red Cross, the cross is fastened in front of the candidates' right shoulder. The general saying, " Brother messenger, by this cross you are made a Knight of the Red Cross, or a brother rosecrucian in the Holy Order of Messiah, having taken upon thyself the second degree of the Order of Messiah, I have the pleasure in the name of Messiah to invest you with the insignia of the preacher's office by fastening by the red ribbon the circular Order of Moses on your right breast, that it may be a symbolic investiture to you of a preacher's gift from Jehovah." The officer then draws his sword and places the flat of the blade on his right shoulder, saying, " Be a valiant knight on the battle-field of Jehovah. In the name of Messiah I seal upon you that love by which He loved the world, when His blood crimson red as this red cross colored the tree on Golgotha. Be you victorious. Preach in your death, as in your life, Amen;" passing the blade of the sword across the chest. These words are only the outline of the second degree, and more will be given in detail in the red book.

The third degree is given separately, but the two first degrees can be given close together, but better given separately, each degree by itself.

The third degree is only conferred on knights of both first and second degrees. The first or apostolic degree of healers is also called the Order of Nephi, and Knights of the White Cross. The candidate must be Knight of the White Cross and Knight of the Red Cross, according to the Order of Moses.

The working order of each degree will be given separately and in detail, and the united working order for the degrees all together. A special book for that purpose will be given to the Order of Messiah containing it all, but the degrees can be known by these outlines.

The third degree, or the Royal Princes of Messiah, is the degree preceding the kingdom, where the degree of king can only be conferred by the King of Kings and the Lord of Lords.

The Knights of the Red Cross being assembled in the Arsenal Hall, can send messengers to the Knights of the Golden Cross, or the Royal Princes of Messiah being assembled in their Temple Hall. By knocking seven times on the door one is admitted to the waiting room, where the assembled princes send him a present given him by the sergeant-at-arms to the candidate from the Order of Moses, or the Knights of the Red Cross, to prepare himself to enter.

At the entrance he is received by the sergeant-at-arms asking him, "Have you a sword." His answer is "yes, I have one." The Sergeant answers, "and I have one, that is two swords, and is sufficient for our defence, because all who wield the sword otherwise shall perish by the sword—follow after me." The candidate follows him into the center of the hall, where he confronts the presiding general. The general asks "Who is that knight?" The sergeant-at-arms answers, "Most Royal prince general, this knight has been valiant on the battle-field of Jehovah and served in the war for the defense of the saints in the church, and shown charity and good works in the world, he has healed the sick and attended the dying under the white cross. He has traveled thousands of miles under the apostolic office of preaching the truth, and shielding the church, and comforting the Order. He has been blessed with spiritual gifts from our king, and with the preaching and spirit of healing, and has fought most victoriously the battle of defense for the truth under the red cross. Now he is seeking to follow his king further, with more endurance and more sacrifices than ever before, and seeks admission." General—"Then let him step forward and sacrifice prayers in the spirit to the Most High God, and let the incense rise like his spirit does, as a sweet perfume before the throne of God. I hail thee, rosecrucian!

The sergeant-at-arms lights the cup of incense and gives the chain to the candidate, who swings the cup before the center of the hall where the yellow light burns. When the degree of Messiah is assembled, all remain standing for a few minutes until this ceremony is over. Then the general approaches him, as it will be designated in the book of ceremonies pertaining to the three degrees.

Calling him by name the general says, "Brother messenger of the Order of Messiah, as you in your heart have prepared yourself to take the degree of Messiah, and you are elected to the honor by the Holy Spirit of prophecy given to the assembled degree of Princes, and the same testimony has borne witness to you in the name of the king, I have the honor to decorate you with the Order and insignia of the Messiah our King, it is the name of Jehovah in Hebrew, written with red letters on a white cross, standing in the golden disc of the sun."

This regalia shall be carried on the left breast in a yellow ribbon, and over the region of the heart.

The general pins the order on the left breast, and says : "As you have brought the holy incense of prayers in the spirit as a sacrifice before the Ancient of Days, and before our King with a devotion to the great power of eternity, you have received the honor to bear this Order, which is the greatest distinction that can be conferred on you, as by that insignia you become one of the elect princes of heavenly royalty to stand on earth ready for the reception of the King.

The sergeant-at-arms approaches the general with a horn filled with oil, and gives it to the adjutant general, who blesses it by keeping it in the left hand and placing his right hand on the top, and remains silent in the spirit of prayer for a few moments. Then he gives the horn to the general. In the absence of a horn a bottle can be used. As the general approaches the candidate face to face, he lifts the horn in the right hand, and at that moment stops, and the entire camp of knights are crossing their arms over their breasts, the right hand to the left shoulder, and the left hand to the right shoulder, and the words are said by all present : " So mote it be in the name of Messiah, King of Kings, and Lord of Lords." The general then pours the oil on the candidate's head (who is seated on a chair with arms crosslaid), and gives the horn to the sergeant-at-arms. The general presiding and two other generals are officiating. The general presiding is anointing the head for a moment, when all three generals put their hands on the candidate's head, and the general says: "I confirm the degree of Royalty upon you as a prince in the Order of Messiah, that the Royal blood of the house of David may be spiritually grafted into your life from adoption by the Messiah at His second coming on earth." The Knights of the Red Cross wear a red belt and a sword with a red hilt. The candidate is commanded to untie his belt, and the general fastens around his loins a golden belt with a sword having a gilt hilt, and says to him, " Mene, Mene, Tekel Upharsin," shall be written upon the designs of all thine enemies. Be victorious, for the Ancient of Days, even the Lord of Hosts, shall fight thy battles until Messiah shall be revealed to thee foot to foot, hand to hand, face to face, breast to breast, and mouth to mouth. Forget never the nobility and rank of thy spirit." The rites of this ceremony will be revealed more in detail in the yellow book.

After the burning of incense on the altar during silent prayer, all are waiting for the spirit of prophecy in which the king comes, and reveals himself, and speaks to the perfect Order of the Messiah degree by the gifts and power from the high. The general approaches from his seat the candidate again, who keeps arms crosslaid, and with his drawn sword makes a cross up and down the chest of the knight saying, " may it always be remembered that you bear the crucified Jesus as a mark on your entire body, that His wounds may be in your hands and feet, and the wound may be found in your side." Then he takes a golden cross made from broad gold ribbons, and pins it in a line from the right of one arm hole to the same place on the other side, and then with the same kind of ribbon he pins a line from the neck down to the waist, saying, " This is the emblem of the degree. May it be to you a protection against evil all your days—may it strike the enemies of the King of Kings with terror, when they shall behold the golden cross on your chest, and may you be valiant, more so than ever you were in the crusade as a Knight of the Red Cross. Being elevated to the rank of Royal Knight of the Golden Cross, and a royal prince messenger, it imposes upon you the most stringent duties. If you have a wife, work as though you had none, and if you have none, live solitary. If you marry a sister of the Order of Messiah, let it be with the consent and approval of the King and according to the spirit of prophecy ; because your life is from now on hidden in the death of Jesus of Nazareth, that you may have the royal priesthood and govern with Messiah. Severe shall your trials be in the work, when you shall be called upon at noon or at midnight to relieve a distressed messenger or a saint of the church, or a stranger who calls for help, or aid, or personal assistance. Thou shalt not stop and question whether to go or not, or into the worthiness of the applicant or not ; but thou shalt go even at the risk of thy life and render the required aid, and fulfil the requested prayer for help, because your Father lets it rain on the fields belonging to the good and the wicked, and His mercy is shining over all the world." The obligations of a messenger of this degree, and of this degree related to another, will be given in the yellow book, or book for the degrees of Knights belonging to the Order of Messiah.

The general says further, "Brother knight of the Golden Cross of the Messiah, being a royal prince of the Order, it becomes necessary that you continue to humble yourself, even as you have done by bearing and exercising the Order of Moses, because there never was a more meek man amongst all Israel ; therefore thou shalt serve thy time as a janitor, and as a sergeant-at-arms of this hall, and serve your brethren of this hall. Also shall it be a duty devolving upon you whenever you shall again visit the arsenal of the Red Cross to serve your brethren, with your right knee bend to the ground and perform the ordinance of foot-washing amongst them. When you enter the armory of the Knights of the White Cross, thou shalt fill the basin with water, and keep the towel ready for use, and be a servant in the ordinance of bathing and sponging, and not officiate as a presiding officer in any of the Orders in the capacity of being a prince, but by being an humble knight of the White or Red Cross, or rank army officer to duty in the army."

After the thanksgiving is sung, the presiding general shall arise with all the knights in a silent benediction, with the emblems of arms cross laid over the breast.

The general extends his hands towards the candidate, who kisses his hand, and at the same time embracing him, saying, "In the name of the King of Kings, even so I receive you as the Father received the prodigal son when he said to his father, I am not worthy to be called thy son, only receive me as one of thy servants; by having entered the degree of the Messiah, thou shalt be all thy life before thy Father in heaven with the mind of the prodigal son, even thou shalt be a son and a prince of the royal household; therefore receive from the King this ring on thy finger, and be from this moment and forever betrothed in His love with the cause of redemption on earth and in heaven, and remain in His love, as His betrothed in the soul of His love forever and forever. As a token of your sincerity and acceptance, kiss this ring. The knight kisses the ring.

You could not gain admittance to this Temple Hall without being divested of your uniform dress belonging to the Red Cross; I hereby present you a new uniform cloak to cover your destitution with, and protect you against cold or severe weather on your mission, even as the Father in his joy presented such a cloak to the prodigal son. Neither were you admitted with shoes on your feet, as the ground is holy, even as Moses was commanded to take off his shoes. Now in token of your heavenly Father's joy over your reception as a son in His household, you are presented with a pair of golden slippers, because He says: "This son has been far off, and has returned to me, and is in love restored to me, and he wishes to remain by me only as one of my servants, but this son was dead to me and is now alive." Therefore remain in your Father's household, not any longer as a servant but as a son, because to the servant He says, "Though you have done all things right, you have only proved yourself to be unprofitable servants as you have only done that which you ought to have done." Concerning the son of the household, he says to the servants: "Let us have great joy and be merry; kill the fatted calf, and invite all the guests to the feast, because my son that I thought to be dead has returned to me." Being now fully equipped as the prodigal son to his Father's supper, you must forever impress upon your mind never to act with any enviousness against your brethren in the rank of highness, but remain humble in their presence, even as you now stand before them as the prodigal son in your Father's house; therefore so shall it be, the last shall be the first and the lowest shall become the most eminent, and those who do not wish to govern shall govern Israel, and govern the world and their own soul. Royal prince, when you visit the brethren, the knight messengers of the different degrees of the Order of Messiah, or you visit the church and preach the first principles, or administer as an elder to the sick, or baptize and confirm members into the church, then remember that you can only enter your Father's home, even with all your most eminent virtues, meek as the prodigal son. May this truth impress itself deep in your soul, that those who are high and eminent in the spirit, even with more elevated rank than the princes in the world, are raised to this position by the grace and love of your heavenly Father, though they have in His sight eaten their food with swine when His spirit visited them in their misery, and drew their hearts to Him until they said, "I will arise and go to my Father's house." When they were afar off, and beheld the old home, there was no demand upon their Father's grace, and when the Father embraced the prodigal son and kissed him, he had no claim on his grace, but said, "I have sinned against heaven and against thy love, because I have ungratefully destroyed my inheritance and forfeited my birthright." Therefore rejoice, for there is no reproach in your Father's heart, because that which was lost is found, and the feast is prepared for your reception in the kingdom." The fullness of the Order gives the rank of royal prince, but not army rank. Captain, colonel and general messenger, you are as you may serve, or as a private messenger.

"It was truly by serving as a faithful messenger that you gained admission to the degrees of the Order, and it was by being admitted into the church by obedience to the first principles of the gospel, you could by degree enter the Order of Messiah and as a volunteer in the army. By the same rule do you now arrive on the third step onwards to the kingdom.

"Your rank of royal prince does not necessarily give you any corresponding rank in the army, and more, you will not be known there from any private messenger, except by the emblems you bear on your breast, and these you have permission to bear in public as well as when the degree of the Order assembles. Princes of this degree receive the highest rank given to the Order, and this helmet (takes a golden helmet in his hand), is only borne by generals of the army. On the front covering the forehead you discover a right triangle standing on its base, and in the triangle is written in Hebrew the name of Jehovah, or I am that I am." What the general further says will be written in the yellow book, expressly for this degree.

Then the general places the helmet on the head of the candidate, saying, "Let this moment be forever called sacred in all your life, and may you be found amongst the 144,000 redeemed from the world, standing on mount Zion, with God's name on your forehead, which signifies supreme wisdom, and glory, and dominion with the lamb that was slain, but now lives forever and forever. Amen."

After the solemn benediction in the spirit, and the salute, and embrace, and the kiss is exchanged, the general approaches again the candidate in the regular form given, and with the holy greeting, saying, " Being a prince of the royal household, you are not any longer a servant, for you are discharged in grace from being a servant, but you are now a son, and have reached to the grace of the sons and daughters of God, and I ask you before the knights of this degree, did you come to this elevation by birthright?" The candidate says yes, or no, or he does not know.

Then the general says, "Very well, if you have not any doubt in your mind that this degree comes to you by birthright, I have the pleasure to ask you to present before this degree the Urim and Thummim, or the seers stone, if you are in possession of such a gift, or do you know the use of such an instrument?" The candidate generally has none. The general says: "Aaron and the sons of Aaron were in possession of such an instrument by birthright, and also Noah, and the patriarchs, and prophets and seers, both ancient and modern. You are equipped as a royal prince in the necessary emblems of your high office, but in that of a seer you are yet according to your own confession, lacking one thing, and that is the seers stone." The general shows a small, round stone, black or grey, and says, keeping the stone in a line between the candidate's eyes, "Brother knight, by this gift was Zion redeemed, and those who were not a people became a people, and those who were low down have been raised high up, and those who were as naught for the world and regarded as the outcast among the nations, have peopled this continent God made great, and you are princes, and sons, and daughters in this adoption. Therefore my brother messenger of this degree, may you also fight the good fight, and gain eternally the crown laid up for those who conquer wrath, and the grabbing selfishness of human nature, by living in the spirit and love of God. By this degree you have received the rank of a general of the host of hosts, but before you can serve as a Knight of the Golden Cross of this degree, it will become necessary for you to humble yourself much before the Almighty God, even as Abraham did when he stood face to face and spoke with Jehovah, and said, "Lord, what am I that thou speakest to me, I am only dust and ashes?" but the Almighty blessed Abraham before all men on earth, and in the same way did He bless Moses, and there was not in all Israel such meek men. If the seers stone shall be of any benefit to you, depends on the Lord, that He will give you besides all other gifts, and the gift of prophecy, the gift of seership. Take this stone in your right hand and place it on the top of your head, and from there to the place above and between your eyes. This sign is that of seer. The officiating general drops the stone into the right hand of the candidate, and says: " Please make the sign of the seer, which shall be given more fully in the book upon this degree. Peace be with you, the peace of God."

"Now you have received the last emblem of the Order of Messiah that can be bestowed on mortal man."

"What you now possess belongs to all prophets and seers by birthright, and many have and possess it by adoption. It will now become a most stringent duty for you to seek into the mysteries of the Godhead, and find the truth of everlasting pleasure, which is in the love of God. You have been educated by degrees in the dealings of God with man, and you stand now prepared to meet the King of the Kingdom, and the Lord and Master of the church. Also be prepared to meet the Patriarch of heaven and the emperor of the world, who is the Father of the church and the ruler of the nations, even as He revealed Himself God the Almighty to Abraham, and the Jehovah to Moses. He reveals himself as the Patriarch of heaven to the Order of Messiah, that we might be blessed by the power and strength of His paternal feelings towards us, and having raised us to the eminence of royal knights and princes of the household, He teaches us the sublime truth to worship with Him the eternity He worships, which cannot be approached by words nor by a sound of the human voice, but is approached in the spirit, and worshipped in the Holy Spirit, and the answer shall also be given to you in the same spirit. Amen."

"Now it will be necessary for you to go to the living water which proceeds from out of all life, and wash your hands and face, and bear a silent testimony before God that your conscience shall remain forever open and free from the guilt of sin against the Holy Spirit, to whom you are from this time most sincerely wedded in your heart."

"Go, wash your hands as an emblem that you will never be found guilty of being a traitor to the cause of Messiah. Neither shall you be found guilty of conspiracy against God or the Order of Messiah, nor be found guilty of bloodshed or ambushing man for that purpose, and should you ever become acquainted with plans for such a purpose, it would be your duty to reveal it without delay to the presiding general of the Order. In token of your sincerity wash your hands and face." When the candidate returns, the general will continue : " During the washing of feet by our Master and King on the night He was betrayed, Peter said to Him, "wash not only my feet, but also my entire body." Jesus answered Him, "whosoever's feet I have washed clean, he is also clean over his entire body." This should impress you with the greatness and dignity of foot-washing, as from the hour you have entered the degree of the White Cross, you have been honored in such a measure, and as an emblem this blessing has been following you, even to your present eminent position in the Order of Messiah. Your soul has borne witness to this council of knights that you have been steadfast, never wavering in the purpose and execution of the will of the Messiah, keeping your hands clean from the blood of this generation. Rejoice, because the Father is I am that I am, that I am, I am, and when you are accosted by night or by day, by an enemy or by a stranger, on the highway, or in your house, in the mountains or in the valleys, and you are asked who are you, then you shall say I am that I am, Jehovah's representative on earth, and your enemy shall not gain power over you to do harm.

"Also in regard to your future, let it be placed in the hands of Messiah to sustain your life in health and strength, and as Jesus spat on the ground and made a paste of clay, and put it on the blind man's eyes, and cured his blindness, so shall ye do the same work. You shall make a paste from the ground, and anoint with it the blind, and the lame, and the deaf, and those who are in the condition of Job and Lazarus, having a body covered with sores and with all kind of disease, and they shall be healed when this anointing is done in the name of the Messiah, and in the power of the Father, and in the prayer of the Spirit with God's power to a knight of the White Cross in the Messiah. Ye shall anoint the wounds or when the ailments are many, only one part of the body, on the naked left breast, below the heart, where the spear pierced on the cross the body of Jesus."

"You shall also remember the night when the angel of death slew all the first-born amongst the Egyptians, and it shall be a sign to you never to be forgotten when a member of any degree of the Order of Messiah is sick. The knights shall assemble in the building of the Order and degree, and continue in silent prayer until the spirit of prophecy makes itself manifest to the circle, and the members of the household shall remain fasting for twenty-four hours, and the father of the family shall kill a dove, or quail, or rabbit, or pigeon, or hare, or antelope, or deer, or lamb, and the legitimate head of the family who is the oldest member of it, either man or woman, and of the Order of Messiah, shall dip the thumb of the left hand in the blood, and remember the crucified Jesus when doing it, and put a mark of blood on the entrance or door frame to the sick room, and if time can be given the angel of death shall not demand him or her to follow through the grave into paradise, but the King of hosts shall appease the angel of death, even the guardian angel of the sick person, and the messengers shall lay hands on the sick in silent prayers in the Holy Spirit, and in the name of Messiah. Amen. Even so shall it be. Then ye shall eat of the meat with the sick, and break the bread and drink the unfermented wine, and as you eat the bread together remember me, and my suffering and death upon the cross. Blessed are those who enter into my glory and remain there. Amen, and Amen. Even so shall I eat the passover lamb with you in the Kingdom of my Father and in His glory, as I ate it with mine apostles on the night of my humiliation."

"Blessed shall you be when you eat the meat, and drink of the wine, and break the bread, and remember me when you eat of that in the Order of Messiah, and blessed shall your household be if you keep my commandments given to you in this Order of the Messiah, for you shall be that I am, and my power shall follow you and rest upon you forever and forever. Amen."

These pages are the outlines of the Order of Messiah, and sufficient for a working basis, which will be contained in the book given to the Order in due time to work on in the different degrees. The stepping stone to the Order is the Gospel of Freedom, or the connecting link between the church, and the churches and the Order.

Also there is no new foundation laid, but only one, which is laid in the first principles of the Gospel of Messiah, and the church remains the church in its re-organization by Joseph as the president and his heir after him. The organization which went into the mountains perished there by their own mistakes, and lost its inspired body of apostles called by revelation from God, and became a political institution of the world, but mine elect shall be gathered to Independence, and surrounding states of the Union.

The Gospel of Freedom is the perfection of the church to be preached as a deliverance for mine elect from church bondage, and the captive shall become at liberty into God's glorious freedom and enter the church, and Order of Messiah, and meet me. Amen. Peace be with you, even the peace which I have in my Father's love. Amen.

MESSAGE FROM JESHUAH, THE MESSIAH.

DISCIPLINE OF THE ORDER OF MESSIAH.

CHAPTER I.

SAN FRANCISCO BAY, August 20, 1887.

1. The Order of Messiah is not the church, but it contains within itself all that which belongs to the church, and more revelation than is found in the church. There is nothing in the Order of Messiah, nor in the kingdom to come, that conflicts with the fundamental principles of the church, or the first principles of the gospel.

2. The Order of the Messiah comes into the world because the church as a body cannot move into the work, but has fallen short of doing this work of preparation now necessary, and because it has its hands full of doing the work of restoration in the world of the first correct principles of the gospel.

3. Therefore the Order of Messiah is an Order of picked men and woman in the gospel service, under the auspices of the spirit of freedom, preparing for the kingdom.

4. As the church could not do the work by its own inherent strength belonging to the preaching of the gospel, it became necessary that the Messiah should do the work Himself by His own special messengers, preluding the day when He in person shall take command with His host of hosts on earth. Therefore the advance divisions are marching before the Kingdom, as the Order of Messiah.

5. This Order is based upon a military discipline belonging to the hosts of heaven, and has in its foundation such regulations, compacts and duties that would be impossible for the church as a body to enter upon according to its own life, welfare, happiness and integrity in the world, but members of the church being so disposed and drawn by the spirit can enter the Order. It may be men and women having once in their lives obeyed the gospel ordinances, and received in the past the spirit of the first principles necessary for the regulation of their lives in the faith of the Messiah.

6. Any membership in the church shall not interfere with the duties or obligations in the Order.

7. Those who have not obeyed the first principles of the church, and wish to become members of the Order, are by baptism passed through the door into the church, and then into the Order, after full obedience to the ordinances of the church.

8. The admission to the Order of Messiah is through the gate of the spirit of prophecy, and by a special ordinance of laying on of hands, or the baptism of fire, also called the endowment, with the power from the kingdom above.

9. As the Order of Messiah is an Order of the kingdom and not of the church, the power to officiate in the Order has to come down from the kingdom which is in heaven, with power not to be found in the church.

10. Therefore in the reorganization the president of the church as the head of the members of the church, who are also members of the Order, can not give them any commands which pertain to the Order, but they receive commands which pertain to the Order from the general in chief, through the department general, and by the general adjutant and in the name of Messiah. The church general can be a counsellor to the president, if called by Messiah through the authority in the church.

11. This close relationship between the church and the Order makes the principles intermarried with each other, and at the same time distinctly apart in the work of restoration and preparation, and endowment in their missions, but the spirit is the same that works it all, and in all, and by all, in his own diversified manner and method, and for a special work to be accomplished. The work of the Order is the work of healers, preachers and prophets, and the Order is a circle of prophets, and none can be accepted into the Order except the brother or sister is a prophet or a prophetess, in the gifts and spirit, and endowment of dreams, and visions, and healings belonging to the speaking and moving, and living in and by the spirit of prophecy.

12. The Order of Messiah is an Order of messengers, or apostles and prophets, and in that respect it does homage to the

president of the church as the prophet, seer and revelator, if he truly and duly not only holds such an office, but also officiates in such a spirit.

13. The third general or church general has not necessarily to be a counsellor, nor to be one of the two counsellors to the president of the church, as he officiates independently as a counsellor from the Order to the president, if he should not be in a hostile relation to the Order from social disorder in the church. He officiates as a third counsellor to the president if he is accepted, and will only represent the Order in its relation to the president and not to the church, as the president will always represent the church.

However, in the true and intimate relation between the Order and the church, the spirit is one with the Order in the same unity of the Messiah, and can only be fully expressed in its true union by the third general of the Order being the counsellor to the president, and at times the right or left hand counsellor in the church.

14. The president of the church cannot by revelation appoint generals in the Order of Messiah, but he can receive from the Lord such revelation to the church that can appoint any general of the Order to be one of the counsellors to the president of the church.

The generals of the Order of Messiah can only be called by a direct message from the Messiah, and a general shall by direct message appoint his vicar, who can officiate in his place during absence, and as his assistant. This vicar exercises the same authority as the general appointed, to act in sickness, absence, or old age, and he will be considered the probable successor to the general. Should any vicar-general by death be called away from earth, the Messiah will for any of the three first generals by special message appoint the new vicar general, so the office shall not be vacant.

15. Any vicar-general of the Order has the same authority as the general he represents, but the work of the generals is exclusively on the spiritual plane.

16. The adjutant general lieutenant's work is on an executive business plane, but he works, and preaches, and teaches in the same spirit as the three generals, and two division commanders and lieutenant generals superior to him.

The vicar generals (but not the general in chief), the Jew and church generals, and lieutenant or major generals, or any of the twelve brigadier generals, either of the twenty-three generals, whoever the mind of Messiah by revelation shall appoint, and upon whom He shall bestow the spirit of the calling to officiate in office, will be mentioned by revelation to the president of the church as his counsellor. Belonging to the Order of Messiah he can represent the Order to the president, while the president of the church though a member of the Order, cannot represent the Order to himself.

17. The Messiah may in extraordinary circumstances call a messenger by appointment and the spirit of prophecy, who is not a general in the Order, and cause the president of the church to receive revelation by which Messiah will call men to be church counsellors who are not numbered amongst the twenty-three generals, nor of the Order.

18. The mission of the general in chief is all over the world, wherever the King shall call upon him to go to organize his forces, and the Messiah shall regulate his messenger's lives by messages given for that purpose, and for the regulation of the Order in its relation to the churches, and to the interior life of the Order by new light which shall be given by the King to the Order.

19. The three general's positions in the Order is in the service of the spirit, and the vicar-general's is of a secular nature to represent the generals, as counsellors do in the church. If the relation between the church and the Order should not be very amiable, the attorney or adjutant lieutenant general shall settle secular difficulties. The church general will the Lord direct concerning the churches, and by revelation to the president of the church, and to the members of the Order, concerning local affairs in the Order of Messiah, is given by the spirit of prophecy and to the general in chief. The attorney adjutant general is by calling, and the spirit of his office, to assist the general in chief, and act as the business general of the Order. His office and the nature of his calling is to remain at the headquarters of the Order, where it by the Lord's message may be appointed, and directed to supervise the interior and exterior business movements of the Order. In case of any of the three

generals' absence or death, the vicar always steps into his place by hereditary right, subject to the spirit of his calling by prophecy. The office of vicar general is not always for active use except as successor; he is on requests and prayers called by message and the spirit of prophecy by the Messiah in the congregation of messengers.

20. The vicar generals belong to the third degree of the Order of Messiah, and are not acting generals in the army, but only in rank belonging to the third degree of the Order.

21. The three vicar generals are not officiating when the generals are at quarters, where they or the generals always must be present. The two lieutenant generals are department commanders, and during absence represented by their adjutants. The third lieutenant general is the attorney adjutant general, with office at headquarters.

22. The general in chief shall have his headquarters on the continent of America, but sends messengers to the other continents. The second general, or the Jew general, shall reside and have headquarters at Jerusalem, Palestine.

23. The general in chief has to travel all over the world because his mission lays all over the world, either by him personally or by his vicar. By re-union of the army he shall always be present at headquarters.

24. The spirit of the calling belonging to the office of general is revealed in the midst of the assembled messengers. No major general can officiate in that position except called by revelation to be the commander of an army corps. The six major generals are each one in command of two brigades, each to be commanded by a brigadier general.

The vicar generals rank with colonels of the army, and Knights of the Golden Cross.

The president of the church of saints can be received in the Order as fully as every member of the church, when he receives such commandment given to him in a special message from the Messiah. However, the president of the church cannot be general in chief, or his vicar general, even though he belongs to the Order, because the spirit of that calling can not rest upon him. Only by special revelation and under certain circumstances which may make an exception, or in emergency, if all three generals and the vicar generals should be killed at the same time, can he officiate in that position until others shall be called by direct message from Messiah to fill the places.

25. This will be sufficient in connection with what is said in former messages to outline the special position for the three head officers in their relation to the church, and its relation and duty to the Order of Messiah. All generals shall not officiate at present, and most of the high offices shall not be filled at present, but the high rank shall be bestowed on a few to commence the work and push the wheel of progress in the Order.

The White Cross Knights, or the healers, are the most numerous, and the bulk of the army, and counts the privates and the subaltern officers from their midst. The working manners and duties of the White Cross is given in a special plain message. Work where the field is ripe, and gather in mine elect in companies of hundred and forty-four messengers of the White Cross, besides officers, till the rank of captain called by the spirit of prophecy speaking in the meetings.

In this manner are regiments organized to colonel, and knights of all degrees can serve as private messengers in the army, but the majors, lieutenant colonels, and colonels shall be knights of the Red Cross of the preachers called rosecrucians, and Knights of the Red Rose. Therefore are the knights of the White Cross called knights of the White Rose, as the knights of the Golden Cross have as emblem the Yellow Rose.

All the generals and knights with the rank of general are Knights of the Golden Cross.

The relief company to each regiment of provision, hospitalier and ambulance, is commanded by a captain, who reports to the colonel for the regiment of seven companies.

To each brigade is to be attached a reserve, and a regiment of hospitalier and ambulance. The reserve shall not be called to active service, but always be in readiness. Women do no military service except as nurses. The name messenger shall be added to all rank in the army, as captain messenger, sergeant messenger, &c.

Every brother and sister of the Gospel of Freedom is designated brother messenger or sister messenger. The words messenger and apostle are synonymous, and the Order of Messiah is an apostolic Order; therefore is the priesthood, and the spirit of the high priesthood of an apostle by ordination, bestowed on every member of the Order, with the power to officiate, equal in power with the twelve apostles of Messiah or the apostles in his church. It is an apostolic order of messengers, with apostolic calling and mission to all the world endowed with prophetic office and appointment, and endowment and power from the Most High God. Amen.

CHAPTER II.

Conducting Meetings.

1. As the entire service is not depending on man, but on God, it shall be conducted accordingly. It matters not what opinion and difference of thought the several members cherish, or in what degree their views differ, the one from the other, as the divine service of the Order is the service of God, in which the spirit serves man to his edification, exaltation and salvation. Therefore the messengers of the Most High God in the Order of Messiah, have to be low and humble in their own estimation; their pride and ambition must all be hidden up in Christ. Their faith must not be founded in their own strength, but it must be the faith, and hope, and strength of Messiah, that they may be found in Him, that His spirit may be by them with the power and strength of God, that the spirit of prophecy may abide with them forever.

When you assemble yourselves together for divine worship, then only members of the Order are present. And worship in the following manner: You shall stand up and pray with uplifted hands to the Most High God of the eternal world, and you shall not pray with words, nor shall you pray with words in the spirit, but you shall collect all your most earnest and holy desires into your mind, and your Father who reads the secrets of the human soul, shall know it ascending to Him from you, and shall fulfil every honest wish, and every earnest desire you ask of Him in the spirit of His love, and in the faith living and moving in the Messiah. This promise He gave me in finishing my mission on the cross, and His words stand good forever and ever. Amen.

This shall be a regulation for opening the regular apostolic prophetic meetings of messengers.

2. When you preach the Gospel of Freedom, or the Messiah before the world, it will at times be necessary to pray with words, especially when you officiate in the name of the church ; remember therefore, when you pray with words, you pray before men and not before God, and the spirit shall not be manifested to you except you pray in the spirit and before God. The church, however, has been a teacher leading to that which you should receive as a more perfect guide, but at the same time the teacher is good to all who need His tuition, but the church is for the world, and the Order for the elect.

The law is a master of good will to men and to those who embraced the faith of Israel, and it became a fruitful teacher of the grace in Christ by the conviction about sin, righteousness and judgment to come, and the law was not done away with, but it is preached to the world up to this day, yet you have a more perfect law, that which by the grace of God is given to you in the perfection of His faith, who loved the world and gave Himself up a sacrifice in the hands of sinful men.

Pray in the spirit and you shall be answered in the spirit, ask in the spirit and you shall receive in the spirit, and power and wisdom to work with shall be given and abide with you. Do not be subject to evil influence, and do not succumb to the evil one, but be valiant as giants in the armor of God, fighting the great battle of Jehovah, and be counted among those who conquered evil and the world, and the adversary's effort in cunning disguise, believing that your battle is not only with flesh and blood, but with the subtle influence around you, and the power of darkness which fills the air you breathe, the ground you walk on, and the waves you cross from shore to shore, following you even among those you bless, and fighting you even with those hands you greet as belonging to friends, but are found to be in the service of the enemy. Therefore try the spirits, whether they are of the Holy Spirit and of His hosts, as there are many spirits going into the world to do mission to humanity, that they may be found to be of the truth as you are in the truth. This is the testimony that I give to my friends, that whatever you ask the Father for in the name of Messiah shall be given to you.

Therefore, when you greet one another, extend the right hand of fellowship to each other as friends. Let it be done in the name of Messiah, and receive all things that you can desire in heaven, and on the earth, in the fellowship with him. This is the power I left behind me on earth, which I have given you. The mantle which Elias left behind to Elisha, and he dashed the waters of Jordan with, and the water divided and he walked across on dry ground, is less than my words left to my elect. I left a power behind me stronger than the rod of Moses, that my friends might dash the dust with, and my Father will call forth all the plagues of Egypt if it were necessary, and done in my name, and more than that, I left behind me as an inheritance the intelligence and power of the Holy Ghost to abide in your souls, and do the work in my name. Therefore Messiah is more than Moses, more than Elias, and more than Abraham understood in the flesh, for in the Order of Messiah is more than at any one time was revealed to man on earth in power and prophecy.

The church shall pray with words, and when you officiate in the church as elders of the church, you shall pray with words, but when you officiate in the Order of Messiah you shall not pray with words, but in the spirit and with the palms of your hands turned to eternity, and you shall receive the fulfilment of your prayers in the spirit.

3. When you preach in the church you shall officiate according to the church custom, and preach the gospel as elders in the church, but when you officiate in the power of Messiah, in the Order of Messiah, you shall not speak as you do in the church, but depend on the movement of the Holy Spirit for all

action according to the spirit of prophecy, tongues and interpretation. Therefore when the Order of Messiah commence meetings, no words are used in the opening service, but all remain after silent prayer seated, waiting for the spirit of inspiration to speak by, as it shall move upon the members present, and by this rule shall they speak and not otherwise. If any has a dream let him relate it, and if any has a vision let him or her tell it to the assembled messengers, and the spirit of interpretation shall be given. In all your transactions lay the matter before the Holy Spirit, and the presiding officer shall put the question on the blackboard written before the Lord, and He shall respond to the request. There shall be no reason given you why the transactions for the benefit, or work in the Order, cannot be done in this manner. It is the only method by which the heavens are governed in my Father's kingdom, and the Order which is the forerunner of the kingdom cannot transact business otherwise.

4. The confirmation by which power is bestowed on the new messenger consists simply in the ordination to the prophetic and apostolic office upon which the Order is based from above. Therefore you shall not admit any saint from the church except by prayer in the spirit, and testimony given in the affirmative by the spirit, or by the spirit of prophecy in the meeting. The affirmation shall always be given in a public meeting after prayer and in the spirit, by the spirit of prophecy to one or more messengers of the Order.

If an answer is not received immediately, then a prayer circle shall be formed and remain in silent prayer till the answer comes for the ordination or against it, and it shall be acted upon accordingly.

5. When election or rejection is settled, and a messenger by the voice of the spirit is elected to be among the Lord's elect, then he or she is to be confirmed in the Gospel of Freedom by the following formula, which has to be repeated aloud : " Upon thee, our fellow servant, do we bestow the spirit of the Gospel of Freedom which is now on earth and manifested to mankind in the Order of Messiah; be faithful and truthful, and serve the truth all your days, and the spirit of the Gospel of Freedom shall manifest himself to you accordingly. Blessed be you our fellow messenger in the name of Messiah. Amen.

These words shall ye say, or about the same as the spirit of prophecy shall direct you to utter them, and you shall let your hands remain on the head of the confirmed messenger brother or sister for a short time, as the spirit shall dictate you to do, and remain in silence and wait, and if it is expedient, the gifts of tongues or the spirit of prophecy shall be manifested to the people or given to the confirmed messenger with great power and strength of evidence and edification to the assemblage: "So mote it be," shall be the united words of all present, and " so mote it be," shall the presiding officer say and finish the ordinance in the hall of Assembly, which is a hall for the Gospel of Freedom.

6. The hall of assembly is for meetings conducted by preaching the Gospel of Freedom, or perfection of the church of restoration in its mission during the tenth hour to all mankind in the churches of christianity. The barracks may be a tent used by the Order and Knights of the White Cross, when in cantonment or entrenched, or in active service. It can also be a building with a white cross on. The Order of Messiah is using arsenal halls for the Knights of the Red Cross to assemble in. Special directions shall be given. These are buildings with a red cross on. The Knights of the Golden Cross come together in a temple hall whenever one can be conveniently built, and the pattern will be given hereafter in detail.

It will be sufficient to say that the hall shall have twelve throne seats. It shall be constructed with two seats to the east and two to the west, and four seats on both sides of the entrance. The chairs and benches are on the middle of the floor facing the east. The entrance shall be in the west. The general in chief of the Order is the presiding officer or grand general of the Order, and shall preside at the re-union of the Knights of the Golden Cross by himself in person, or by his vicar during his absence.

The barracks or armory for the Knights of the White Cross, the arsenal hall for the Knights of the Red Cross, and the temple hall for the Knights of the Golden Cross, will be described in detail in a special book concerning the working of the degrees.

There shall be a perpetual light in the center of the temple hall, or barracks, or arsenal, wherever worship is made. Resembling the King, the eternal light, and the Most High God, governing with the supreme power of eternity.

The building or tent shall be constructed according to the ground plan given, being a circle divided into sixteen parts, two parts for entrance east, and two for the entrance west. The balance gives six seats on each side of both entrances. The presiding officer is seated north, resembling the north pole, as the tent or hall is resembling the earth. The Knights hoist the White Cross in a red flag over the tent, or there is placed a White Cross. In the center is hanging a lantern with white glass, and a perpetual light. Where the White Cross can afford to keep their own barracks or armory, the walls inside and outside are painted white. The battle flag for the Knights of the White Cross, has a golden sword resting on a red ground.

Where the Knights of the Red Cross are assembled, is in the center a small light burning within a lantern of red glass. For this degree of the Red Cross is the light an emblem never to be extinguished, but shall burn there forever, or as long as the place is used for worship, and as long as the emblem of the Order of Messiah is above the entrance, and as long as the flag of the Order is seen on the mast above the tent or house. The flag being the red cross of heaven, with a golden sword thrown on the white ground of the banner.

Around the center of the arsenal hall is a passage and a railing, and above and under the loft is seen twelve lights, gas or candle, to lighten the hall. There shall be around the center four cups resting on the railing, each one of them for offering of incense or sweet perfume before God, as the high priest did from the holy in the temple.

The center light differs in color according to the different degrees of the Order which may be in occupation of the place.

In the armory where the Knights of the White Cross are assembled, the center light is enclosed in a lantern of white glass.

In the arsenal hall where the Knights of the Red Cross are assembled, the center light is red, or the lantern is of red glass.

When a messenger of the Gospel of Freedom wishes to join the degree of the White Cross under the patronage of Nephi, he has to send in his request signed by two Knights of the White Cross to recommend him. The application is then posted on a board in the ante or waiting room, or entrance to the degree of the Order. The application remains posted for seven, fourteen, or twenty-one days, and the candidate is either accepted or rejected by the ballot; accepted if all are white balls; rejected on one black ball. Whatever the report may be, it is given to the general of the degree, and the vote is laid before the Lord and King, and His answer is awaited by the spirit and gift of prophecy either in the affirmative or negative. Should the answer be in the affirmative and the brother has been elected with white balls, the general shall declare the brother to be a candidate for the degree. Should the Lord declare the brother a candidate, and he should have received one or more black balls, then the general shall request the Knights who threw the black balls to leave the armory, and they will go away, and in harmony with the balance the candidate enters the armory and is received and passes into the degree.

Should the candidate be elected by the ballot, and the answer from the Lord not be in favor of his being received into the degree, he is informed of it, and will have to withdraw his application for seven times seven weeks, before he makes a new application. This is a regulation for all degrees, and for passing from one degree to another up to the highest.

7. Every messenger belongs to the Gospel of Freedom, and is accepted into the Freedom by an ordinance of confirmation, as he is received into the army by the holy anointing to be a soldier of the Host of Hosts.

The pledge of fidelity to the King is taken in the following manner: The presiding officer requests the messenger to put his hand on the hilt of the sword which is extended to him, and says: "Brother messenger, wilt thou promise to be a faithful soldier in the army of the King, that His word may proceed out of your mouth as a two-edged sword, that it may penetrate the souls of men, and conquer the world into the obedience to the Master and King. Do you promise that in the name of the Messiah, and by the help of your God and Father?" The candidate responding yes! The officer answers "then I declare you worthy to advance further on the way of our king to become a Knight of the White Cross."

8. As none can be a messenger unless he or she has been ordained previously to the Melchisedek priesthood, or the priesthood after the sons and daughters of God, it will be necessary to confer the ordination on those who are not already ordained, before they can be accepted in the Gospel of Freedom. That being the case, all women who are entering the Gospel of Freedom, and have not the priesthood, are to be ordained elderesses, and after that to receive the ordinance of confirmation into the Gospel. The same thing must take place with the brethren who are not elders, that they may receive the fullness of the priesthood.

Also it must be remembered that the entrance to the Order is through the church of Christ, as He is the door, and those who are baptized in Him according to the restoration, and in the name and authority given by Jesus in accordance with the first principles of the gospel, shall be considered acceptable to the Order, because the messengers do not believe in re-baptism nor re-ordination, because the work being done in God cannot be rendered imperfect by man's own faithless condition, but as often as a person returns to the Father's home he is received with joy, and God's promises are eternal and are good for eternity, as they are never broken by God, but may be put aside by men. Therefore the Order of Messiah cannot confer rebaptism nor re-ordination. Some members of the church may have been dismembered, but it does not make the ordinance conferred upon them dead and void. They may have been cut off from a body of believers, from a branch of the church, but no person who ever lived on earth had authority to make God's promises null and void, nor to cut men and women off from God, nor has it ever been invested in any priesthood as an authority from God. Those who are for us are not against us, is as true as those who are not against us are for us. The person who is severed or has severed himself from the church is not necessarily severed from God, neither in his baptism, confirmation or ordination, and much more some in the church in apparently good standing, have removed themselves far off from all ordinances in the church in an eternal sense, but nobody would say to them that God in their behalf has made all His promises null and void.

Therefore when an apostate from the church shall wish to enter into the Order of Messiah, there shall be no hindrance for him because of his apostacy from the church, nor can the church by any protest hinder him from entering the Order, and being recognized on his original baptism and ordination. But if a Catholic, or Lutheran, or Methodist, or Baptist, or any other denomination shall apply for admission, it must be given in the following manner :

The first principles to be obeyed are not recognized by any of the churches except in the restoration of the Gospel by Joseph Smith, but have to be obeyed by all the Lord's people; and secondly, after baptism and confirmation shall the person be considered a member in the church. In the Gospel of Freedom he becomes a messenger, but remains in the church, and bears a ribbon of green, blue and red—men on the breast, and women around the waist, with two slips hanging down to the left hip. Blue is love, green is hope, and red is faith. Such a person may be considered a member of the church of Jesus Christ. Have always sufficient charity from the King to receive a brother, when sufficient charity is found in the Lord to ordain him to the most holy priesthood, and the messengers shall have found him worthy. Knights of the Order of Messiah can step into the place of the church and perform the rites of baptism, confirmation, ordination, &c. The messenger of the Order of Messiah is a member of the church and will forever remain so to be, provided the church will continue to accept him in his place as he goes on to higher degrees. Should the church object, it would not alter his course, and he or she must be satisfied by being a son or daughter of God, and if the church should banish such a person, then God will never banish even the lowest amongst His messengers.

In the same way that degrees for men in the Order of Messiah are formed, are they also formed and organized for women, except that the armory, arsenal, or temple hall are not occupied during the same hours by the women as by the men. There is not a degree nor anything in a degree that cannot be conferred on a woman. She can receive the Golden Cross and be general presiding in this degree, but not in the army. She enters the degree of the Golden Cross as a girl or mature woman not married, but is allowed, if she chooses, to marry a single man of the same degree whom she loves, and according to prophecy, and it is her duty to learn, and teach, and live the heavenly companionship in love and fidelity.

In the army women cannot reach higher rank than healer at the hospitaliers or ambulances. She cannot serve in the army as soldier or officer, but as a nurse and healer in the relief corps.

9. A messenger can rise to the rank of general in the Knights of the Golden Cross, but it is not the rank of active general in the army. The general in chief of the Order is the grand general of the army, with military rank as a commander in chief of the army in the field.

The general for the Jews, my messenger David, the second general of the Order, shall be represented by vicar until he in person can arrive at his headquarters at Jerusalem. The third general of the Order, the general to all the churches of christianity, and the church of saints, my messenger John, my apostle to the church at Utah, shall receive his endowment in the work by doing my will, and the power to conquer hindrances by, if he receives me in the spirit with great meekness, as Moses did, then the spirit and power of Moses shall abide with him.

He shall deliver the elect of my children from bondage, and into the Gospel of Freedom, and direct their way to Missouri, Iowa, Arkansas, Kansas and Nebraska. This work which he shall superintend as the messenger in my spirit and by my Father's blessing, shall he be assisted in by a host of faithful messengers called by the spirit of prophecy and revelation into my work. Therefore let him not falter, nor be disheartened, but go where the spirit shall guide him by dreams and visions, and lift up a loud voice of warning, and exhortation, and consolation, and my blessing and the peace of my Father shall follow my work. I will lead him into a new and happy future, as I wish to all my servants, that he may settle in peace and content at Independence, Missouri, and build himself a house and a home of rest and comfort, when he returns from his work and his mission to the scattered messengers and the saints of the church. Look up and rejoice, because the Son of Man is coming hastily to those who love him. Amen.

10. The office of adjutant general or attorney general, the third lieutenant general of the army, shall be at the headquarters of the Order, and at the office of the general in chief of the Order and his vicar, and be located at Independence, Missouri, with a branch office at Jerusalem, Palestine, working under the directions from headquarters, except when the general in chief resides at Jerusalem.

The general in chief shall not be represented by his vicar at Independence, except when my beloved messenger Peter, the grand general of the Order of Messiah, shall receive command to tarry at Jerusalem, and be engaged in the diplomatic work for the gathering of the Jews, and assisting and directing the work of my beloved messenger David, my general to the Jews. David is in my hands and I will restore him into health and strength to do my work, if he will listen to the voice of the spirit, and receive Him even as he shall receive this work. Amen.

The general in chief shall have no vicar at Jerusalem. His vicar shall reside at headquarters on the American continent. The general in chief will direct the general movement of the Order through all Europe from the delegation of the adjutant general's branch office at Jerusalem, where the grand general shall reside when working in my name on the other continents. By the spirit of prophecy and revelation I shall fill the offices of the generals and vicars, and I shall give to them the spirit of their calling to fill their position by, and make them mighty and valiant in the warfare for the King, and on the battle-field for Jehovah. I will endow them according to their spiritual development to receive it by, and not as in former days when they received promises and not the gifts, because they turned against my spirit, and became hardened in their souls, and contrary to govern.

11. The Order of Messiah in the first degree represents the Knights of the White Cross, or the healers. This degree derives its duties, and obligations, and work from the first heaven, that the spirit of regeneration from that heaven may come down on earth with all the benefits, improvements and healings to humanity. The Knight of the White Cross is an hospitalier, ambulancer and healer. His duty brings him in a familiar

relation with the art of healing, which he shall study and know in the spirit of Messiah. Being the priest of reform, he must be versed in the spirit of nature and apply the spirit of healing, which is the power in the spirit of God for the purpose of relieving pain and curing diseases.

He shall teach what is beneficial for man and what is hurtful to him, and advocate fruitful and temperate living, and his life shall be regulated as a pattern for men and women to imitate and live by. One of the great hindrances for the spirit of God is the trials of all kinds of ailments men confess to be subject to, but the perfect work of the spirit is in a perfect healthy man. Therefore shall diseases not be tolerated nor accepted as normal to exist in man with God's dominant spirit in the soul, because the body is only the expression of the interior man, who is the real man, and has the power to exercise, command, and control, and remodel the physical organism. If you can believe it, even so shall it be to you, and according to your faith. Diseases are conditions originating in the domain of soul, and from the mind. These conditions can be harmonized. Say to the inharmonious conditions of the vital power to be gone, and they will exist by degree no more. Man has the power in God to do all these things, if he accepts the power invested in his soul from God, and he has the moral courage and positive belief, but the will of God is supreme, and he is working in accordance and in harmony with it. The perdition of the world is self-love, the mother of all diseases and contentions, which are of darkness and not of the light. The salvation is to receive the truth, that you are in God, and man has to receive God's love within him as the light necessary for his individual consciousness of life and growth, even as the sunlight is necessary for the plant to grow by. The great mission in healing diseases is to heal the soul, palliate the suffering, and remove that mental condition which caused the disorder and inharmony. The art of healing revealed to man by the great masters appeals to the vital power of nature or spirit, and is based on the law of removing conditions from the sick person, by the soul of corresponding things, or substituting to the soul a corresponding condition, as person's fright and grief can be cured by those filled with fright, and grief, and sympathy is as the dynamics applied to inharmonious conditions in correspondence to the soul.

Man is a microcosm and the mirror of the soul of nature, in which soul manifests itself to the world, and the human body contains in itself thirty-five different elements of nature on earth, and every part in the organic and inorganic life has its expression corresponding to some condition of the human soul, which can be applied in corresponding conditions of discord or accord dynamically, which is spiritually remedied to counterbalance diseases, or specific aberrations and expressions by symptoms known and observed by the sufferer. This healing art has to be studied and applied by every Knight of the White Cross, as a science in the great work of Messiah. In the spirit of every particle in nature is a healing, as in every organism is a correspondence for or against another organism. Pray for knowledge. Light, air and water are the three factors which flow in abundance richly, to give health and strength to all life manifested in the flesh of man and animals.

Live in the freedom of nature where you have admission to light and air, and breathe its healing power with expanded lungs, and receive vitality to the blood, and strength to the nerves, by the life which the sunlight imparts to the air. Use fresh water freely internally, and externally for bathing, and do not omit the daily sponge bath all over the body, because the great protection against all diseases is given to that person who keeps the skin clean, vigorous and active, as a secretive organ most essential and important for happiness, health and prosperity in life.

Many people die young and arrive in the spirit world before their allotted time, because they did not know sufficient on earth to keep their skin clean and powerful. Others invoke the spirit continually to heal them, and call on the elders to come with oil and anoint them in the Lord's name, and lay on of hands for the grace to be healed, but they do not open the windows for the bad air to escape.

The Holy Spirit will enter and heal in the pure balmy breeze which sweeps over the gardens, and bathes the pine forests. The holy angels bear health and light to those who love the light, and do not live behind dark curtains and window blinds which exclude the sunlight from the room. People ask the Father in the name of Messiah to purify their souls and remove discord and disease, but they do not purify their own persons with clean clothes and garments ventilated and cleansed from filth. Also they enter baptism as an assurance company for their souls, thinking that sins are remitted they commit daily. They should enter the bath-room, or walk into the sea or lake with a desire to clean their bodies from impurity, and invigorate the physical frame.

Do first all you know in truth and from the conviction in the spirit, and if you need wisdom pray and call on God, that you may gain His blessing, and He will hear and answer you by the spirit of prophecy, and by laying on of hands, and anointing with oil of the sick and suffering. The spirit counseled you to use herbs and make teas for the sick, but it is better not to use any drugs, as it is no food for the body, and the healing power is not in the derangements which drugs inflict by alterating the system. Therefore when the perfection comes in the Gospel of Freedom, all drugs, and spices, and narcotics shall be abandoned, and all stimulating liquors, and beverages, and tobacco, and tea, and coffee shall be abandoned for general use as it is now indulged in, because it over stimulates and enervates man, and makes him grow old and crippled, and shortens his life on earth. I will put days and years, and scores of years to all those person's lives who follow these rules of abstinence and frugality. The curse of the human life at present consists largely in its wants. Man should want nothing except that he most absolutely needs, and his wants will be very few and his happiness great.

Drugs and drug stores should not exist except for chemical use, but not to sell ingredients which men and women swallow down in the stomach. Drugs are an abuse and poison to mankind, and make the soul dull and stupid, and destroy happiness and welfare. The sanitary use of water as my servant Vincent taught the world, is good and useful, and a natural stimulating power. Medicine must be prepared without any visible drug to be seen or tested. They must be spiritualized as man's soul, and be vitalized dynamic specifics, according to the law of affinity, or correspondence promulgated by my servant Samuel. Soul force is the regulation for man, and he can use the soul of thing and regulate by the similarity corresponding discording conditions in the soul manifested by the symptoms. When these cease to exist health is restored without alteration and by a negative process. The only rational way of cure is by the spirit of God, and His vital power from angels, man and spirits to restore balance and health in life, and not by drug alterations. Laying on of hands is the spiritual science of healing and as old as man, and is not confined to the head except in the ministerial service as an ordinance. All love and attraction, all affinity and friendship between persons is based upon the law of soul affinity, or similarity of the spiritual magnetic sphere of life where the weak is cured by the strong person. Soul love contains in itself a true healing for man. Ill will and anger is cause for diseases, depletion of life power, disorder and too negative or positive conditions are speaking aloud to man and woman by symptoms.

Love is the union of life, it sounds in both souls at once, and repeats its language simultaneously in two as one. Love is the origin of man and health. The inorganic electro magnetism is crude to organic life, and can only serve as a counter irritant. It cannot be assimilated, nor digested, nor absorbed, or retained as part of the human organism. It cannot be digested any more than minerals, there cannot be a constituent of the human body except when by the organic process they become a part of the body, as iron does in the organic combination, but electro-magnetism is not the organic vita, nor can it be retained in the organic cellular living tissues, interwoven with the life of organic magnetic soul force. Inorganic magnetism is a passing by current through the organism, and by its similarity of correspondence conveys into action a certain amount of the organic or vital magnetism, which is perfected in proportion to the development and perfection of the constructive cell. Electro-magnetism can be used with great benefit to allay irritation and pains, especially during the prime of human life, but becomes always disastrous to old age and in general depletion of the organism. The action is in correspondence and congenial with young and middle aged persons, and gives strength by stimulating into action the latent stored up vitality. To the category of stimulants belongs also the alterative method of the alloeopathic school of medicine. It is true that alteratives can be used, but it is a very dangerous method for general health and longevity, and a very rudimental philosophy of diseases and their causes.

Drugs are spiritually a discord to humanity. Nothing but ignorance would apply drugs internally, but the method corresponds to the development of man, and his present condition and rudimental state of living. Drugs are for anasthetics and external uses if for any at all, but even there the human will or water makes all drugs superfluous. By a higher development of man, when the spiritual science can be applied and understood, no person will surrender his person for the gain of doctors to experimental alterations and poisonous drugs. In the spiritual worlds are that class of men consciously impressed with thoughts of love, to redeem humanity from drugs. They are organizing for such efforts, but their obstacle is the profound ignorance of man as a spiritual developed being, and the utter impossibility in his present rude and semi-barbarian state of society to apply truth, as a general rule to his brain life. The method advocated in the heavens is now striving to come down in the kingdom on earth. When man indulges in intoxicating drinks, he is equally only an easy prey for drug doctors and their deception, and the use of strong boiled coffee or tea, where the coffeine and theaine is doing the most disastrous work on the nerve globules.

The utter ignorance of humanity and the tradition that drugs cure diseases, is simply nothing less than ridiculous to children in the spirit world, as such an assertion is without spiritual truth, and without the slightest foundation in truth and reason to any matured spiritual being.

The process of healing is an inherent power in the integrity of the soul, which by self action must and will preserve its individuality, and comply to eternal laws of life reactive for the preservation. Therefore symptoms have not to be fought nor to be put down, nor suppressed, "nor dug up by root," as all such ideas are fallacies of healing and impositions in the divine code of common sense.

Symptoms are the language of the soul in its expressions through flesh and blood. He tells the tale of his woe and discord in the effort to restore balance and health, and in the same degree the disturbance is mortal, his energies are aroused in the most intense pain or efforts to restore health, but what do the doctors? They say it well but do it not. They say, viz:

medicatrix natura, but they destroy that healing principle in humanity by their drugs and depleting processes. In the place of supporting the subtle language, and study and grouping symptoms, they ignore them as man ignores an enemy, and wage a war with pains. In the place of using the soul of things in highly dynamized preparation, corresponding to the similarity or group of symptoms combined with the pathological presentation for such a condition, derived by the provings of drugs and poisons on the persons in health, the doctors do the very opposite—they destroy, they silence, they paralyze the effort of the soul to restore health and balance, and for each treatment the organism grows more feeble and weak, and premature death is the result and the inevitable cause of some doctors work for humanity.

God heals and drugs kill. Such a farce may appear extremely laughable when viewed from the stand point in the spirit, and those who practiced the old method of bleeding, and blistering, and purging, and calomel, morphine and chinin treatment are those most amused over their own folly, but it does not better society on earth, as for a long time doctors have followers who fight for drugs as if they were saviors, when in fact their teaching reveals that they do not do the thing they claim for truth, but arrive in all serious cases to the very opposite of healing. Their claim to be of truth, drugs prove to be falsehoods. For these reasons come the Knights of the White Cross and the Order of Messiah as the healers to man. Laying on of hands has never been understood by the church, and cannot be comprehended except in the conception of the man in God, and not only God in man, which is comparatively a very weak position, and shaky as a platform to heal on.

When the Son of Man cured diseases, it was done by the power of God and not by the power of man. It was done with that interior conviction that God was manifested in the flesh, and all power was given to man which is in heaven and upon earth. I did not come to heal diseases, but I came to call man to repentance, not to the repentance to obey the law of Moses because Israel lived by it, but to a higher repentance, that of man in God, that God might be everything and man nothing but Him and only Him. In that teaching I lived, and I did cure all diseases, and my healings were not mine but His work, that

His name should be glorified by it and not mine, and to establish such a repentance to God did I die as I had lived, and commended my spirit into His hands.

The curing of diseases as doctors call it, can be done rationally by applying the soul of things, or dynamically prepared remedies, by which the soul power of the physical organism or the soul, is operated on by soul. Also you have the mesmeric, psychometric and psychological healing, and the healing by the spirit magnetism or by spiritual agencies, and the healing by the Holy Spirit.

The divine spirit circle of the third heaven distributes the power to the external world. It depends upon the faith in God by which man invokes the supreme power to do the work, or the power which does it in and by man as the medium. Although there is only one power supremely through all the universe, and the world moves in that power, only very few persons identify themselves with it as the element in which they live by healing and gifts in the name of Messiah. This Holy Spirit power from on high is governing the spirit life, and the souls of men and women on earth, who pray God in the name of the Son and in His love and follow after Him in the regeneration full of His spirit power. That is the authority by the Messiah to live in that power. His power by the messengers shall work great things, the blind to see, the deaf to hear, the lame to walk, and the preaching of the Gospel of Freedom to those suffering in bondage.

The world labors in great pain under the law full of contention in souls without love. The selfishness which permeates natural man is the great hindrance for the power of God to be revealed in man on earth. Mankind is naturally animal, with the propensities of his fellow creatures, mentally filled with deception, and falsehood, and hate to the truth.

This condition barricades the ways of angels, and the departed progressive spirits weep over humanity, but do nothing where no kind of emotion is in the soul to attach the love of God to. "Why does God or spirits not speak themselves to me," is the common question. Because you are not in submission to that spirit of love which is in them, as the development by which you ever will see God and know of Him even as the Messiah knows him. " Why does not God cure me if He cures anybody," are the common words from the lips of sick persons. Because you are not in His light of healing, and diseases is your natural condition or discord in your relation to God and His spirit. Man is moving on between animal and spirit, between his own ways and the ways of God. Move in the faith and trust of God and you shall be healed, because you suffer the discord of the flesh in the discord of the soul, and according to your own faith which has no power to live by nor to be healed by, on account of your spiritual death. That condition gives man the low rank only a little above the animal in his field, devoid of spiritual gifts and spiritual power, and without a God.

The Knights of the White Cross being the healers have an especial mission to regulate the physical and social affairs of man, and regulate diet and diminishing the use of meat, as the flesh of animals makes man hard, selfish, cruel and bloodthirsty for wars and conquest. Man's principal diet shall be fruit and grain, because for that are his teeth made in the beginning. The new wine used to my remembrance in my Father's kingdom shall be unfermented, and fermented wine shall not be used except in want of unfermented, and then mixed three-fourths with water, which is my will the church shall use in preference to fresh colored water. Marriage shall be contracted in love, and by two souls in the love of the spirit, or marriage does not exist except in name, and is dead in the spirit and in truth. The Knight of the White Cross has to study and teach by his own life conjugal bliss and harmony, that man may marry in the spirit of love and freedom, not for money, nor for the slavery to wealth, or other considerations, but in love to possess a strong and healthy offspring. Children not born in love are under a curse, as the marriage is they were reared in. All things belong to you if you remain in God's love.

The many duties of the Order of Nephi will be taught in the "white book" belonging to that degree. The counsel is now as it was to Israel to intermarry in distant relations as much as possible. It may be wrong for the world, but you are a chosen people and it is right for Israel according to the spirit of God, and your relations shall be preserved from the world.

Abraham married his half sister, Isaac his cousin, and Jacob his cousin, and each tribe intermarried, and they multiplied and became a strong people, because my spirit contended with them and dwelt upon them, as long as they followed my precepts and walked upon my ways. A man shall not marry that woman who gave birth to him, nor shall a daughter marry that man by whom her mother conceived her, because that relation is sacred and shall not be broken, nor shall children intermarry who are born of the same mother, because that relation is sacred and shall not be broken by any marriage relation, but other family relations shall not be a restrain from heaven, but a command to join together in loving companionship. My people are a holy people, and my spirit dwells upon them, and in my love they shall multiply if they remain in my love one to another, they shall prosper on earth in freedom and love. However, be subject to regulations made by the world, and by governments and rulers on earth, and obey the laws of the country where you are living. The spirit of prophecy shall guide you and bear testimony to you forever.

The Gospel of Freedom is preached to Israel, and the spirit of perfection in that gospel is in subjection to the spirit of God. In this unconditional submission is the blessing given to man, that he shall live above the law and in my spirit. Freedom exists only in the holiness which is in God, and your lives are there in His glorious freedom, and you are free indeed in the truth by the servitude to the holy spirit of God. By the law you are not free, but in bonds to the curse attached to the law. Neither are you under the spirit of love one to another in God, because you condemn one another for not keeping the law you are in bonds to keep, and the law does not make you free in the spirit but is debarring you from the grace of God. The servant under the Gospel of Freedom is not to judge but to save the world from selfishness, the root to all evil in man's nature. If you are in the freedom of the spirit you are under the law of God's love, and the laws of the world cannot affect you nor disturb the peace of your heart in God.

The laws of the world are the introduction to civilization, and regulations to be kept of the society, but the perfection of the law is the spirit of God's love to man and above the written testimony to Moses. When the world legislates it does it in good faith, according to its own spirit and the voice of the people, but when the holy spirit legislates it does it according to that love to man which is in God. By that love you obey the laws of the world, and much more the perfection of God's love in your hearts filled with charity and good works.

Freedom in the Messiah does not condemn, but the laws of the world condemn the erring brother. God is not in man's love, because man's love is evil and not of truth, therefore man must be found in God's love or perish in self love.

That is the glory of God, that you heal the sick and raise the dead in the spirit into that love. "Say only one word and my servant will be healed," is the power and spirit of the Gospel of Freedom. Psychological healing is soul force from a strong mind operating on discording conditions of the human body, commanding them in the power of God to disappear by restoring and reinstating the dispensed person's soul into unity and harmony of the entire man, that the lame may walk, and the obstructed vision is reinstated in clearness of sight by the power of God.

The work of the first heaven is to restore and deliver those persons arriving daily from the deformities and ailments they carry with them into spirit life, and as God's will is done in heaven shall it be done on earth, when man responds to His love. You have to be developed into health before you can receive the gift of healing, and by the strength in God heal the weak and sick on earth.

The spirit of freedom lived in Abraham and the patriarchs. This spirit is the mind of the Ancient of Days. Man shall again see God in the freedom and holiness of His pure spirit. In the power of that spirit speak a word, and it shall be fulfilled, and whosoever you touch with your hands with prayer and command in His spirit to be healed shall be healed according to the faith of acceptance, because it shall come to the applicant according to the faith in God, and the love of God in His soul.

All the manifestations of the Gospel of Messiah which move spiritualism shall be revealed to mankind before the Son of man comes. The dead shall rise and speak to many in the flesh, and eat and drink with them, and dwell in their houses, and the Messiah, and His twelve apostles from past days in Judea, shall appear visible to His friends. The first resurrection is the permanent power of materialization, established on earth as in the forty days I went out and in with my disciples.

I am the resurrection and the life, and I have the power in my hand, even as I have received it and shown it to my elect. The resurrection in the materialized body of my elect shall be known to my friends, whether the world shall accept the evidence or not. That is the bread of life to all souls who are hungry for my advent, to eat with the Messiah when He comes again, and He is manifested in the power of eternity before all heaven and to all on earth.

Be rich in God even if you are poor in the world, because the world shall perish, but your riches of life shall be in Him who is living forever. Study into the various gifts and seek them in the spirit, and by the spirit photography shall much truth be revealed to earth. Receive your departed friends, listen to the voice of your guardian angels, and live the truth in all your actions. Observe the baptism for dead friends and relatives as a token of love for those departed in ignorance and darkness.

Join together prayer circles in the spirit, and I will come to you and stand in your midst and teach you. I am the Alpha and Omega, the one who was and continues to be, and my name will last forever. Therefore fear not the lightning from men, because all flesh withers as the grass, but my words are life eternal and power, and you shall live by them in the power of Messiah and the eternal light. Fear falsehoods, because the spirit of the world is bound up in falsehoods. Cure the sick, but do not presume to do it only by the knowledge of men, but by the wisdom and spirit of my Father. Say only a word with my power resting upon you, and in my spirit, and for my name's sake, and it shall be fulfilled according to your words. I will send out my messengers to cast fire on earth, and all the world shall be in a flame by the Gospel of Freedom before the Son of man comes. Amen.

The second degree, the Knights of the Red Cross, also called the Rosicrucians, are the preachers and defenders of the truth. They are the spiritual embodiment of the crusades to attain by the two-edged sword which comes out from my mouth, that which could not be attained by many years of bloody contest with the followers of Mohammed. It has been a puzzle for many generations why the conquest of Minor Asia and Northern Africa was allowed to be made by the Arabs. Why was it allowed by God, because the spirit had left the congregations. When they apostatized from the living truth into the dead letter of dogmatism, then the destroyer did his work. Surely there was no power left to resist the invasion. The condition of the christians was enervated and stagnated, and falsehoods bred an odor offensive everywhere, and nations became an easy prey for the fresh and vigorous branch of Ismael, and his people sprung up as a reform amongst the idolatrous tribes of Arabia, superior in their philosophy to the sickening falsehoods of the churches. The crusade was a chivalrous battle for the dignity of the cross, but it did not repair the lost hope, nor did it convert Islam, and Palestine sunk back into the hands of the enemy, that the words of prophecy should be fulfilled until the fullness of time for the Gentiles. It may appear that God banished the soil of the promised land, when He banishes nothing, but Israel banished its own light, and its own race, and its own soil. Even as it went with Babylon and Nineveh also went it with Canaan, and the haughty Capernaum lifted in its pride towards heaven, and built on the mighty bluffs at the lake shore is now cast down into the hell of destruction and desolation. When the preachers go out amongst the nations they point to the past history with warning finger and voice before all the congregations, that if God did not spare His chosen people, nor the mighty nations of Babylon, and Assyria, and Persia, and Macedonia, and Rome, nor shall He spare the American nation, nor any other nation which persecutes the light and kills His messengers. Men may say even as the Jews did, we have it all, we have Moses and the prophets, but their forefathers killed the prophets, and they built monuments over their graves, and killed the prophets who came in their own generation and did not repent. Their priesthood became as vipers filled with deadly poison, even as a church priesthood will be, when the spirit of prophecy departs from it.

Lift up a warning voice before the Son of Man comes, and inquire into the truth and nothing but the truth, and even so conduct your lives. Do not preach of yourselves, nor of your own wisdom, even you shall seek after knowledge by day and by night. Do not depend upon what man knows, because before the tribunal of God he knows nothing, but depend upon the inspiration which comes down from heaven and shall fill your souls with the unspeakable peace and glory of my Father above all that which can be uttered by a human tongue. Live in that knowledge and despise none, but love all the light bearers on earth, love spiritualism, and love every spirit, and every man and woman who comes to you with truth on their lips, and with truth in their mediumship, and with truth in their materialization and inspiration. Many are called upon and only few are my elect, therefore beware that those ye despise shall not come up and sit in judgment against you.

My friends and messenger rosicrucians fight the good battle and strive onwards until the crown of regeneration shall be pressed over your brows as kings in my Father's kingdom on earth. Let nothing detain you, because those who lose their lives as rosicrucians shall find them a thousand times again. I am the true vine, and every branch which has its root in me shall live and bear much fruit. Gather out my people from bondage and into the Gospel of Freedom, and teach them my will by the power and inspiration of the spirit of prophecy, and ye shall be mighty in the midst of this continent. Say to those who are rich to forget their wealth for my sake, because the Son of man had not on earth that much as he could lean his head to. Therefore ye rich on earth be poor and meek in the spirit, and I will make you rich eternally, and come forth and dedicate of your superfluous means to the building of my temple at Independence, even as the command was given before, also do I give it to my people now, that it may be built in this generation as a holy edifice before all the world. Amen.

Preach that at every meeting and before all the congregations, until the spirit has moved upon the hearts of my elect to fulfil my command to be done now. For that purpose I am calling you out from the mountains where you have accumulated wealth, and out from the great cities, and from the fields, and stores, and from the other side of the earth, to donate in my holy name and before my Father the gifts of that love God planted in your hearts to the building of my temple on the spot designated, near Kansas City.

This work shall not be omitted, but be a prominent part of your crusade with the army for the blessing of mankind. The spirit of my Father's love shall teach you for the balance, and move your hearts and souls in the channel of all truth as far as you remain in the intensity of that love, which is the essence of all truth in heaven and on earth. Peace be in your footsteps and peace be in your words, and peace follow your life if you conduct it in the peace of holiness.

I have called you rosicrucians that you might know by that I have called you to investigate into all knowledge and wisdom, which springs forth in God's love and is associated by the spirit of eternal truth.

Be not ashamed of spiritualism because it is not wanted on earth in the christian churches. Neither was my work wanted on earth amongst Israel. Come to spiritualism and learn, and gather in truth on earth and in heaven under one head, that all may be perfected in the love of God. Even so I say to you "I will gather in my harvest from fields of christianity you did not cultivate, and from a people prepared for me, which the churches counted not to be great, but they were great before the spirit of my heavenly Father's love. Therefore thus says the spirit, even the holy spirit of God, " I will make those a people in my kingdom who were in the spirit on earth and did not know my name, and I will make spiritualism a chosen keystone to the portal arch and entrance to your Father's house." Cultivate fraternity with all the mediums, because those who are not against us are of us in the same spirit of tolerance and peace.

Believe me I have called you to the righteousness which is in the spirit of God, and not to that which is in man. Like man is subject to the Messiah, also shall woman be one in God's love to her husband, because he is her honor by having assumed his name, even of the Messiah is the honor to that man who receives his priesthood and adopts His name. Woman shall be in subjection to the holy spirit of love in her own soul, and in that united to the man in her love. This is the supreme law which rules the heavens and earth, and is never contradicted except by unholy unions, devoid of love and lived in contest. Without subjection there is no love, because love is always in subjection to its own life. Even so the man that loves a woman in the love of God renders her worship in that divine love, but her love honors him in the same love, even as he honors the Messiah. This law shall never be broken in the Order after my name, and even as I love the church, also shall a man love a woman, and when she rejoices in rebellion she is not in love and shall be rejected of him, even as God rejected the church when it affiliated and falsified itself with the world for gain's sake, and quenched my spirit, and laid heavy burdens and chains of bondage on my people, because my love had no resting place in their hearts. That woman who pretends love to a man and rebels against him, is in the spirit of the arch traitor and the father of perdition. Thou shalt cast her from thy heart as if she were a serpent full of deadly poison, and clean thy hands in the name of God, that thy fingers shalt not become as a leper's because thou touched her. Blessed are the women who remain in the spirit of holiness, and walk in the love of God, and blessed the man who shall receive such a wife from God. Blessed is the man who loves a woman more dear than his own body, and loves her in that divine worship which is in the love of God to him. Most unfortunate are those who pretend to sell love for luxury, display, money and high living, because they are in accusations against each other, but there are no accusations in the freedom and love of God, but long suffering, holiness, charity and peace.

A knight shall not marry except by revelation and the spirit of prophecy, and in such a manner be very cautious and avoid the divorces of the world as superfluous in the Order of Messiah. In all marriage teach and preach to be in accord with the love of heaven. Marry within the degree and within the Order, and marry in the peace of love in your soul as in the mind of the Messiah, because such is the heavenly companionship in the glory of the summer land, where love begotten by love gives birth to spirits of love, bright as the morning star in God's love.

In the intensity of your love man and angels arrive at the truth of wisdom, and to the works of charity. In the divine worship by which you love one another, you are loving God in

His love. Fear not your enemies, do not tremble for the power of darkness, because light is bright in love, and you shall not be entangled in the snares of the flesh if you remain in love. The crime of perversion and infanticide is not found in the spirit of love nor by a holy people. Perversion makes misfit of sexes, and the greatest of all curses to toil together as oxen under a heavy yoke. Preach the word of love to woman in prostitution, teach her the dignity of her being, and that only love can redeem her. Teach that incarceration and seclusion in convents does not solve the problem of love, which is the interior attachment of soul to another being of the other sex, and that devoted love returned to the heart again.

All the mysteries of love and knowledge about the summer land belong to the second degree, as it belongs to the second heaven. Therefore is marriage on earth mentioned in connection with that spirit of love, and the mutual development of soul-power in that love, which is the essence of the life in the summer land. This intense love always adorns the spiritual companions and is only in a few instances realized on earth. Teach a careful selection of mates, and by your spirit guides and the spirit of prophecy, superior is love to all other considerations that should have any weight in selecting a wife or a husband. Love endures all tribulation, it asks for nothing but its own life, and permission to serve its own ideal, and gives up everything to be in the blessed presence of the beloved, which is worth much more than the world's treasures. Being the fountain of life, love is at the same time the cream of life itself, and the cause of power through all eternity. In that love is the divine life to man and woman in which they are to receive the love of God and enter the celestial world, which is the glory of the third heaven above all human understanding. Work, preach, teach and live in that love, and your lives are in the truth of your entire being. Amen.

The princes in the Order of Messiah, or Knights of the Golden Cross, must live in the continued flow of inspiration without end, as a stream of living water to be poured constantly into their souls. Thus life is the power in God. This inspiration is without beginning or end, because it is eternally as God is eternal, and it is God. A knight of this degree must be born of the spirit in every breath, and every step, and every move, and every word on his lips. He must live in the element of the living power in God the Father, and His Holy Spirit. This divine life must manifest itself to the world by a continued sacrifice in the labor he performs, for God's work in an untiring love, ready to lay down his life to find it eternally. Charity born in tears of love he offers the king, because nobody had a greater love than the Messiah who laid down his life in the love of God for a world filled with hate against Him. It shall be the duty of the Knights of the Golden Cross to guard over that power of inspiration, and the spirit of prophecy shall not depart from the Order or from the church, and if the power of God should be diminished, He shall call upon the Knights of the Red Cross to assist him in preaching a crusade against the churches and the Order, that the light and spirit of prophecy shall not be extinct as in former days, because Israel departed from the love, and light, and life which is in God. "Therefore thus says the Lord thy God, I will raise up a high tower in Zion, and I will put watchmen there after my own heart to guard my people, and I will make them speak with flows of inspiration, and their words shall be streams of life, and I will give them power to protect mine elect, and those who are gathered in from afar off to remain in the truth of the living word, which comes out from God to give life to the world. And they shall speak with tongues of angels, and sing hymns from Paradise, and blessed are those who receive them because they receive me. I will raise up a golden cross on that tower, and it shall be known from one end of the world to another, and my messengers shall walk in the golden light from the celestial world." Amen.

All the knowledge belonging to the third heaven, which can be made intelligible to man, belongs to this degree, and my watchmen shall be seen by day and by night on the tower which I have built in the midst of Zion, that my work may be done even as I have received the command from my Heavenly Father. My friends, remain in my love as I have remained in His love, and all things are yours as they are mine. Remember charity is the pearl of life. Live with your love in the spirit of charity, willing to make sacrifices for charity's sake, that your love may be perfected to each other, and love in the love of the heavenly companionship, and harvest the fruit of love by spiritual children born to you in the eternal life. Blessed are those who receive my words because they receive both me and my Father. I have much to say to the Knights of the Golden Cross, or the degree of prophets and seers, but it shall mostly be given in symbols, and be read in the yellow book.

Every degree shall be fully understood by the works illustrated for the knights to perform, but the necessary hints are given to you. My blessing I give to the honest of heart who read these words, that they may receive life to enlighten their understanding about God's love, but those who are blind and mute in the spirit will despise my mission to man and hate the light. Those shall be angry and persecute my messengers and kill some of them, and make others suffer.

Be as living witnesses in the spirit, and of a never ceasing prayer in your hearts. Pray always in your soul, and truth shall flow to you in God's love and give you charity. Pray for spiritual gifts, and knowledge, and the "raising of the dead," that the departed may appear again materialized and in the form on earth, and pray that the spirit of prophecy may always abide with you. Despise not God's gift in man or woman, because He works in His own way, and not in the ways of man, which are counterfeits to His work. That which is low down in the pride, and arrogance, and self-conceit of the world, has God made great to work out His design with, and magnify His name by.

Blessed are you if you love the light, and remain in my love as the children of the light, because my blessing belongs to them, even the blessing I bestowed on my apostles when on Mount Olive I departed from them. The same power do I seal on the heads of my messengers. Go out in all the world—preach the Gospel of Freedom and deliverance to all nations, and prepare the world by the Order of Messiah for the kingdom to come. The coming of the Son of man is near at hand, when He shall appear visible and tangible before all of you.

Peace be with you, my peace follow you, which is the peace of my Father's love which burns in your hearts.

Amen and Amen.

www.ingramcontent.com/pod-product-compliance
Lightning Source LLC
Chambersburg PA
CBHW022333230426
43664CB00040B/477